Bilingualism and Language Contact:
Spanish, English, and
Native American Languages

Bilingual Education Series

GARY D. KELLER, *Editor*

GUADALUPE VALDÉS, ANTHONY G. LOZANO, and RODOLFO
    GARCÍA-MOYA, editors
    Teaching Spanish to the Hispanic Bilingual: Issues,
    Aims, and Methods

JOSHUA A. FISHMAN and GARY D. KELLER, editors
    Bilingual Education for Hispanic Students in the
    United States

FLORENCE BARKIN, ELIZABETH BRANDT, and JACOB ORN-
    STEIN-GALICIA, editors
    Bilingualism and Language Contact: Spanish,
    English, and Native American Languages

Bilingualism and Language Contact:

Spanish, English, and Native American Languages

Edited by

FLORENCE BARKIN   *Arizona State University*

ELIZABETH A. BRANDT   *Arizona State University*

JACOB ORNSTEIN-GALICIA   *University of Texas— El Paso*

Teachers College, Columbia University
New York and London, 1982

Published by Teachers College Press, 1234 Amsterdam Avenue, New York, N.Y. 10027

Library of Congress Cataloging in Publication Data

Main entry under title:

Bilingualism and language contact.

   (Bilingual education series ;   )
   1. Sociolinguistics–Southwestern States–Addresses, essays, lectures. 2. Languages in contact–Southwestern States–Addresses, essays, lectures. 3. Language and languages–Study and teaching–Southwestern States–Addresses, essays, lectures. 4. Sociolinguistics–Mexico–Addresses, essays, lectures. 5. Languages in contact–Mexico–Addresses, essays, lectures. 6. Language and languages–Study and teaching–Mexico–Addresses, essays, lectures. I. Barkin, Florence. II. Brandt, Elizabeth. III. Ornstein-Galicia, Jacob, 1915– .   IV. Series
P40.45.U5B5   404′.2   81-21503
                         AACR2

ISBN 0-8077-2671-0

Manufactured in the United States of America
87 86 85 84 83 82   1 2 3 4 5 6

Contents

Preface

In the summer of 1978, Jacob Ornstein-Galicia invited a small group of scholars together for an international conference on border linguistics sponsored by the Southwest Cross-cultural Ethnic Studies Center and the Inter-American Center at the University of Texas at El Paso. That conference provided the initial stimulus for the development of a new perspective for the study of languages and varieties in the U.S. Borderlands. We decided to develop a volume to explore this theme, with several of the conference papers as a nucleus for the collection. Additional articles were then commissioned and selected to deal with topics we saw as important to the development of this perspective.

As researchers and teachers located at major institutions within the Borderlands, we also felt a need for a collection of sociolinguistic papers to provide a background for the study of the linguistic diversity which surrounds us. While there are many volumes dealing with bilingualism, there are very few which provide a survey of all the languages and varieties within a region.

We believe that the volume will serve as a useful reference work for scholars, students, and teachers and lead to the development of 1) a new framework for the study of language contact and diversity; 2) a greater concern with the processes of language contact and bilingualism; and 3) a deeper appreciation of the necessity for socially grounded studies of linguistic phenomena.

We would like to express our thanks to all of those who made this work possible: to Chris MacCrate, for his valuable editorial assistance; to Guido Weigend, dean of the College of Liberal Arts at Arizona State University, for his support of the project; to the Departments of Anthropology and Foreign Languages at Arizona State University for their services; and to Barbara Beckner, and others, for typing this manuscript.

Introduction

It has been a quarter-century since the appearance of Uriel Weinreich's ground-breaking *Languages in Contact* (1953). Since then, a spate of collections have offered themselves to those interested in bilingualism, sociolinguistics, applied linguistics, and general linguistics. Interestingly enough, there have been relatively few volumes devoted primarily to language contact. With no false modesty, we might cite among these *Sociolinguistic Studies in Language Contact* (Mackey & Ornstein, 1979). In the preface, Mackey observes, "The study of language contact has been central to no single discipline, although many sciences have studied the phenomenon to the extent that it might throw light upon some of their particular problems." Possibly it is indeed the very breadth and number of effects of languages in contact that prevents individuals from undertaking collections on this topic, fearing that they may not do it justice. Perhaps with more valor than discretion, the three editors have ventured forth in an attempt to do such justice.

We are concerned in this volume with the Borderlands, an area difficult to define precisely, but which we take to include the U.S. Southwest (Arizona, New Mexico, California, Colorado, Texas, Utah, and perhaps Oklahoma), and northern Mexico (Sonora, Chihuahua, and Baja). The land is an enormous area of mountain and desert, both beautiful and fragile. It is also land crossed by both political and social boundaries, many of which are recent. While political divisions allow individuals to claim citizenship in either the United States or Mexico, social and economic boundaries are not so definite. Where the same languages are spoken on either side of the border, the need to communicate for economic and social purposes necessitates a redefinition of the Borderlands, one that is socially based. With respect to the United States and Mexico, the border has moved, causing the languages of certain groups in the Borderlands to lose their original political recognition and to become secondary, rather than primary, languages of the newly defined nations. While the existence of the languages still may be recognized, their status has changed from official to subordinate. The permeability of the border makes the language situation very complex.

The complexity is even greater with respect to Native American languages in the region. There are a few Native American languages, such as Apache and Yaqui, which are spoken on both sides of the U.S./Mexican border and where there is regular contact between the speakers of these languages on both sides of the border. For the majority of the other Indian languages in the border area, Indian communities enjoy partial political autonomy and tribal self-determination, yet Indian communities and individuals are still embedded in the larger sociopolitical complex of their nations and the region as a whole. Thus, for Native Americans, as well as English- and Spanish-speakers, the relevant borders are political, economic, and social.

As is evident from the title of the book, we are also dealing with bi- and multi-lingualism. Our work is distinguished from other collections on this subject primarily in its relation to language contact. We are less concerned with bilingualism as an outcome than as a process. We have selected our authors for their holistic, data-based, socially situated analyses of the processes involved in language contact. It is clear that in the Borderlands languages and varieties of languages serve to differentiate and maintain distinctiveness both within and between groups and individuals. Diversity persists because of interaction.

The book is divided into five sections. The articles in part I, "Perspectives," introduce the unique concerns of Borderlands scholars. They survey past research on Spanish and Native American languages and describe the need for the development of a broad regional, international, and interethnic theoretical orientation, contextually grounded in multiple social realities.

Part II, "Native American Languages in Contact," focuses on Native American speech communities within the broad framework of the ethnography of communication. The papers deal primarily with language contact between Native American languages, Spanish, and English.

The papers in part III, "Spanish in the Borderlands," study the sources of geographically and socially conditioned speech variation. They provide a broad survey of the dimensions of variation and consider selected variables in their social contexts.

Part IV, "Teaching and Learning," explores the teaching and learning process in language education. The papers in this section all stress the fact that unexpected outcomes may result unless there is a clear realization of cultural and social factors.

Part V is concerned with "Language Maintenance, Language Shift, and Language Use." This is a theme running throughout the entire volume, as the contributors discuss the complex patterns of language contact among Native American languages, Spanish, and English, patterns that also reflect the history of contact in the Borderlands. Since the Borderlands is unique as a multilingual, multiethnic, and multinational geographical area, the maintenance of individual languages there becomes a cultural, social and sometimes political issue for their speakers.

There does not yet exist a linguistics or sociolinguistics of the Borderlands. The Borderlands, as an area of study, has only begun to develop. There is, however, a Consortium of Border institutions and an organization of Border-lands Scholars. In 1976, the *Rocky Mountain Social Sciences Journal* pro-duced a special double issue of commissioned articles with the express purpose of assessing the status of Borderlands studies. The present volume is an initial contribution to a perspective that we hope to foster. At this preliminary stage, we have neglected varieties of English other than Indian Englishes (see Leap, this volume), and research on both Spanish and Native American languages in northern Mexico outside the immediate border area. It is our hope that this volume will lead to increased research in these areas, to the development of regional models, and to extensive areal and typological studies.

I | Perspectives

OVERVIEW

The papers in this section have two goals: first, to survey past research on Spanish and Native American languages in the Borderlands; and second, to provide contextually based research perspectives for the study of bilingualism and language contact in the region.

Guadalupe Valdés demonstrates the importance of studying Spanish in contact with English in an area where Spanish is not a minority language and where, as a consequence, its functions are not limited. She explores the characteristics of the population in the Ciudad Juárez/El Paso region, an urban area approaching a population of one million, and provides a comprehensive discussion of the social contexts of Spanish and English usage.

Juan M. Lope Blanch, coordinator of a monumental project involving the study of *la norma culta* (the educated standard) in the principal cities in Latin America, recognizes the importance of describing the Spanish of the Borderlands and makes a plea for publication of well-conceived and carefully executed studies describing Spanish dialects of this area, even if they do not comply with the particular theoretical approach in vogue at the time. He explains that he consciously omitted the Spanish of the Southwest from his project, since he felt that individual and institutional resources for research were far more abundant in the United States than in Latin America.

Elizabeth Brandt reviews past research on Native American languages and develops a research agenda that stresses an areal-typological perspective. She argues for greater attention to the community's research needs, while still maintaining state-of-the-art quality. Each of the papers in this section is meant to stimulate further research leading to the development of a linguistics of the Borderlands that is contextually grounded in multiple social realities.

1 | Bilingualism in a Mexican Border City: A Research Agenda

GUADALUPE VALDÉS
New Mexico State University

RESEARCH ON SPANISH/ENGLISH LANGUAGE CONTACT

Recent research on Spanish/English language contact on the North American continent has focused on the effects and characteristics of such linguistic contact among Hispanic minorities in the United States. Much work has been done, from both a purely linguistic and a sociolinguistic perspective. More recently, because of the interests of educators in this country, attention has also focused on the locus of language contact, the bilingual individual himself.

There is much, however, that is not yet understood about the Spanish language in contact with English. The available research has increased our knowledge about the nature of English/Spanish bilingualism in minority groups. It has not, however, focused on the Spanish language itself. It has not, for example, attempted to differentiate between those effects on Spanish which may be strictly a result of this language's minority status in the United States and those effects which might in any case be expected for Spanish in contact with the globally prestigious English language in various other types of settings.

While in general we can speculate or hypothesize about the possible presence or absence of transfer phenomena in those other kinds of contact settings, there is no evidence at present to substantiate such speculation. For example, while one can hypothesize that code switching between Spanish and English might have low acceptance in situations in which bilinguals take pride in keeping their two languages apart, we have no empirical evidence that this is actually the case. We have little information about the effects on the Spanish language of sustained contact with English outside of the United States and Puerto Rico. At the same time, existing theory would have us assume that Spanish in contact with English might exhibit other, or different, or less frequent instances of transfer when it does not occupy the position of minority language. However, until another type of contact situation has been studied in some depth and the

3

results have been compared with those obtained among Hispanic minorities in the United States, such theoretical assumptions must be questioned.

The purpose of this paper is to suggest a context in which our present assumptions about Spanish/English language contact, based upon the observations of minority groups in the United States, might be questioned. Essentially this paper will: 1) Describe a Spanish/English contact area which differs significantly from those that have been described to date and, most important, in which Spanish does not occupy a position of lesser value than English. 2) Outline the types of questions that might be answered about bilingualism in general and about Spanish/English language contact specifically, by a thorough study of such a community.

THE STUDY OF BILINGUALISM ALONG THE U.S.–MEXICAN BORDER

It has long been an established fact that language contact as it occurs across national boundaries presents characteristics which are not identical to those found in other language-contact settings, such as contexts in which immigrant bilingualism is the norm, contexts in which bilingualism exists because a colonial language has been adopted as a national language, and so forth. Indeed, for some time researchers have involved themselves in the study of language borders in Europe and South America (Alsace-Lorraine, Levy, 1929; the German-Dutch border, Kloss, 1930; the German-Danish border, Bock, 1938; and Spanish/Portuguese language contact along the Uruguay-Brazil border, Rona, 1959, 1963). The U.S.–Mexican border, however, has not been the subject of such study. Little is known, for example, about intergroup communication between border cities, and even less is known about why and when monolingual members of each language group become bilingual.

In the light of the importance of studying Spanish in contact with English in contexts in which Spanish is not limited in function because of its minority status, the study of the effects of contact between Spanish and English on the Mexican side of the border becomes particularly attractive. Not only is the type and frequency of language contact likely to be significantly different from that found within Hispanic communities in the United States, but, more important, the position of the Spanish language itself, its general status as the national language, and its use in interaction in situations varying from the most formal to the most intimate contrasts with both its prestige and function among U.S. Hispanics.

THE JUÁREZ/EL PASO BORDER

The two largest cities on the U.S.-Mexican border are Ciudad Juárez (often called simply Juárez), which is located in the Mexican state of Chihuahua, and

El Paso, which is located at the extreme western tip of the state of Texas. The Rio Grande (known in Mexico as the Río Bravo) forms a boundary between the two cities and the two countries. The cities are located in an arid region between two mountain chains. While population figures vary, in general most estimates agree with Goodson, Bolds, and Palmore (1974), who cite a population of 401,270 for El Paso in 1974, and with Palmore, Roth, Foster, and James (1974), who predicted a population of 699,867 for Juárez by 1980.

Characteristics of El Paso

El Paso is in many ways a typical American city of its size. It does, however, reflect the long-term contact with the Mexican border. For example, domestic labor is cheap and plentiful in El Paso, a fact which has allowed many women who have preschool children to become active members of the El Paso labor pool. El Pasoans habitually cross the Mexican border, not only as tourists, but also as customers who seek bargains in barber and beauty shops and other such establishments and in the purchase of gasoline, fruits and vegetables, meat, liquor, soda pop, and other goods. Promotion literature for the El Paso area emphasizes the advantages to be derived from the proximity of Mexico and seeks to attract tourists who, because of their interest in Juárez, may tangentially bring benefits to the El Paso community.

The economies of the two cities are essentially interdependent. The El Paso downtown area, an area which in other cities of the same size has already declined, has been kept alive because of the walk-across traffic of shoppers from Juárez who seek goods either unavailable in Juárez or more expensive there. Events such as the devaluation of the peso in 1976 have resulted in serious problems for the El Paso merchants. During 1976, these merchants sought federal disaster aid for the area because of the impact of reduced shopping by Mexican nationals.

Characteristics of the Population of Juárez

Owing to both natural population growth and constant migration from the interior of Mexico, Juárez has a rate of growth of 5.7% annually, greater than the average rate of growth, 3.3%, for Mexico as a whole. It is estimated that only 48% of the city's population is native to the general area. It is estimated also that 65.6% of its residents are 23 years old or younger, the largest concentration of population centering around the ages of 6 to 11.

CHARACTERISTICS OF THE MIGRANT POPULATION
According to Antonio Ugalde (1974), who has studied the urbanization process of one Juárez *colonia popular,* the news of opportunities available on the border brings large numbers of peasants and transients from the states of Coa-

huila, Durango, Zacatecas, and the southern part of Chihuahua. Few families migrate directly from their place of birth to the border, however. It has been found that most individuals migrate in steps, beginning with a move to an urban area close to their birthplace and ending with their arrival in Juárez. When interviewed, most individuals indicate that while proximity to the United States was a factor in their choosing Juárez, most came because they hoped to be near friends and family who had already settled in the city.

Only 45% of the individuals questioned by Ugalde had worked in the United States, either legally or illegally. Working there was generally perceived by these respondents as a temporary solution during extended periods of unemployment or during a financial crisis at home. Crossing to the United States seemed a good opportunity to make large amounts of money in a relatively short length of time. Few, however, seemed interested in living in the United States, a claim which is supported by the relatively short periods of residency reported by these same persons. Only 20% of the residents of the *colonia* studied by Ugalde had spent a year or more outside of Mexico; 58% had spent 4 months or less.

EMPLOYMENT

Residents of Juárez can be divided into two principal categories: persons who are employed in El Paso, and persons who are employed in Juárez.

Those who are employed in Juárez have jobs that include the entire range of occupations normally found in Latin American cities of the same size. One finds major professionals and executives of large concerns, lesser professionals and executives of medium-sized concerns, semiprofessionals and administrators of small businesses, technicians and owners of petty businesses, skilled workmen, semiskilled workmen, and unskilled workers. Income levels vary greatly, and class divisions are rigid. Membership in what have been termed euphemistically *las clases acomodadas* is dependent on both family ties and socioeconomic level.

Persons who are employed in El Paso legally are known as Green-Card commuters. These commuters have the status of legal aliens in the United States, but prefer to reside on the Mexican side of the border. Martínez (1978) cites studies conducted by the U.S. Immigration and Naturalization Service which estimate that in 1973, 40,000 Green-Carders crossed the El Paso/Juárez border daily. A related group consists of U.S. citizens (persons who were born in El Paso) who reside in Juárez. In 1973, it was estimated that 19,000 U.S. citizens of all ages were residing in Mexico.

One tenth of all Green-Carders in the El Paso area are thought to work in agriculture, with nearly one-third in industry and over one-fourth in sales and service jobs. It is estimated also that about 40% of the income generated by *juarenses* derives from commuter employment in El Paso.

EDUCATION

In a study entitled "The Ciudad Juárez Plan for Comprehensive Socio-Economic Development: A Model for Northern Mexican Border Cities," Palmore et al. (1974) found that 42% of the population ages 15 and over complete primary school; 28.1% receive a secondary-school education; 18.1% attend a preparatory or vocational school. The current potential number of students seeking university education in Juárez is thought to be 12,461.

Juárez has 2 universities, 9 preparatory or vocational schools, and 57 secondary schools. The city's primary schools accommodate a potential number of 483 children per school.

Educational facilities in Juárez are complemented by facilities available in El Paso. Traditionally, children of upper-middle-class families are not sent to Mexican public schools. In Juárez, this results in children being sent to El Paso schools (private one-sex academies, parochial schools that accept students who pay tuition, public schools that accept out-of-state students on a tuition basis) or to a handful of "accepted" private schools in Juárez. Other families, who may value an English-language education for various reasons, but who cannot afford to pay out-of-state or private-school tuition, often use a variety of interesting ploys in order to send their children to El Paso public schools. Currently, attendance at the University of Texas at El Paso is also high, as is that at the newly established El Paso Community College.

Children who attend school in El Paso ordinarily commute daily, along with Green-Carders, and spend an 8-hour period in El Paso, returning home in the late afternoon.

GENERAL OVERVIEW

To the casual visitor, Juárez does indeed resemble a *Babilonia pocha* (a culturally corrupted Babylon). Its ties with the interior are loose, a situation which, in the past, has contributed to its reputation. However, overall, Juárez is a typical provincial Mexican city, down to its very Spanish *Casino*. The striking contrast between rich and poor is as apparent as it tends to be in Mexico City. One finds exclusive neighborhoods made up of palatial residences, while *colonias populares*, where *paracaidistas*, or squatters, live in cardboard shacks, surround the city on all sides.

As befits a city which depends on tourism, one finds gaudy tourist joints and curio shops, along with the very tastefully designed PRONAF shopping center (Programa Nacional Fronterizo), which serves as a showcase for Mexican arts and crafts. There are parts of the city which are strictly tourist areas, others which cater to both groups (the Juárez racetrack, the bullrings, certain restaurants), and others which serve an exclusively Mexican clientele (the Juárez Country Club, and certain restaurants, shops, and shopping areas).

Recent radical change in the Mexican government's policy toward border communities has resulted in careful attention to economic planning in Juárez. This turn of events has had a profound impact on the city. The presence of both the PRONAF, as well as the Border Industrialization Program (BIP), has aided considerably in transforming Juárez into one of the most important urban centers in Mexico. The PRONAF program has contributed to the promotion of Mexico as a whole and has increased tourism in general. The BIP program, begun in 1965, has led to the establishment of over 100 predominantly foreign-owned factories in the Juárez area. These twin plants, or *maquiladoras,* involve a system in which U.S.-manufactured component items are exported to Mexico for labor-intensive processing and then imported to the United States again, where duty is paid only on the value added through labor. The plants help reduce unemployment in Mexico and benefit U.S. firms through the use of inexpensive semiskilled labor.

More recently, in an attempt to reduce the amount of shopping habitually done by Mexicans in the United States, the Mexican government established a special program involving the importation of *artículos gancho* (enticement products). Under the guidelines of this program, merchants residing in designated border zones may import popular American products duty free for resale in their communities. Mexican merchants agree, however, to stock their stores with at least 50% Mexican products. In this way, Mexican merchants make profits that otherwise would go to foreigners. The impressive growth of the *gancho* business was curtailed somewhat by the peso devaluation in 1976.

Summarizing briefly, it can be said that while Juárez does indeed have many characteristics of the popular concept of "border town," in many ways it is much more than this. The great majority of its residents work in Juárez in commerce, industry, and service professions. Their livelihood is only tangentially connected to the fact that the city happens to be on the border. The recent aggressive programs established for the *zonas fronterizas* are an important factor in the city's determination to break its economic dependence on the United States.

LANGUAGE USE IN JUÁREZ

Except in the tourist areas, all communication in Juárez takes place in Spanish. Spanish is the expected language for all exchanges among its residents. Superficially at least, Juárez does not appear to be a bilingual city; that is to say, there is no evidence that activities are normally carried out in two languages by its residents or even that persons who are bilingual choose to address other bilinguals in anything other than Spanish. In the street, English is heard only in the tourist areas of the city. It is the language that all street vendors, sales clerks, and waiters there normally select to address customers and potential customers. Indeed Juárez residents who may find themselves in these parts of town must clearly identify themselves as Mexican nationals, in order for the communication to proceed in Spanish. Physical appearance alone is not sufficient, because of the fact that visitors from the United States, Chicanos whose ability in Spanish may be limited, clearly prefer to be addressed in English.

The three daily newspapers are written in Spanish and do not contain sections in which English is used. While much advertising is carried by the dailies for El Paso stores, all such advertisements are carefully worded to order to avoid the use of English. These advertisements often go to great lengths to provide Spanish names for new or "trendy" items for which there are no established equivalents.

All Juárez broadcasting stations use only Spanish, and, again, great care seems to be taken to avoid the use of English in advertising on the air. The two television channels (one originating in Juárez and the other in Mexico City) also use only Spanish. Advertising in general, including billboards and handbills, is found only in Spanish.

The language of the schools is Spanish. English is taught as a foreign language at the secondary level and, at certain private schools, at the elementary level. Specialized *institutos* and *academias* claim to be involved in intensive language teaching. These institutions seem to be quite popular and advertise widely. Most of these language schools schedule 2- or 3-hour daily sessions at different times of the day and evening in order to accommodate working adults.

Attitudes Toward English

In a preliminary study carried out in 7 *zonas comerciales* (business areas) in the Juárez area by the author, 50 out of 50 persons interviewed rated English as *very important* for Juárez residents. When asked if English were *equal to, less important than,* or *more important than* other languages for worldwide communication, 35 respondents ranked it as *more important,* and the remaining 15 ranked it as *equal to* other languages. Not a single individual questioned, however, ranked English as *more important* than Spanish. Twenty-four individuals thought English to be *just as important* as Spanish, and 26 thought it to be *less important.* When questioned further, most individuals favored a policy which would make English a regular part of the elementary-school curriculum.

Negative attitudes toward bilingualism in general, of the type usually present in the popular mind in the United States, were not reflected. There was a general feeling that since it was "normal" and "useful" for individuals who live in Juárez to learn English, they might as well do so in childhood. All individuals questioned agreed that childhood was the ideal time to acquire another language.

Of the 50 individuals questioned, 18 had received a part of their education in El Paso schools or currently had children enrolled in El Paso schools. None of them seemed concerned about the "immersion" aspects of their own or their children's language experience. The general feeling seemed to be that Spanish would not be "damaged" by such a process, and, further, that a temporary academic setback would be overcome as soon as English could be acquired.

Use of English by Juárez Residents

While it has been established above that Juárez residents normally do not use English for most exchanges with other residents of the city, a large number of individuals might reasonably be expected to be in contact with English-speaking persons at least part of the time on a daily or frequent basis. Such individuals can be divided into two large groups; persons who potentially interact with monolingual English-speakers in El Paso, and those who potentially interact with monolingual English-speakers in Juárez.

PERSONS WHO USE OR ARE EXPOSED TO ENGLISH IN EL PASO
Potentially, this group of Juárez residents includes individuals who are employed on the U.S. side of the border. In its widest sense, it includes illegal aliens, Green-Carders, U.S. citizens residing in Juárez, and any other group which might be employed in El Paso. Since the principal occupations of this group of persons as a whole (as reflected by the U.S. Immigration and Naturalization Service) are in the areas of agriculture, construction, and sales, there is some doubt about the exact needs of persons in this group for English-language communication skills. One might legitimately conjecture that persons involved in sales or service would ordinarily be expected to have some command of English, although most El Paso retail stores and similar business establishments tend to hire persons who can communicate with their Spanish-speaking monolingual clientele. This entire question needs to be studied further.

A second group of Juárez residents who might be expected to use English in El Paso includes children and young people who are attending El Paso schools. Ordinarily such youngsters will spend their entire school day using or listening to English in the classroom environment. (It is doubtful that many Juárez parents whose main objective is that their children be immersed in an English-language environment enroll their sons or daughters in bilingual programs in which Spanish is the primary language.)

It must not be assumed, however, that because children use English in the classroom they will also do so outside the classroom during the normal school day. Juárez children generally cluster together, and some do not make friends with their English-speaking monolingual peers. Many schools enforce a "no Spanish" rule at the request of tuition-paying parents. In any event, it can be assumed that children who attend El Paso schools for a reasonable length of time will acquire English-language skills.

A third group of individuals who might be expected to use or be exposed to English in El Paso includes persons who shop there, those who conduct business of various sorts in that city, and those who spend part of their leisure time in the El Paso area. While it is certainly possible for a Juárez resident to shop in El Paso without speaking English because of the interest most stores have in wooing Juárez customers, it is also possible that certain categories of business might not have bilingual employees. This is especially true of establishments such as banks, real estate companies, travel agencies, and the like, that do not have a large Juárez clientele. One could conjecture, therefore, that those individuals who frequently shop or conduct business in such establishments will have worked out a means for communicating with the English-speaking monolinguals involved. In some cases, such adaptation includes the use of pidginlike forms by both speakers.

On the other hand, people from Juárez who frequently see movies or plays in El Paso have, at least, a receptive control of the language. This activity is quite common for Juárez residents, particularly on Sunday, because of the overcrowded condition of most Juárez movie theaters.

PERSONS WHO USE OR ARE EXPOSED TO ENGLISH IN JUÁREZ
Potentially, also, Juárez residents who listen to El Paso radio or watch El Paso television, see an American movie which is not dubbed but has subtitles, or work in the kind of establishment (restaurant, store, bank, racetrack, bullring) which might be visited by English-speaking tourists are exposed to English in Juárez. It is difficult to ascertain, however, how much English persons who work in tourist areas must actually control. The same preliminary questionnaire mentioned above failed to probe deeply enough into this general area. Individuals tend to downplay their English-language skills in standard self-report scales and at the same time list a variety of complex activities they have carried out in English. Extensive recording must be carried out of the speech of persons engaged in the "trade" activities and perhaps in formal interview settings.

It is difficult to conjecture how many people are actually involved in activities in which they come into contact with English-speaking monolinguals. In each tourist area of the city, there are certainly several hundred such persons. On the other hand, a copy of the regular Sunday edition of Juárez's largest daily, *El Fronterizo,* included only 3 out of 57 help-wanted advertisements that called for English-language skills.

A second group of persons who might use English in Juárez itself is also potentially very large. It includes all individuals who in one context or another have learned English at some time and who might find themselves in a situation in which a "secret" language is needed. Not surprisingly, English is used by parents to speak to each other when they do not want their children to understand. In the same way, young people who have attended schools in El Paso will often speak to each other in English when they do not wish to be understood by parents, grandparents, servants, and others. One can easily hypothesize that many other Juárez bilinguals do this also. Indeed, the one exception to the primarily-Spanish rule for public interaction among Juárez residents might involve exactly such a situation.

Language Contact in the El Paso/Juárez Area: A Summary

Summarizing briefly, it can be said that language contact does indeed take place across the United States–Mexican border. Examining only the extent to which English might be used or needed by Juárez residents has made obvious, however, that many features of language contact need to be studied more fully. It is clear that the Juárez area cannot be called a bilingual area in the same sense in which the literature has referred to Puerto Rican or Chicano barrios in the United States, where English and Spanish often are used by the same individuals among themselves and also separately in certain contexts. Indeed, it is uncertain whether one can really refer to the Juárez side of the border alone as a bilingual community at all. Definitions established for other contact situations may not be useful in this one.

At the same time, the differences between this border situation and contexts in which Spanish is a minority language are clearly evident. Juárez residents for the most part are comfortable living in Mexico, think of themselves as Mexican (which, in their minds, is different from being Chicano or Mexican American), and learn English for instrumental and economic reasons. Few desire, in a general sense, to become American, or to be accepted by Americans. *Juarenses* are essentially *border people* needing and taking advantage of the best of both countries. It is this fact which makes the study of Juárez particularly important.

The final section of this paper will be devoted to a discussion of exactly how the study of such border people can contribute to existing knowledge about bilingualism in general and specifically to our understanding of Spanish/English language contact.

LANGUAGE CONTACT IN THE EL PASO/JUÁREZ AREA: QUESTIONS FOR RESEARCH

Language Acquisition

A number of important questions can be studied in the El Paso/Juárez area which are basic to the understanding of second-language acquisition in both natural and classroom settings. For example, it is known that many individuals of different ages, from different educational and socioeconomic levels, learn English at some point in their lives if they remain in Juárez. It would be interesting, therefore, to determine exactly how these factors influence learning. Is there an ideal age for learning English? Is childhood really the most efficient age? How does educational background affect the rate of learning? Can different levels of motivation relating to socioeconomic background be determined? What are the effects of the various language-learning contexts, specifically: 1) language immersion in El Paso schools; 2) language immersion in the work setting; 3) formal instruction in Juárez, with subsequent immersion; 4) formal instruction alone; 5) various types of formal instruction (methods, teacher-student ratio, etc.); 6) exposure to English on television, radio, and movies; 7) exposure to English through older siblings or other members of the family?

Potentially, a very large number of studies can be designed. Records can be found for individuals who have attended various language schools in the Juárez area, and newly arrived migrants can be studied from the moment of initial exposure.

Language and Education

The entire question of language and its role in education is one which has caused much controversy in the United States. It has been claimed that language is a key factor in the educational process and therefore the underlying cause of the academic problems of Hispanics in the United States. Current educational thinking in the United States holds that children who speak languages other than English must receive their basic education in their own language.

While one would not disagree that language is one of several factors involved in academic problems of non-English-speaking children, it is clear that there are other equally important aspects which have not been focused on. Conclusions about the importance of language are based on the study of minority populations. However, it is not known how upper-middle-class children who speak languages other than English might succeed in traditional English-only programs, as opposed to children of the same language group but of low socioeconomic background. Where there are such upper-middle-class children in the United States, they are generally not monolingual speakers of minority languages. Loss of original language is still the norm among most immigrant groups. Thus a basic comparison cannot be made in the United States. Educators can only speculate, on the basis of the Culver City (Cohen, 1975) and Canadian findings (Lambert and Tucker, 1972), that middle-class children might respond well to total-immersion programs.

Juárez, with its long tradition of educating upper-middle-class children in El Paso schools, provides a very large group with which a comparison could be made. One private school in the area, for example, has academic records, including standardized test reports, going back over a 25-year period. There is much evidence suggesting that middle-class Mexican children who are products of immersion programs derive important benefits from bilingualism and often outdistance monolingual English-speaking peers in general achievement.

Recently Cummins (1977) and Skutnabb-Kangas (1979) have raised new questions concerning the relationship between language development in L_1 (the first language) and subsequent development in L_2 (the second language). It is conjectured by some that, while meaningful, the social-class factor may not be of great importance in predicting either proficiency in L_2 or academic achievement. The more precise predictor, it has been argued, is the level of language development attained in L_1.

The Juárez area is again an ideal setting for the study of such questions. Because children from Juárez of different backgrounds, ages, and abilities have attended El Paso schools of different types, it is possible to gather data on the academic histories not only of upper-middle-class children, but also of lower-middle-class and working-class children. It is equally possible to compare the performance of Juárez children who have entered El Paso schools at different levels. It is frequently the case that Juárez children complete 6 years of elementary schooling in Mexico and then transfer to begin high school work in El Paso. Patterns vary, however, and it would be possible to identify groups of children of different socioeconomic levels who have entered various types of English-language schools after different experiences in the Mexican school system. It is possible also, at the same time, to explore the impact on both language acquisition and academic achievement of the ethnic backgrounds of students and teachers and the neighborhood setting of the schools in question.

The Presence and Frequency of Language-Contact Phenomena

The study of Spanish/English language-contact phenomena (such as integration, interference, and code switching) is of particular interest because of the potential comparison which can be made with contact features that have been studied in Chicano and Puerto Rican Spanish. Extensive, well-planned recording in Juárez, which would include a broad range of speech situations and individuals, could reveal interesting aspects about the following:

1. The presence of integrated borrowings from English in the speech of individuals of different educational and socioeconomic backgrounds, bilingual and monolingual
2. The attitude toward such borrowings among bilingual and monolingual speakers of various ages and backgrounds
3. The presence of transfer (involuntary) from English in the speech of bilinguals of various ages, backgrounds, and proficiency levels

4. The attitude toward such transfer by bilinguals and monolinguals of the various types mentioned
5. The presence of acceptance of code switching among bilinguals of the various types mentioned
6. The presence of pidginlike codes

Juárez provides a context in which one could examine the very direct aspects of language-learning modes and environments against the presence of language-contact phenomena, the effect of residency in the United States and interaction with U.S. Hispanics, the effect of specialized education in a specific discipline carried out in English on professionals who subsequently work in Spanish, and finally, the effect of American television. While such a study, particularly one that focuses on frequency of use of either transfer features or integrated borrowings, presents the same methodological problems of quantification that have plagued studies in the United States, it is nevertheless important to emphasize its place in our understanding of what have been considered basic processes in language-contact settings.

Types of Bilingualism

A no less serious methodological problem than that mentioned above is encountered in approaching the measurement of bilingualism. It is reasonable to expect, therefore, that levels and types of bilingualism as they are found in the Juárez area cannot be measured with absolute accuracy either. At the same time, it is clear that the various situations and contexts which result in exposure to and use of English in Juárez have produced varying levels of proficiency in English-language skills. A researcher focusing on this problem, then, might wish to develop a method for assessing both receptive and productive English-language skills in individuals who range from educated professionals to illiterate laborers. One might want to determine, for example, the number of registers controlled by an individual in Spanish, as well as his total functioning capacity in a wide variety of settings. One could then compare his English-language "range" with that of his Spanish. In this way, one could differentiate between individuals who can use both languages in the same functional contexts (for example, who can give formal lectures in both Spanish and English) and individuals who cannot do so in either language, or who can use only one of their languages in most contexts. Essentially, this type of study would be asking such questions as:

1. If an individual uses an "elaborated" code in one language, will he acquire it in another?
2. Will an individual normally acquire only those levels (registers) of language that he already uses in his native language?

3. How well do productive skills exercised in a limited domain (e.g., selling curios) transfer to other domains?
4. Is there a difference between individuals who learn English for instrumental reasons (i.e., the desire to work in the United States) and those individuals who believe that all educated persons should speak more than one language?
5. How do self-report data on English-language proficiency correlate with other language measures?
6. Do individuals who learn English in an American environment and who have learned and continued to use Spanish in a totally Mexican environment become "coordinate" bilinguals?
7. How do these individuals compare with others who have begun their study of English in Juárez?
8. Can the "compound"/"coordinate" distinction be supported in this setting and for these groups of bilinguals?

The questions which can be asked and answered about language contact and bilingualism by a study of Ciudad Juárez are clearly many. Few questions, however, as has been made evident above, are simple and direct. In most cases, in order to obtain benefits from studies in this context, researchers will have to address questions which, precisely because of their complexity, have only been studied superficially or have not been addressed in other settings. One would hope that current interest in border research might, however, bring this or similar contexts to the attention of investigators in general.

REFERENCES

Bock, K. N. Graenseegnenes Sprog: Mellemslesvigs sprogforhold. In F. V. Jessen (Ed.), *Haandbog i det slesvigske Sprogsmaals Historie, 1900–1937* (Vol. 3). Copenhagen: C. A. Reitzel, 1938.

Cohen, Andrew. *A sociolinguistic approach to bilingual education: Experiments in the American Southwest.* Rowley, Mass.: Newbury House, 1975.

Cummins, J. The cognitive development of bilingual children: A review of current research. *Indian Journal of Applied Linguistics,* 1978, *4.*

Goodson, S., Bolds, J., & Palmore, G. Industrial location: El Paso, Texas. *The El Paso Economic Review,* 1974, *11*(9), 1–4.

Kloss, H. Die niederlandisch-deutsche Sprachgrenze, insbesondere in der Grafshaft Bentheim. *Deutsche Akademie Mitteilungen,* 1930, 96–109.

Lambert, Wallace E., and Tucker, G. Richard. *Bilingual education of children: The St. Lambert Experiment.* Rowley, Mass.: Newbury House, 1972.

Levy, P. *Historie linguistique d'Alsace et de Lorraine* (2 Vols.). Paris: Societé d'editión, Les Belles Lettres, 1929.

Martinez, O. J. *Border boom town: Ciudad Juárez since 1848.* Austin, Tex.: University of Texas Press, 1978.

Palmore, G. L., Roth, T. P., Foster, J. R., & James, D. D. The Ciudad Juárez plan for comprehensive socio-economic development: A model for Northern Mexican border cities. *El Paso Economic Review,* 1974, *11*(6), 1–4.

Rona, J. P. *El dialecto fronterizo del norte del Uruguay.* Montevideo, Uruguay: Adolfo Linardi, 1959.

——. La frontera lingüística entre el portugués y el español en el norte del Uruguay (Porto Alegre, Brazil). *Revista Veritas,* 1963.

Skutnabb-Kangas, T. *Language in the process of cultural assimilation and structural incorporation of linguistic minorities.* Rosslyn, Va.: National Clearinghouse for Bilingual Education, 1979.

Ugalde, A. *The urbanization process of a poor Mexican neighborhood.* Austin, Tex.: University of Texas Press, 1974.

2 | La Investigación del Español en México y en el Suroeste de los Estados Unidos: Posibilidades de Aproximación

JUAN M. LOPE BLANCH
Universidad Nacional Autónoma de México

El tema que se me ha pedido que presente ante ustedes me parece bastante complejo y de muy difícil resolución. La tarea de coordinar, armonizar o siquiera aproximar los intereses de diversos investigadores es, en verdad, tarea ingrata y de resultados dudosos. El pesimismo que estas palabras muestran está plenamente justificado en mi caso. He tenido ya varias experiencias en ese campo, y siempre han surgido dificultades más o menos graves.

Investigar, trabajar individualmente, estudiar los problemas que a uno le interesan, es placentero y puede inclusive resultar fácil. Pero aproximar actitudes, reunir voluntades y coordinar intereses múltiples me parecen empresas enormes, por no decir que utópicas. Mis actividades como coordinador del "Proyecto de estudio *coordinado* de la norma lingüística culta de las principales ciudades de América y de la Península Ibérica" han tropezado con no pocos obstáculos y han tenido que vencer dificultades de muy diversa naturaleza. Claro está que, al cabo de quince años, me cabe la satisfacción de advertir que ese Proyecto ha sido la actividad más provechosa y feliz de todas las respaldadas por el Programa Interamericano de Lingüística y Enseñanza de Idiomas, satisfacción que probablemente ha sido la causa de que aceptara hablar ante ustedes en torno al delicado tema que los organizadores de esta conferencia tan gentilmente me propusieron.

Trataré, pues, de someter a su consideración algunas sugerencias sobre la posibilidad de aproximar, en alguna medida, las investigaciones que se están haciendo o pueden hacerse en el futuro en torno al español hablado al norte y al sur del Río Bravo.

Se me ocurre pensar que tal aproximación podría intentarse a través de tres caminos básicos: 1) el "oficial" o institucional; 2) el personal o individual; 3) una combinación de ambos.

18

Esta última posibilidad sería, sin duda, la más provechosa, pero también la más compleja, puesto que presupone la existencia de las dos anteriores. Pero se sabe que un proyecto institucional que no contara con la colaboración de investigadores personalmente interesados, no podría pasar de la etapa de gestación. Y sabe también que una investigación amplia, iniciada por acuerdo exclusivamente personal, pero sin contar con un sólido respaldo institucional, correría el peligro de morir en su infancia o de quedar trunca e incompleta. Habría, pues, que tratar de reunir intereses personales e institucionales.

Cuando concebí el "Proyecto de estudio de la norma urbana de Hispanoamérica" y más aún cuando esbocé el "Proyecto de delimitación de las zonas dialectales de México," excluí de ambas empresas los territorios hispanohablantes que hoy forman parte de los Estados Unidos. No influyó en esa decisión, por supuesto, ninguna causa de carácter discriminatorio, sino todo lo contrario. Actué así pensando que en todo el sur de los Estados Unidos había en aquel entonces mucha más capacidad—institucional e individual—para llevar a cabo esas empresas. Con posterioridad, he ido advirtiendo que también en los Estados Unidos se produce una acusada falta de coordinación entre unas y otras instituciones universitarias o filológicas.

Pero claro está que ya entonces pensaba—como sigo hoy pensando—que el estudio del español hablado en el *norte* de América queda grave y dolorosamente incompleto si abarca sólo el actual territorio de México y olvida el suroeste de los Estados Unidos. Juzgo de primera importancia estudiar conjuntamente las hablas hispánicas del norte y del sur de nuestra larga frontera. Pero me pregunto—y me hago la pregunta con pocas esperanzas de obtener respuesta afirmativa—si habría alguien en los Estados Unidos, actualmente, que se interesara por hacer ese trabajo con los propósitos y los métodos fundamentales del proyecto hispanoamericano. Mi suposición de que la respuesta sería negativa me parece prueba contundente de nuestro actual distanciamiento.

Trataré de presentar las directrices fundamentales del proyecto hispanoamericano, para que sea posible apreciar su distanciamiento respecto de las investigaciones que suelen llevarse a cabo en el suroeste de los Estados Unidos.

A las instituciones filológicas de Hispanoamérica y de España—a los estudiosos o investigadores que a ellas representaban—les pareció de primordial importancia llegar al conocimiento—al simple y puro conocimiento—de la actual realidad lingüística de sus respectivos países, vista a través de la norma general, *estándar,* propia de sus ciudades capitales. (Sólo en este sentido se concibió el proyecto como estudio de la "Norma culta urbana," pero no como consecuencia de actitudes elitistas o de afanes de corrección purista.)

A todos nosotros nos pareció necesario alcanzar un conocimiento general, global, del estado que guarda la lengua española actualmente en las principales ciudades del mundo hispánico. Tal conocimiento podría servir como punto de partida para posteriores investigaciones más especializadas, más particulares y concretas en su alcance. Nuestro propósito inicial era, por lo tanto, simplemente *descriptivo,* sin mayores complejidades. Al llegar a este punto me asalta de nuevo la duda de que, en esta época, coloreada por los intensos y complejos matices de la sociolingüística, difícilmente podría encontrarse en los Estados Unidos a un grupo de investigadores interesado en *describir* simplemente el estado actual del español hablado en el suroeste del país. Y parece que aún menos cabría esperar que esas personas, de existir, pudieran interesar en la empresa a las instituciones oficiales sin cuyo concurso la tarea sería prácticamente irrealizable. Porque—podrían todos ellos objetar—¿por qué abrazar finalidades y métodos propios de los comienzos de siglo, cuando el progreso de la lingüística ha abierto nuevos y más brillantes horizontes?

Y sin embargo nosotros, los investigadores hispanoamericanos, pensamos que era necesario comenzar desde el principio, casi desde cero, con esos propósitos antiguos, por la sencilla razón de que *eso*—ese estado del conocimiento lingüístico propio de la primera mitad del siglo—no se había alcanzado todavía en la mayor parte de nuestros países. Allí donde se hubiese cumplido y superado esa etapa del conocimiento, sería posible y conveniente adentrarse por nuevos caminos científicos; pero el estudio del español americano general estaba todavía "en pañales," y nos pareció conveniente ponerle pantalón corto antes de vestirlo de largo o de smoking. . . .

Tras esta breve justificación de nuestro "anacrónico" proyecto, vuelvo a mi anterior consideración sobre los caminos que tal vez permitiesen llegar a una aproximación en las investigaciones lingüísticas sobre el español de México y el del sur de los Estados Unidos.

Decía que me parece necesario contar con algún respaldo oficial o institucional si se quiere garantizar la continuidad de los trabajos. Empresas de largo alcance, como son éstas, requieren de plazos amplios para su ejecución, del concurso de varios investigadores, y de financiamientos sólidos. Todo lo cual sólo puede ser proporcionado por alguna institución universitaria o de similar naturaleza.

Supongo que no podremos ahora, en esta conferencia de desarrollo tan breve, estudiar y analizar la cuestión. La presenta como una simple sugerencia, con la remota esperanza de que caiga en terreno propicio y abonado. Aún más: pecando tal vez de optimista—y para no decepcionar a los organizadores de este coloquio, que algo tendrían en mente al proponerme el tema de mi intervención—, me atrevo a imaginar que acaso no fuera totalmente imposible pensar en organizar un sistema de información que nos permitiera estar al tanto de las investigaciones que sobre el español se realicen al norte y al sur de nuestra frontera. Del conocimiento de lo que unos y otros estemos haciendo puede nacer el interés recíproco y el deseo de colaboración, pero si no sabemos qué hacen los demás, será imposible que podamos armonizar o aproximar intereses.

Pienso, pues, que tal vez fuera posible organizar una especie de "banco de datos," similar a los que han organizado otras instituciones científicas en América. Lo imagino ahora como una sencilla y modesta "Oficina de información sobre el español del norte de América" o algo semejante. Sería un simple centro de documentación al que deberían hacerse llegar informes sobre investigaciones en proyecto o en curso, de manera que desde allí se pudieran después reproducir y distribuir entre todos los interesados—instituciones o personas—por la investigación del español mexicano o estadounidense. Faltaría, por supuesto, determinar quién podría hacerse responsable del funcionamiento de esa oficina, y qué institución le proporcionaría el respaldo indispensable. No me parece utópico suponer que cualquiera de nuestras universidades estaría ampliamente capacitada para ello: la Universidad de Texas, en cualquiera de sus extensiones o recintos, la de California, o la propia Universidad Nacional Autónoma de México. Dejo caer, así, la semilla; tal vez germine la idea, y tengamos algún día tan necesaria oficina de información lingüística.

Si la cooperación institucional resulta indispensable, no lo es menos la aproximación o coordinación de intereses personales. También es necesario armonizar posiciones diversas y aún antagónicas. Por supuesto que las investigaciones sobre el español que se hagan al norte y al sur de la frontera tendrán, casi necesariamente, distintos enfoques. Y digo "necesariamente" por una simple y obvia razón: no es el mismo, ni mucho menos, el *status* de la lengua española en México (o en Venezuela, Colombia o la Argentina) que en el sur de los Estados Unidos. Lengua oficial (y a veces prácticamente única) en el primer caso, pero lengua de una minoría en el segundo. Y claro está que esa diferente situación de la lengua en los dos distintos territorios engendra una gran diversidad de problemas, de intereses científicos, de propósitos en el estudio.

Las implicaciones sociales que la "hispanofonía" tiene en el suroeste de los Estados Unidos son muy diferentes de las que tiene en México. De ahí que la orientación sociolingüística resulte básica, fundamental, en los estudios que se emprendan en los Estados Unidos, un tanto que los propósitos esencialmente descriptivos—dialectológicos en el sentido más estrecho de este término—son primordiales en los estudios relativos al español mexicano. Pero claro está que estas dos orientaciones no tienen por qué considerarse antagónicas y ni siquiera diversas, sino verdaderamente complementarias. Además de que la "dialectología vertical," no obstante sus profundas implicaciones sociológicas, no deja de ser pura y verdadera *dialectología,* según he dicho en otro lugar.

Por cierto que, al proyectar el estudio—descriptivo—del habla culta urbana, pensé que debía concebirse como un primer paso de una investigación dialectal más amplia, que se extendería, en etapas de trabajo posteriores, a los demás estratos sociales de la población. Así, estando ya muy avanzado el estudio de la norma culta mexicana, hemos iniciado ahora, en el Centro de Lingüística Hispánica de la Universidad Nacional Autónoma de México, investigaciones sobre la norma urbana popular, con resultados de indudable interés. Personalmente, he hecho una breve confrontación entre la cláusula propia del habla culta—en su promedio—y la típica del habla popular, y he llegado a conclusiones en cierto modo sorprendentes. Como lo ha sido advertir que la estructura de la cláusula culta se acerca bastante más a la estructura propia de la cláusula escrita que a la del habla inculta, con lo cual cabe pensar que el supuesto divorcio entre lengua hablada y lengua escrita acaso no sea más que producto de las murmuraciones de las malas lenguas, y que la desavenencia sea más acusada en el caso de la pareja formada por habla culta y habla popular. Pero no es éste el momento de tratar este asunto. Consideremos, en cambio, otros antagonismos que sí se relacionan con nuestro tema general. Permítanme detenerme en torno a uno muy particular, en el que creo que cabe alcanzar la armonía: el de polimorfismo y variación libre frente a condicionamiento sociológico.

No todas las variaciones libres son "libres," en efecto, pero no deja de haber variaciones verdaderamente libres, que dan lugar a las situaciones lingüísticas de polimorfismo puro. Entiendo por polimorfismo, en un sentido muy amplio, la concurrencia de dos o más formas lingüísticas—fonéticas, gramaticales o léxicas—que alternan libremente para desempeñar una misma función, tanto dentro de un sistema dialectal (habla de una localidad o región) cuanto en un sistema idiolectal o individual, polimorfismo este último que es el único que Jacques Allières considera verdadero y estricto polimorfismo. Claro está que este polimorfismo idiolectal es el determinante del polimorfismo dialectal, puesto que todo dialecto es la suma o reunión de múltiples hablas individuales; y claro está también que el polimorfismo dialectal permitirá distinguir entre dialectos—locales, regionales o aún nacionales—más coherentes y uniformes que otros, más polimórficos.

En ambos casos, cabe distinguir entre: 1) polimorfismo condicionado en alguna medida por A) factores lingüísticos, y B) factores socioculturales; y 2) polimorfismo libre, no condicionado, o polimorfismo "puro." Creo que, ante todo, hay que atender a los condicionamientos de carácter lingüístico, que suelen ser los más productivos e importantes, y luego prestar atención a los condicionamientos de carácter sociológico.

En la articulación del fonema /r/ en México, por ejemplo, observamos que las realizaciones asibiladas—sordas o sonoras y breves o largas [ř, r̄, ř̥, r̥̄]— alcanzan un porcentaje del 22%: [Ř] = 22%. Advertimos después que el total de articulaciones asibiladas [Ř] se distribuye de la siguiente manera:

1. en posición final de palabra ante pausa = 90%
2. en posición implosiva interior de palabra = 6%
3. en contacto posterior con /t/ = 4%[1]

Podemos entonces concluir que la asibilación de /r/ en el habla mexicana actual está condicionada—determinada mayoritariamente—por su posición dentro del contexto: por la posición final absoluta (factor lingüístico).

Si atendemos ahora a posibles condicionamientos sociológicos, advertimos que las realizaciones asibiladas se distribuyen del siguiente modo:

20% en hombres jóvenes incultos
24% en mujeres jóvenes incultas
18% en hombres adultos incultos
19% en mujeres adultas incultas
21% en hombres viejos incultos
17% en mujeres viejas incultas
21% en hombres jóvenes cultos
22% en mujeres jóvenes cultas
. . . . etcétera.

De todo lo cual *no* podremos concluir que el fenómeno sea propio de las mujeres de la primera generación carentes de instrucción escolar o familiar, no obstante que haya sido en su agrupación sociológica donde el fenómeno haya alcanzado un ligeramente superior porcentaje de incidencia (24%). Y ello, por la sencilla razón de que la diferencia porcentual es muy levemente superior a la de otras agrupaciones, y por el hecho inevitable de que, establecidas las agrupaciones de acuerdo con esos tres factores sociológicos, alguna de ellas habría de resultar ser la de índice superior y otra cualquiera la de índice inferior. (No es éste el momento de discutir qué intervalo porcentual mínimo podría considerarse sintomático de diferencias sociológicas.) No parece, pues, estar condicionado el fenómeno en cuestión por factores sociales.

En cambio, el hecho de que podamos observar que en la articulación de la -*r* final ante pausa, en un mismo hablante, en una misma situación y en idénticas condiciones de discurso, presente la siguientes realizaciones: [r] = 24%, [ɹ] = 26%, [ř] = 17%, [ř̃] = 15%, y [r̄] = 18%, sí nos permite concluir que el habla de ese informante—dentro ya de una particular situación y de un determinado contexto *lingüístico*—es obviamente polimórfica, y con polimorfismo libre o *puro*.

Sirva este ejemplo como muestra de la posibilidad de existencia del polimorfismo puro o de la variación libre. Posibilidad que la naturaleza misma del fenómeno en sí, explica, suficientemente. Quiero decir que el polimorfismo debe ser considerado como hecho inherente a cualquier sistema lingüístico, y no como un fenómeno ajeno a la lengua y excepcional en ella. Si una lengua no es un sistema estático e inmutable en sí mismo, y si su naturaleza es *dinámica,* el cambio no deberá considerarse ajeno a ella, sino parte integrante de ella misma y efecto de su dinamismo natural. Si, por otro lado, el cambio lingüístico—

como señaló Menéndez Pidal—tiene en muchos casos una duración *multisecular,* las situaciones de conflicto entre formas concurrentes pueden también mantenerse a lo largo de varios siglos, originando un polimorfismo sumamente duradero. En consecuencia—y a despecho de Saussure por un lado y de Chomsky por otro—, al establecer las obvias y necesarias relaciones entre la naturaleza dinámica de la lengua y la multisecularidad del cambio lingüístico, se comprenderá que el estado normal o natural de toda lengua—de todo dialecto—habrá de ser el estado polimórfico.

Y, repito, la polimorfía podrá estar muchas veces determinada por factores lingüísticos o sociológicos. Pero otras veces será el resultado simple y llano del ejercicio de las múltiples posibilidades que ofrece el sistema mismo. Y ello, tanto en el dominio fonético, cuanto en el morfosintáctico o en el lexicológico. No puedo descubrir ningún condicionamiento preciso en la alternancia, por ejemplo, de formas varias de la expresión dubitativa (del tipo "No sé si *está* / *estará* / *esté* bien así"), ni en la colocación del pronombre personal átono en el habla mexicana de nuestros días ("voy a hacer*lo* en seguida" / "*lo* voy a hacer en seguida"), ni en el orden de los elementos de ciertos períodos ("se lo daré cuando llegue / cuando llegue se lo daré"). Debo, pues, interpretarlos como casos de polimorfismo puro. Fenómeno cuya existencia no es posible negar, como tampoco lo sería ignorar los casos de condicionamiento sociológico—en el sentido amplio del término—, que hoy ya nadie parece poner en duda. Debemos, pues, aproximarnos en ambos sentidos, rehuyendo adoptar posturas extremas o excluyentes de otras alternativas.

En la preparación del atlas lingüístico general del español de México decidí entrevistar a un mínimo de siete informantes en cada localidad. Tomé esta decisión, a pesar de los inconvenientes materiales que para la ejecución de la empresa suponía, en primer lugar por mi consciencia del acusado estado polimórfico de las hablas mexicanas; pero también, aunque fuese en segundo término, por mi deseo de descubrir problemas de carácter sociolingüístico. Cierto es que la atención a sólo siete informantes en cada población había de resultar insuficiente para cualquier análisis de finalidades sociolingüísticas; pero no es menos cierto que ese procedimiento nos ha permitido *detectar* fenómenos o problemas de muy posible condicionamiento sociológico, que investigaciones posteriores y específicas podrán tratar de analizar detenidamente. Hemos podido, así, encontrar *síntomas* de hechos hasta ahora desconocidos que exigen un estudio pormenorizado, no ya geolingüístico, sino sociolingüístico.

Las investigaciones sobre el español del suroeste de los Estados Unidos podrían también beneficiarse si trataran de aproximarse a nuestros propósitos y procedimientos. El análisis detenido de problemas concretos y muy particulares de raíz sociológica no choca con el estudio—previo, a mi entender—de las realidades lingüísticas, dialectales, del español hablado en esta amplia región de los Estados Unidos. La visión general, global, de esa realidad lingüística puede servir como marco de referencia para las investigaciones monográficas. Y en este dominio es mucho lo que falta por hacer. Me decía hace unos momentos el Dr. Anthony Lozano que el Profesor Roland Ross, autor de un estudio descriptivo general del español hablado en San Luis, Colorado, no piensa publicar ya su investigación, como tal, por considerar que había sido concebida y ejecutada con propósitos esencialmente descriptivos y con métodos diferentes de los que se han ido generalizando durante los últimos años. Me parece que es ésta una decisión lamentable. Si el estudio de un dialecto tan singular e interesante como el de San Luis ha sido hecho con responsabilidad y honestidad—y supongo que así ha sido hecho—, será siempre un estudio válido y científico, que contribuirá a enriquecer nuestro conocimiento del español norteamericano, aunque no coincida con los propósitos ni los métodos de otros estudios "más modernos." El Profesor Ross ha trabajado por cubrir una de las lagunas generales que había en la lingüística hispano-norteamericana; no debería dejar la laguna abierta para los demás. Su decisión de mantener inédito el fruto de su esfuerzo parece una prueba inequívoca más de que es preciso que nos aproximemos, mutuamente, quienes estamos interesados en estudiar el español hablado en estas regiones.

NOTA

1. Porcentajes ficticios, usados sólo a manera de ejemplo teórico.

3 | A Research Agenda for Native American Languages

ELIZABETH A. BRANDT
Arizona State University

This paper selectively surveys past research on Native American languages in the Borderlands and points out realistic dimensions for future research. In the development of the research agenda, I have followed the lead of my coeditor, Jacob Ornstein, who stated in 1971, "Returning now to our own Southwest, there are enough tasks here for the study of bilingualism/biculturalism to involve hundreds of individuals for goodness knows how many lifetimes" (p. 323). He developed a list of some 60 specific research targets for Southwestern languages, many of which remain to be accomplished. I recommend his list to you and have developed my own as a supplement specific for Native American languages (see appendix, p. 40).

This survey of the literature focuses most strongly on the languages spoken in that vast area of mountain and desert which covers most of Northern Mexico and the present U.S. Southwest. This area has been called the "Gran Chichemeca" or "Chichemec Sea" by Riley and Hedrick (1978) and represented the northern frontier of the rich Puebloan cultures of the Southwest. It was a constant sphere of prehistoric interaction. Kelly (1974) argues in a controversial thesis that trading groups known by others as *trocadores, pochteca,* or *puchteca* maintained a far-flung network of social contact and traded widely (Sahlins, 1965) throughout this region. Goods such as macaw feathers, copper bells, and shells from the Pacific were brought to the Southwest and traded for turquoise and pottery. Kelly and others even suggest that some traders were resident in areas such as Chaco Canyon in New Mexico and Casas Grandes in Chihuahua, with other contacts extending to California on the west and Kan-

This paper is a greatly revised version of a paper entitled "A realistic agenda for a border linguist" presented at a conference on border linguistics sponsored by the Cross-cultural Ethnic Studies Center and the Inter-American Center of the University of Texas at El Paso in July 1978. I wish to acknowledge the assistance of Cliff Hughes, David Schwartz, and, especially, Chris MacCrate, in searching the literature. Their assistance brought the paper to completion. I am solely responsible for the views and interpretations of the literature expressed here.

sas, Texas, and Oklahoma on the east. The height of this contact seems to have been in the century from A.D. 1150 to 1250. Although Kelly's ideas that traders also brought views on religion and architecture and were actually resident in Pueblo communities are highly controversial, the existence of trade and contact in this region in prehistoric and protohistoric times is not. It is solidly supported by archeological evidence prior to A.D. 1150 and was maintained after that. We have reports of Mexican Indians in the Southwest that date from the fifteenth century onward, and reports of Pueblo Indians in Mexico (Riley, 1975). The presence of Aztec loanwords in U.S. Southwest Spanish and the prevalence of Montezuma legends and dances in the pueblos is evidence that the clear contact between the Southwest and Mexico has affected language and culture. McQuown (1976) surveys American Indian linguistics during the Spanish period. Developments in archeology have led to a regional view of the Borderlands, and work is beginning in Northern Sonora which is resulting in revisions of the prehistory of the region. Let us hope that this broader perspective, which focuses on contact, trade, and transmission of ideas without regard to the recent boundary, will also continue to develop in our studies of multiculturalism and multilingualism, which should be seen not as recent developments, but as the continuation of ancient patterns of relationship.

LANGUAGE RELATIONSHIPS

The patterns of language relationships clearly show the historic connections of cultures and peoples in the Borderlands. The largest and most widely dispersed language family is that of Uto-Aztecan, which includes such southwestern representatives as Hopi, Northern and Southern Paiute, and possibly Keresan (Davis, 1979, p. 412), and such Mexican representatives as the Aztecic family and northern Mexican languages such as Cora, Huichol, Opata, and many others (Steele, 1979). Campbell (1979) mentions a Sonoran grouping of Uto-Aztecan. Representatives are also found in the U.S. Great Basin region and in California. The larger grouping, Aztec-Tanoan (Whorf and Trager, 1937), which united Kiowa (Oklahoma) and the Tanoan languages (New Mexican Pueblo languages) has been recently called into question (Campbell, 1979; Davis, 1979), as has Mexican Penutian (Campbell, 1979) and some relationships with Hokan. I refer the reader to Campbell and Mithun (1979a) for the most recent assessment of language classifications and historical and comparative research on Native American languages. There are clear-cut genetic relationships that are not in doubt between languages in the core of the Southwest—California, the Great Basin, Oklahoma, Texas, Sonora, and Chihuahua. As Campbell and Mithun (1979a) point out, other relationships have been postulated in the past on the basis of far less evidence and need careful reevaluation. Campbell (1979) also points out that the Middle American languages show unity only in the south. Areal-typological work is just beginning in the U.S. Southwest (Sherzer & Bauman, 1972; Sherzer, 1976), but it may be that areal features will be found that unite the languages of Northern Mexico and the Southwest. There are some languages, such as Yaqui, Apache, and Kickapoo, which are found on both sides of the border, but represent recent population movements. This chapter will focus primarily on the languages found in Arizona and New Mexico. Basically, four linguistic stocks are represented in the Southwest: Athabaskan (Navajo and Apache), Yuman (Yavapai, Walapai, Cocopa, Havasupai, and so forth), Kiowa-Tanoan (Northern and Southern Tiwa, Tewa, Towa, and Kiowa), Uto-Aztecan (Pima, Papago, Hopi, and possibly Keres), as well as some isolates such as Zuni.

LANGUAGE CONTACT

The evidence from language relationships clearly shows contact between inhabitants of Mexico and the United States over many centuries. The archeological evidence also argues for contact. The existence of groupings such as Sonoran Uto-Aztecan may point to finer subdivisions and spheres of influence. Although there are loanwords from the Aztec language in many of the Native American languages of the region and in Spanish, the majority of the evidence points to the spread of these terms through Spanish, and thus to bi- or multilingualism in Spanish, rather than direct bilingualism in Native American languages. There is as yet no evidence for the presence of any pidgin, creole, or lingua franca that may have united the Borderlands in prehistoric times. Gunnerson (1974) presents evidence that Apache may have served this function during the seventeenth century. She also discusses the possibility that the name *Apache* may be derived from Nahuatl *mapachtli,* "raccoon," via Spanish *mapache.* Three possible reasons for the connection are suggested: 1) the custom among the Southern Athabaskans of painting the eyes and orbital areas to resemble a raccoon's mask; 2) the raiding of cultivated fields, a trait shared by the Southern Athabaskans and the raccoon; or 3) the accumulation of stones in cairns along trails for trail marking and the animal's pack-rat characteristics (p. 58).

Bi- or tri-lingualism in some Native American languages, English, and Spanish has been found in the twentieth century, with English replacing Spanish in most Indian communities. A great many Native American languages are currently spoken only by those over 30 and may be extinct before the end of this century. In the whole region, the three most flourishing languages, in order of number of speakers, are Navajo, Pima-Papago, and Apache, having respectively 130,000, 15,000, and 9,000 speakers (U.S. Bureau of Indian Affairs, 1980). Brandt and MacCrate (1979) present limited evidence for the presence of an American Indian Pidgin English (AIPE) in the Southwest during the late nineteenth century. While there has clearly been contact, borrowing, and extensive recent bi- and multi-lingualism on the part of speakers of Native American languages, the large number of distinct languages spoken has also served as a social barrier or boundary. Monolinguals are still found, especially among the Navajo. In some communities, Indian children still begin school without knowing English. In other cases, the children are either bilingual in their native language and English or monolingual speakers of Indian English. As Leap (this volume) points out, the fact that they are speakers of Indian English does not mean that aspects of their native-language structures are not present in their English. The use of Indian English is often stigmatized in schools. In some cases, children are even referred to speech pathologists to "correct their speech problems," without the realization that they speak another dialect of English (Nelson-Barber, 1980). For a study of Pima English, see Nelson-Barber (1981).

RESEARCH REVIEW

A survey of some significant research on Native American languages in the United States, concentrating primarily on the period from 1953 to the present, follows. Assessments of the state of Southwestern linguistic research start with Newman's 1953 paper given at a special symposium of the American Anthropological Association and published as a special issue of the *American Anthropologist* in 1954. This session stimulated much research and interest in the Southwest. It was followed in 1967 by the publication of *Studies in Southwestern Ethnolinguistics* (Hymes & Bittle), with an introduction by Newman. The late sixties marked the beginning of a renaissance in the study of Native American languages, and the field expanded with an influx of new scholars who received their degrees in the sixties and seventies. In 1971, the Southwestern Anthropological Association and the American Ethnological Association met in Tucson, and the session on "Bilingualism in the Southwest" generated much enthusiasm, resulting in the publication of the papers from the meeting under Paul Turner's editorship (Turner, 1973). A second, revised edition of Turner's book is in press. A series, *Current Trends in Linguistics,* under the general editorship of Thomas Sebeok, produced a volume surveying the scholarship to date for many Native American languages in 1976. In 1974, the Linguistic Society of America, in its second golden-anniversary symposium, focused on Native American languages. A collection of papers from this meeting was published in 1976 (Chafe) and contained several articles relevant for our area (Hale, 1976; McQuown, 1976; Voegelin & Voegelin, 1976). The first of two proposed volumes on the Southwest in the new *Handbook of North American Indians* (Ortiz, 1980) has appeared, and the volume on Native American languages is forthcoming (Goddard, in press). Campbell and

Mithun (1979b) have edited a collection of papers dealing with language history and classification that surveys some of the languages in this area.

In 1972, the first Southwest Areal Languages and Linguistics Workshop (SWALLOW) was held under the impetus of Ornstein and has continued yearly. The proceedings of this conference, published yearly, are a valuable resource (see Bills, 1974; Harvey & Heiser, 1975; and Barkin & Brandt, 1980, for examples). The Linguistic Association of the Southwest (LASSO) publishes a journal which covers topics on all Southwestern languages and also meets yearly. There are several specialist conferences that are of critical importance in stimulating research. The most established is the Uto-Aztecan conference, which produces regular proceedings. In the last two years, both the Athabaskan scholars and the Kiowa-Tanoanists have met to exchange data and discuss theories and problems. The Yumanists have held several summer workshops and produced occasional proceedings. All of these conferences, and the production of newsletters, have generated an explosion of research in the past ten years. On the national scene, the insights gained from the study of Native American languages have contributed to theoretical linguistics, and special sessions have taken place at national and international meetings. A shortcoming of traditional Native American linguistics was the focus on word lists for historical comparison, and phonologies, to the detriment of syntactic, semantic, and sociolinguistic work. To some extent this is still the case, especially for semantics, but the period since the mid-sixties has shown an increasing number of syntactic studies such as Lindenfeld's work on Yaqui syntax (1973), Langacker's (1976) massive survey of 20 Uto-Aztecan languages, Kendall (1976) on Yavapai, Kroskrity (1977) on Arizona Tewa, and Zaharlick (1978) on Picuris, to mention only a few. The long tradition of Apachean scholarship, especially for Navajo, has stimulated the development of textbooks for the teaching of Navajo (Young, 1973; Goosen, 1967). Young and Morgan (1980) have just published the culmination of their work on Navajo in the form of a grammatical treatise and a massive dictionary. Pedagogical materials have been available for Navajo, but more materials have been developed by the Rough Rock School, the Navajo Community College, and the Native American Materials Development Center in Albuquerque, which has also produced materials in Apache. Kalactaca (1978) has produced a series of materials in Hopi. Bilingual programs have led to the production of limited materials in the native languages, especially for the primary grades, but bilingual dictionaries are still lacking for many languages.

Many more languages have been described in recent dissertations. For Yuman, there has been recent work by Kendall on Yavapai (1976), Shaterian on Yavapai phonology (1971), and Crawford on Cocopa (1966), as well as Harwell on Maricopa (1976), Press (1975) on Chemehuevi, Seiden (1963) and Kozlowski (1972) on Havasupai, and Gorbet on Diegueño (1974). For Apachean, we have Greenfield's work on White Mountain Apache (1972), Kari (1976) on Navajo, and Witherspoon's work on Navajo semantics (1971, 1977). In Tanoan studies, there is Brandt (1970a, 1970b) on Sandia and Leap (1970) on Isleta, Zaharlick on Picuris (1978), and Kroskrity (1977) on Arizona Tewa.

The most significant development in the area of Native American language studies is that in 1978 the first two Ph.D.'s in linguistics were granted to Native Americans. Paul Platero, a Navajo, and Laverne Masayevsa Jeanne, a Hopi, received their Ph.D.'s from MIT. Both have published extensively, and Platero was instrumental in founding a research group in Navajo linguistics and a journal, *Papers on Navajo Linguistics.* Ken Hale, at MIT, has initiated the training of Native American linguists to work on their own languages. Albert Alvarez, a Papago, has also published on Papago linguistics (1969, 1970). As more and more Native Americans begin and continue to work on their own languages, we will achieve new insights that only native speakers can contribute and work that may be responsive to the needs and desires of Native American communities.

The last ten years have also seen the establishment of programs and centers for the study of Southwestern languages directed by Native Americans in many of the regional universities, such as the program at the University of Albuquerque and the University of Arizona, continuing programs at the University of New Mexico and Arizona State University, and centers such as the Native American Materials Development Center in Albuquerque.

Although this basic descriptive activity is much welcomed, there is still a need for additional descriptive work on a continuing basis for all of the languages, with special attention to syntax and semantics. These descriptions should be sociolinguistically relevant, detailing the diversity and usage within the community. Where possible, descriptions should provide comparisons with older material, since several investigators have demonstrated rapid linguistic change (Brandt, 1970b; Greenfield, 1973a).

In comments on Newman's survey of Southwestern linguistics in 1953, Swadesh (1954, p. 639) stated, "The most serious lack is dictionaries, for these are a prime requisite for analyzing cultural meanings and for reconstructing history." Hoijer (1954, p. 637) stated that there were "only the merest beginnings of dependable historical research in linguistics." We now have dictionaries available in Navajo (Morgan & Young, 1954; Young & Morgan, 1980), White Mountain Apache (Perry, 1972), and Papago (Saxton, 1969). A great many specialized dictionaries and lexicons are in use in connection with bilingual education materials, many of which have limited circulation.

A need still exists, though, for more extensive lexicographical work in a form usable by community members and educational personnel, as well as linguists. The White Mountain Apache dictionary, for example, goes only from English to Apache, effectively limiting its use for many purposes. Orthographies used in preparation of such materials must be carefully designed, and accepted by the community. In some areas, computerized dictionaries and lexicons may be most useful, as well as specialized retrieval systems. The computer can also be of use in speeding up the lengthy process of dictionary making by programming morpheme or word-structure constraints and using the resulting output with a team approach to secure meanings and usage. For further information on this approach, see V. Carroll (1968) or contact the author for unpublished material.

The appearance of new grammars and dictionaries gives us for the first time sufficient reliable data on which to base more extensive historical studies and discussions of language relationships. We have come a long way since Hoijer's statement. There has been much excellent historical work and reconstruction done for Uto-Aztecan, though some controversies about classification remain; see Steele (1979) for a discussion. Still, the work on Uto-Aztecan sets the standards for the other languages in the area. The specialist conferences have done much to foster this research. The work of the Alaska Native Languages Center, which has done extensive work on Northern and Pacific Athabaskan, has also been a major stimulus in the development of careful comparative work for all of Athabaskan; see Krauss (1979) for a review which also includes the Southwest. This article has the best description of the Apachean and Uto-Aztecan languages.

A prime topic that remains to be investigated is the nature of the possible relationship between Uto-Aztecan and Kiowa-Tanoan. Leap and I, as Tanoan specialists, have questioned whether there was a relationship, as has Davis (1979). For the Tanoan branch, there is now sufficient recent data for work on Proto-Tanoan, although more extensive data would be welcomed on Towa (Jemez). Kiowa has been described by E. C. Trager (1960), and a dissertation has just been completed by Laurel Watkins (1980). Zaharlick (1978) completed a dissertation on Picuris (Northern Tiwa) syntax. Her recent work focuses on the passive in Tanoan. She reports that with the new material from Watkins, Picuris and Kiowa appear to be very similar and may not belong to separate groupings (1978). Each Southern Tiwa language has now been described (Brandt, 1970a; Leap, 1970), and material is also available on Tewa (Dozier, 1956; Spiers, 1969; Kroskrity, 1977). Processes of pidginization and creolization may have occurred within Tanoan. G. Trager (1966) suspected that Picuris had been influenced and that Tewa might also be a creole. Kroskrity is investigating Tewa-Navajo similarities and has in preparation an exhaustive bibliography on Tanoan (see also his article, this volume). The anthropological archives at the Smithsonian have a wealth of material available on Tanoan languages, including a marvelous Taos grammar by Carobeth Tucker Harrington Laird and 8 cubic feet of Tewa material by J. P. Harrington. No doubt there are other undiscovered jewels. The case of Isleta del Sur remains interesting. In the late sixties, G. Trager and M. E. Smith attempted to determine if any Southern Tiwa was still being spoken, without noticeable success. Given the cultural revitalization of this community, perhaps a look at language would also be in order again, as well as one at the communities of Senecu and Socorro. Keresan still remains linguistically unaffiliated; perhaps some enterprising student will find a relationship. Keresan has also contributed words and songs to a number of other Pueblo communities, and an interesting study could be made that could also shed new light on the cultural history of the Southwest (see, for example, Rood, 1973).

ORTHOGRAPHY, LITERACY, AND LANGUAGE ENGINEERING

In Ornstein's (1973) inventory of tasks, no. 9 is that of studying the status of the reduction to writing of Indian languages, and no. 10 that of determining the status of standardization, codification, and other "language engineering" efforts applied to Indian languages. It seems appropriate to report on progress in these areas.

The great majority of languages in the Southwest have orthographies which have been designed by linguists and language missionaries, though relatively few of these orthographies are in widespread use. In some cases, there are competing orthographies, as is the case with Papago. Many have been designed without consideration of the community's needs, wishes, or input, or are strongly identified with special interests. Orthographies are in use in bilingual programs, instructional materials, newspapers and newsletters, and for religious purposes. Literacy classes are currently being held in many communities, and language classes using materials in the native language are found in many communities and in some area universities.

A stress on orthography and literacy should not blind us to the importance of other media for language teaching and materials development. A number of native-language radio programs exist in the Southwest and are a potent force for communication within large reservations. The San Carlos Apache are in the process of developing radio lessons in Apache. Tape libraries are also in use and could be more extensively utilized. The use of video recordings and discs, and of cable and satellite transmission for television have also not been exploited. All of the latter have the advantage of preserving an oral mode.

Relatively little research has focused on the indigenous development of writing systems for general- or special-purpose uses, nor on the choices available to bilingual Native Americans (but see Spolsky and Irvine, this volume). Basso and Andersen (1973) discuss the development and use of a writing system developed by Silas John, the Apache prophet. Young (1972) and Holm (1973) both survey written Navajo. The Yaquis of Mexico, and later Arizona, made extensive use of a rough orthography developed by the Jesuits in the seventeenth century for personal communications. Sands has shown the importance of this orthography in the period between 1880 and 1927, when it constituted the only means of contact between Yaquis in Mexico and Arizona (Sands, 1978). Three volumes on the Yaqui have been produced by the University of Arizona Press, including the autobiography of Refugio Savala (Sands, 1979), initially written almost exclusively in Yaqui. These volumes use a Yaqui orthography that will probably become standard.

Only two writing systems have been reported as having been developed independently by Native Americans: the syllabic system of Cherokee developed by Sequoyah, and the pictorial system of Silas John (Basso & Andersen, 1973). If one considers the hieroglyphic and logographic systems of Mesoamerica, it is clear that Native Americans have not developed alphabetic systems and, indeed, prefer not to use writing systems for the native language at all. We need to understand these facts. Are there other systems, including pictographs and petroglyphs, which could be described? Navajos continue to make pictographs in the Gallup area. Some Isletas wrote in Isleta, using a modified English alphabet, during World War II in order to circumvent censorship.

There are documents in the New Mexico archives that seem to have been written in Spanish by Pueblo governors in the eighteenth century. A number of documents and memoirs written by Native Americans in Arizona in English are emerging and in the process of publication. Excerpts from a manuscript by Mike Burns (1929), a Yavapai, relating the story of the Apache troubles in Arizona, have been published in Corbusier (1969). This work will add much to our knowledge of the history of southwestern culture and is also relevant to the question of "the Indian Englishes" and "Spanishes" in the area. I issue a call for new studies in the ethnography of writing in our area.

Another research topic that has been neglected and is of the utmost importance is Native American opposition to writing and literacy, particularly as it relates to the recording of religious and ceremonial material. As an orthographocentric white, I am only now beginning to see the complexity of Native American attitudes toward the process of recording in any form, especially a written one. This area has enormous ramifications for all work concerning language and bilingual/multilingual work. We are dealing with religious, political, aesthetic, and very deeply felt emotional issues here, and virtually no attention has been given to them. I have explored this question in a very preliminary way (Brandt, 1980, 1981).

The last area of concern here touches on the ethnography of communication (Hymes, 1967), the necessity for the creation of specialized lexicons and an examination of the process involved, both past and present. There is some suggestion in the literature that Apaches, upon encountering a new item, assigned it a provisional Spanish name until its true name in Apache could be ascertained. This fits with the comments of Sapir (1921) about the Athabaskan preference for coining new terms while resisting acculturative influence. Alvarez (1969, 1970) found it necessary to create new linguistic terminology for Papago in his grammatical sketch of the language written in Papago. Bahr (1975a) has argued for the necessity of legal Papago to protect the rights of monolingual Papagos. Why do some languages create and some borrow? What use is made of interim solutions and languages, as in the Apache case? Who creates new lexicons, and how do the processes of adoption or rejection take place?

CONTACT PHENOMENA AND AREAL LINGUISTICS

Given the recent descriptive work, we are in a much better position to assess the extent of borrowings within and between Native American languages and Spanish and English, and to discuss differential patterns such as those noted earlier for Athabaskan and discussed by Dozier for Tewa and Yaqui (1956). Lindenfeld's work on Spanish and Yaqui (1971) is a valuable recent addition to this literature. Specialized lexical studies such as Bright's (1960) should be encouraged, along with studies of other specific domains such as color, kinship, and plant and animal taxonomies, whether of indigenous or borrowed origin, so as to tie in with work on linguistic universals (Berlin & Kay, 1969; Berlin et al., 1973) and the recent psychological work of Rosch (1975). There have been relatively few studies of Native American code switching. Radio programs in the native languages provide a valuable source of information and also show the adaptation of items of English and Spanish origin to the linguistic structure.

Most Native American communities show a complex pattern of multilingualism, and continued study of this is needed. The recent work on Southwest Indian English (Dubois, 1977; Leap, 1977; St. Clair & Leap, 1981) represents a research topic with major educational implications (see Leap, this volume).

The work of Valdés-Fallis (1977), Dubois (1977), and others on the extent of historical bi- or multi-lingualism among Native American groups should continue and be extended to other groups. A prime topic is the question of whether a lingua franca existed, given the extensive trade in the Borderlands.

The use of interpreters by the Spanish and the Anglos is frequently mentioned. Riley (1975) mentions the Spanish practice of kidnapping Native Americans and returning them to Mexico or Spain until they learned Spanish and could be used as interpreters on other journeys. Individual women attached to soldiers also served as interpreters. On the Arizona frontier, interpreters were often Native American captives who had lived with other groups, though the famous scout and interpreter Tom Horn was trained by being adopted by an Apache band, having already learned Spanish from work with freighters before he became a scout for Sieber. A variety of routes seem to have been taken toward the learning of English and Spanish—always as a second or third language.

For Native American languages, evidence is mounting that there are not only possible creoles, such as Tewa and Picuris (mentioned earlier), but also the presence of American Indian pidgin English (AIPE) in the border areas.

The thesis of AIPE in the west was first advanced by Dillard (1972, 1975) who discusses the presence of Chinese Pidgin English and Chinese English in the west and also suggests that pidgin English was transmitted to Native Americans by blacks who joined Texas Seminoles. Drechsel (1977) lists several marginal languages in the border area: an Indian-Spanish-English pidgin spoken along the Brazos trail in the nineteenth century, Mobilian or the Choctaw/ Chicasaw trade language, and an Afro-Seminole creole in the Mexico-Texas area.

In another article, Drechsel (1976, p. 73) suggests that AIPE, while its existence cannot be denied, is structurally and functionally a kind of style or register, or perhaps foreigner "talk" or broken English, since it retains so much easily understandable English and Indian languages seem not to have had a lasting or intense influence on it. Dubois (1977) has examined the evidence for Dillard's claims for Mescalero Apache in southern New Mexico and finds it unconvincing, agreeing with Drechsel that it more likely represents "broken English."

I want to encourage the difficult and often frustrating search for materials which bear on documenting the existence or spread of pidgin and creole varieties in the Borderlands and to add some new attestations to this controversial area from the Arizona frontier.

Davis (1915) reported about a Yuma:

> One of the scouts, a Yuma corporal, who spoke quite good English, was very indignant at our eating horses and refused to join in the feast. "Him poor horse, work fo' you alla day, no much get eat in mountain. Cally you all day. Fall down; you kill, eat. Damn! No good."

Davis (p. 167) also reported the following speech by an Apache when at Camp Apache in the White Mountains of Arizona:

> "Tabac! Tabac! . . . Injun grass; your horse eat 'um. Injun water; your horse, he drink 'um. Injun wood; white man burn 'um. Tabac! Tabac!"

Dr. Corbusier, who served with the army in the West from 1869 to 1886 (1969, p. 105), quoted two Paiute girls who took care of his first child when he was stationed at Camp McDermit in Nevada as saying, "Papoose yarowling heap hungry." The term *yarowling* is possibly from Paiute *yaru,* "hoarse"

(Sapir, 1931). Corbusier (p. 212) also reports a comment by Yellow Face (Quatha-hooa-hooba) at the Fort Grant infirmary, when he was given the all-purpose medicine quinine: "Schsquinine? No like Schsquinine! Go all same schwizie, schwizie in head."

As far as sources are concerned, one cannot determine whether Dillard's hypothesis is correct or not. A variety of tribes provided scouts during the Indian Wars, Texas Seminoles among them. Corbusier (p. 210) mentions the presence of the "colored 9th and 10th calvalry" at Fort Grant in the Arizona territory and also mentions their having Chinese cooks on two occasions (pp. 92, 110) and staying at a hotel run by a Chinese person at Ehrenberg on the Colorado River (p. 129). Browne (1868, p. 390) recounts an interaction between a party of Paiute Indians who were collecting taxes and some Chinese workers:

> "Me Piute cappen. Me kill plenty Melican [American (?)] man. Dis my lan'. You payee me, John. No payee me, gottam me killee you! ... D——'n Melican man! Me no sabbe Melican man! Me Piute cappen. S'pose you no payee me fifty dollar, me killee you!"

This example demonstrates that Chinese pidgin English was at least an occasional medium of discourse between differing groups.

These quotations, a fraction of the many we have collected, demonstrate many of the characteristics of American Indian pidgin English discussed by Miller (1967) and Leechman and Hall (1955). Further research is needed to explore this controversial area, and I feel confident that my continuing research will answer the questions raised. Certainly there was both a black and a Chinese presence on the frontier, and verifiable contact between these groups and Native Americans. Brandt and MacCrate discuss these issues and provide additional evidence (1979).

An areal-typological perspective began to emerge for the Southwest at the Tucson meetings in 1971. Sherzer and Bauman (1972) have emphasized the importance of areal studies for disclosing cultural contact, and in their survey of scholarship on North American Indian languages have set up a series of linguistic traits which are a start towards the definition of various geographical areas. Sherzer (1976) has published the major areal-typological study of Southwestern languages. Kroskrity is currently involved in areal research which shows three traits that are similar in Navajo and Tewa: 1) presence of classificatory verbs; 2) subject-object ranking and constraints on passive and active sentences; and 3) similar constraints on relative clause formation. He also has in preparation an exhaustive bibliography of Tanoan which should prove very useful to researchers.

Interest in the border area is also part of a general interest in language universals in linguistics. G. Trager (1939), in his article "*Cottonwood* Equals

Tree," showed the presence of highly similar semantic structures across both Native American languages and Spanish. Continuing studies, especially those comparing syntactic and semantic variables, must be done, and done in conjunction with attention to structures in border Spanish.

ACQUISITION OF LANGUAGE AND COMMUNICATIVE COMPETENCE

There is a great gap in the literature when we consider studies of Native American language acquisition. These are urgently needed. Speech clinicians and audiologists who have tested San Carlos and White Mountain Apache children report that language acquisition in Apache is much ahead of white norms (Dorman & Hannley, 1978). The same clinicians have also reported that there is a much higher incidence of both genetic and environmental hearing loss at early ages, which in other populations seems to disrupt language acquisition to a much greater extent than it does for Apache children. This suggests that something very different is occurring in language acquisition among Apache children and that additional attention to speech and language disorders must be part of our concern. Linguists have virtually ignored the whole area of disorders, and yet it has tremendous educational implications. In many communities, the description of language acquisition must be of bilingual acquisition or of Indian English (Dubois, 1977). Beyond simple studies of the acquisition of a phonological system, there must be attention to syntax and semantics.

We must also consider the recent evidence emerging on the patterns of hemispheric dominance in bilinguals (Vaid & Lambert, 1979; Genesee, 1980). Studies to date suggest that relevant factors are: age of L_2 acquisition, sex, initial versus advanced bilingualism, and formal versus informal language learning. Scott, Hynd, Hunt, and Weed (1979), Hynd (1980), and F. Carroll (1978), working with Navajo and Hopi speakers, all found more right hemisphere involvement in speech for these languages. Brandt and Dorman are currently attempting to replicate their findings. If substantiated, they may reflect bilingualism, typological factors of the languages in question, preferred strategies of language acquisition, or slower response times.

Along with such studies, there is a need for research on communicative competence in whatever varieties or codes are used, whether by children or adults. Philips (1972) has done a wonderful study of Warm Springs Indian children in the community and the classroom, detailing their conversational patterns. Her work should be emulated in the Southwest. Studies of turn taking, the existence of turn-taking systems, conversational repair, and correction and hesitation phenomena are urgently needed, particularly for use in the classroom. Do bi- or multi-lingual children exhibit several different systems or only one?

THE ETHNOGRAPHY OF SPEAKING

Basso (1970, 1974, 1976, 1979) has made the largest contribution to the ethnography of speaking in the Southwest. Some interesting material is also emerging from Mexican languages, but there is much to be done. A great many special varieties of language are found in the Southwest, such as warpath language, special ritual languages, gender-linked differences in speech, the special register of Pueblo clowns, Apache "wise words," and a great many literary forms. Some of these varieties cannot be described because of their sacredness, but others may. There is also a need to focus on aesthetics as a shaping force in language and art. Sands (1978) suggests that the communication between the Arizona and the Mexican Yaqui is maintained primarily for aesthetic reasons. Witherspoon (1977) has just completed a magnificent analysis of the role of language in Navajo philosophy which should be read by everyone interested in the Southwest. Bahr (1975b) has compared Papago ritual oratory to Japanese haiku and is currently at work on an analysis of Papago song cycles which are also reminiscent of haiku, and extraordinarily beautiful. More and more materials such as legends, myths, and song and dance are available and being used in bilingual classrooms. Undoubtedly new forms will also emerge from this process.

SUMMARY

In this survey of research on Native American languages, I have not attempted to be exhaustive. A bibliography on Navajo language and linguistics alone would run to several thousand entries. The literature on bilingual and bicultural education for these languages is easily accessible and widely known. I have undoubtedly overlooked areas of importance and neglected to mention related sources. My purpose has been to stress issues that need additional attention and research goals that can realistically be accomplished. The immediate concerns are: continuing stress on solid linguistic and sociolinguistic description, especially by native speakers; production of bilingual dictionaries; archival and historical research bearing on language relationships, language contact, and possible processes of pidginization and creolization; studies of language acquisition and communicative competence; continuing development of an areal perspective, especially one uniting the languages in the Borderlands; attention to language and speech disorders; attention to the sociolinguistics of literacy or ethnography of literacy; and consideration of the importance of verbal art and aesthetic factors. In order for the areal perspective to develop, we need a broader temporal and spatial perspective and increased contact across present geopolitical and ethnic boundaries. The study of these languages must first and foremost contribute to the communities of those who speak them. Linguistic and language studies can aid communities, and linguists must strive to develop ways to meet community needs by making research more accessible to users. This is not to say that research must all be applied and nontheoretical, for the Borderlands is one of the richest areas for the study of language contact, bi- and multi-lingualism, and language death and attrition (see Hale, 1976, for a discussion of this issue). It is to say that research must be considerate of its contribution in both the scholarly sense and the community sense. These two aims are not in conflict. Communities deserve the best research possible, in the form of state-of-the-art publications. These works, along with the novel suggestions coming from the community level, will result in an advancement of that state and will benefit all concerned.

APPENDIX: A RESEARCH AGENDA

1. Continuing basic description of Native American languages with special attention to syntax, semantics, and tonal systems which have barely been described
   a. Sociolinguistically relevant descriptions
   b. Where possible, comparison to earlier material
   c. Publication of texts and natural speech genres
2. Production of more extensive and usable dictionaries and lexicons which are multipurpose. Orthographies used must have community acceptance and must be developed by the community of users.
   a. In some areas, use of computer technology for production and retrieval
   b. Computerized lexicography in initial production
3. Continued examination of language relationships and historical reconstruction
   a. Reconsideration of evidence for the Uto-Aztecan and Kiowa-Tanoan relationship
   b. Reconstruction of Tanoan
   c. Search for possible pidgin/creole relationships, especially within northern Tiwa (Taos-Picuris) and Tewa
   d. Study of language situation at Isleta del Sur, Senecu, and Socorro
   e. Search for an affiliation for Keresan and study of Keresan loans into other Pueblo languages
   f. Publication of specialized bibliographies, including archival material on Native American languages for use by language researchers
   g. Development of data banking for material on Native American languages, where desirable
4. Study and understanding of Native American attitudes toward recording, writing, and literacy
   a. Continuing development of functional orthographies, where desired
   b. Publication of relevant materials in a bilingual or monolingual format
   c. Innovative approaches to materials development, using radio, audiotape, videotape, cable and satellite television; development of tape libraries
   d. Development of the ethnography of writing and literacy; study of pictographs and petroglyphs
   e. Study and publication of texts in English and Spanish by Native Americans, including increased availability of oral and videotaped materials

    f. Study of multilingual choices in writing systems

    g. Study of the development, rejection, or spread of new lexicons, including the use of interim languages such as Spanish or English

    h. Examination of factors responsible for borrowing as opposed to new creation of terms

5. Examination of contact phenomena such as pidgins and creoles between Native American languages or between them and European ones. Studies of the possibility of special registers. Investigation of Chinese/black/Native American contacts

    a. Relexification hypothesis

    b. Monogenetic/polygenetic origins

    c. Lingua francas

    d. Sign language

6. Study of borrowings between Native American languages or between them and European ones

7. Historical sociolinguistic descriptions

8. Investigation of Indian Englishes and Spanishes

9. Study of bi- and multi-lingual code switching

10. Studies of special lexical domains, especially when they have cross-cultural interest, such as color or plant and animal taxonomies

11. Examination of the role of interpreters

12. Identification of areal similarities: development of areal perspective

13. Studies of language acquisition, both monolingual and bilingual; also the acquisition of communicative competence

14. Studies of pause phenomena, hesitation, nonverbal behavior

15. Examination of turn taking, question and answer sequencing, conversational repair, speech act theory, discourse

16. Special attention to speech and language disorders

17. Speech perception studies

18. Development of "ethnographies of communication" detailing everyday language use, the language of the classroom, and special uses of language, such as ritual language, gender-marked speech, and special literary forms

19. Special attention to aesthetic factors in language and verbal art, and in play

20. Relation of Native American forms to similar ones in other traditions

21. Description of Native American attitudes toward language and its role—importance in the culture

22. Typological studies

23. Development of a border perspective focusing on possible similarities in northern Mexico

REFERENCES

Alvarez, A. ?o?odam ñe?oki há- idag. Unpublished manuscript. Massachusetts Institute of Technology, Department of Linguistics, 1969.

Alvarez, A., & Hale, K. Toward a manual of Papago grammar: Some phonological terms. *International Journal of American Linguistics,* 1970, *36,* 83–97.

Bahr, D. M., Gregorio, J., Lopez, D. I. & Alvarez, A. *Piman shamanism and staying sickness (Ka:cim mumkodag)*. Tucson: University of Arizona Press, 1973.

——. Language policy and the birth of writing among the Papagos. In G. C. Harvey & M. F. Heiser (Eds.), *Southwest languages and linguistics in educational perspective*. San Diego, Calif.: Institute for Cultural Pluralism, 1975. (a)

——. *Pima and Papago ritual oratory: A study of three texts*. San Francisco: Indian Historian Press, 1975. (b)

Barkin, F., & Brandt, E. (Eds.). *Speaking, singing and teaching: A multidisciplinary approach to language variation*. Proceedings of the Eighth Annual Southwest Areal Languages and Linguistics Workshop. Anthropological Research Paper, No. 20. Tempe: Arizona State University, 1980.

Bartlett, J. R. *Personal narrative of explorations and incidents in Texas, New Mexico, California, Sonora, and Chihuahua*. New York: D. Appleton, 1854.

Basso, K. To give up on words: Silence in Western Apache culture. *Southwestern Journal of Anthropology*, 1970, *26*, 213–30.

——. The ethnography of writing. In R. Bauman & J. Sherzer (Eds.), *Explorations in the ethnography of speaking*. London: Cambridge University Press, 1974.

——. "Wise words" of the Western Apache: Metaphor and cultural theory. In K. Basso & H. A. Selby (Eds.), *Meaning in Anthropology*. Albuquerque: University of New Mexico Press, 1976.

——. *Portraits of "The Whiteman."* Cambridge, England: Cambridge University Press, 1979.

Basso, K., & Andersen, N. A Western Apache writing system: The symbols of Silas John. *Science*, 1973, *180*, 1013–22.

Berlin, B., Breedlove, D. E., & Raven, P. H. General principles of classification nomenclature in folk biology. *American Anthropologist*, 1973, *75*, 214–42.

Berlin, B., & Kay, P. *Basic color terms*. Berkeley, Calif.: University of California Press, 1969.

Bills, G. (Ed.). *Southwest areal linguistics*. San Diego, Calif.: Institute for Cultural Pluralism, 1974.

Brandt, E. A. On the origins of linguistic stratification: The Sandia case. *Anthropological Linguistics*, 1970, *12*, 46–50. (a)

——. Sandia Pueblo: A linguistic and ethnolinguistic investigation. Doctoral diss., Southern Methodist University, 1970. (b)

——. The role of secrecy in a Pueblo society. In T. C. Blackburn (Ed.), *Flowers of the wind. Papers on ritual, myth and symbolism in California and the Southwest*. Ballena Press Anthropological Papers, No. 8. Socorro, N. Mexico: Ballena Press, 1977.

——. On secrecy and control of knowledge: Taos Pueblo. In S. Tefft (Ed.), *Secrecy. A cross-cultural perspective*. New York: Human Sciences Press, 1980.

——. Native American attitudes toward literacy and recording in the Southwest. *Journal of the Linguistic Association of the Southwest*, 1981, *4*, 152–60.

Brandt, E., & MacCrate, C. 'Make like seem heap Injun': Pidginization in the Southwest. Paper presented at the Forty-third International Congress of Americanists, Vancouver, Canada, Aug. 1979.

Bright, W. Animals of acculturation. In *The California Indian languages*, University of California Publications in Linguistics, No. 4. Berkeley: University of California, 1960, pp. 215–46.

Browne, J. R. *Adventures in the Apache country*. New York: Harper, 1868.

Burns, Mike. The Indian side of the question: Stories by Mike Burns, Mohave-Apache. Unpublished manuscript in the collection of the Sharlott Hall Museum, Prescott, Ariz.; copy also in the Smithsonian Institution, Washington, D.C., 1929.

Campbell, L. Middle American languages. In L. Campbell & M. Mithun (Eds.), *The languages of Native America*. Austin: University of Texas Press, 1979.

Campbell, L., & Mithun, M. Introduction: North American Indian historical linguistics in current perspective. In L. Campbell & M. Mithun (Eds.), *The languages of Native America*. Austin: University of Texas Press, 1979. (a)

Campbell, L., & Mithun, M. (Eds.). *The languages of Native America*. Austin: University of Texas Press, 1979. (b)

Carroll, F. W. Cerebral dominance for language: A dichotic-listening study of Navajo-English bilinguals. In H. H. Key, S. G. McCollough, & J. B. Sawyer (Eds.), *The bilingual in a pluralistic society. Proceedings of the Sixth Southwest Areal Languages and Linguistics Workshop*. Long Beach, Calif.: California State University, 1978.

——. Neurolinguistic processing of a second language: Experimental evidence. In R. Scarella & S. Krashen (Eds.), *Research in second language acquisition. Los Angeles Second Language Research Forum*. New York: Newbury House, 1979.

Carroll, V. Generative elicitation techniques in Polynesian lexicography. *Oceanic Linguistics*, 1968, *5*, 59–70.

Chafe, W. (Ed.). *American Indian languages and American linguistics*. Lisse, Belgium: Peter De Ridder Press, 1976.

Corbusier, W. T. *Verde to San Carlos. Recollections of a famous Army surgeon and his observant family on the western frontier, 1869–1886*. Tucson, Ariz.: Dale Stuart King, 1969.

Crawford, J. M. The Cocopa language. Doctoral diss., University of California at Berkeley, 1966.

——. *Mobilian trade jargon*. Knoxville: University of Tennessee Press, 1978.

Davis, A. Pioneer days in Arizona by one who was there. Manuscript in the collection of the Arizona Historical Foundation, Tempe, Ariz. 1915.

Davis, I. Linguistic clues to Northern Rio Grande prehistory. *El Palacio*, 1959, *66*, 73–84.

——. Keresan-Caddoan comparisons. *International Journal of American Linguistics*, 1974, *40*, 265–67.

——. The Kiowa-Tanoan, Keresan, and Zuni languages. In L. Campbell & M. Mithun (Eds.), *The languages of Native America*. Austin: University of Texas Press, 1979.

Dillard, J. L. *Black English*. New York: Random House, 1972.

——. *All-American English*. New York: Random House, 1975.

Dorman, M. & Hannley, M. Personal communication, fall, 1978.

Dozier, E. Two examples of linguistic acculturation: The Yaqui of Sonora and the Tewa of New Mexico. *Language*, 1956, *32*, 1946–57.

Drechsel, E. J. "Ha now me stomany that!": A summary of pidginization and creolization of North American Indian languages. *International Journal of the Sociology of Language,* 1976, *7,* 63–82.

——. Historical problems and issues in the study of North American Indian marginal languages. In W. L. Leap (Ed.), *Studies in Southwestern Indian English.* San Antonio, Tex.: Trinity University Press, 1977.

Dubois, B. L. Spanish, English, and the Mescalero Apache. In W. L. Leap (Ed.), *Studies in Southwestern Indian English.* San Antonio, Tex.: Trinity University Press, 1977.

Dubois, B. L., & Hoffer, B. (Eds.). *Papers in Southwestern English. I: Research, techniques and prospects.* San Antonio, Tex.: Trinity University Press, 1975.

Genesee, F. Bilingual brains? Paper presented at the Neurolinguistics Conference, Albuquerque, July 1980.

Goddard, I. (Ed.). *Native American languages.* In *Handbook of North American Indians* (Vol. 17). Washington, D.C.: Smithsonian Institution, in press.

Goosen, I. W. *Navajo made easier.* Flagstaff, Ariz.: Northland Press, 1967.

Gorbet, L. Relativization and complementation in Diegueño: Noun phrases as nouns. Doctoral diss., University of California at San Diego, 1974.

Greenfield, P. J. The phonological hierarchy of the White Mountain dialect of Western Apache. Doctoral diss., University of Arizona, 1972. *Dissertation Abstracts International,* (1972) 1973, *33,* 2450B. University Microfilms No. 72-31, 852. (b)

——. Cultural conservatism as an inhibitor of linguistic change: A possible Apache case. *International Journal of American Linguistics,* 1973, *39,* 98–104. (a)

Gunnerson, D. *The Jicarilla Apaches. A study in survival.* DeKalb: Northern Illinois University Press, 1974.

Hale, K. Theoretical linguistics in relation to American Indian communities. In W. L. Chafe (Ed.), *American Indian languages and American linguistics.* Lisse, Belgium: Peter de Ridder Press, 1976.

Harvey, G., & Heiser, M. F. (Eds.). *Southwest languages and linguistics in educational perspective.* San Diego, Calif.: Institute for Cultural Pluralism, 1975.

Harwell, H. Reading and writing in Maricopa (the alphabet) as approved by the Maricopa Community meeting, August 9, 1976. *Pima-Maricopa Echo, 4* (18), 1976.

Hoijer, H. Comments on Newman. *American Anthropologist,* 1954, *56*(4), 637–38.

——. A Navajo lexicon. University of California Publications in Linguistics, No. 78. Berkeley: University of California, 1974.

Holm, W. Some aspects of Navajo orthography. Doctoral diss., University of California at San Diego, 1973.

Horn, T. *Life of Tom Horn.* Denver: Louthon, 1904.

Hymes, D., & Bittle, W. E. (Eds.). *Studies in Southwestern ethnolinguistics.* The Hague: Mouton, 1967.

Hynd, G. W. Acculturation and the lateralization of speech in the bilingual Native American. *International Journal of Neuroscience,* 1980, *11,* 1–7.

Kalactaca, M. *Lessons in Hopi.* R. W. Langacker (Ed.). Tucson: University of Arizona Press, 1978.

Kari, J. M. *Navajo verb prefix phonology.* New York: Garland, 1976.

Kari, J. M., & Spolsky, B. Athapaskan language maintenance and bilingualism. In

G. Bills (Ed.), *Southwest areal linguistics.* San Diego, Calif.: Institute for Cultural Pluralism, 1974.

Kelly, J. C. Speculations on the culture history of Northwestern Mesoamerica. In B. Bell (Ed.), *The Archeology of West Mexico.* Ajijic, Jalisco, Mexico: West Mexican Society for Advanced Study, 1974.

Kendall, M. *Selected problems in Yavapai syntax.* New York: Garland, 1976.

Kozlowski, E. Havasupai simple sentences. Doctoral diss., Indiana University, 1972.

Krauss, M. Na-Dene and Eskimo-Aleut. In L. Campbell & M. Mithun (Eds.), *The languages of Native America.* Austin: University of Texas Press, 1979.

Kroskrity, P. V. Aspects of Arizona Tewa language structure and use. Doctoral diss., University of Arizona, 1977.

Langacker, R. W. Non-distinct arguments in Uto-Aztecan. University of California Publications in Linguistics, No. 82. Berkeley: University of California, 1976.

Leap, W. L. The language of Isleta, New Mexico. Doctoral diss., Southern Methodist University, 1970.

Leap, W. L. (Ed.). *Studies in Southwestern Indian English.* San Antonio, Tex.: Trinity University Press, 1977.

Leechman, D., & Hall, R. A. American Indian Pidgin English and its grammatical peculiarities. *American Speech, 1955, 30, 163–71.*

Lindenfeld, J. A transformational grammar of Yaqui. Doctoral diss., University of California at Los Angeles, 1969.

——. Semantic categorization as a deterrent to grammatical borrowing: A Yaqui example. *International Journal of American Linguistics, 1971, 37, 6–14.*

——. *Yaqui syntax.* University of California Publications in Linguistics, No. 76. Berkeley: University of California, 1973.

McQuown, N. A.. American Indian linguistics in New Spain. In W. L. Chafe (Ed.), *American Indian languages and American linguistics.* Lisse, Belgium: Peter De Ridder Press, 1976.

Miller, M. R. Attestations of American Indian Pidgin English. *American Speech, 1967, 42, 142–47.*

Miller, W. R. The ethnography of speaking. In I. Goddard (Ed.), *Handbook of North American Indians* (Vol. 15). Washington D.C.: Smithsonian Institution, in press.

Morgan, W., and Young, R. W. (Eds.). *Navajo historical selections.* Lawrence, Kans.: Bureau of Indian Affairs, Haskell Institute, 1954.

Nelson-Barber, S. Personal communication, Apr. 1980.

——. Phonological variations of Pima English. In R. St. Clair & W. L. Leap (Eds.), *American Indian language renewal.* Arlington, Va.: National Clearinghouse for Bilingual Education, 1981.

Newman, S. American Indian linguistics in the Southwest. *American Anthropologist, 1954, 56, 626–34.*

——. Comparison of Zuni and California Penutian. *International Journal of American Linguistics*, 1964, *30,* 1–13.

Nichols, M. Linguistic reconstruction of Proto Western Numic and its ethnographic implications. In C. M. Aikens (Ed.), *Great Basin Anthropological Conference 1970: Selected papers.* University of Oregon Anthropological Papers, No. 1. Eugene: University of Oregon, 1971.

Ornstein, J. Toward an inventory of interdisciplinary tasks in research on U.S. Southwest bilingualism/biculturalism. In P. Turner (Ed.), *Bilingualism in the Southwest.* Tucson: University of Arizona Press, 1973.

Ortiz, A. (Ed.). *Southwest.* In *Handbook of North American Indians* (Vol. 9). Washington, D.C.: Smithsonian Institution, 1980.

Perry, E. *Western Apache dictionary.* Fort Apache, Ariz.: White Mountain Apache Tribe, 1972.

Philips, S. U. Participant structures and communicative competence: Warm Springs children in community and classroom. In C. B. Cazden, V. P. John, & D. Hymes (Eds.), *Functions of language in the classroom.* New York: Teachers College Press, 1972.

Press, M. A grammar of Chemehuevi. Doctoral diss., University of California at Los Angeles, 1975.

Riley, C. L. Pueblo Indians in Mesoamerica: The early historic period. In T. R. Frisbie (Ed.), *Collected papers in honor of Florence Hawley Ellis.* Papers of the Archeological Society of New Mexico, No. 2. Norman, Okla.: Hooper, 1975.

Riley, C. L., & Hedrick, B. C. *Across the Chichemec Sea.* Carbondale: Southern Illinois Press, 1978.

Rood, D. S. Swadesh's Keres-Caddo comparison. *International Journal of American Linguistics,* 1973, *39,* 189–91.

Rosch, E. Cognitive representation of semantic categories. *Journal of Experimental Psychology,* 1975, *104,* 192–233.

Sahlins, M. D. On the sociology of primitive exchange. In *The relevance of models for social anthropology.* New York: Praeger, 1965.

St. Clair, R., & Leap, W. L. (Eds.). *American Indian language renewal.* Arlington, Va.: National Clearinghouse for Bilingual Education, 1981.

Sands, K. Personal communication, Apr. 1978.

—— (Ed.). *The autobiography of Refugio Savala.* Tucson: University of Arizona Press, 1979.

Sapir, E. *Language.* New York: Harcourt Brace, 1921.

——. Southern Paiute dictionary. *Proceedings of the American Academy of Arts and Sciences,* Vol. 65, No. 3. Cambridge, Mass.: American Academy of Arts and Sciences, 1931.

Saxton, D., & Saxton, L. *Dictionary: Papago and Pima to English, O'odham-Milgahn: English to Papago and Pima, Mil-gahn-O'odham.* Tucson: University of Arizona Press, 1969.

Scott, S., Hynd, G. W., Hunt, L., & Weed, W. Cerebral speech lateralization in the Native American Navajo. *Neuropsychologia,* 1979, *17,* 89–92.

Sebeok, T. (Ed.). *Current trends in linguistics* (Vol. 13). *Native Languages of North America,* pt. 3. The Hague: Mouton, 1976.

Seiden, W. Havasupai phonology and morphology. Doctoral diss., Indiana University, 1963.

Shaterian, A. Yavapai phonology. Unpublished manuscript, 1971.

Sherzer, J. *An areal-typological study of American Indian languages north of Mexico.* Amsterdam: North-Holland, 1976.

Sherzer, J., & Bauman, R. Areal studies and culture history. *Southwestern Journal of Anthropology,* 1972, *28,* 131–53.

Spiers, R. H. *Tewa Hi? Short dictionary of Tewa*. Santa Ana, Calif.: Summer Institute of Linguistics, 1969.

Steele, S. Uto-Aztecan: An assessment for historical and comparative linguistics. In L. Campbell & M. Mithun (Eds.), *The languages of Native America*. Austin: University of Texas Press, 1979.

Swadesh, M. Comments on Newman. *American Anthropologist*, 1954, *56*(4), 639–42.

Trager, E. C. The Kiowa language. A grammatical study. Doctoral diss., University of Pennsylvania, 1960.

Trager, G. L. "Cottonwood" = "tree." A Southwestern linguistic trait. *International Journal of American Linguistics*, 1939, *9*, 117–18.

———. Tewa as "pidgin" Tanoan. Paper presented at annual meeting of the American Anthropological Association, Denver, Nov. 1966.

Turner, P. (Ed.). *Bilingualism in the Southwest*. Tucson: University of Arizona Press, 1973.

United States Bureau of Indian Affairs. 1980 census. Phoenix, Ariz.: Area Office, U.S. Bureau of Indian Affairs, 1980.

Vaid, J., & Lambert, W. E. Differential cerebral involvement in the cognitive functioning of bilinguals. *Brain and Language*, 1979, *8*, 92–100.

Valdés-Fallis, G. Early day communicative relations of the Mescalero Apache with Spanish speakers, 1540–1846. In B. L. Dubois & B. Hoffer (Eds.), *Southwest areal linguistics then and now*. San Antonio, Tex.: Trinity University Press, 1977.

Voegelin, C. F., & Voegelin, F. M. Some recent (and not so recent) attempts to interpret semantics of native languages in North America. In W. L. Chafe (Ed.), *American Indian languages and linguistics*. Lisse, Belgium: Peter de Ridder Press, 1976.

Wall, L., & Morgan, W. *Navajo-English dictionary*. Window Rock, Ariz.: Navajo Agency, Branch of Education, 1958.

Watkins, L. J. A grammar of Kiowa. Doctoral diss., University of Kansas, 1980.

Whorf, B. L., & Trager, G. L. The relationship of Uto-Aztecan and Tanoan. *American Anthropologist*, 1937, *39*, 609–24.

Witherspoon, G. Navajo categories of objects at rest. *American Anthropologist*, 1971, *73*, 110–27.

———. *Language and art in the Navajo universe*. Ann Arbor: University of Michigan Press, 1977.

Young, R. W. Semantics as a determiner of linguistic comprehension across language and cultural boundaries. Doctoral diss., University of New Mexico, 1971.

———. *Written Navajo: A brief history*. University of New Mexico, Navajo Reading Study Progress Report, No. 19. Albuquerque: University of New Mexico, 1972.

———. The development of semantic categories in Spanish-English and Navajo-English bilingual children. In P. Turner (Ed.), *Bilingualism in the Southwest*. Tucson: University of Arizona Press, 1973.

Young, R. W., & Morgan, W. *The Navajo language. A grammar and colloquial dictionary*. Albuquerque: University of New Mexico Press, 1980.

Zaharlick, A. M. Picuris syntax. Doctoral diss., American University, 1978.

———. Personal communication, 23 Feb. 1981.

II | Native American Languages in Contact

OVERVIEW

The theme of this section is the complex pattern of language contact between speakers of the large number of Native American languages and speakers of Spanish and English. If the reader is unfamiliar with many of the Native American languages, Brandt (in part I) provides a broad overview. Speakers of Native American languages were first in the Borderlands, and the region is still home to the largest number of Indian people in the United States. The three most widely spoken Indian languages (Navajo, Papago, and Apache) are found within this region. It should be remembered that both Native Americans and Chicanos are territorial minorities in the Borderlands, in contrast to ethnic minorities in other areas. The Navajo reservation, for example, encompasses a territory larger than many of the eastern states.

Paul V. Kroskrity's paper is a masterful study of language contact through time in a single speech community, that of the Arizona Tewa. He takes a holistic view of the process of language contact, stressing the social values and outcomes of contact. This is a major contribution to the development of a typology of the outcomes of language contact.

Bernard Spolsky and Patricia Irvine add to a developing concern with the *process* of language contact by focusing on the outcomes of literacy in American Indian vernacular in the native language. They do for writing what Kroskrity has done for speech. Their paper is a contribution to the developing field of the sociolinguistics of literacy.

Ralph Cooley and Philip Lujan also describe "situated speech"—in this case, actual speeches given in English by Native American students. The authors relate the rhetorical styles used in English to traditional Native American forms of discourse. Ina C. Siler and Diana Labadie-Wondergem develop this material further by relating these rhetorical styles to their cultural origins.

William L. Leap discusses the nature of Indian "Englishes" in a broad summary of the field he pioneered, showing the relevance of this research to the educational concerns of Indian communities. From the data available, it appears that the advent of bilingualism in English in many Native American communities is very recent, dating only to the first two decades of this century. The shift from some Indian languages to English has been even more recent, occurring for many communities in the last generation. Even in situations such as these, however, he shows that aspects of the native language structures are not lost, but appear in the variety of English used by the community. The Indian Englishes, Leap asserts, are distinct varieties of English which deserve scholarly attention.

Because of the wide range of American Indian languages and the large number of communities, we are able to deal with only a few in this section. Our hope is that these studies will serve as models and stimuli for the study of contact between Indian languages, Spanish, and English.

4 Language Contact and Linguistic Diffusion: The Arizona Tewa Speech Community

PAUL V. KROSKRITY
University of California at Los Angeles

Within Southwestern linguistic scholarship, as within anthropological linguistics in general, the treatment of language contact has been characterized by a preoccupation with the "products" of diffusion, rather than with the diffusion "process" itself (e.g., Hoijer, 1939; Trager, 1944; Spencer, 1947; Miller, 1959–60). As Gumperz and Wilson (1971, p. 151) observe, "Students of bilingualism and language contact so far have concentrated primarily on the end effects of these diffusion processes. There has been almost no direct investigation of the actual mechanisms involved." While this focus on the linguistic artifacts of diffusion rather than the linguistic processes which create them has made possible some descriptive accomplishments notable for their taxonomic precision (e.g. Casagrande, 1954–55), it has nevertheless seriously undermined a *holistic* approach to language contact. By a holistic approach, I mean one in which contact is examined from the complementary perspectives of language structure (autonomous linguistics) and language use (the ethnography of communication and sociolinguistics). Within such an approach, the former perspective

This article represents a revised version of an earlier article (Kroskrity, 1980a) and is used by permission of the Anthropological Research Papers, Arizona State University. It is based on research on Tewa conducted from 1973 to 1978 in Tewa Village, Polacca, and Keams Canyon, Arizona, and on Navajo conducted in 1977 in Klagetoh, Arizona. The research was variously supported by the Graduate School of Indiana University, the Phillips Fund of the American Philosophical Society, and the Melville and Elizabeth Jacobs Research Fund of the Whatcom Museum of History and Art. To these institutions I express my gratitude for their support. In addition, I would like to thank Betsy Brandt and Carl and Flo Voegelin for useful comments on previous drafts of the present chapter. The present chapter may presuppose some familiarity with the Arizona Tewa. Dozier's (1954) ethnography remains the best introduction to the relevant social and cultural background. As for the transcription of the Arizona Tewa examples to follow, the phonemes are: 1) consonants: p, t, k, p', t', k', ' (written as ' here), kʷ, kʷ', kʸ, kʰʸ, b, d, g, c, c', s, h, hʸ, m, n, l, w, and y; 2) vowels: i, e, ɛ (low-mid, front), a, u, and o. In addition, Arizona Tewa distinguishes length (V·), tone (2, V́ = high, V = low), and nasality (Ṽ).

supplies information concerning code-internal factors which may facilitate or inhibit borrowing. The latter provides information as to the degree of awareness, nature of social evaluation, and situated meaning with which members of a particular speech community may have endowed a particular linguistic trait.

One of the consequences of the failure to examine language contact in its sociocultural context is a dearth of insight into the nature of the sociocultural concomitants of linguistic diffusion. Just what are the sociocultural factors which promote or inhibit diffusion? What types of diffusion (e.g., lexical or grammatical, phonological or syntactic) are the expected outcomes of such conditions as multilingualism and interethnic interaction? In an attempt to address these and comparable questions, the Indiologist Franklin Southworth (1971, p. 256) has called for a "more precise sociolinguistic typology of outcomes of language contact." More recently, these and similar issues have resurfaced in the investigation of the more inclusive phenomenon of *language attrition* (Lambert, 1980, p. 1). While this new research focus will attract some much needed interdisciplinary interest in the future, the sociolinguistic typology of contact currently exists in only the most rudimentary form.

In the present paper, I seek to contribute to such a typology by examining some significant portions of the contact history of the present Arizona Tewa speech community, as well as that of its ancestors over the past 500 years. In this manner, data will be reported for the contact of Arizona Tewa and its antecedents with (in receding temporal order) English in the twentieth century, Hopi since the eighteenth century, Spanish from the sixteenth century, and Apachean in prehistoric times. First I will report, in abbreviated form, the findings of my recent research in the Arizona Tewa speech community. This study examines language contact and incipient change as it is manifested in the form of patterned, interindividual linguistic variation. Since the change is ongoing, and since it therefore offers an opportunity to view language contact directly in its sociocultural context, I will devote considerable attention to this particularly instructive instance. The remaining instances of language contact will be examined as case studies in which a holistic view of language contact must be achieved by the more indirect means of ethnohistorical investigation and inferences from linguistic data.

CONTACT OF ARIZONA TEWA WITH OTHER LANGUAGES

Contact with English

As in other Pueblo communities like Sandia, Acoma, and Cochiti, where similar situations have been reported (Fox, 1959; Brandt, 1970; Maring, 1975), the speech of younger members of the speech community exhibits considerable linguistic acculturation, or what may be better termed, following Weinreich

(1953, p. 1), *linguistic interference.* Most of these younger speakers, in contrast to their elders, employ English as the dominant language and exhibit what is perceived by the older speakers as an impaired proficiency in Tewa and often little or no proficiency in Hopi, except for some kin terms and polite expressions.

Yet despite the fact that the older members of the speech community view the Arizona Tewa speech of the young people as defective, they seldom, if ever—as at Acoma (Maring, 1975, p. 480), offer correction. The perceived deficiencies in the speech of the young are located by older speakers in the phenomenon of lexical attrition and the replacement of indigenous terms by their English counterparts. Though sociocultural change has prompted some adaptive "shifts" (Herzog, 1941) in the lexicons of older speakers, younger Tewa have abandoned the formerly productive strategies of semantically extending native terms or compounding two or more such terms in order to create lexical resources for nontraditional concepts. For example, the oldest word for 'automotive vehicle' was *wa ʾ-teʾge*—literally, 'wind wagon'. This word has been replaced in the lexicons of all but the oldest speakers by /athu/, a phonemically retouched loan from English *auto.* Today, younger speakers— those 30 years of age or less—simply employ [kar] in utterances that are otherwise encoded in Tewa, despite the fact that [r] does not occur in the Arizona Tewa grammars of older speakers at either a phonemic or phonetic level of analysis. Older Tewa also cite two additional kinds of evidence in support of their claim that younger Tewa possess a diminished proficiency in their native language. Younger people, they claim, no longer command vocabulary items associated with such native economic activities as planting, hunting, herding, and related activities. Even more serious is their charge that younger people have forgotten all but the morphologically most fundamental verbs. Many young people openly concede that they no longer know how to "say a whole sentence in one word," as one young man phrased it, though they view this inability as a consequence of changes associated with modernization and not, as their elders often maintain, as evidence of moral degeneration.

As with other social variables—ones which I have treated more fully elsewhere (Kroskrity, 1977, pp. 241–49)—to which linguistic variation is attributed in the members' account, the covarying linguistic phenomena are primarily located at the lexical level. This finding closely parallels that of Gumperz and Wilson's Kupwar study in which they observed that lexical items and their inflectional properties appear to provide the phenomenal basis for the folk perception of what constitutes the defining attributes of a given language (Gumperz & Wilson, 1971, pp. 101–2). Though the Arizona Tewa perceive age-based variation as primarily a lexical phenomenon, the speech of younger Arizona Tewa, as we shall see, exhibits striking syntactic and semantic differences from the speech of their seniors. In fact, as at Acoma (Maring, 1975, p.

Table 4.1: Age-Based Syntactic/Semantic Variation in Arizona
Tewa Speech

Age Groups (Range in Years)	Percentage of Phrasal Conjunctions Realized as NP-á-dí NP	Percentage of Passives Which Accord with Condition: Subject of Passive Verb = +animate
1 (20–30)	90/84	74/46
2 (30–50)	48/44	90/84
3 (50 or more)	38/42	98/94

Note. Percentages are recorded in the following manner: Elicited Response Score/Spontaneous Speech Score.

480), it appears that grammatical interference from English is at least as significant at these subsystem levels as it is at those which are more recognized by members of the Arizona Tewa speech community.

Consider table 4.1, which represents an abbreviated summary of my findings regarding syntactic and semantic variation within the Arizona Tewa speech community (cf. Kroskrity 1978b, p. 242).

Group 1 consisted of members under 30 years of age. In this group, age correlated with ignorance of the ceremonial subcode, use of English as a preferred language in intragroup interaction, and replacement (approximately 30%) of native vocabulary in the Arizona Tewa code with corresponding English terms.[1] Group 2 consisted of members between the ages of 30 and 50. Like the younger group, members of this group displayed no command of the ceremonial subcode. By "no command," I mean that they lacked generative capacity, in the following sense: In regard to song and narrative production, I mean the ability to not only repeat previously composed songs and oral texts, but also to compose new songs and texts in the traditional style. Members of Group 2 did, however, differ from members of Group 1 in two important respects. First, they used all of the codes in their linguistic repertoires with approximately equal facility and in accordance with a more "context-sensitive" notion of appropriateness.[2] Second, they exhibited greater *compartmentalization* of codes, as manifested in relatively little (less than 10%) lexical replacement. Compartmentalization here refers to the symbolic strategy, on the part of multilinguals, of maintaining two or more distinct codes as discrete languages by minimizing their unilateral or reciprocal influence in grammar or lexicon (cf. Gumperz, 1968, p. 386).

Group 3 consisted of members of 50 or more years of age. They characteristically displayed familiarity with the ceremonial subcode, in contrast to the members of both other groups. Like members of Group 2, they also exhibited

a more balanced implementation of all of the component codes in their linguistic repertoire and comparable code-switching behavior.

In the first task represented above, I attempted to measure differential pro-
pensities to realize instances of phrasal conjunction in the surface/structure
pattern [NP-á-dí NP (NP and NP) Verb Complex$_s$]. For example, the translation equivalent of 'the man and the woman' may be alternatively realized in
Arizona Tewa as any of the following logically equivalent expressions:

1. sen-ná-dí kʷiyó da-cu·de-'ɛ'ɛ (man-EMPHATIC-ASSOCIATIONAL
   woman 3d:dual:stative-enter): *The man and the woman are entering.*[3]
2. sen-ná-dí kʷiyó-wá-dí da-cu·de-'ɛ'ɛ (man-EMPHATIC-ASSOCIA-
   TIONAL woman-EMPHATIC-ASSOCIATIONAL 3d:dual: sta-
   tive-enter): *The man and the woman are entering.*[4]
3. sen kʷiyó-wá-dí da-cu·de-'ɛ'ɛ (man woman-EMPHATIC-ASSOCIA-
   TIONAL 3d:dual:stative-enter): *The man and the woman are
   entering.*

Table 4.1 shows that speakers of Group 1 make frequent use of phrasal conjunctions which are realized as the first of the three alternatives (i.e., [NP-á-dí
NP Verb Complex$_s$]). Both the elicited responses and the spontaneous speech
of this group indicate that though speakers of groups 2 and 3 realize less than
half of their utterances involving phrasal conjunction in this manner, speakers
of group 1 approach uniformity in their reliance on this variant as the sole
means of realizing phrasal conjunction.

Moving to the second measure, we should note that all dialects of Tewa, like
Navajo—an Apachean language for which a comparable phenomenon has
been previously attested (Hale, 1973; Creamer, 1974)—exhibit semantic constraints on the well-formedness of passivelike and active sentences. In Navajo,
entities designated by nouns may be hierarchically ranked, providing a basis
for a rule of semantic interpretation which declares as ill-formed those sentences in which the hierarchically inferior noun precedes the superior noun in
surface structure. The comparable Arizona Tewa phenomenon employs not an
elaborate hierarchy, but rather a simple binary discrimination between animate and nonanimate nouns. Thus in Arizona Tewa, the only "ranking" of any
significance is the superiority of animate nouns (e.g., people, animals) to inanimate nouns. Inanimate nouns therefore can never be the subject of a passive
sentence in Arizona Tewa.

Another difference between these languages is that in Tewa, in contrast to
Navajo, the logical subject (or AGENT argument) is marked by the postposition /dí/. In other words, linear order of noun phrases in Arizona Tewa need
not reflect their grammatical relations, since this information is morphologically encoded in Tewa passive sentences. A consequence of these differences is
that the rule of semantic interpretation must be restated in the Tewa case so

as to refer not to the serial order of noun phrases but rather to the occupant of the grammatical relation "subject of" a passive verb. These observations are exemplified by sentences 4 through 7 below.

4. nɛ-'i sen he-'i pɛh mán-hey (this man that deer 3d subject:3d object:passive-kill): *This man killed that deer.*

5. he-'i pɛh nɛ-'i sen-dí 'ó-hey (that deer this man-ASSOCIATIONAL 3d subject:3d object:passive-kill): *That deer was killed by this man.*

6. he-'i sen nɛ-'i p'o mán-su-n (that man this water 3d subject:3d object:active-drink-TENSE): *That man drank this water.*

7. *nɛ-'i p'o he-'i sen-dí 'ó-su-n (this water that man-ASSOCIA-TIONAL 3d subject:3d object:passive-drink-TENSE): *This water was drunk by that man.*

Sentences 4 and 5 represent an active-passive alternation in which the passive sentence is semantically well formed partially because the surface subject fulfills the condition of animacy. When this condition is violated, as in 7—the passive alternative of 6—the result is an unacceptable, semantically ill-formed sentence.

Here again, group 1 exhibits notable differences in speech behavior from that of groups 2 and 3. Whereas speakers of these other groups consistently observe the semantic constraint in both elicited and spontaneous speech, speakers of group 1 only approximate this in the careful, more self-monitored style permitted by the elicited response—an indication which suggests that some stylistic control based on reflection and perhaps recollection of traditional notions of semantic well-formedness of the passive prompts such a response. But while this knowledge appears retrievable in situations where it is made problematic for the speaker—such as during the task of translation—the spontaneous speech score on this linguistic variable indicates that when problematicity for the speaker shifts away from linguistic production, adherence to the semantic constraint approaches random frequencies.

In contrast to the statistically insignificant differences which prevail between these and other measures employed for groups 2 and 3, group 1 manifests consistent and marked differences. Collectively these indicators reveal a pattern of grammatical interference from English in the internalized Arizona Tewa grammars of group 1. In order to substantiate this claim, two issues must be adequately addressed. First, the observed differences must be ones predisposed by a consideration of the surface facts of English. Two, some evidence must also be advanced to account for why differential interference exists. Since English is included in the repertoire of all the Arizona Tewa speakers sampled, why is it only members of group 1, the younger speakers, who provide demonstrable evidence of linguistic interference? In order to deal with each of these points, a brief review of some linguistic and ethnographic details is necessary.

Regarding the former, an examination of the linguistic evidence cited above clearly demonstrates that the grammar of English does provide a plausible source of grammatical interference for the observed pattern. The pattern of phrasal conjunction most widely employed by speakers of group 1 is that which is structurally isomorphic with its English counterpart: [NP-á-dí NP$_{NP}$], [NP and NP$_{NP}$]. Though aware of the traditional semantic condition on the semantic well-formedness of passive sentences which is regularly observed by members of groups 2 and 3 in both elicited and spontaneous speech, members of group 1 do not systematically produce sentences which accord with this semantic condition in their spontaneous speech. The fact that less than half of the sentences in this sample were realized in what, from the perspective of older speakers, constitutes a grammatically well-formed manner suggests that the Tewa passive is undergoing reanalysis in the speech of younger Tewa on the model of English, in which no comparable semantic constraint exists.

Collectively, then, linguistic interference has proven to be a plausible explanation for the patterned differences in the internalized grammars of younger Arizona Tewa speakers. The internalized grammatical rules which underlie production and interpretation of phrasal conjunctions and passives in English and Arizona Tewa thus appear to have converged (Gumperz & Wilson, 1971), or at least to have approximated convergence insofar as these phenomena are concerned. The compartmentalization of codes which accounts for the relative lack of grammatical interference in the speech of groups 2 and 3 no longer acts as a nearly impermeable barrier between coexisting codes in the linguistic repertoire of younger speakers. The presence of both lexical and grammatical interference in the speech of younger members of the Arizona Tewa speech community testifies to the breakdown of compartmentalization as a symbolic strategy for maintaining the distinctiveness of coexisting codes within the same code matrix.

Having illustrated the plausibility of an interpretation of grammatical interference from English as the cause of the patterned variation in these instances of syntactic and semantic behavior, it seems appropriate to return to the question of why the younger speakers' speech exhibits such a marked degree of linguistic interference from English. Foremost among the responsible factors is the formation of a new and influential "reference group" (Shibutani, 1962) which has informally recruited a majority of the younger people. This new reference group of peers has been fostered by the formal education provided by the federal government, nurtured by the increasing penetration of the mass media into the reservation, and transported from the urban-based boarding schools which most Arizona Tewa attend for the duration of their secondary education. There the fact that English is the sole language of instruction and the only common language for young Indians of various Southwestern tribes, though important, is perhaps not as significant as the removal of younger people from the traditional socializing influences of kinsmen and other community members. When subsistence agriculture played a major role in the economy of the reservation, the practical activities of planting, cultivating, and herding constituted an obligatory part of one's informal education, an education which entailed significant intergenerational interaction with kinsmen and community members. Today subsistence patterns have yielded to a cash economy in which the economic security of a household depends heavily on the wage work or salaried employment of at least one of its members. Yet for young people, the slim economic base of the reservation provides few opportunities and acts as a "push-factor" (W. Hodge, 1971, p. 349), a force which encourages abandonment of the reservation in either a physical sense (actual urban migration) or a psychological one (adoption of a nontraditional, "urban" orientation).

In keeping with this urban orientation, English is employed as the preferred language of intragroup interaction, and since such interaction comprises the bulk of all of their interpersonal relations (a testament to the diminished influence of family and other kinsmen), English may be properly regarded as the dominant language of the vast majority of young people. Whereas the Arizona Tewa language continues to serve as a badge of ethnicity for older speakers, younger members have adopted English as a symbol of their nontraditional orientation. Their habitual use of English even in response to remarks addressed to them in Arizona Tewa by their parents violates traditional expectations regarding code-switching behavior and both signals the disparity of values attached to the component codes of the linguistic repertoire by members of different generations and symbolically invokes a competing nontraditional perspective from which meanings are differently assigned to actions and objects. By so responding, young people manifest both their rejection of more traditional norms and values as factors to be considered in the generation of appropriate behavior and their allegiance to a new reference group from whose perspective they prefer to formulate and evaluate their actions.

A direct examination of the contact between English and Arizona Tewa has proven instructive in regard to at least three issues. First, it clearly demonstrates the differences between the folk and analytical perspectives as they pertain to the salience of linguistic phenomena. In contrast to linguists, who tend to equate a language with its grammar (Bolinger 1973, p. 8), nonlinguist members of speech communities appear to regard a language as consubstantial with its lexicon. The significance of this observation resides in its implications for diffusion: If grammatical phenomena are less subject to the awareness of members of a speech community, and therefore less subject to the evaluation which such awareness would permit, then we, as analysts, must be prepared for differences in both pattern and rate of change in lexical and grammatical diffusion. The fact that no marked differences in rate or pattern of diffusion for grammar and lexicon have been established in this case study may be variously attributed to 1) the relatively short history of contact with English in the form of stable multilingualism (approximately 60 years) and 2) the relatively narrow focus of this study. In other words, the present study cannot be understood as a refutation of the observation concerning salience and its implications for change. Thus, while this study has demonstrated the existence of the disparity between folk and analytical perceptions of language, it has not documented the significance of this difference in shaping differential patterns of linguistic diffusion.

A second observation which should also be noted is the facilitating role of multilingualism in producing linguistic diffusion. In linguistic terms, the role of multilingualism is to introduce variants, at one or more subsystem levels, which represent instances of linguistic interference. The chance of such variants being both "innovated" and propagated is further enhanced by *societal multilingualism* (as opposed to *individual multilingualism*) (Miller, 1978, p. 613), which both increases the likelihood of independent innovations and promotes a more uniform evaluation of variants, further assisting propagation.

A final instructive observation here is the relationship of language and ethnicity. Compartmentalization and its antithesis, convergence, are significantly influenced at both lexical and grammatical levels by the symbolic roles occupied by the languages in contact. I will defer a discussion of language and ethnicity until I can provide evidence from the Hopi contact situation, since this instance is particularly effective in demonstrating the importance of ethnicity to language contact.

Contact with Hopi

In marked contrast to the convergence described above, the relationship of Tewa to Hopi in the linguistic repertoires of Arizona Tewa speakers has been and continues to be one of almost complete compartmentalization. Despite nearly three centuries of contact between the two codes and stable societal multilingualism during most of this period, a single phonological innovation remains the only candidate for an instance of grammatical diffusion. Arizona Tewa, unlike all the Rio Grande Tewa dialects (Speirs, 1966), possesses a voiced lateral phoneme (/l/). Table 4.2 provides examples of cognate forms in the two dialects which, with the exception of some regular correspondences and partial reduplication, differ only in the addition of the /l/ segment.

It should be emphasized here that one need not interpret the apparent innovation of an /l/ phoneme in Arizona Tewa as a product of language contact with the Hopi. In every other Kiowa-Tanoan language, /l/ appears medially. Whether or not /l/ can be reconstructed for Proto-Kiowa-Tanoan in medial position remains, as Kenneth Hale (1967, p. 116) has stated, an unsolved problem. Thus, it appears that the presence of /l/ in Arizona Tewa is at least as attributable to genetic retention of a family trait as it is to diffusion from Hopi.

Perhaps even more surprising than this lack of grammatical diffusion is the

Table 4.2: Tewa Dialects and /l/

Arizona Tewa	Rio Grande Tewa	Translation
-cála	-cá'	to cut
ni·li	ni·	chicken
p'ólo	p'ô	road
-tɛle	-tɛ	to pull
wo·lo	wo·	medicine
ka·la	ka·	leaf
na·la	na·	aspen
t'ólo'	t'ó·	sage
-mi·li	-bi·	to turn
me·le	be·	bowl, ball

Note. Some of the productive correspondences between initial conso-
nants in Arizona Tewa (AT) and Rio Grande Tewa (RG T) are: AT /d/
= RG T /r/; AT /pʰ/ = RG T /f/; AT /y/ = RG T /j/; AT /kʸ/ =
RG T /č/; AT /kʰ/ = RG T /x/; AT /m/ = RG T /b/.

virtual absence of lexical borrowing, despite the fact that lexical items are usually less difficult to absorb. The Arizona Tewa have adopted Hopi placenames
and some designations for a few cultural concepts (e.g., Dozier, 1954, p. 305).
But such loans are never phonologically integrated into Tewa, and more important, they never represent a replacement—or even an alternate—for a preex-
isting Tewa lexical item. The Hopi case thus appears aberrant. Despite coresidence with the Hopi and considerable social accommodation to them, as well
as intermarriage and stable societal bilingualism in the two codes, very little
linguistic diffusion of any type can be detected. Why? The answer, in part,
hinges on the relationship of language and ethnicity, thereby involving the symbolic role of the Tewa language for the Arizona Tewa.

The long period of coresidence on First Mesa, after the migration of the
ancestors of the Arizona Tewa from their former Rio Grande pueblos, manifested itself in considerable borrowing from the Hopi. As Barth observes (1969,
pp. 15–16),

> Entailed in ethnic boundary maintenance are also situations of social contact
> between persons of different cultures: ethnic groups only persist as significant
> units if they imply marked differences in behavior, i.e., persisting cultural dif-
> ferences. Yet where persons of different cultures interact, one would expect those
> differences to be reduced, since interaction both requires and generates a con-
> gruence of codes and values.

In the Arizona Tewa case, increased interaction with the Hopi generated a
discernible congruence of codes and values in the areas of kinship behavior and

ceremonial organization. While the terminology of the kin terms closely resembles that of the Rio Grande Tewa, the kinship system itself is structurally akin to the Hopi system, featuring matrilineal emphasis and strict matrilocal residence (Eggan, 1950, p. 41; Dozier, 1955). These features represent a marked departure from the more patrilineal emphasis and patrilocal residence patterns which typify traditional Rio Grande Tewa kinship behavior. Clans were also borrowed from the Hopi and equated with Hopi clans either nominally or mythologically. Changes in kinship structure permitted intermarriage between members of the two groups to occur without disrupting social patterns. The establishment of clans facilitated the legitimization of Tewa land-holdings, since the Hopi viewed all property as belonging to the clan. Both of these developments may be construed as attempts by the Hopi and the Tewa to enlarge kinship networks and to ensure economic security and stability. In addition, the Arizona Tewa have borrowed the Kachina cult (Eggan, 1950, p. 164). Dozier summarizes these changes in the following manner: "It is interesting that when elements could be incorporated within the Tewa pattern without endangering cultural aloofness, borrowing was in order" (Dozier, 1951, p. 61). Dozier's statement may seem somewhat paradoxical. Despite extensive borrowing from the Hopi, the Arizona Tewa still retain a distinct culture and a discrete status as a separate ethnic group. Yet how is this accomplished?

The answer to this problem is at least partially a symbolic one. As interethnic interaction over a long period of time has reduced the total inventory of tangible sociocultural differences which formerly characterized the two groups, the persisting differences assue a new symbolic function as badges of identity, or in Barth's terms, "diacritica of ethnicity" (Barth, 1969; Jackson, 1974). For the Arizona Tewa, one of the most significant of these diacritica continues to be language. The Arizona Tewa language, as an exclusive possession of the Arizona Tewa themselves, serves as tangible evidence of persisting differences between them and their Hopi neighbors, differences which attest to the penetration of the present by the past.

This instance of contact of Arizona Tewa with Hopi thus proves especially instructive in illustrating how the symbolic function of a language as an emblem of ethnicity can insulate it from diffusional processes, even in instances of stable societal multilingualism.

Contact with Spanish

This pattern is somewhat replicated in the case of contact with Spanish, but whereas in the Hopi situation I was able to isolate at least one candidate for phonological borrowing, however dubious, in the Spanish case, borrowing appears to be strictly limited to the lexicon. Table 4.3 provides a list of Spanish loanwords in Arizona Tewa which can be established with relative certainty.

Table 4.3: Spanish Loanwords in Arizona Tewa

Arizona Tewa	Spanish Source	Translation
bán	pan	(wheat) bread
cini	chili	chili
ci·yo	cuchillo	knife
kʰa·pe	cafe	coffee
kula·nto	cilantro	coriander
kʷenu	cabrio	goat
limon	limon	lemon
mansana	manzana	apple
melo·ni	melon	melon
mu·la	mula, mulo	mule
mu·lu	burro	donkey
mu·sa	miza	cat
sani·ya	sandia	watermelon
tomati	tomate	tomato
'u·ba	uva	grape
wak'a	vaca	cow
wa·yu	caballo	horse

Note. For further discussion of this table, consult P. V. Kroskrity, Inferences from Spanish loans in Arizona Tewa, *Anthropological Linguistics 20,* 1978, 340–50.

Perhaps the most noteworthy aspect of this list is its brevity. Despite the fact that the Tano, the ancestors of the Arizona Tewa, were subjected to the most intensive contact of any of the Eastern pueblo villages during the century-long contact period before the Pueblo Revolts of 1680 and 1696, only 17 loanwords exist. Qualitative analysis of these loanwords reveals the superficial nature of the borrowing. They are primarily labels for the Spanish "imports": plant-derived foodstuffs (2, 4, 5, 7–9, 13–15) and domesticated animals (6, 10–12, 16–17).

Unlike Rio Grande Tewa, which has borrowed a considerable amount of religious and governmental terminology from Spanish (Dozier, 1964, p. 514), Arizona Tewa exhibits only loanwords that refer to the material innovations offered by the Spanish. Thus, whereas Dozier provides Rio Grande Tewa examples such as *kumpáreʰ* (from Spanish *compadre,* godfather), *konfesâ* (from Spanish *confesión,* confession), and *piʰkâ* from Spanish *fiscal,* official) comparable loanwords are conspicuously absent in Arizona Tewa. This difference is, of course, partially due to the fact that the Tano escaped a prolonged period of contact with the Spanish, after reconquest, by migrating to First Mesa. The superficiality of linguistic borrowing is further evidenced by the lack of lexical elaboration afforded to the terms introduced by the Spanish. In contrast to Rio Grande Tewa, which has admitted loanwords that often preserve the gender and age distinctions of the source language, Arizona Tewa has borrowed only a single undifferentiated lexeme, to which other native terms must be compounded to yield comparable semantic distinctions. Thus, whereas Rio Grande Tewa possesses loanwords that lexically distinguish 'stallion' from 'mare' and 'calf' from 'cow,' Arizona Tewa, as Table 4.4 indicates, has borrowed only one term per species, to which the native terms for *man, boy, girl,* and so forth must be appended to yield greater specificity.

Thus, in an analysis of Spanish loanwords in Arizona Tewa showing their scarcity, selection from restricted semantic domains, and lack of lexical elaboration, we have found evidence of extreme compartmentalization, which we can infer to be the linguistic response to the intolerance and suppression accompanying the early Spanish colonial program (Dozier, 1964, pp. 148–49). Despite the shared experience of the initial 100 years of Spanish domination before the migration of the Tano, in the wake of the Pueblo Revolt of 1696, the ancestors of the Arizona Tewa disrupted the otherwise ongoing acculturative influence of the Spanish that the more tolerant Eastern Pueblo adaptation permitted. The relative lack, both quantitatively and qualitatively, of Spanish loanwords which I have documented for Arizona Tewa and the absence of any vestige of the Spanish-Catholic ceremonial system continue to provide contemporary indices of different historical adaptations to Spanish culture contact (Dozier, 1958).

Here the contrast between patterns of admission of Spanish loanwords in Arizona and Rio Grande Tewa should not be explained solely by reference to the longer period of direct contact experienced by the Rio Grande Tewa, although this is certainly important. Of key significance is the fact that during this longer period of contact a more peaceful and varied relationship between the Spanish and Pueblo groups was effected, thus providing a symbolic environment more conducive to diffusional processes, both cultural (Ortiz, 1969, pp. 62–71) and linguistic.[5]

Table 4.4: Contrastive Elaboration of Spanish Loans in Tewa

Spanish	Rio Grande Tewa	Arizona Tewa	Translation
vaca	wá·siʰ	wak'a-kʷiyó	bovine-woman = cow
becerro	beceroʰ	wak'a-e·nu	bovine-boy = calf
yegua	ǰe·waʰ	wa·yu-kʷiyó	horse-woman = mare
caballo	kavaǰuh	wa·yu-sen	horse-man = stallion

Contact with Apachean

In contrast to the previous contact situations which have been described, the contact between Tewa and Apachean, which I infer from apparent linguistic diffusion, occurred in a past so remote that it precedes the historical period in the American Southwest. Also in contrast to the preceding contact situations, the contact and diffusion which I delineate here is not restricted to the present Arizona Tewa speech community or that of its Tano ancestors. Since the apparent diffusion appears in all dialects of Tewa, the relevant contact with Apachean must be traced back to a relatively undifferentiated speech community which is ancestral to all of the historic, Tewa-speaking pueblos. My objective here is to briefly summarize my preliminary findings in regard to Tewa-Apachean diffusion (Kroskrity, 1981).

The evidential basis for the claim of Tewa-Apachean diffusion consists of four observations.

First, the Tewa passive (as exemplified by sentences 4–6 above) is characterized by 1) the occurrence of passive prefixes; 2) the semantic foregrounding of Patient-Subjects; 3) agent marking; and 4) a semantic constraint on Subjects (i.e., that they be +animate).[6] While the latter two of these represent traits shared by other Kiowa-Tanoan languages, the former two are not replicated elsewhere in the family. In all of the other Kiowa-Tanoan languages, "passives" simply appear to be sentences containing verbs inflected for intransitivity which permit an AGENT argument; they lack distinctive passive prefixes. The Tewa passive not only represents a family anomaly in this regard, but a Southwestern one as well. With the exception of the Apachean languages, no other neighbor possesses a comparable phenomenon. Navajo, for example, not only has an analogous passivelike prefix, but also the other features, except for agent marking. Yet while the presence of agent marking can be explained in Tewa as the result of genetic inheritance, the other characteristics cannot be similarly dismissed. Since only three other causes of linguistic similarity exist—language universals, diffusion, and accidental convergence—and since these similarities cannot be dismissed as language-particular manifestations of language universals, only two possibilities remain: chance and diffusion.

Second, as Larry Gorbet (1977) has recently demonstrated, relative clauses in both Tewa and Navajo are structurally similar to those of many other Southwestern languages. Most of these languages possess "headless" relative clauses—relative clauses which lack a syntactic head noun and have a lexical instance of the semantic head in the embedded sentence. Examples 8 and 9 illustrate representative relative clauses in Tewa and Navajo respectively.

8.   na· he-'i sen c'a·ndi **'u·ba-p'o** mán-sun 'i dó-kumɛ (I that man yesterday **grape-water** 3d subject:3d object: active-drank it 1st subject:3d object:active-buy): *I bought the wine which that man drank yesterday.*

9. Hastiin **bịịh** bit'adéldooh-ę́ę̣ neiis'ah (man **deer** I:shot-RELATIV-
   IZER butcher): *The man butchered the deer which I shot* (Hale &
   Platero, 1974).

In each example the semantic head has been set in boldface type to emphasize
its location in the embedded sentence. My interest here, however, is not merely
to exemplify the "headless" nature of these relative clauses, but rather to focus
attention on the relativizing morphemes as well. In Tewa, the third person pronoun positioned immediately after an embedded sentence functions as the
relativizer. When suffixed to nonsentential material, such as uninflected verb
stems, the same pronoun also functions as a simple nominalizer. So common
is this occurrence of the constituent *'i* that J. P. Harrington (1910, p. 498)
ignored its basic role as the third person pronoun and translated it as "that
already referred to," thus capturing its anaphoric function. The only other language in the Southwest with a recognizable anaphor as a relativizer is Navajo,
where, as example 10 demonstrates, the relativizer is attributed a meaning very
similar to that previously provided for Tewa *'i*.

10. ⱡii-ę́ę̣ dilwo' (horse-"aforementioned" fast): *The aforementioned
    horse is fast.*

As with Tewa, the relativizer in Navajo is a multifunctional constituent which,
in addition to its relativizing function, can be employed in nominalizations and
in the formation of adjectival or appositive structures. Here Sapir (1935, p.
136) reminds us that what I have referred to as the relativizer appears to be
an Athabaskan family trait, though a trait more elaborately developed in the
Apachean languages, where it has not been restricted to the formation of
sobriquets (as in non-Apachean Athabaskan). An additional similarity, and
one which cannot be treated as a retention from Proto-Athabaskan on the part
of languages such as Navajo, is that in both Tewa and Navajo, "headed" relative clauses exist as unpreferred stylistic alternatives.

Third, classificatory verbs in Tewa and in Navajo reveal apparent similarities which warrant examination as instances of linguistic diffusion. These verbs
"assign to their object nouns certain qualities of number, shape, texture. . . .
The verb stem has a meaning which refers to the shape of the noun and the
noun has a shape which permits it to occur with that stem" (Davidson, Elford,
& Hoijer, 1963, p. 30). Hoijer's (1945) study of classificatory verbs in Apachean discriminated 12 frequently occurring classes. In contrast to this elaborate classificatory system, the Tewa classification, according to Anna Speirs
(1974, p. 56), discriminates only 5 classes. Though comparable classifications
exist in the other Kiowa-Tanoan languages, the available comparative data
suggest that Tewa alone has developed a containerized class. The presence of
this apparent innovation in Tewa and the existence of an Apachean analog
further suggests the possibility of diffusion.

Fourth, some lexical evidence also suggests diffusion.[7] This evidence consists of grammatical morphemes and "content" words. Briefly stated, among the Tewa grammatical morphemes are several postpositions, a possessive morpheme (/-bi/), and a numeral suffix (/-di/), which display striking phonetic and semantic similarities to comparable Apachean forms. As for "content" words, preliminary areal-comparative inspection reveals some similarities in the words for 'deer' (AT pɛh˙, Navajo bįįh), 'grease' (RGT ką˙, Navajo k'ah), and 'coyote' (AT bayɛnah, Chiracahua Apache ⁿba'ye) (Hoijer, 1946, p. 59) which are quite striking when one considers the phonological differences in these languages.

Though a more definitive assessment of this evidence awaits some much-needed genetic-historical linguistic research on language families represented in the Southwest, the discernible pattern at present seems best explained by linguistic diffusion. What are the ethnohistorical implications of such an interpretation? Any account of language change and, of course, language contact is not merely a depiction of the collision of disembodied verbal symbolic systems but, implicitly, an account of speech communities as well. The pattern of diffusion which I have briefly sketched would seem to presuppose considerable individual, if not societal, bilingualism in these languages and significant, stable networks of communication between the two groups. Does the ethnohistorical literature meet these expectations? Initially it might appear that it does not. Nowhere do we find extensive documentation which explicitly acknowledges Indian bilingualism in these languages. The record, however, must be viewed as a less than systematic collection of impressions by untrained Spanish observers. If we attend to the indirect references to interethnic relations between Pueblo Indians and Apacheans offered by the Spanish documents, we find mention of several key "institutions" which could well have promoted considerable bilingualism. These include: 1) the existence of periodic and regular trade fairs for the regulation of commerce between Pueblos and Apacheans; 2) the tradition of winter settlement by Apachean groups just outside the limits of various pueblos; 3) the military alliances between Pueblos and Apacheans during the frequent outbreaks of interpueblo hostility; and 4) the tradition of seeking refuge among Apacheans by individual Pueblo Indians, their families, and even larger segments of villages on occasions of exceptionally extreme oppressive actions by the Spanish (F. Hodge, 1907, pp. 356–57; Hammond & Rey, 1966, pp. 345, 484; Hester, 1971, p. 51; Schroeder, 1972, p. 55). This evidence of sustained interethnic relations which is available in some sixteenth- and seventeenth-century records withers in later documents, particularly those after the Pueblo Revolts of 1680 and 1696. Spanish colonial disruption of precontact inter-Indian relations gradually transformed these more amicable relations into the typical raiding patterns and attendant hostile relations between the Navajo, the most "puebloized" of all Apachean groups, and the Pueblos in more recent historical times. Thus the historical plausibility demonstrated above complements the linguistic interpretation of diffusion.

FACTORS AFFECTING DIFFUSION

Cases of diffusion such as the Tewa-Apachean instance outlined above represent a special challenge for the student of linguistic diffusion. No direct observation of sociolinguistic processes is available to the researcher, and the indirect view provided by ethnohistorical investigation is too fragmentary to permit a reconstruction of the relevant details of the contact situation. In such cases, the products of diffusion may, themselves, represent an important source of inferences concerning the sociocultural contexts of language contact.[8] But whether evidence of linguistic diffusion can be effectively employed in illuminating the past or not depends critically upon our success as researchers in developing a sociolinguistic typology of the outcomes of language contact as an interpretive guide. As I stated in my initial paragraph, the tendency to view diffusion largely in terms of its products has inhibited the development of a holistic approach stressing the relations among linguistic, social, and cultural systems. Thus, instead of elucidating systems, we must first confront the more rudimentary taxonomic task of identifying the relevant variables.

Code-Internal Properties

All natural languages exhibit certain structural problems at various subsystem levels (gaps, ambiguities, exceptions, complications, vestigial forms, etc.) which may actually predispose borrowing, if the potential source language provides compatible resources (lexical, grammatical, etc.) for resolving these problems (e.g., the borrowing of a specialized subordinating morpheme from Spanish by Yaqui [Lindenfeld, 1974]). Another code-internal source of diffusion which can be detected is the tendency of speakers to regularize analogous structures in two or more languages so as to effect a convergence of codes. Examples of this are provided by Gumperz and Wilson's (1971) Kupwar study and the interference of English in the grammar of the younger Tewa speakers.

Code Functions

The symbolic or functional role that a language plays in expressive or instrumental tasks influences its candidacy for diffusion—witness the relative imperviousness of Arizona Tewa in its contact with both Spanish and Hopi. We can infer a well-circumscribed role for Spanish in the linguistic repertoires of the Tano in pre-Pueblo Revolt times—that of economic and political subordination. Such a functional specialization of Spanish must actually have promoted compartmentalization, thereby minimizing the influence of Spanish on coexisting codes in the linguistic repertoire. In the case of contact with Hopi, a language which has assumed a more diversified usage pattern (Kroskrity, 1977, p. 209), the emblematic significance which most Arizona Tewa attribute to their native language has served to insulate it from diffusion despite the long duration of stable contact with Hopi.

Multilingualism

The facilitating role of multilingualism in effecting diffusion is reaffirmed in the preceding studies. While some stray lexical borrowings can occur in non-multilingual situations, more elaborate lexical borrowing and borrowing at other subsystem levels seem to presuppose multilingualism. The distinction between societal and individual multilingualism (as in Miller, 1978, p. 614) is useful not only in distinguishing the degree to which members of a speech community share a second code, but also in pointing out our ignorance concerning the types and degrees of diffusion which correlate with each of these types of multilingualism. Lacking an instructive, ethnographic analogy for a contact situation involving significant individual multilingualism and lacking a knowledge of what diffusion is produced in that contact situation, I have no principled basis for interpreting societal or individual bilingualism as an informing factor in Tewa-Navajo diffusion.

Language Attitudes

The often remarked "linguistic conservatism" of the Pueblos (Sherzer, 1976, p. 233) has clearly had an influence on diffusion in the American Southwest, though scholars disagree in their interpretation of its impact on multilingualism and diffusion. Wick Miller (1978, p. 613) seems to conclude that the "extreme ethnocentrism" of the Pueblos manifested itself in the form of a denigration of second-language–learning, whereas I (Kroskrity, 1980b) contend that it was not bilingualism itself that was so devalued, but rather the language mixing, or linguistic interference, which bilingualism could produce. Further ethnographic work must be undertaken on language attitudes and their implications for linguistic behavior in the Pueblo Southwest. One thing, however, is certain: The patterns of diffusion which we will be able to elucidate in the Pueblo Southwest will differ markedly from, say, those of the Northwest Coast, where language attitudes actually promote diffusion, rather than inhibit it (Miller, 1978, p. 611).

Popular Awareness as a Factor in Diffusion

The study of contact between Arizona Tewa and English summarized earlier replicates some of the findings of Gumperz and Wilson (1971, p. 161) in regard to the popular salience of linguistic phenomena. Gumperz and Wilson found that such phenomena can be ranked in accordance with their degree of popular awareness. Most available to such awareness are the "content word" nouns. Significantly less available are adverbs, conjunctions, postpositions, and other grammatical phenomena. The implications for diffusion are clear: Linguistic elements of high popular salience will be subject to the symbolic evaluation of the speaker, a factor which, given the cultural predisposition to devalue interference, could inhibit diffusion. Those elements of low popular salience, the more grammatical (as opposed to lexical) elements, would escape such evaluation. Recall the pattern of diffusion between Tewa and Apachean: some apparent grammatical borrowing, little lexical borrowing. This pattern may well be the product of the differential diffusability of these linguistic phenomena.

NOTES

1. My use of nonsyntactic and nonsemantic criteria to rank speakers was, in part, an attempt to detail for the reader those manifestations which first suggested the relevance of age as an explanatory variable.

2. By "context-sensitive" notion of appropriateness, I mean to designate, however imperfectly, a code-switching strategy in which code selection and code switching are guided by a speaker's consultation of such contextual features as participants, setting, topic, etc. In other words, I mean a strategy in which codes are actually switched in reference to such contextual features. The code switching of younger Tewa, in contrast, appears to be insensitive to traditional notions of appropriateness. Terming the traditional code-switching strategy as *context-sensitive* is somewhat inappropriate, since it implies that the younger speakers' strategy is utterly immune to considerations of social context, when, in fact, this context is only differently construed and evaluated.

3. The ASSOCIATIONAL postposition /-dí/ is a polysemous constituent, variously interpreted as *with, by, and,* etc., depending upon its immediate syntactic environment.

4. [ná] and [wá] are allomorphs of /-á-/, the emphatic, which are derived by morphophonemic rule. For specific details, consult Kroskrity, 1977, p. 131.

5. Though it is true that Rio Grande Tewa experienced more linguistic borrowing from Spanish than did Arizona Tewa, I do not mean to suggest that such borrowing ever flourished. Dozier (1964), in a classic article which contrasts borrowing from Spanish in Yaqui and Rio Grande Tewa, clearly demonstrates the comparative lack of linguistic borrowing in Rio Grande Tewa. The Arizona Tewa case simply represents an even more extreme instance of compartmentalization.

6. This Arizona Tewa semantic constraint on the well-formedness of passives may seem qualitatively different from the ranking of nouns (Creamer, 1974) which occurs in Navajo. Yet the existence of more elaborate, hierarchical ranking constraints in both Rio Grande Tewa and Jemez confirms the fact that the Tewa and Navajo constraints are truly analogous systems and not merely superficially similar—a possible, though misguided, interpretation of the more vestigial manifestation of the constraint currently operating in Arizona Tewa.

7.   This statement is the result of preliminary efforts to ascertain the existence of such loans. A definitive statement on the status of lexical borrowing between these two languages must await the compilation of an Arizona Tewa dictionary.

8.   For a more elaborate statement of this position, see Sherzer and Bauman, 1972.

REFERENCES

Barth, F. *Ethnic groups and boundaries.* Boston: Little, Brown, 1969.

Bolinger, D. Getting the words in. In R. I. McDavid & A. R. Duckert (Eds.), *Lexicography in English.* Annals of the New York Academy of Sciences, No. 211. New York: New York Academy of Sciences, 1973.

Brandt, E. A. On the origins of linguistic stratification. *Anthropological Linguistics,* 1970, *12,* 46–51.

Casagrande, J. B. Comanche linguistic acculturation (3 Vols.). *International Journal of American Linguistics,* 1954, *20,* 140–51, 217–37; 1955, *21,* 8–25.

Creamer, M. H. Ranking in Navajo nouns. *Diné Bizaad Nánil'ịịh / Navajo Language Review,* 1974, *1,* 29–39.

Davidson, W., Elford, L. W., & Hoijer, H. Athapascan classificatory verb stems. In H. Hoijer (Ed.), *Studies in the Athapascan languages.* University of California Publications in Linguistics, No. 29. Berkeley: University of California Press, 1963.

Dozier, E. P. Resistance to acculturation and assimilation in an Indian pueblo. *American Anthropologist,* 1951, *53,* 56–66.

——. *The Hopi-Tewa of Arizona.* University of California Publications in American Archaeology and Ethnology, Vol. 44, No. 3. Berkeley: University of California Press, 1954.

——. Kinship and linguistic change among the Arizona Tewa. *International Journal of American Linguistics,* 1955, *21,* 242–57.

——. Cultural matrix of singing and chanting in Tewa pueblos. *International Journal of American Linguistics,* 1958, *24,* 268–72.

——. Two examples of linguistic acculturation: The Yaqui of Sonora and the Tewa of New Mexico. In D. Hymes (Ed.), *Language in culture and society.* New York: Harper & Row, 1964. (Originally published in *Language,* 1951, *32,* 146–51).

Eggan, F. *Social organization of the western pueblos.* Chicago: University of Chicago Press, 1950.

Fox, J. R. A note on Cochiti linguistics. In C. H. Lange (Ed.), *Cochiti, a New Mexican pueblo, past and present.* Carbondale: University of Southern Illinois Press, 1959.

Gorbet, L. Headless relatives in the southwest: Are they related? *Proceedings of the Berkeley Linguistics Society,* No. 3, pp. 270–78. Berkeley: University of California, 1977.

Gumperz, J. J. The speech community. *International Encyclopedia of the Social Sciences,* 1968, *9,* 381–86.

Gumperz, J. J., & Wilson, R. Convergence and creolization: A case study from the Indo-Aryan/Dravidian border. In D. Hymes (Ed.), *Pidginization and creolization of languages.* London: Cambridge University Press, 1971.

Hale, K. Toward a reconstruction of Kiowa-Tanoan phonology. *International Journal of American Linguistics,* 1967, *33,* 112–21.

———. A note on subject-object inversion in Navajo. In B. Kachru (Ed.), *Issues in linguistics.* Urbana: University of Illinois Press, 1973.

Hale, K., & Platero, P. Aspects of Navajo anaphora: Relativization and pronominalization. *Diné Bizaad Nanil'ı̨ı̨h / Navajo Language Review,* 1974, *1,* 9–28.

Hammond, G. P., & Rey, A. *The rediscovery of New Mexico.* Albuquerque: University of New Mexico Press, 1966.

Harrington, J. P. A brief description of the Tewa language. *American Anthropologist,* 1910, *7,* 497–504.

Herzog, G. Culture change and language: Shifts in the Pima vocabulary. In L. Spier (Ed.), *Language, culture, and personality.* Menasha, Wis.: Sapir Memorial Fund, 1941.

Hester, J. J. Navajo culture change: From 1550 to 1960 and beyond. In K. Basso & M. Opler (Eds.), *Apachean culture history.* Tucson: University of Arizona Press, 1971.

Hodge, F. W. *Handbook of American Indians north of Mexico.* Bureau of American Ethnology, Bull. 30, Pt. 1. Washington, D.C.: U.S. Government Printing Office, 1907.

Hodge, W. H. Navajo urban migration: An analysis from the perspective of the family. In J. O. Waddell & O. M. Watson (Eds.), *The American Indian in urban society.* Boston: Little, Brown, 1971.

Hoijer, H. Chiracahua loan-words from Spanish. *Language,* 1939, *15,* 110–15.

———. Classificatory verb stems in Apachean languages. *International Journal of American Linguistics,* 1945, *11,* 13–23.

———. Chiracahua Apache. In H. Hoijer (Ed.), *Linguistic structures of Native America.* Viking Fund Publications in Anthropology, No. 6. New York: Wenner-Gren Foundation for Anthropological Research, 1946.

Jackson, J. Language identity of the Colombian Vaupés Indians. In R. Bauman & J. Sherzer (Eds.), *Explorations in the ethnography of speaking.* London: Cambridge University Press, 1974.

Kroskrity, P. V. Aspects of Arizona Tewa language structure and language use. Doctoral diss., Indiana University, 1977. *Dissertation Abstracts International,* 1978, *38,* 5564-A. (University Microfilms No. 7800139, 301.)

———. Aspects of syntactic and semantic variation within the Arizona Tewa speech community. *Anthropological Linguistics,* 1978, *20,* 235–57.(a)

———. Inferences from Spanish loans in Arizona Tewa. *Anthropological Linguistics,* 1978, *20,* 340–50.(b)

———. Language contact and linguistic diffusion: The Arizona Tewa speech community. In F. Barkin & E. A. Brandt (Eds.), *Speaking, singing, and teaching: A multidisciplinary approach to language variation.* Proceedings of the Eighth Annual Southwest Areal Languages and Linguistics Workshop. Anthropological Research Papers, No. 20. Tempe: Arizona State University, 1980.(a)

———.On "linguistic conservatism" in the Pueblo Southwest. Paper presented at the Conference on American Indian Languages held in conjunction with the Seventy-ninth Annual Meeting of the American Anthropological Association, Washington, D.C., Dec. 1980.(b)

——. Toward a sociolinguistic history of the Tewa. Paper presented at the School of American Research Advanced Seminar on the Tewa, Sante Fe, 1981.

Lambert, R. D. Language skill attrition, conference initiates research in new subfield. *Linguistic Reporter,* 1980, *23,* 1–3.

Lindenfeld, J. Spanish influences in Yaqui syntax. Paper presented at the Conference on American Indian Languages held in conjunction with the Seventy-third Annual Meeting of the American Anthropological Association, Mexico City, Nov. 1974.

Maring, J. M. Speech variation in Acoma Keresan. In M. D. Kinkade (Ed.), *Linguistics and anthropology in honor of C. F. Voegelin.* Lisse, Belgium: Peter de Ridder Press, 1975.

Miller, W. R. Spanish loanwords in Acoma, I, II. *International Journal of American Linguistics,* 1959, *25,* 147–53; 1960, *26,* 41–49.

——. Multilingualism in its social context in aboriginal North America. *Proceedings of the Berkeley Linguistics Society,* No. 4, pp. 610–16. Berkeley: University of California, 1978.

Ortiz, A. *The Tewa World.* Chicago: University of Chicago Press, 1969.

Sapir, E. A type of Athabaskan relative. *International Journal of American Linguistics,* 1935, *2,* 136–42.

Schroeder, A. H. Rio Grande ethnohistory. In A. Ortiz (Ed.), *New Perspectives on the pueblos.* Albuquerque: University of New Mexico Press, 1972.

Sherzer, J. *An areal-typological study of American Indian languages north of Mexico.* Amsterdam: North Holland, 1976.

Sherzer, J., & Bauman, R. Areal studies and culture history. *Southwest Journal of Anthropology,* 1972, *28,* 131–53.

Shibutani, T. Reference groups and social control. In A. M. Rose (Ed.), *Human behavior and social processes.* Boston: Houghton Mifflin, 1962.

Southworth, F. C. Detecting prior creolization: An analysis of the historical origins of Marathi. In D. Hymes (Ed.), *Pidginization and creolization of languages.* London: Cambridge University Press, 1971.

Speirs, A. Classificatory verb stems in Tewa. *Studies in Linguistics,* 1974, *24,* 45–64.

Speirs, R. H. Some aspects of the structure of Rio Grande Tewa. Doctoral diss., State University of New York at Buffalo, 1966. *Dissertation Abstracts International,* 1966, *27,* 762A–763A. (University Microfilms No. 66-7987, 203).

Spencer, R. F. Spanish loanwords in Keresan. *Southwest Journal of Anthropology,* 1947, *3,* 130–46.

Trager, G. L. Spanish and English loanwords in Taos. *International Journal of American Linguistics,* 1944, *10,* 144–58.

Weinreich, U. *Languages in contact.* New York: Linguistic Circle of New York, 1953.

5 | Sociolinguistic Aspects of the Acceptance of Literacy in the Vernacular

BERNARD SPOLSKY and PATRICIA IRVINE
University of New Mexico

Among the most debated questions in the development of language-education policy for minorities is that of the choice of language for initial literacy teaching. Traditional colonial policies in Africa, for example, followed one of two approaches: The French and Portuguese assumed that the acquisition of literacy was a basic step in civilization and that it could be usefully achieved only in the standard metropolitan language. The British, Belgians, and Germans, on the other hand, accepted the desirability of initial literacy in the vernacular, with literacy in the standard metropolitan language being taught much later in the system to a much smaller number of pupils.

In the twentieth century, the view that initial reading teaching should take place in the vernacular has been widely held, with support in international organizations (UNESCO, for example) and international missionary groups such as the Summer Institute for Linguistics, and expressed in national language policies, including the U.S. Bilingual Education Act and Soviet policy. With all of this, there is still no conclusive evidence, as Engle (1975) has shown, that there is a clear advantage in initial literacy being taught in the vernacular rather than the standard language.

This paper focuses not so much on the question of initial literacy but on a related question which concerns the acceptance of literacy in the vernacular by the vernacular-speaking community. We argue that rejection, or nonaccept-

This article represents a greatly revised version of an article in F. Barkin & E. A. Brandt (Eds.), *Speaking, singing, and teaching: A multidisciplinary approach to language variation,* Anthropological Research Papers, No. 20 (Tempe: Arizona State University, 1980) and is used by permission. The work reported in the paper is supported in part by a grant from the National Institute of Education to the University of New Mexico for a historical and comparative study of the sociolinguistics of literacy. The principal investigators are Bernard Spolsky, Guillermina Engelbrecht, and Leroy Ortiz.

ance of literacy in the vernacular or native language can in fact be perceived as a method of attempting to maintain the integrity of a traditional culture. In addition, we will suggest some questions which appear to be fundamental to a sociolinguistics of literacy.

Two cases of the acceptance of vernacular literacy in the nineteenth century are particularly striking. First, in New Zealand, literacy among the Maori people started with missionary contact in 1820. By 1870, most Maoris were reported to be literate in their own language, and a book was written to teach them English literacy through Maori. By 1900, more items written in Maori than in English had been published in New Zealand. Another example of rapid acceptance of vernacular literacy is that of the Cherokee, a special case among American Indians. In 1821, Sequoyah, a Cherokee, developed a syllabary which was accepted and immediately implemented. Within a decade, 90% of the western Cherokee were literate in their own language (White, 1962; Walker, 1969).

In other cases, acceptance of literacy in the vernacular has been minimal. Orthographies have been developed for various Micronesian languages, for example, and some materials have been printed, but on the whole, literacy is restricted to some churchgoers and a few pilot bilingual programs. In the case of the Pueblo communities of the Southwest, until very recently there was actual opposition by speakers to the development of literacy in their native language, but acceptance of literacy in English (Brandt, in press).

The case of only minimal acceptance of native-language literacy which we have had most opportunity to learn about is that of the Navajo. Although literacy in the Navajo language was introduced in the early 1900s and a standard orthography accepted in 1937, there has been no "rush to literacy" among the Navajos (Young, 1977). At the moment, Navajo literacy is limited to those who have learned it through contact with missionaries, and some teachers and students at the three or four schools with active bilingual programs. We do not point this out to denigrate the success of these programs, but rather to focus on the contrasting general lack of acceptance by the Navajo population. Such literacy as exists is likely to be in English. In fact, anyone literate in Navajo is probably also literate in English.

Why is it, then, that some people enthusiastically accept, and use, vernacular literacy while others seem to be indifferent or actually opposed to it? The opposition, it turns out, does not necessarily extend to literacy in the standard language. In fact, in most cases standard literacy appears to be considered desirable and appropriate.

In the Navajo situation, Navajo is spoken not just in the homes in the community, but is appropriate for contact with the government bureaucracy (which provides interpreters when necessary), for legal proceedings, for governmental activities at the chapter and tribal level, and for local radio broadcasts. On the other hand, English is used for reading and writing in almost all situations: All forms and reports filled out in Bureau of Indian Affairs (BIA) and tribal government offices are in English, records of law cases are kept in English, and minutes of chapter-house meetings of the tribal council are written in English. The tribal newspaper is in English, and local radio broadcasting includes many English programs, for which Navajo radio announcers use English scripts (Spolsky & Holm, 1971). Essentially, then, the situation can be characterized as kind of diglossia: Navajo is the preferred and appropriate language for oral use, and English the most frequently used language for writing.

It becomes clear, especially when looking at the Navajo case, that literacy is more than just a technical skill that can be considered independently of a social context. Among the Navajo, oral and written language varieties serve distinctly different social functions. As a preliminary step to understanding why vernacular literacy is not acceptable to some groups, we have to discover how the written use of language functions in society.

What happens when vernacular literacy is added to the linguistic repertoire of a community? Using Fishman's (1971) concept of sociolinguistic domain, which he defines as a function of the intersection of setting, topic, and participants, we offer two related observations to support our view that nonacceptance of vernacular literacy may be an attempt to maintain the integrity of a traditional culture.

First, *literacy in the vernacular seems most likely to be accepted when there already exists a domain or domains in which literacy is perceived as being useful by members of the vernacular-speaking community.* Among both the Cherokee and the Maori, our paradigm cases of acceptance, literacy came to function in domains that existed prior to the introduction of writing. In traditional Maori schools, learning involved the memorization of a large body of traditional lore. Best (1923) reports the reactions of the missionary teachers in the late nineteenth century when, for the first time, their students wrote down the traditional material, rather than memorizing it: They performed over the books the same ceremony that they previously had performed over a learner who had committed the material to memory. Cherokee shamans also wrote down, in their new orthography, various formulas for performing sacred rituals and magic. Recognizing the dangers of having committed their secret knowledge to paper, they are reported to have mislabeled the pages, giving misleading headings to the information. Both of these are cases where a preliterate society rapidly accepted literacy, and where it found use in a traditional domain. Moreover, these examples are instructive in showing some of the tensions which arise when traditional domains come in contact with modernizing influences such as writing.

A second, related observation is that *literacy in the vernacular is most likely to be accepted in domains or for communicative functions that are perceived as congruent with the traditional social and cultural pattern of a group.* To put this another way, when the introduction of literacy is associated with a second language, an alien culture, and modern, technological functions, literacy in these new domains is preferred in the alien, second, or standard language.

Since the Navajo case provides the most poignant illustration of this, it is necessary to briefly recount the circumstances under which literacy was introduced. We can group efforts to introduce literacy to the Navajos into three major periods:

1. The earliest period is associated with Catholic and Protestant missionaries, linguists, and ethnologists, all of whom developed different orthographies. The Protestant missionaries translated portions of the Bible, and were the only ones in this group to attempt teaching literacy to the general population. Their motive was to spread Christianity.

2. In the 1930s, BIA policy was to promote literacy among Navajo children and adults. A standard orthography was developed and accepted, and in 1943 a Navajo newspaper began publication. According to Kluckhohn and Leighton (1962), a major factor in the government's support of vernacular literacy at this time was the need to disseminate information about policies such as livestock reduction and to involve Navajos in the war effort. After the war, Navajos who had worked off the reservation or had served in the armed forces found that their lack of English had placed them at a disadvantage and demanded better English programs. The government policy became one of assimilation, with relocation training programs focused on English, and Navajo literacy efforts were dropped (Young, 1977).

3. Current efforts at promoting Navajo literacy are associated with bilingual programs and the move towards community-controlled schools. Here vernacular literacy has been seen as a transitional step to learning English more easily.

In short, the functions of literacy among the Navajo have, in the past, been directly linked to religious beliefs alien to their culture and to colonial government policies such as stock reduction and relocation, and are now associated with transitional bilingual programs.

Robert Young (1977), in writing about the history of Navajo literacy, sums up what seems to be the origin of the current attitude of Navajos towards vernacular literacy: "The idea of writing had been introduced to the Navajo with the English language at a period when the institutions of Navajo culture, including the Navajo language, were held in low esteem. Consequently, many people looked upon English as the proper language in which to write" (p. 469).

In recent history, literacy has most often been introduced to preliterate societies through missionaries, the activities of a colonizing government, or in company with the technological changes that lead to increased contact with a literate group. The result is major pressure towards literacy in a second language, for the modern purposes of the colonizing group. In this situation it is not surprising to find that the question of which language to use for literacy involves at the very center some of the basic tensions facing any traditional society undergoing modernization. There appear to be two equally difficult courses to follow. A group can resist the pressure toward cultural innovation, as many traditional Navajos have done; those who choose to modernize can do so by learning English and carrying out in English the functions associated with modernization, including reading and writing. Or, a group can integrate the alien functions associated with a second language into the traditional culture, as the Maori did. Their conversion to Christianity was rapid, and acceptance of other cultural and economic notions from the Victorian missionaries was inevitable, and also happened quickly. With the wholesale acceptance of the new values, it was reasonable to continue to express the new values in the traditional language, and thus to develop an extensive literacy in the vernacular. This comparatively rapid assimilation, however, lessened the ability of the Maori people to resist the next stage, when, after 1870, all of the schools started insisting on literacy in English rather than in Maori. Within 50 years, the force of Maori literacy had been weakened, and within 100 years the language itself was endangered, and very few children were still growing up speaking Maori. In this analysis, then, acceptance of literacy in the vernacular can be seen as a sign of a culture's greater readiness to accept assimilation to the majority culture and as a possible first step to submersion.

In presenting this argument, we are building on Charles Voegelin's (1959) suggestion that word borrowing may be seen as a method of maintaining the purity of traditional language and culture. When speakers of a language come across, or are presented with, a new object, they have many choices about how to name it. One choice is to extend the meaning of a native word to cover it; thus, the Hopi might have chosen to use a traditional word meaning 'tunic' to refer to the kind of shirt that you buy in a store. Voegelin argued, however, that by choosing instead to use the English loanword to refer to the new item, they kept the native word to be used in its purity for the native object. From this point of view, code switching, word borrowing, and acceptance of literacy in the standard language, rather than the vernacular, might all be seen as ways in which the speakers of a language attempt to maintain the integrity of their own culture.

Complicating this issue is the symbolic value that defenders of a language give to its development into a standard language. To the Navajo nationalists who are committed to preventing the loss of their language and culture in the face of the pervasive influence of English, literacy in Navajo is crucial as a symbol of positive cultural identity. A major tension is therefore set up between traditional resistance to literacy, on the one hand, and nationalist fervor on the other; the paradox would appear to be that both groups have the same goal, but they approach it with opposing policies.

Any resolution of this paradox is going to require a more thorough analysis of how literacy functions in a community than is available at present. What is needed is a sociolinguistic approach which would, at the very least, involve such dimensions as Fishman's concept of domain; language choice as well as language variety (style, register, and degree of formality); and choice of oral or written channel. Field observations might comprise the first step in developing a model. The uses or functions of writing within a given community would be described in a number of settings, such as home, church, community center, and work sites. In each setting, it would be observed whether writing is used and, if so, how much and in which language. Investigators would also note 1) the topics handled by writing, and 2) the participants (i.e., writer and reader in each written communicative act).

Observations of the functions of literacy in a bilingual school setting, for example, might focus on the differential use of the vernacular and the standard language. A subsequent comparison of the functions of literacy which are valued in the community with those valued in the school setting would be of practical value for language-education policymakers.

Not only would a mapping of the functions of literacy serve the particular needs of any community, but we expect that descriptive maps could be compared in order to see if any larger sociolinguistic patterns are clearly involved in the adoption or rejection of literacy. By asking the following questions, it might be possible to identify principal factors that need to be taken into account in planning for vernacular literacy:

1. Under what circumstances do certain groups of people accept literacy in the vernacular? What conditions prompt groups to move towards literacy in the standard language? What are the tensions that arise in each of the decisions?

2. Was literacy in either the vernacular or the standard language generated from within the group, or was it introduced from the outside? For what purposes, and with what consequences?

3. What are the functions of literacy in the community? Who writes, who reads, about what topics, in what settings? Which language is used? If more than one, is there a diglossic or functional differentiation of language?

4. To what extent are the functions associated with literacy indigenous to the culture, and to what extent do they derive from technological and social change associated with contact with modernized society? To what extent has change occurred over time?

5. To what extent are school-related literacy programs, including teaching practices, curriculum, and materials, developed or planned on the basis of knowledge of the sociolinguistic situation in the community? What functions of language do the schools appear to value? Are they the ones that the community also values?

In this paper, we have tried to relate the sociolinguistic concept of domain to the functions of literacy in a community in order to support our view that the Navajo people may be maintaining the integrity of their traditional culture by not accepting literacy in their own language. We have furthermore attempted to show the need for a sociolinguistic approach to looking at the complex functions of literacy in any society, and have suggested a number of questions to guide research and model making in this area. It now seems clear that the issue of whether or not to teach initial literacy in the vernacular cannot be answered simply "yes" or "no," but rather "it depends." A sociolinguistic analysis is needed to make explicit the conditions upon which such a decision depends. We look forward to the development of a model which will allow us to make better-informed policy decisions concerning language education.

REFERENCES

Best, E. *The Maori school of learning; its objects, methods and ceremonial.* Wellington, New Zealand: Government Printer, 1923.

Brandt, E. A. Native American attitudes toward literacy and recording in the Southwest. *Journal of the Linguistic Association of the Southwest,* in press.

Engle, P. O. The use of vernacular languages in education. *Papers in Applied Linguistics.* Washington, D.C.: Center for Applied Linguistics, 1975.

Fishman, J. (Ed.). *Advances in the sociology of language* (Vol. 1). The Hague: Mouton, 1971.

Kluckhohn, C., and Leighton, D. *The Navajo.* Garden City, N.Y.: Natural History Library, 1962.

Spolsky, B., and Holm, W. Literacy in the vernacular: The case of Navajo. *Navajo Reading Study Progress Report No. 8.* Albuquerque: Navajo Reading Study, University of New Mexico, 1971.

Voegelin, C. F. An expanding language, Hopi. *Plateau,* 1959, *32,* 33–39.

Walker, W. Notes on native writing systems and the design of native literacy programs. *Anthropological Linguistics,* 1969, *11,* 148–66.

White, J. On the revival of printing in the Cherokee language. *Current Anthropology,* 1962, *3.*

Young, R. A history of written Navajo. In J. Fishman (Ed.), *Advances in the creation and revision of writing systems.* The Hague: Mouton, 1977.

6 | A Structural Analysis of Speeches by Native American Students

RALPH COOLEY and PHILIP LUJAN
University of Oklahoma

Public speeches by Native Americans are often stereotyped by whites as "unorganized" or "rambling." Careful listening, however, reveals considerable similarity among these speeches. Further, Native Americans are easily able to separate bad speeches from good ones and to rate speakers according to their speaking skills. These last observations lead us to suspect that, rather than lacking structure, these speeches are organized according to different structural principles than are speeches by whites. The lack of understanding of these different principles on the part of whites, then, is a major contributing factor in the stereotype. This paper is an attempt to remedy that problem by offering a description of the structural principles by which at least some Native Americans organize their speeches.

Our approach recognizes that these speeches are performances and that the speaker has assumed a responsibility to the audience for a "display of communicative competence" (Bauman, 1977, p. 11), although this responsibility is somewhat limited in one of our data-gathering situations, the college classroom, where student speeches (whether enthusiastically or reluctantly delivered) are recognized by all to be the accomplishments of neophytes. In that situation, the student has assumed only a responsibility for an attempt at competence, with the expectation that she or he will fall short in some way. In addition to this modification, we differ from Bauman in that our analysis is primarily text-centered. Such an orientation seems appropriate because the

A shorter version of the analysis of the student data (Cooley, 1979) was presented at the 1979 annual meeting of the Berkeley Linguistics Society and subsequently was published in the proceedings of that meeting. We appreciate the Society's willingness to allow that version to be incorporated into this more complete one. This version has been slightly adapted from Cooley and Lujan's article in F. Barkin & E. A. Brandt (Eds.), *Speaking, singing, and teaching: A multidisciplinary approach to language variation,* Anthropological Research Papers, No. 20 (Tempe: Arizona State University, 1980) and is used by permission of that university. This paper owes a great deal to a group of graduate students who participated with Ralph Cooley in a graduate seminar in the fall of 1978. We appreciate their enthusiasm, contributions, and help, although the responsibility for the work presented here remains ours.

structure of that text is precisely what the stereotype of Native American speeches is about and what is being evaluated by the students and the teacher in the class.

John Gumperz (1979) points out that the structural patterns with which we are concerned in this paper are very pervasive, outlasting first-language proficiency and dialect phenomena. Nevertheless, there are many other behaviors, both verbal and nonverbal, in these data which seem likely to reveal interesting performance processes. One cannot do everything at once, and we were led to begin with the question of structure by the obvious immediate relevance to the stereotype.

Cooley and Babich (1979) examined Native American speeches in an attempt to furnish teachers with sufficient knowledge about their structures so that they could begin to attack the stereotype. In that paper and in another by Cooley (1979), it was argued that one should not use traditional rhetorical analytic methods and categories to analyze these speeches, since those methods and categories are themselves founded in Western cultural norms (Young, Becker, & Pike, 1970), while Philipsen (1972) has shown that at least one Native American culture, the Navajo, values speech behaviors which operate within a different rhetorical framework.

We offer here an analytic system which examines four phenomena in speeches by Native Americans: 1) the organization and progression of topics, paying particular attention to the relation of topics to each other and to the subject of the speech; 2) the organization which holds within each topic; 3) the structure of the transitions between topics; and 4) the use of reference as a cohesive device, following Halliday and Hasan (1973). The choice of these phenomena and the constructs used to analyze them follows very naturally from the stereotype, which expresses a perceived lack of organization of subject material.

We will examine a series of 12 speeches by Native Americans from various tribes in Oklahoma. Of these speeches, 8 were delivered by students in "Principles of Communication," an introductory course given in the Department of Communication and the Native American Studies Program at the University of Oklahoma. The students were all monolingual in English and were from 4 different Oklahoma tribes. The speeches varied in length from 3 minutes, 45 seconds to nearly 17 minutes. All of them were simultaneously video- and audio-recorded, with the permission of the entire class.

In addition to the 8 student speeches, we include in these data 4 speeches by 3 nonstudents, all older, prestigious Native Americans. These speeches vary in length from 4 minutes to 30 minutes. Only 1 was videotaped, but all were audiotaped with the full knowledge of the speaker. The elders' speeches are of two types: 2 of them are actual speeches made before an audience; the other 2 were recorded for a hypothetical situation; the speakers had been asked to prepare a speech in advance and deliver it "as if" they were speaking to an audience from their tribe on some ceremonial occasion. These elder speakers were Kiowa, Creek, and Cherokee.

We chose these two populations for the following reasons: The students bear the brunt of the stereotype in school situations where they are required to speak in public and are judged by white audiences and teachers. It is then crucial to examine these school-situated performances precisely in order to garner the most telling evidence concerning the stereotype. The elders were chosen because it seemed likely that experienced speakers serve as culturally appropriate models from whom the students have learned something about how to speak properly in public. We must note here that there are many Native American tribes in the United States, and even more who call themselves Native American on this continent. There is no coherent body of literature which examines the cultural similarities or differences between these modern societies. Hardly any literature examining the communication behaviors of modern Native Americans exists at all. We make no attempt here to generalize beyond the population which the individuals who supplied our data represent. Nevertheless, we have received considerable anecdotal feedback from Native Americans and from whites who work with them suggesting that the phenomena we are characterizing here do exist elsewhere in this country. A rigorous examination of the validity of these anecdotes would be welcomed.

THE DATA

Before proceeding, it is necessary to define the constructs which we have used in analyzing the structure of these speeches. There are six: topic, topic-change point, organization, information points, cohesive devices, and reported speech. *Topic* is defined as the speaker's talk about one, and only one, content area. Typically a speech will consist of several topics, all related to the subject of the speech in some way. Those places in the speech where the speaker moves from one topic to another are noted as *topic-change points.* The points themselves are not of interest; instead we are interested in the manner in which transition from topic to topic across those points is achieved by the speaker. The perceived relationships which hold between topics, the way those relationships are made evident at topic change points, and the relationships between information points within topics are defined as the *organization* of the speech. An *information point* occurs within topics and is defined as talk about one aspect of the topic's content.

Cohesive devices, discussed at length in Halliday and Hasan (1973), mark coreferential relationships and tie parts of the speech together, making it a unified text. Cohesive devices are not structural units, but are markers of semantic relations which hold in a text. Cohesion by the use of reference, the device investigated here, is achieved by employing pronouns or other words which stand in the place of the original referent noun. These words can either refer backward to a coreferent which has already occurred, or forward to one which has not. *Reported speech* is the attribution of information or a statement to someone other than oneself, but not through direct quotation. Reported speech is introduced by phrases such as "I was told that . . . ", or "What was told to me was . . . ."

The analysis of all speeches was done from transcripts made from the audiotapes. First the transcript was divided into topics; then topic-change points were marked and information points were noted. Next the cohesive devices were annotated, and finally occurrences of reported speech were noted.

STUDENT SPEECHES

Organization of Topics

There is a great deal of variation in the details of organization in these speeches, as one would expect. Nevertheless, strong similarities in the general patterns of organization exist. The typical speech consists of 3 to 5 topics, depending on its length, which are related to the subject of the speech in that they are parts of it. For example, a speech on the "Moonie Cult" has three topics: Rev. Moon, recruiting techniques, and brainwashing. These three topics are offered by the speaker in a sequence which does not demonstrate any relation between them, except through their relation to the subject of the speech. In other words, there is no overt organizational pattern which holds between the topics, but they all can be seen to relate to the subject.

Example 1

1   This will be on the Moonie cult, which is a cult started
2   by a gentleman who created every Moonie, which is, I guess,
3   a religious being that has no denomination, supposed to be
4   a unified—any denomination that you want. And he was
5   from Korea. He escaped Korea when the U.S. overcame this
6   POW camp where he was in jail at the time, and he went to
7   New York where he started his religious cult. He started
8   out as a Presbyterian, and he went to the Unification Church,
9   which he started and designed himself. I was supposed to
10 talk over brainwashing techniques that the cults used.
11 What they do is they—the Moonies like people who are edu-
12 cated or getting educated, that are young. They usually
13 have their own college canvassers recruiting, looking for
14 people that are depressed waiting for classes that had a
15 test, people who are worried about something, like low-

16   morale people. And they invite them over to the group,
17   which consists of a lot of smiling faces and a lot of young
18   people, and try to impress them in that sort of state. The
19   object of their recruiting is to get the person to stay
20   over a while and visit and live with them for a little
21   while. And what was told to me was the best time to get a
22   recruit was late in the week, and if it was possible to
23   keep him over and have him miss class the beginning of the
24   next week, chances were that they had them in the cult.
25   And brainwashing is a big controversy right now. . . .

At line 9, the speaker concludes his first topic, Rev. Moon, and begins the
next, which is announced as "brainwashing techniques," but which turns out
to be recruiting techniques. At line 24 he concludes that topic, and returns to
brainwashing at line 25. There are no overt markers of the relation between
Rev. Moon and recruiting, or between recruiting and brainwashing. The
speaker merely moves from one topic to the next at the topic-change point.

In speeches where the speaker begins with an overtly marked introduction,
there is often a brief outline of the planned speech which takes the form "first
I will . . . , next I will . . . , and finally I will . . . ." Example 2, lines 1 through
5, shows such an introduction.

Example 2

1   OK, my part of the symposium is dealing with some of the
2   reasons or causes that lead to suicide. And I attempted
3   to cover three specific areas; and I started with Indian
4   reservations, and went on down to the urban society, and
5   I also covered the area of boarding schools. And I found
6   that on a reservation that the living conditions were. . . .

Speakers who use these phrases in their introduction often introduce each topic
with a similar phrase. In lines 5 and 6, the speaker introduces his first topic
with "and I found that on a reservation". This speaker goes on to introduce his
second topic with "I went on to research some more in the urban areas," and
his third with "and the last topic I attempt to do some research on was boarding
schools." These transitional phrases serve to announce a topic change and to
show the listener where the speaker is in the speech by relating each topic to
the introduction, but they do not demonstrate any relationship between the
topics. As transitions, they operate very abruptly, and often they are simply
not there, in which case the topic is changed without announcement, as in the
last line of example 1.

In only 1 of the 8 student speeches was there any explicit marking of the
relationship between a topic and its immediately adjacent neighbor. This
speech is easily recognizable as being different from the others, and it is this

feature that makes it so. In all of the other speeches, the only relationship between topics is implicit, through their relationship to the subject of the speech.

Organization Within Topics

Organization of information within the topic is very much like the organization between topics. Example 3 illustrates a single topic (suicide in boarding schools), which has four information points: prior problems of students, staffing problems, intertribal conflict, and alcoholism. Even though the topic is a unified text, there are no overt marks of the relationship between these four points, excepting their occurrence in the topic.

Example 3

1   . . . and the last topic I attempt to do some research on was
2   boarding schools. And I have a statement here that was
3   made by Laslow and [?] on psychosocial adjustment of
4   Indian youth, and this is from the *American Journal of*
5   *Psychiatry*. It states that there is a high incidence of
6   suicide among the American Indians on reservations and in
7   Indian schools. Part of the boarding school problems were
8   that there were behavior problems in the children before
9   they even attended schools. Like a lot of them didn't—
10 this was the only place they had to go. There were no
11 parents, and they had been in a lot of foster homes and
12 stuff, and finally they get old enough to go to boarding
13 school they ship them off. They come there with a problem,
14 you know. And it's the boarding school, how it's set up,
15 a lot of times there isn't enough staff there to suit every
16 child, you know, to help everybody like it should be.
17 There was also some tribal conflict within the many tribes
18 that integrated into the boarding school. I guess attemp-
19 ting suicide was putting oneself into a situation where he
20 might be beat up to the point of death. An' also alcohol
21 and drugs, like I say.

Cohesion

Within topics, the text is strongly cohesive, and most of the cohesion is realized by pronouns which are coreferential with nouns and other pronouns elsewhere in that topic. Of the four cohesive types which Halliday and Hasan (1973) discuss, this type, reference, is used an overwhelming percentage of the time. Notice its use in the following speech.

Example 4

1 The first instance of Indian Militancy was, I guess, well
2 not really the first, but when the papers and everything
3 started writing about it and started coming into public
4 view, was the occupation of Alcatraz, and that was in San
5 Francisco Bay. These Indians, which weren't really Cali-
6 fornia Indians, they were Indians from all over the
7 United States and there really wasn't that many California
8 Indians in the group that occupied the island. But the
9 reason they took it over was because of an old treaty that
10 said the government when it's not using any land it should
11 revert back to the original owners, which was the Native
12 Americans. They had a lot of plans for this place, you
13 know. They wanted to turn it into a cultural school, also
14 a spiritual center, a museum. It was in San Francisco
15 Bay, but in San Francisco the Native American Center there
16 had burned down, and so they didn't really have any place
17 to go. They lasted out for about two winters, but all the
18 time they was holding out, you know, there was always con-
19 frontations with the federal marshals, which blockaded
20 medical supplies, food, and sanitation facilities.
21 Finally, in the spring of 1970, they cut off their elec-
22 tricity and water, but it wasn't until June of 1971 that
23 they finally, you know, gave up. It was called the war of
24 attrition, but, you know, they really didn't accomplish
25 that much, but what they did accomplish they knew that they
26 had to carry on and do something else . . .

In this example, there are 30 markers of coreferentiality, and 24 of these are third-person pronouns, either *they* or *it*. The longest cohesive string begins with "these Indians," in line 5, is 16 markers long, and ends on line 25. All but two of these markers, "group" (line 8) and "Native Americans" (line 11–12), are occurrences of the pronoun *they*. The use of this device makes cohesion within topics very strong, if somewhat repetitious. A very important fact, however, is that cohesive devices are not used across topic-change points, even in the one student speech which is recognizably atypical.

Reported Speech

One particular pattern of reported speech occurs quite regularly throughout the corpus of these student speeches. A phrase, often with an intransitive or passive verb, precedes the information obtained from a source, which is described in the form of a "that" clause. This pattern, in one of two variants, occurs more than half the time that reported speech is used.

    a. "It was stated that they thought that . . . they thought that polyandry existed because it was associated with extreme poverty."

    b. "I have a statement here . . . , and it states that there is a high incidence of suicide among the American Indians on reservations."

or

    c. "And what was told to me was . . . the best time to get a recruit was late in the week."

    d. "This one report was surprised that it was . . . the white people are trying to destroy us."

The remaining occurrences were varied:

    e. "In this book I read on the suicide among American Indians. . . . It covered the one area on the Cheyenne reservation."

    f. I think I studied in my class that . . . that most divorces, they marry again."

It must be noted that these speakers do not always use this device; often they cite the data with no reference to the sources at all. Nevertheless, these types of referencing phrases occur often enough to stand out. The fact that they occur initially and involve these types of verbs shifts the focus from the content of the information cited to its source, giving the speeches a flavor of speaker as reporter, rather than source.

In summary, student speeches can be characterized as follows: They consist of several topics, presented in sequence, with no overt attempt to explicate the relationship between them. Topic changes occur suddenly, rarely with more than an introductory phrase. Within topics there is tight cohesion, most frequently effected by the use of coreference. Cohesive ties across topic-change points do not occur, leaving only the implicit commonality of subject area across all the topics to bind them into a text. In addition, where the source of information is noted, the particular type of reported speech which occurs focuses on the source of the information which the speaker is using, rather than on the information itself.

ELDERS' SPEECHES

Like the students' speeches, there is a considerable variation in the elders' speeches. In general, as would be expected, they represent much more sophisticated performances than the students' speeches. The two "as if" speeches fall together in one class, with a high degree of formality and ceremonial phrasing (see examples 5 and 6). The other two are much more informative and are therefore more similar to the students' speeches (see example 7). Nevertheless, certain similarities exist between these four speeches.

Example 5

1	We are gathered here for a great purpose, and we are grate-
2	ful that this event took place so we could all come togeth-
3	er. And it should be like this. But first I address my
4	elders, my brothers, my sisters, my friends, and acknowledge
5	their presence, your presence. I have been asked to speak,
6	and yet my words fall short. I may not measure up to what
7	you already know, and I may not even add to what you already
8	know. But because this time has been allotted me, I'm go-
9	ing to try to fulfill the wishes of the people here, and
10	say to you that time was when elders got together in this
11	manner and they used to enjoy one another's fellowship,
12	company. Today, soon as a meeting of this kind is over
13	with, all we see immediately is dust, people in a hurry,
14	going home. It wasn't that way way back there. Our old
15	people found it hard to leave one another, sometimes they
16	would embrace one another, shed tears, and give words of
17	encouragement one to another as they left. And today we
18	spend a lot of time talking about love. But to live it is
19	another thing. We live in such a way so that people might
20	say of us, is that the kind of love he was talking about?
21	So we live in a day when we need to be cautious, and re-
22	gardless of what position in life that you might attain in
23	this life, don't forget that the foundation upon which you
24	came from, those that made it possible for you to stand and
25	to see people eye to eye and not be ashamed, was because of
26	the suffering of our elders, who made it possible for us.
27	Let us never forget that fact. I don't care how far in life
28	you go, you go as a result of the elders that went through
29	a lot of suffering in our behalf. And never forget, that
30	blood flows in our veins today. And if we can express love,
31	and give help to our fellow men, then do it. Go out with
32	all the knowledge you can attain. Let it be tempered with
33	the same kind of love they had for people. We thought they
34	were shortsighted. They couldn't read or write, but they
35	knew about life. They saw way ahead, even beyond our time.
36	They saw the little ones that's not even born yet, that's
37	gonna come up, they saw the kind of world that was awaiting

38   them, they saw ahead far beyond our sight. But let us
39   catch the same spirit in which they lived, and thereby live
40   in harmony with one another, and express the true love
41   flowing through our veins because of them.

This complete text of an "as if" speech consists of an introduction and a conclusion, separated by a discussion of three topics: leaving, love, and the elders' foundation. Again, adjacent topics are related more implicitly than explicitly, and the speaker does not use cohesive devices to bridge topic-change points. There are, however, two important differences between this and the students' speeches. The constant reference to elders—there are 20 occurrences of this word, or of a pronoun or a lexical substitute for it, in 41 lines—makes the entire speech strongly cohesive. In addition, the conclusion is designed so that it refers back to each of the topics, reinforcing them and emphasizing their unity.

The next example is a typical excerpt from a long ceremonial speech given in an "as if" situation.

Example 6

1   Thank you, thank you, members of the family and descendants
2   of Chief Sitting Bear and Chief White Bear for permitting
3   me to be your announcer during your recognition of one of
4   your illustrious young men who recently returned from the
5   late war in Viet Nam. This is initiation day, as you know,
6   this is a Saturday in October. We gather here, in Anadar-
7   ko at the_____campground annually, and it's good that we
8   have a beautiful day to observe these beautiful old customs.
9   My name is _____, and I'm a member of the public relations
10   department here, the Kiowa Veteran's association, and I'm
11   happy to serve you people in whatever your desires are this
12   afternoon, because this is part of my job. But let me ask
13   your indulgence in the use of our own tribal language. I
14   must apologize that I have not had much practice recently,
15   actually for the past 45 or so years, or longer
16   even, to use this language properly, but I will do the best
17   I can, because this family has asked me to serve in this
18   capacity. I will try to serve in that capacity to honor
19   Mr._____, whom I will give the Kiowa name_____ at this
20   time. Because I believe I have the authority in the contem-
21   porary world, in modern days, because the old people are
22   gone. He's my nephew, and this is why I take the liberty to
23   give him a Kiowa name, _____. _____ refers to young chief-

24   tains, or chiefs, war chiefs, and certainly his illustri-
25   ous parents bear this out. So I was a commissioned officer
26   in World War II, and served overseas, and this is why I am
27   one of the officers of the Kiowa Veteran's Association, and
28   Tongkonga, an ancient warrior society that we have decided
29   to revive, to be a part of our Kiowa Veteran's Organization.

There is a topic change at line 18, where the speaker moves from the introduction to the first topic, and another in the middle of line 25. In the introductory phrase to the first topic, "I will try to serve in that capacity," there is a cohesive tie to the phrase "this capacity" in the previous sentence, and this cohesion helps to place the first topic, the naming, in the context of the speech. However, at the next topic-change point (line 25), there is neither cohesion between the two topics nor is there any use of structural devices to show the relationship between them.

Example 7, an excerpt from a longer speech of the informative type, appears not to have a great deal of explicitly stated organization.

Example 7

1   . . . so then we had a school election. And the election got
2   so bad that I knew that the superintendent was driving up
3   and down the street with a shotgun laying across his lap.
4   Then I told my wife that we'd better move out of here. So
5   we went to South Dakota. And we like to starved to death
6   and froze to death up in South Dakota. All these things
7   I'm saying is because when I lived and grew up in the com-
8   munity south of here, my Daddy could talk Creek and Chero-
9   kee. My Grandpa could talk Cherokee, and English, but my
10   Grandpa could read Cherokee. And they never did teach me
11   to talk Cherokee. And if you don't know how to talk Chero-
12   kee, don't let anybody teach you to talk it either. You
13   sure get into trouble. From what I have observed after
14   goin' to school, my Grandpa was the man in charge of the
15   family. The things that we were doing I know now were our
16   customs. We use to invite people who lived near _____ com-
17   munity, they were my cousins, and they'd come over and
18   visit us, and we'd get up early in the morning. We'd all
19   go down and wash by the running water in the cold and in
20   the fog. Then that night we'd go to Grandpa's house, and
21   then he'd put some water in a big old black kettle like he
22   would do when he was getting ready to cook hog. Get it
23   real hot, then put the old covered wagon and make a tent out

24   of it. That's the way we used to take our sauna. These
25   were to get us in good health and be able to attend school
26   in the rural areas regularly.

In this example, there is no explicitly stated relationship between many of the topics. The second topic, which begins on line 6, is introduced by a transitional phrase containing a cohesive reference to the previous topic, but that device does not explicate the relationship between the topics. In line 13, the topic is changed with neither cohesive reference nor any statement of the relationship between the new topic and the old. This speech continues for half an hour, using much the same structure. Most of the time the topic is changed without introduction and with neither structural nor cohesive ties to the previous topic.

In the 4 elders' speeches, we find the same basic structural components which are so apparent in the student's speeches. Topics are more implicitly than explicitly related. These speakers use transitional sentences and cohesive devices more frequently and much more effectively than the students do, but they still make no attempt to tie each topic to its neighbor, and so the relationships between topics remain implicit, rather than being made explicit.

CONCLUSION

Although the data base which we have used is small, this analysis allows us to conclude that it is quite likely that the students are modeling the way they structure their speeches after the elders. Within speeches from each group and across all the speeches we found that, overwhelmingly, speeches were organized according to the implicit relationships between topics. Some speakers were more explicit that others in both groups, but even the most explicit depended more on the implicit relations between topics for organization than on any explicit marking of those relations. This implicit organization is reinforced by the lack of across-topic cohesion. Again, the degree of cohesion varies from speech to speech, but even in the most cohesive speech (probably example 5), there is little or no attempt to tie adjacent topics together.

Finally, in the student speeches, information sources were referenced in a manner which focused on the source, rather than on the information or the speaker. We did not find this behavior in the elder's speeches, possibly owing to the limited size of the sample.

Our goal in this investigation has been to examine these speeches in light of the stereotype. The analysis shows that they are not randomly constructed, but are all organized according to principles which are very different from those to which their evaluators are accustomed. This fact seems to be the source of the stereotype. Elsewhere in this volume, there are comparisons with Western rhetorical traditions and an examination of the pedogogical implications of these differing communication behaviors. All of us who have been involved in this investigation hope that this presentation will stimulate further investigations of culturally determined communication behaviors and their impact on communication.

REFERENCES

Bauman, R. *Verbal art as performance.* Rowley, Mass.: Newbury House, 1977.

Cooley, R. Spokes in a wheel: A linguistic and rhetorical analysis of Native American public discourse. In C. Chiarello, J. Kingston, E. Sweeser, et al., (Eds.), *Proceedings of the Fifth Annual Meeting of the Berkeley Linguistics Society.* Berkeley: Berkeley Linguistics Society, 1979.

Cooley, R., & Babich, R. *The Structure of Native American public speeches.* Paper presented at the Second Annual Southeastern Native American Bilingual Education Conference. Mar. 1979.

Gumperz, J. Personal communication, Feb. 1979.

Halliday, M. A. K., & Hasan, R. *Cohesion in spoken and written English.* London: Longmans, 1973.

Philipsen, G. Navajo world view and culture patterns of speech: A case study in ethnorhetoric. *Speech Monographs,* 1972, *39,* 132–39.

Young, R. E., Becker, A. L., & Pike, K. L. *Rhetoric: Discovery and Change.* New York: Harcourt, Brace, & World, 1970.

7 | Cultural Factors in the Organization of Speeches by Native Americans

INA C. SILER
Northern Illinois University

DIANA LABADIE-WONDERGEM
California State University

During the past 20 years, the United States has attempted to compensate for the injustices imposed upon ethnic minority groups by instituting various programs intended to enable minorities to catch up with the overculture both economically and educationally. Even though these programs have been in existence for some time, the overculture still appears to be ambivalent about incorporating the values and customs of minority groups into any of its institutions. Lujan and Dobkins (1978) state that the dominant culture wants to preserve the minority culture's traditions, yet continues to pressure the minority culture to conform to its expectations. This pressure probably is present in the classroom, since the classroom is an agent of the overculture. Therefore, if minority students fail to measure up to acceptable standards of the overculture, they are penalized. The Native American student is one who is faced with this dilemma.

We are particularly concerned with the problems facing Anglo teachers when they evaluate Native American student speeches. Cooley and Lujan (this volume) indicate that Native Americans organize their speeches differently than Anglos do. The organization of Native American speeches often leads the Anglo listener to conclude that they are rambling, difficult to follow, and move from topic to topic without any transitions. Moreover, Cooley and Lujan report that the patterns in the students' speeches also are present in speeches made

This article is based on a paper presented at the Eighth Annual Southwest Areal Language and Linguistics Workshop, Tempe, Ariz., Apr. 1979, and originally appeared in F. Barkin & E. A. Brandt (Eds.), *Speaking, singing, and teaching: A multidisciplinary approach to language variation,* Anthropological Research Papers, No. 20 (Tempe: Arizona State University, 1980). This revised version is used by permission. The speech data cited in this article were collected by Ralph Cooley and Philip Lujan, and are used here with their permission. These data are discussed in their chapter in this book, "A structural analysis of speeches by Native American students," where the complete texts of sample speeches may also be found.

by some Native American elders. This phenomenon led us to believe that the structure of speeches by Native American students did not indicate that the students had no knowledge of how to organize speeches, but were examples of a different style entirely. Just as Anglo speakers have reasons for organizing their speeches a certain way and for using particular rhetorical strategies, so might Native American speakers have reasons for structuring their speeches as they do. Although the speakers observed by Cooley and Lujan represent only five tribes from the Southwestern part of the United States, the characteristics identified in the majority of the speeches suggest that Native Americans in general might organize their speeches in similar ways. Therefore, in this article, we attempt to identify the aspects of Native American culture that might explain the structural patterns in their speeches.

THE RELATIONSHIP BETWEEN CULTURE AND COMMUNICATION

Ong (1973) states that the important characteristics of a culture seem to be deeply rooted in the communication patterns of its members. Isolating the culturally significant communication patterns and determining their functions within the culture are the first steps in highlighting the reciprocal relationship between a culture and the behaviors of its members. There is little reference to communication behaviors—that is, conversational interaction, joking, and rhetorical style—in the literature about Native Americans, but research into the communication behaviors in other cultures supports the relationship between culture and communication.

Thomas Kochman (1970), who has conducted ethnographic investigations of Black American verbal behavior, describes several different types of speech behaviors and their functions within that culture. For example, he talks about a stylized way of talking to whites called *shuckin.* This communication behavior serves two functions. First, it is a way of humbling oneself before whites, and second, it demonstrates one's ability to handle a possible conflict situation successfully. When black students carry these behaviors into the classroom, they create confusion for teachers, who consider the behaviors unacceptable there.

Abrahams (1977) discusses the role of speech making as a reflection of culture in St. Vincent in the West Indies. The expert speaker must demonstrate the ability to handle conflict situations. The speaker creates dissonance in the listeners, encourages them to respond verbally, and then, through oratorical skills, eliminates the dissonance. Responding appropriately to anxiety-producing situations is a valued skill for the Vincentian which is demonstrated through public discourse.

The relationship between culture and communication can be further exemplified by examining the research of sociolinguists (see Gumperz, 1972; Hymes,

1974; and Bauman, 1975). Their area of research, which is referred to as the ethnography of speaking, focuses on societal norms and values governing speech acts, and the principles and strategies underlying the acts. They report that the organization of speech events in some cultures is directly related to the values, traditions, and norms of the cultures (Bauman & Scherzer, 1974). They also believe that these characteristics hold true in other cultures. Cooley (1979a), summarizing the position that ethnography of speaking takes, indicates that variation in communication, regardless of whether the focus is on linguistic phenomena or speaking behaviors, is governed by socially determined rules. These rules are subject to social interpretation, hence to societal pressures. The pressures affect a minority culture's use of the overculture's communication behaviors, and eventually the use of their own communication behaviors.

Although there has been little research reported on Native American speaking style, other aspects of Native American communication behavior have been explored. For example, Dumont (1972), John (1972), Philips (1972), and Lujan and Dobkins (1978) report that silence is a communication behavior that is valued in Native American culture. John argues that Navajo children tend to approach their world visually, rather than verbally, through quiet, persistent exploration. If this is true in other Native American cultures, Anglo teachers may perceive these students as reticent and unintelligent, when in fact students may be exhibiting communication behavior that is valued in their tribe (Lujan & Dobkins).

St. Clair (1980) found that the written compositions of Native American students also reflect aspects of their culture. For example, he observed that students representing tribes from the Northwest frequently used visual metaphors in their written compositions. He argues that the use of the visual metaphor is an outgrowth of the strong oral tradition in Native American cultures. Further, he argues that because oral cultures provide cognitive patterns distinctively different from those of print cultures, subsequent behaviors probably will be different from the behaviors emanating from print cultures.

The research on communication in non-Indian cultures, sociolinguistic literature, and the limited research available on Native American communication behaviors suggest that communication and culture are interwoven. When people perceive themselves as part of a specific culture, they also perceive themselves as being part of a specific communication community. The overall communication behaviors not only seem to serve different functions within the culture; they also mirror that culture.

TRANSMISSION OF CULTURE

An examination of the method of transmission of Native American culture also supports the argument that the students' speeches were not aimless ramblings, but examples of learned patterns of stylistic discourse. In some traditional Native American cultures, the family is very important. The family unit generally is an extended one; it might include grandparents, uncles, aunts, and cousins. All share the responsibility of raising the children. In particular, the elders of a family assume the responsibility for educating, entertaining, and caring for the children (Spencer & Jennings, 1977).

In the Ramah Navajo tribe, a young man received formal instruction concerning the religious ceremonies from his father or any other older male in the clan (Kluckhohn, 1962). Vanderwerth (1971) found that young Indian men interested in becoming speakers often attended tribal meetings to get examples of appropriate delivery and styles of argument from the tribal elders. These examples indicate that in the past, the older members of the tribe were very instrumental in the transmission of culture to the younger members. Although some of the children today who go away to school are not exposed to family traditions, they are still exposed to elders at the tribal level. Alex Labadie (1978), an Osage tribal leader, states that the elders are important members of the tribe. They are the initiators of events such as dances, dedications, and powwows, and the main speakers at these events. As the leaders of tribal communities, they serve as role models for the younger Indians.

The fact that in some Native American societies the ability to speak in public is a skill taught by the elders to the younger generation suggests to us that the student speakers may have developed their style of speaking by observing experienced speakers in their tribes.

SOME CULTURAL EXPLANATIONS FOR SPEECHES

Cooley and Lujan identified areas of speaking style which were handled similarly by the Native American speakers in their data. Of these, two are relevant to our discussion: topical organization and cohesion. The ways in which the speakers organized their topics and gave coherence to their speeches appear to be closely linked to Native American cultures.

Topical Organization

In general, the speeches tended to consist of 3 to 5 topics, all of which seemed to relate to the subject of the speech. However, no explicitly stated relationships between the topics existed. Speakers did not overtly indicate the relationship between the different topics, but simply moved from one to another. This pattern appeared in the majority of the speeches examined, and is regarded by Cooley and Lujan as the norm. Only 1 of the 12 speeches analyzed had explicit markers of topic change indicating how the topics related to each other and to the general subject of the speech. That speech was recognizably different from the others.

In speeches that follow traditional Western rhetorical norms, the transitional phrase acts as a signpost to the listener, telling him where the speaker has been, where he is now, and where he is going. The speaker's credibility is determined in part by his ability to demonstrate skill as an expert speaker. As Wilson and Arnold (1976) indicate, the speaker is expected to overtly lead listeners to the goal. Some introductory-level speech-communication texts even provide a list of appropriate transitional phrases and statements (Wilson & Arnold; Monroe & Ehninger, 1976).

According to Western norms, the speaker is also expected to organize the speech in a manner that will make it easy for the listeners to follow. Wilson and Arnold (pp. 156–64) describe 11 different ways to organize a speech. An organizing strategy should fit the topic and purpose of the speech. However, all speakers analyzed by Cooley and Lujan used the topical plan of organization.

Native American rhetorical norms appear to be quite different from Western norms. Native American norms merely require that the speaker provide information to the listeners. This information must be carefully selected and ordered. However, it is not the speaker's responsibility to overtly lead the listener to the goal (Philipsen, 1972). The listener is responsible for deciding the importance and relevance of each information point. Through this technique, the listener assumes an active role in the public-speaking event and appears to have more freedom to decide whether a change in his attitude will occur. This makes persuasive and even informative speaking in Native American cultures very different from Anglo speaking.

Cohesion

Cooley and Lujan also point out that the Native American student speeches they examined contain cohesive devices which mark co-referential relationships and tie the parts of the speech together, making it a unified text. They explain that cohesion using reference is achieved by substituting pronouns or other words for the original referent noun. They find that cohesion by means of reference (usually with pronouns) is used very frequently in the student speeches. However, and most significantly, the devices are not used across topic-change points.

Once again we compare Native American norms to Western norms. Native American speakers do not take on the role of leading the listener through the speech. As we stated earlier, it is the listener's responsibility to decide on the importance of each topic and to relate the topics to each other. To use cohesion as a device to relate topics is as inappropriate as it is to show that relationship with structural devices such as transitions and internal summaries.

Criteria for Effective Speaking

Marcellus Williams (1978), a Creek elder, cites several criteria important for judging a speaker's abilities. They help to clarify the patterns uncovered by Cooley and Lujan. He states that a good speaker must be knowledgeable about the members of the tribe, know the challenges of today, the needs of the time, and how to cope with the present from past knowledge. In addition, an organized speech should contain visual analogies, illustrations, and personification to create a picture in the minds of the listeners. Last, the speaker should be modest, making statements that imply that he is not worthy of speaking. Mr. Williams further explains that disclaimers are used to indicate the speaker's unworthiness, and to ask permission of the elders to speak. He refers to this as speaking through someone else, as not being sufficiently honorable or knowledgeable to give the intended message. Although disclaimers were observed in the elders' speeches, they were missing in the student speeches. We suggest that they did not occur in a class assignment because there was no one of whom to ask permission to speak. Moreover, since the speech resulted from an assignment, such behavior was patently inappropriate.

DISCUSSION

The overall organization of Native American speeches can best be illustrated through a rhetorical model. The subject of the speech can be viewed as the hub of a wheel, with the speaker on the rim. The speaker proceeds through the speech, moving along the rim to offer the audience a series of different perspectives on the subject. The different perspectives, or topics, represent the spokes of the wheel and appear as though they are being presented serially. All of the topics relate to the subject of the speech, but are separate from each other. The listener should determine the extent to which the topics are separate. If this analogy characterizes the structure of the speeches, identifying relationships among topics will be difficult unless the listener is familiar with the style.

In Native American cultures, the speaker is responsible for sharing with the audience knowledge about a subject, and the listener is responsible for determining the worth of the information. Any indication of the relationship among topics might be interpreted as an attempt to lead the audience towards a decision. This rhetorical strategy would be considered inappropriate. The spokes-on-the-wheel model seems to capture the essence of the structure of Native American speeches, including the different responsibilities of both speakers and listeners. To paraphrase one of the speakers in Cooley and Lujan's data, the speaker may supply the pieces in the puzzle, but it is up to the audience to make a picture out of them.

REFERENCES

Abrahams, R. The training of the man of words in talking sweet. In R. Bauman (Ed.), *Verbal art as performance.* Rowley, Mass.: Newbury House, 1977.

Bauman, R. Verbal art as performance. *American Anthropologist,* 1975, *77,* 290–311.

Bauman, R., & Scherzer, J. Introduction. In R. Bauman and J. Scherzer (Eds.), *Explorations in the ethnography of speaking.* London: Cambridge University Press, 1974.

Cooley, R. Language attitudes and policies in the United States: Their impact on Native American culture. Paper presented at the meeting of the Society for Intercultural Education, Training, and Research, Mexico City, Mar. 1979. (a)

——. Spokes in a wheel: A linguistic and rhetorical analysis of Native American public discourse. In C. Chiarello, J. Kingston, E. Sweeser, et al., (Eds.), *Proceedings of the fifth annual meeting of the Berkeley Linguistics Society.* Berkeley: Berkeley Linguistics Society, 1979. (b)

Dumont, R. V. Learning English and how to be silent: Studies in Sioux and Cherokee classrooms. In C. Cazden, V. John, & D. Hymes (Eds.), *Functions of language in the classroom.* New York: Teachers College Press, 1972.

Gumperz, J. Introduction. In J. Gumperz & D. Hymes (Eds.), *Directions in sociolinguistics: The ethnography of communication.* New York: Holt, Rinehart & Winston, 1972.

Hymes, D. Ways of speaking. In R. Bauman & J. Scherzer (Eds.), *Explorations in the ethnography of speaking.* London: Cambridge University Press, 1974.

John, V. Styles of learning—styles of teaching: Reflections on the education of Navajo children. In C. Cazden, V. John, & D. Hymes (Eds.), *Functions of language in the classroom.* New York: Teachers College Press, 1972.

Kluckhohn, C. Some social and personal aspects of Navajo ceremonial patterns. In R. Kluckhohn (Ed.), *Culture and behavior: Selected essays of Clyde Kluckhohn.* New York: Free Press of Glencoe, 1962.

Kochman, T. Toward an ethnography of Black American speech behavior. In N. Whitten & J. Szwed (Eds.), *Afro-American anthropology.* New York: Free Press, 1970.

Labadie, A. Interview, 20 Dec. 1978.

Lujan, P., & Dobkins, D. *Communicative reticence: The Native American in the college classroom.* Paper presented at the meeting of the Speech Communication Association, Minneapolis, Nov. 1978.

Monroe, A. H., & Ehninger, D. *Principles and types of speech communication.* Glenview, Ill.: Scott, Foresman, 1976.

Ong, W. World as view and world as event. In M. Prosser (Ed.), *Intercommunications among nations and peoples.* New York: Harper & Row, 1973.

Philips, S. U. Participant structures and communicative competence: Warm Springs children in community and classroom. In C. Cazden, V. John, & D. Hymes (Eds.), *Functions of language in the classroom.* New York: Teachers College Press, 1972.

Philipsen, G. Navajo world view and culture patterns of speech: A case study in eth-norhetoric. *Speech Monographs,* 1972, *39,* 132–39.

St. Clair, R. *Visual metaphor in Native American rhetoric.* Paper presented at the meeting of the Midwest Modern Language Association, Minneapolis, Nov. 1980.

Spencer, R. F., Jennings, J. D., Johnson, E., et al. *The Native Americans* (2nd ed.). New York: Harper & Row, 1977.

Vanderwerth, W. C. *Indian oratory: Famous speeches.* Norman: University of Oklahoma Press, 1971.

Williams, M. Interview, 23 Sept. 1978.

Wilson, J., & Arnold, C. C. *Dimensions of public communication.* Boston: Allyn & Bacon, 1976.

8 | The Study of Indian English in the U.S. Southwest: Retrospect and Prospect

WILLIAM L. LEAP
The American University

> The English variety in question, *American Indian* English or *Native American* English, is used by persons in reservation communities and urban Indian enclaves when the Indianness of a discussion topic, of the conversational situation, or of the participants themselves needs formal linguistic marking. While such Indian English usage does not preclude simultaneous control over standard English styles, such a diglossic balance is not always effected by all speakers. Frequently, Indian English is the first form, and may remain the only form, of English language expression acquired by the community membership. Since analysis tends to reveal Indian English grammatical and phonological structures as replications of the groups' Indian language detail, this acquisition process may involve nothing more than the addition of English lexical synonyms to complement one's existing, or developing Indian language facility. In this sense, Indian English can be characterized as a means of talking to the outside world (literally) in Indian terms. For this reason, I view Indian English as a continuation of the speakers' native language tradition; in situations where the Indian language itself is no longer a part of the community's verbal repertoire, it may be the *only* continuation of that tradition which now remains. (Leap, 1975, p. 1)

I advanced the claims in the preceding paragraph in 1975, as the opening to a discussion of possibilities for the study of American Indian English in the

An earlier draft of this paper was presented at the Seventh Annual Southwest Areal Languages and Linguistics Workshop (SWALLOW VII) held at Boulder, Colo., 20–22 April 1978. The development of the argument since that time has profited from discussions with, among others, Ruth Landman, Gina Harvey, Dick Heiser, Betsy Brandt, Ron Scollen, Steve Stout, Amy Zaharlick, Walt Wolfram, Forrest Cuch, Pat Locke, and Gill Garcia. The present statement is my own, however. The data discussed in the fourth section are taken from a field research project supported in part by an American University Faculty Summer research grant, awarded to me in 1974. The data in section five are taken from a research project funded by National Institute of Education grant no. NIE-G-77-0006. I continue to remain grateful to both parties for their support of those phases of my work.

U.S. Southwest and elsewhere. At the time, to my knowledge, only the variety of Indian English spoken at Isleta Pueblo, New Mexico, had been given any attention by linguistic scholarship. There were many who argued, in the absence of available data, that American Indian English was merely "another" nonstandard English code, Indian only in the sense of the speaker's ethnic background. The treatment of Indian English within the schools of the U.S. Southwest was affected accordingly.

Since then, as can be seen by a review of the bibliography accompanying this paper, the Indian English question has begun to receive increasing amounts of attention. The number of persons working in the area of sociolinguistics has expanded, and the degree of individual interests in this topic has also intensified. No longer can the students of Indian English in the U.S. Southwest be counted on the fingers of two hands. Graduate students as well as undergraduates have joined the ranks. Indian English–related dissertations on Mohave English, Laguna English, and Mobilian trade jargon have been completed. Papers on Indian English themes have been read at a variety of regional, national, and international meetings. The Southwest, and, in particular, the border area, has remained the focal point for these studies, though the impact of scholarship from Alaskan and now from Canadian sources has begun to be evidenced as well.

Today, there is a literature on American Indian English, something woefully lacking as recently as 1975. A recently published monograph (M. Miller, 1977) contrasts the acquisition of English by a group of black students in Maryland with the acquisition of English among Pima Indian children. There is a collection of papers (Leap, Ed., 1977) which surveys aspects of the phonology, syntax, history, social variability, and educational implications of several of these codes. Single articles has appeared in journals, though the privately circulated research report (Kalactaca & Kuhlman, 1977; Wolfram, Christian, Leap, & Potter, 1979) remains an equally viable part of the data base. It is no longer necessary for scholars or concerned educators to rely solely on handouts, marginal notes, or scraps of recollection from late-night telephone calls to gain comparative, historical, or practical perspectives on issues confronting their interests in the Indian English question.

A legitimization of interests has emerged from these discussions and the increasing scope given to their circulation. The same legitimization has come as the funding agencies have recognized the worthiness of Indian English–focused research proposals and responded with awards. Since 1975, the National Institute of Education has awarded support to Wolfram and Leap to explore the impact of Indian English fluency on student acquisition of reading and writing skills (Wolfram, Christian, Leap, & Potter, 1979); to Leap and McNett to explore the impact of language skills and other factors on Indian student math learning and math avoidance (Leap, McNett et al., 1981); and to other scholars for similar purposes. The National Endowment for the Humanities has assisted Betty Lou Dubois to continue her archival studies of the historical backgrounds of Mescalero Indian English. The fact of these awards is important to present interests: They show that the agencies view such research concerns (and with them, the existence of Indian English itself) as a legitimate part of the mandate given by Congress to the funding agency. This sets a precedent for future applications.

The linguistic and educational realities of Indian English codes have not been recognized only within the profession. The "village English" of Alaska's rural Eskimo and Indian communities became central in the enforcement proceedings brought against the Alaskan State Department of Education by the U.S. Office for Civil Rights between 1976 and 1978. The Office for Civil Rights was not willing to accept Lau-compliance plans from the state's rural education attendance areas if the plans attempted to assess the language needs of the native students exclusively in terms of their ancestral language dominance. The students' concurrently held levels of English proficiency also had to be determined; then the correlation and overlap between each speaker's native-language and English-language proficiency levels had to be ascertained, and the plan proposed to remediate the students' needs for English-language skill had to be developed in terms of all of those considerations.

The definition of eligibility for services under programs funded by Title VII of the Elementary and Secondary Education Act (ESEA, or the Bilingual Education Act), likewise has come to reflect a growing awareness of the educational reality of Indian English. The reauthorization language passed by Congress in 1978 refers to "limited English proficiency," not "limited English-speaking ability," as was formerly the case. Moreover, along with those persons whose native language is other than English, the new definition of limited English proficiency includes persons who come from environments where a language other than English is dominant, *as well as* "individuals who are American Indian and Alaskan Native students and who come from environments where a language other than English has had a significant impact on their level of English language proficiency" (Public Law 95–561, see references). This makes it the intent of Congress that Title VII services be extended to students from Indian and Alaskan native backgrounds, who, because they are dominantly or exclusively fluent in an Indian English code might otherwise *not* be considered to have difficulty speaking, reading, writing, or understanding the English language within their appropriate age and grade levels, or to have other educationally relatable English-language needs. Already, two Indian-focused Title VII projects in the U.S. Southwest have applied for and been awarded funding under this provision of the Bilingual Education Act. Their proposals to the Office of Bilingual Education and Minority Language Affairs provide ample demonstration of the fact that an Indian student's English fluency does not guarantee the student's having English proficiency. Such is especially the case when the English variety spoken differs systematically from the grammatical conventions of standard English, and the pragmatic and other usage skills that the student controls differ from the performance patterns which speakers of standard English expect from participants in English conversations (Leap, 1978).

The discovery that differences in grammar and in usage do separate Indian English varieties from standard English has been the single most important insight to emerge from Indian English scholarship to date. That discovery marked a significant advance over previous attempts to account for the structure of Indian English codes, most of which were carried out in terms of their "deletion of the verb *to be*," "absence of $-Z_1$ suffix," or other features which the nonstandard codes did not possess. Now, armed with the discovery that Indian English varieties are systematic, are "regular," and thus are as well-formed as are other such varieties of English, scholars have begun to push their inquiry beyond the level of basic description and have started to probe the significance of these differences for language learning, classroom performance, employability, and other such issues. Such inquiries, I predict, will constitute the thrust of Indian English scholarship in the 1980s, much as clarification of descriptive questions served as our theme for the past 10 years. The reasons for this prediction will be explored in the following paragraphs.

The idea that the English varieties spoken by members of American Indian speech communities have their own, unique grammatical characteristics, and thus are not mere imitations of standard language codes, is of recent origin. Of course, the contrasts distinguishing Indian English and standard English at certain levels had long been recognized by English-as-a-second-language scholarship. Yet with the exception of Robert Wilson's comments about "dormitory English" (cited in Harvey, 1974), the nature of the linguistic and sociolinguistic factors giving rise to these contrasts did not begin to be explored until the early 1970s. Ohannessian, in her report on the teaching of English to American Indians, put the matter quite succinctly. In 1967 she wrote, "There are no descriptions of varieties of English spoken by Indians" (1967, p. 11).

Research completed since that time has greatly advanced our understanding of these codes. Certain general facts about Indian English, which remained obscure as long as the codes were studied in terms of standard English-based descriptive models, now seem abundantly clear.

First, the surface structures of the English used in Indian speech communities contain reflexes of the phonemic patterning and phonological constraints which are characteristic of the community's traditional (Indian) language. This condition cannot be viewed merely as an interference phenomenon. Standard English details are not being "predictably" altered in these codes, but are

being replaced, in whole or significant part, by Indian-language–based phonological constraints. Such is found to be the case *whether or not* the individual
speaker is fluent in the ancestral language of that community. Data provided
in Harvey (1974), Leap (1973, 1977b), Nelson-Barber (1981), Penfield
(1977), Scollen (1979), Stout (1977b), and Alford (1974) all provide support
and illustration for this claim.

Second, Indian-language grammatical rules have priority over the corresponding English grammatical rules in the formation of subordinate clauses,
the marking of cross-reference relationships between nouns and verbs, and in
other morphemic and syntactic constructions in the surface structure. A formal
statement of this claim is given in Leap (1974). Supplementary examples are
found for Isletan English in Leap (1974, 1977c), and for Tewa English in Leap
(1980).

Third, the semantic component of the community's Indian language may
likewise directly affect the formation and marking conventions found in the
resulting English surface constructions. The commonly attested use of single
rather than multiple negation to indicate nonpositive alternatives to an otherwise affirmed condition (Leap, 1977c) is one example of structures which may
emerge from such influences. The cognitive parallels to these conditions are
discussed in Scollen (1977) and his related essays.

Fourth, constructions commonly attested in other nonstandard English varieties may also be found within Indian English codes. The presence of distrib-
utivelike uses of uninflected *be* in Isletan English (Leap, 1977d) is one example
of this phenomenon. Usually constructions of this type cannot be accounted for
by reference to standard English or to Indian-language grammatical rules.
Bickerton (1975) notes the presence of such constructions in postcreole communities. Their presence in Indian English–speaking communities may reflect
something of the processes underlying the formation and maintenance of their
English repertoire, but this mode of explanation for these features has not been
systematically explored. Diffusion from other nonstandard English codes (Dillard, 1972) is a second, competing explanation for this condition.

Fifth, the range of factors which enter into sentence-formation processes in
each of these speech communities gives a high degree of structural uniqueness
to each of these Indian English codes. To date, studies of the English varieties
used within the following tribal contexts have been completed: Northern Athabaskan (Scollen, 1977, passim); Northern Cheyenne (Alford, 1974); Hopi
(Penfield, 1977); Isleta (Leap, 1973, passim); Laguna Keresan (Stout, 1977b;
Wolfram, Christian, Leap, & Potter, 1979); Makah (Fleisher, 1981); Mohave
(Penfield, 1977); Navajo (Harvey, 1974; Penfield, 1977); Papago (Kuhlman
& Longoni, 1975); Pima (Kalactaca & Kuhlman, 1977; M. Miller, 1977,
1981; Nelson-Barber, 1981); Santa Ana Keresan (Stout, 1977a); San Juan
Tewa (Leap, 1980; Wolfram, Christian, Leap, & Potter, 1979); Shoshone (W.

Miller, 1967); and Ute (Penfield, 1977). In each of these instances, to the extent that documentation is provided in the discussion, specific details from each tribe's ancestral language tradition appear to affect the design of the phonology, grammar, semantics, and usage patterns of the tribe's English code. Numerous points of contrast distinguish each Indian-language tradition from every other Indian-language tradition in America. Those differences alone assure that the combination of standard language, nonstandard detail, and Indian-language conventions found to underlie one Indian English variety need never be found in any second variety. Each Indian English code appears to be best understood as a unique configuration of linguistic, social, historical, and cultural influences. This is why, in previous publications, I have found it appropriate to posit the existence of over 200 different Indian Englishes within the United States alone. The tribally specific nature of these codes assures us that there could be as many different varieties of American Indian English as there are distinctive Indian-language traditions. Given dialect, geographical variation, and other such factors, there could be even more Indian English varieties than that.

Along with the sharpening of descriptive perspectives on these codes has come advances in other areas of Indian English research: the acquisition of Indian English fluency (Miller, 1977; Dubois, 1978); sociolinguistic and pragmatic functioning (Philips, 1973, 1974; Stout, 1977b); the overlap with reading and writing (Wolfram, Christian, Leap, & Potter, 1979) and the development of mathematical skills (Leap, McNett et al., 1981). General implications for the formation of educational policy have begun to be advanced, as well (Harvey, 1977, passim).

Of equal importance have been the strengthening of historical perspectives which can be brought to the interpretation of these codes. Here the work of Dubois (1977, 1978) and Valdés-Fallis (1977) has been of particular interest, in that they remain the only systematic attempts to use ethnohistorical records to clarify Indian-, Spanish-, and English-language usage and contact patterns for any *single* tribe within the Southwest.

Their studies have had implications far beyond Mescalero linguistic history. In reporting on one portion of their findings, for example, Dubois writes: "For the period 1846–1880, Spanish was the vehicle for communicative interaction with Anglo-Americans, . . . particularly with the Mescalero" (1977, p. 191). In fact, as subsequent citations in the article point out, English was still a linguistic novelty among the Mescalero people as late as 1900. That date correlates well with M. Miller's observation that "apparently there were no Pima-English contacts until the nineteenth century . . . , [and] it was not until about 1920 that Pimas can be said to have begun the *learning* of English to any great extent" (1977, pp. 105–6, emphasis mine). Bodine, in his study of Taos linguistic acculturation (1962), gives a comparable date for the introduction of

English fluency within Taos Pueblo. Working with comparable data for Isleta Pueblo, Hutchinson (1977) found that the pueblo's "language preference has shifted from Spanish to English in the last 95 years" and that "the shift was not effected until relatively late in Isleta's contact history" (p. 173).

These attempts to draw intertribal comparisons of language histories are preliminary in scope. Still they point to an important observation: Indian English, at least in the tribal/community–specific sense in which it is known today, appears to be a linguistic phenomenon recently added to the verbal repertoires of the Southwestern tribal speech communities. How this addition came to occur, and at what point in a community's language history it can be said that a "new" component has been added to the verbal repertoire are questions which now must be given attention. Brandt and MacCrate (1979) have argued, for example, that individual Southwestern Indians knew and used some form of English long before the time when community- or tribal-level acquisition is said to have occurred. M. Miller (1977, p. 105) suspects that among the Pima there may have been a "small knot" of bilingual individuals who engaged in political or commercial negotiation with outsiders long before other members of the tribe became exposed to English fluency. Attempts to determine how much English these persons may have known—or what kind of English they controlled, for that matter—must ultimately be made in the light of the American Indian pidgin English question. It is clear from the discussions of Leechman and Hall (1955), M. Miller (1967), Haas (1975), Johnson (1975), Crawford (1978), Goddard (1977), and especially Drechsel (1976, 1977) that pidgin English codes were in use in the Northeast, the Southeast, the Northwest Coast, and elsewhere shortly after European contact with the tribal peoples of these areas had begun. In some cases, data suggest that there were intertribal pidgins in use before the European arrival and that English vocabulary, with necessary modification, was merely grafted onto the existing pidgin sentence structures and into the rules that underlay their formation. Had such pidgin languages existed in the precontact Southwest, or had an Indian-Spanish pidgin emerged out of the Hispanic colonial period, it would be easy to treat Southwestern Indian English today as the present-day continuation of an older, long established interlanguage tradition. Successive stages of relexification would then be posited to account for the predominance of English vocabulary and English surface morphology within the contemporary codes, a pattern that is hardly atypical of the histories of pidgin languages in other parts of the world.

Whether precontact or Indian-Hispanic pidgin languages existed in the U.S. Southwest is another matter entirely. If there are documents containing evidence of their presence, the documents have yet to be identified. And before dismissing the lack of data to the contrary as evidence in support of such codes' formation, it is useful to look at the patterns of multilingualism long maintained by Tanoan- and Keresan-speaking pueblo communities along the Rio Grande, and by the more migratory tribes living in areas adjacent to them, to determine whether the use of such pidgins, given their interlanguage basis, would have been consistent with their principles of language usage and verbal etiquette.

Tradition found it more appropriate, for example, for trading partners or friends from different tribal and language backgrounds to acquire some level of fluency in each other's ancestral language. People were not expected to compromise the richness and explicitness of their own linguistic traditions by recourse to the pidginization process and its more limited and restricted by-products. This tradition favoring individual-level multilingualism within these communities remains quite viable today, even within the so-called acculturated tribes (Dozier, 1956; Barber, 1973; Leap, 1973). In such contexts, the formation or maintenance of any single language to serve as a regional or area-wide, neutral, function-specific means of communication would be highly inappropriate. When faced with the need to interact with English-speakers (or with speakers from any other nonindigenous language tradition, for that matter), tribes could have designated individual members to develop the necessary fluency and then to serve as linguistic intermediaries when the occasion for translation arose; or, if conditions warranted, the community as a whole could have been encouraged to acquire skills in the outside tongue. Among the Rio Grande pueblos, the earliest attestations of community-wide English fluency coincide with the earliest opportunities for community-level uses of such fluency. Dubois's and Miller's studies, cited above, show that this correlation was not restricted solely to central New Mexico.

Viewed in historical terms, the presence of the Indian English varieties of the U.S. Southwest provide a powerful illustration of a speech community's collective ability to apply its language-learning skills to practical, communication-related problem solving. Referring to the outcome of such instances of community-level linguistic creativity as a language "hybrid," divorced from any single linguistic tradition or stable linguistic base, containing characteristics of neither of the grammars from which it was derived, will certainly underestimate the significance those codes assume under these circumstances. It will seriously shortchange appreciation of the language abilities of the persons who form and use those codes as well.

It is very important, especially in the Borderland areas, where the outcome of language contact can take on so many differing forms, that an accurate picture of speaker skills be kept in mind when any discussion of community-specific language realities is being attempted. But not all scholars exploring the linguistic complexity in the U.S. Southwest bring the objective perspective on local language conditions which such historically based conditions might warrant. In fact, some scholars have preferred to refer to local conditions strictly in terms of more generally derived explanatory frameworks, even though, when given closer inspection, the relevance of those frameworks to local conditions and to the historical traditions which underlie them prove highly suspect.

One such framework, used until recently to describe (and thereby account for) the Indian English codes used in the U.S. Southwest, was offered by the phrase *limited English-speaking ability*. The popularity of this phrase can undoubtedly be traced to its pivotal position within the eligibility requirements for support under Title VII, the Bilingual Education Act. Until 1978, to receive funding from Title VII, students in a school had to manifest limited English-speaking ability, and data had to be presented in the proposal to demonstrate that this was so. Standardized test scores often supplied the data used for such purposes, the implication being that students who do not score successfully on standardized language arts tests do poorly because of their own language arts deficiencies. School-leaving data were also frequently provided, the implication being that students leave school because they are unable to communicate effectively within the classroom.

Whether the courses of study supported under Title VII funds actually brought about changes in the students' language limitations is another matter. The whole question of the impact of bilingual education on student educational achievement remains at best unclear (Engel, 1975; Epstein, 1977; American Institutes for Research, 1977). Perhaps because of the continuing uncertainty, and perhaps because of the changes in the Title VII Act in 1978 which broadened the criteria defining student eligibility for Title VII support, educators began searching for a concept which would summarize minority student English-language problems and do so in a format making school-based intervention, regardless of how limited its impact, an absolute social necessity.

This concept, *semilingualism,* was found within the European literature and has slowly begun to appear in discussions among American scholars as well. In its earliest use, semilingualism referred to a particular kind of linguistic situation found among the children of Finnish migrants now resident and attending school in Sweden. The two leading proponents of this concept, Tove Skutnabb-Kangas and Pertti Toukomaa, described the situation as one where "a migrant child does not have proper command of the language of the host country but has no proficiency in his mother tongue, either" (Toukomaa & Skutnabb-Kangas, 1977, p. 2). Paulston (1975, p. 390) notes Loman's reference to semilingualism as a type of " 'faulty linguistic competence' . . . especially observed in individuals who have, since childhood, had contact with two languages without sufficient or adequate training and stimulation in either of them." Then Paulston continues, in her own words: "By knowing two languages poorly, the children know no language well and this condition has negative emotional, psychological, cognitive, linguistic and scholastic consequences" (p. 390).

All proponents of the concept agree that bilingual instruction, beginning with intensive language arts training in the home language during the pre-school years, is the only remedy appropriate for this situation. Even critics of the inadequacy and "hidden agenda" quality of language-related educational policies in America seem willing to accept the validity of the concept and of the rationale for school-based intervention which it presents.

The linguistic condition described by the term semilingualism has been linked by some to American Indian speech communities. Burnaby (1980) has raised some telling questions about the accuracy of attempts to interpret language needs in Indian education in such terms. Elsewhere (Leap, 1981) I have raised additional objections. I doubt that such statements will be sufficient to prevent connections being drawn between Indian student educational needs and semilingual theory. Parallels to the difficulties in communication, the repression of emotions, the inhibited nature of student commentary, and other such reflexes of the "emotional, psychological, cognitive, linguistic, and scholastic consequences" attributed to student semilingualism can readily be found within numerous American Indian classroom contexts. Consider, for example, the statements of a sixth grader from a New Mexican pueblo community as she responds to a request to retell a particular story:

Q. Now you tell that story back to me.
A. Tom Black was a cowboy. (Pause.) I don't know, I forgot the story, I do not like to listen to stories.
Q. Want me to repeat it again? (Interviewer does so.)
A. OK. Tom Black was a cowboy. Uh, let's see. I forgot that, the first one.
Q. What did he do?
A. Bought a pickup truck, and he went to the rodeo.
Q. Right.
A. (Laugh.) I forgot.
Q. What did he do at the rodeo?
A. He won a bucking contest or whatever, he won a gold saddle.
Q. What did he do then?
A. I forgot. (Pause.) He put it in his pickup.
Q. Yes, he did.
A. I forgot the last part.
Q. Then he went home?
A. Yes.

Yet this same "repressed, inhibited, non-spontaneous" English speaker evidenced a total reversal in her evidenced control over her expressive language arts and cognitive skills when, during the concluding portion of the interview, she was asked to make up a story about a picture drawn by one of her classmates. The discussion ran as follows:

Q.   This is a picture, tell me about it.
A.   First, you have to tell me what it is.
Q.   What does it look like?
A.   Like a dog or coyote.
Q.   Which do you want it to be?
A.   A coyote.
Q.   OK, it's a coyote, tell me about it.
A.   It's howling.
Q.   It's howling?
A.   Yes. (Pause.) Want me to tell you a story?
Q.   Yes.
A.   Can I pretend like there was children in this house? . . . Once upon a time, there were two little childrens on a top of the hill. Their house is built in the middle of the hills. But there is another hill on the other side; there was, it was a full moon and there was a coyot-. And they were by themself, their parents were not around. And they started hearing this howling sounds. And they got scared, and they did not know what it was. So they went out, and they saw it was a coyot- (abrupt pause)—That enough?

Is this child semilingual? Accurate assessments of her mastery of English and of her ability to employ English for problem-solving purposes within structured environments are not going to be found if generalizations are drawn solely from her performance on one of these tasks. School-related language proficiency involves effective performance skills in a variety of domains and task-related contexts. Any effort to determine a student's level of proficiency in any language must be carried out in terms which are equally inclusive.

Such has not been the nature of the efforts used to assemble the data from which conclusions about student semilingualism have been drawn. Acting almost as if Labov (1969) and related essays had never appeared, Toukomaa and Skutnabb-Kangas relied on standardized tests of nonverbal intelligence and of picture vocabulary to measure the language skills and cognitive skills of the Finnish immigrant children living in Sweden. The tests of Swedish and Finnish language ability showed that these children were, "on the average, two to three years behind their monolingual peers, both in Finland and in Sweden. Thus the children did not know either language near as well as the monolingual children" (1977, p. 2).

Their conclusions require particular attention within the present context. Neither linguistic data nor direct observations of student language usage were consulted here. Toukomaa and Skutnabb-Kangas have not looked at the sentence-formation skills already mastered by these children, nor have they attempted to construct test situations like the one described above, where students can formally demonstrate their language attainment. In a parallel discussion (Leap, 1981), I describe the rule-governed complexity underlying sentences formed by Indian students who, if judged solely in terms of standard tests or other narrowly constructed assessments of language skill, would be said to possess semilingual English fluency. Here, I want to stress how much of the cultural reality underlying these codes is being ignored when conclusions about verbal skills are drawn from such a limited data base. As has been argued in earlier sections of this essay, the presence of American Indian English in the U.S. Southwest can be attributed, structurally, to the application of Indian-language grammatical constraints to English-language sentence-formation tasks, and, historically, to the rules of bilingual etiquette developed and still maintained within the speakers' tribal speech community. Since the existence of these codes is so directly dependent on the structural and historical realities, it seems highly inappropriate to overlook them when fluency in these codes is to be described.

The question remains, however: Does a student's proficiency in his tribe's Indian English variety act as a barrier to school-related achievement? Several recently completed research projects have explored aspects of this question. The findings of one of these (Wolfram, Christian, Leap, & Potter, 1979), will be briefly reviewed here.

Funding for this project was awarded by the National Institute for Education. The project was designed to examine the Indian English codes used in two pueblo Indian communities (San Juan and Laguna) and to determine the effect which fluency in those codes might have on an elementary-school student's reading and writing skills. Data from free-flowing conversations with adults and children from each community, student oral-reading performance on selected, graded reading passages, and sets of writing samples provided the data for the analysis. San Juan Tewa and Laguna Keresan not being at all historically relatable, comparisons of the spoken and written English materials from each site offered broader perspectives on language-specific influences which might be structuring the responses in the sample.

Two of the findings from the analysis of the writing samples are particularly relevant to this discussion. First, we did not find the level of unique, language-specific details in the English samples from either pueblo which previous studies had identified in other locales. Students from each pueblo did manifest distinctive examples of reading- and writing-related errors, however, and in some instances these errors could be directly related to Indian-language influences. In other instances, these errors seemed to be characteristic of the mistakes that students at these grade levels would make, regardless of language background. And there were cases where students from both pueblo contexts seemed to share the same types of skills problems, whether those errors were common to other student populations or not.

It was the frequency with which these errors appeared within the respective samples which ultimately proved to be most significant to this study. Students from Laguna pueblo, for example, made fewer spelling errors than did students from San Juan; otherwise, they manifested high incidences of Indian-language–related influences in their reading and writing samples. San Juan students, in contrast, made a smaller number of errors overall, but spelling as well as context-specific errors were significantly represented within that sample.

The analysis was complicated by an additional fact, anticipated in Leap (1977a) but not previously explored in systematic terms: Any error which could be related to a spoken-Indian-language source could have any number of possible sources within the spoken-language grammar or elsewhere. The complexity at issue here is illustrated by the occurrence of the uninflected verb *dance* in the following writing sample:

American Indian Day

1   American Indian Day was
2   Thursday September 22nd. In
3 x the morning they Dance the
4   Eagle Dance and the Harvest
5   Dance.
6   And the butterfly Dance.
7 x Some of the Classmates Dance.
8   in the afternoon. We Did
9   not have School.

Dance can be explained by reference to any one (or combination) of the following sources, not all of which are limited solely to the Indian English circumstance:

1. Phonological reduction of final position -[sd] cluster in the spoken English favors the absence of the *d* in the spelling of the verb.
2. Syntactic convention, from Indian-language narrative style, allows the tense of the whole story to be marked only once—in the first verb construction of the text. Hence, *was* in line 1, and hence *dance* in lines 3 and 7.
3. Semantic contrasts from the Indian language allows continuous, non-restricted action to be denoted by verb base and $=\emptyset$ suffix.
4. General nonstandard English conventions allow action "distributed" at various points in time to be marked by uninflected verb forms.
5. General "error-related" tendencies of all students learning to write English show deletion, in earlier years, of the second of two elements in a cluster, especially if each element has its own grammatical function.

6. For that matter, cluster "simplification" of this sort can occur for any population that is learning to write one of the languages they commonly speak.

Thus the analysis of the student writing samples shows that student Indian English fluency can have a negative impact on school-related performance tasks. Phonological as well as syntactic and lexical influences from the Indian English grammar may be working individually or jointly to condition the presence of nonstandard and nonacceptable constructions within these students' written prose. It must be stressed, however, that the negative impact may not be due to the influence of individual rules, so much as to the influence of rule configurations—rules working in a "conspiracy," jointly favoring the use of certain surface-level constructions in those paragraphs, and jointly discouraging the use of other such constructions. So, while the possibility of spoken Indian English influencing a student's reading and writing skills remains significantly high at each pueblo, the specific influences which will emerge in each case are not so predictable before the fact. Those influences, this analysis shows, are governed by the combination of ancestral, nonstandard, and standard English rules which jointly characterize the community's Indian English tradition. And for that reason, these influences can only be described and assessed in equally site-specific terms.

The most favorable prospects for the study of Indian English are to be found in the continuation of that sort of site-specific inquiry. Similarly, however, we need to be able to examine site-specific findings in larger comparative and interpretive perspectives. Good science always demands clarification of the nonobvious from its practitioners; no less of a demand should be made of linguistic analysis.

Many comparative and interpretive tasks need to be undertaken. Some of them have been highlighted or otherwise referred to in preceding sections. Some additional suggestions can be offered here.

Within the area of Indian English phonology, we need to determine whether tone (i.e., segmental, rather than suprasegmental pitch) exists in Indian English when the ancestral language of the speakers still retains such phenomena. Except for Stout's discussion of schwa-intrusion in Santa Ana English (1977a), we have virtually no information on the phonotactic systems used in any of these codes. The match between underlying Indian-language grammatical categories and the rather unimaginative morphology of English surface structure has only been briefly explored. The solutions developed to allow surface-level word classification for each Indian English code, given that the morphemic inventory available for the purpose is so meager, raise interesting questions about grammaticality, as my brief discussion of the many uses of the

-/z/ suffix has demonstrated (Leap, 1977a). On the level of syntax, the overlap between Indian-language grammatical rules and the "gradient tendency" seen in postcreole contexts needs to be explored. If, as Stout and Erting (1977) and Fleisher (1981) have argued, Indian English may be a postcreole phenomenon in some communities, we must be prepared to see some grammars of Indian English containing a large number of rules which cannot be derived from ancestral or English-language sources; what that will do to the intertribal communication in English is another matter, and one equally worthy of attention. And finally, the interplay between language proficiency and socioeconomic background needs attention, if only to determine whether, as is always *said* to be the case by non-Indian educators, the more economically successful the person, the more proficient he will be (or become) in standard English. Stout's dissertation (1977b) has only begun to look at the relevant variables for *one* Indian community.

The educational implications which can be drawn from such studies are clear. Additional issues related to education also need exploration in their own right. Strategies used to open and close spoken English paragraphs, the processes of question asking, as contrasted to question formation, and the relationship between pronunciation and spelling as discussed above are only three examples. The scope and the detail which the study of such issues will provide cannot be anticipated by reference to studies of other varieties of vernacular English. The tribalness of the speaker's language tradition and of the speaker's cultural background remains, here as elsewhere, the significant variable with which the analysis must contend. The prospects for Indian-language scholarship in the coming decade center on a continuation of current commitments to determine, in as many ways as are possible, exactly what significance that variable has for Indian English and Indian educational equity.

REFERENCES

Alford, D. K. The Cheyenne dialect of English and its educational implications. Unpublished manuscript, Lame Deer, Mont.: Northern Cheyenne Title VII project, 1974.

American Institutes for Research. *Evaluation of bilingual education programs: Final report on contract no. OEC 0-74-9331.* Palo Alto, Calif.: American Institutes for Research, 1977.

Barber, C. G. Trilingualism in an Arizona Yaqui village. In Paul Turner (Ed.), *Bilingualism in the Southwest.* Tucson: University of Arizona Press, 1973.

Bickerton, D. *Dynamics of a creole continuum.* London: Cambridge University Press, 1975.

Bodine, J. J. Taos names: A clue to linguistic acculturation. *Anthropological Linguistics, 1962, 10,* 23–27.

Brandt, E., & MacCrate, C. 'Make like seem heap Injun': Pidginization in the South-west. Paper presented at the Forty-third International Congress of Americanists, Vancouver, Aug. 1979.

Burnaby, B. *Languages and their roles in educating native children.* Ontario Institute for Studies in Education, Informal Series No. 16. Toronto: Ontario Institute for Studies in Education, 1980.

Crawford, J. *The Mobilian trade jargon.* Knoxville: University of Tennessee Press, 1978.

Dillard, J. L. *Black English.* New York: Random House, 1972.

Dozier, E. Two examples of linguistic acculturation. *Language,* 1956, *32,* 146–57.

Drechsel, E. J. 'Ha now me stomany that!': A summary of pidginization and creolization of North American Indian languages. *International Journal of the Sociology of Language,* 1976, *7,* 63–82.

——. Historical problems and issues in the study of North American marginal languages. In W. L. Leap (Ed.), *Studies in Southwestern Indian English.* San Antonio, Tex.: Trinity University Press, 1977.

Dubois, B. L. Spanish, English, and the Mescalero Apache. In W. L. Leap (Ed.), *Studies in Southwestern Indian English.* San Antonio, Tex.: Trinity University Press, 1977.

——. A case study of Native American child bidialectalism in English: Phonological, morphological and syntactic evidence. *Anthropological Linguistics,* 1978, *20,* 1–13.

Engel, P. L. The use of the vernacular languages in education. *Review of Educational Research,* 1975, *45,* 283–325.

Epstein, N. *Language, ethnicity and the schools.* Washington, D.C.: Institute for Educational Leadership, 1977.

Fleisher, M. The educational implications of American Indian English. In R. St. Clair & W. L. Leap (Eds.), *American Indian language renewal.* Arlington, Va.: National Clearinghouse for Bilingual Education, 1981.

Goddard, I. Some early examples of American Indian pidgin English from New England. *International Journal of American Linguistics,* 1977, *43,* 37–41.

Haas, M. What is Mobilian? In J. Crawford (Ed.), *Studies in Southeastern Indian languages.* Athens: University of Georgia Press, 1975.

Harvey, G. C. Dormitory English: Implications for the teacher. In G. Bills (Ed.), *Southwest areal linguistics.* San Diego, Calif.: Institute for Cultural Pluralism, 1974.

——. Some observations about Red English and standard English in the classroom. In W. L. Leap (Ed.), *Studies in Southwestern Indian English.* San Antonio, Tex.: Trinity University Press, 1977.

Hutchinson, M. Naming preferences as an index to language history at Isleta, New Mexico. In W. L. Leap (Ed.), *Studies in Southwestern Indian English.* San Antonio, Tex.: Trinity University Press, 1977.

Johnson, S. Chinook jargon variations: Toward the compleat Chinooker. Paper presented at the International Conference on Pidgins and Creoles, Honolulu, Jan. 1975.

Kalactaca, M., & Kuhlman, N. Sacaton School District language assessment project: Preliminary report. Unpublished manuscript, San Diego: National Training Resource Center, 1977.

Kuhlman, N., & Longoni, R. Indian English and its implications for education. In G. Harvey & M. F. Heiser (Eds.), *Southwest languages and linguistics in educational perspective.* San Diego: Institute for Cultural Pluralism, 1975.

Labov, W. The logic of non-standard English. In *Georgetown University roundtable on languages and linguistics,* No. 22, pp. 1–31. Washington, D.C.: Georgetown University, 1969.

Leap, W. L. Language pluralism in a Southwestern pueblo: Some comments on Isletan English. In Paul Turner (Ed.), *Bilingualism in the Southwest.* Tucson: University of Arizona Press, 1973.

——. On grammaticality in Native American English: The evidence from Isleta. *International Journal of the Sociology of Language,* 1974, *2,* 79–89.

——. Prospects for American Indian English linguistic research. In B. L. Dubois & B.Hoffer (Eds.), *Papers in Southwest Indian English. I: Research techniques and prospects.* San Antonio, Tex.: Trinity University Press, 1975.

——. A note on subject-verb agreement in Isletan English. In W. L. Leap (Ed.), *Studies in Southwestern Indian English.* San Antonio, Tex.: Trinity University Press, 1977. (a)

——. On consonant simplification in Isletan English and elsewhere. In W. L. Leap (Ed.), *Studies in Southwestern Indian English.* San Antonio, Tex.: Trinity University Press, 1977. (b)

——. Two examples of Isletan English syntax. In W. L. Leap (Ed.), *Studies in Southwestern Indian English.* San Antonio, Tex.: Trinity University Press, 1977. (c)

——. Uninflected BE in Isletan English: A problem in accountability. In W. L. Leap (Ed.), *Studies in Southwestern Indian English.* San Antonio, Tex.: Trinity University Press, 1977. (d)

——. American Indian English and its implications for bilingual education. In *Georgetown University roundtable on languages and linguistics,* International dimensions of bilingual education. Washington, D.C.: Georgetown University, 1978.

——. Cleft and pseudo-cleft in Tewa English. In F. Barkin & E. Brandt (Eds.), *Speaking, singing and teaching: A multidisciplinary approach to language variation.* Proceedings of the Eighth Annual Southwest Areal Languages and Linguistics Workshop. Anthropological Research Papers, No. 20, pp. 179–91. Tempe: Arizona State University, 1980.

——. Educational politics and the 'semilingualism conspiracy'. In R. St. Clair & W. L. Leap (Eds.), *American Indian language renewal.* Arlington, Va.: National Clearinghouse for Bilingual Education, 1981.

Leap, W. L. (Ed.). *Studies in Southwestern Indian English.* San Antonio, Tex.: Trinity University Press, 1977.

Leap, W. L., McNett, C., et al. *Dimensions of math avoidance among American Indian elementary school students: Final report on NIE grant NIE-G-79-0086.* Washington, D.C.: American University, 1981.

Leechman, D., & Hall, R. A. American Indian pidgin English: Attestations and grammatical peculiarities. *American Speech,* 1955, *30,* 163–71.

Miller, M. R. Attestations of American Indian Pidgin English. *American Speech,* 1967, *42,* 142–47.

———. *Children of the Salt River: first and second language acquisition among Pima children.* Indiana University Publications, Language Science Monographs, No. 16. Bloomington: Indiana University, 1977.

———. English acquisition by monolingual or bilingual Pima Indian children. In R. St. Clair & W. L. Leap (Eds.), *American Indian language renewal.* Arlington, Va.: National Clearinghouse for Bilingual Education, 1981.

Miller, W. R. Report to the Center for Applied Linguistics on the teaching of English to American Indians. Unpublished manuscript, Arlington, Va.: Center for Applied Linguistics, 1967.

Nelson-Barber, S. Phonological variations of Pima English. In R. St. Clair & W. L. Leap (Eds.), *American Indian language renewal.* Arlington, Va.: National Clearinghouse for Bilingual Education, 1981.

Ohannessian, S. *The study of the problems of teaching English to American Indians.* Washington, D.C.: Center for Applied Linguistics, 1967.

Paulston, C. B. Ethnic relations and bilingual education: Accounting for contradictory data. In R. Troike & N. Modiano (Eds.), *Proceedings of the First Inter-American Conference on Bilingual Education.* Arlington, Va.: Center for Applied Linguistics, 1975.

Penfield, S. Some examples of Southwestern Indian English compared. In W. L. Leap (Ed.), *Studies in Southwestern Indian English.* San Antonio, Tex.: Trinity University Press, 1977.

Philips, S. Participant structure and communicative competence: Warm Springs children in community and classroom. In C. Cazden, V. John, & D. Hymes (Eds.), *Functions of language in the classroom.* New York: Teachers College Press, 1973.

———. Warm Springs 'Indian time': How the regulation of participation affects the progression of events. In R. Bauman & J. Sherzer (Eds.), *Explorations in the ethnography of speaking.* London: Cambridge University Press, 1974.

Public Law 95-561. *The Educational Amendments of 1978.* 92 STAT. 2143. Washington, D.C.: U.S. Government Printing Office.

Scollen, R. *The context of the informant narrative performance: From sociolinguistics to ethnolinguistics at Fort Chipewyan, Alberta.* Ottawa: National Museum of Man, 1977.

———. Two hundred thirty-six years of variability in Chipewyan consonants. *International Journal of American Linguistics,* 1979, *45,* 332–43.

Stout, S. O. A comment on selective control in English expression at Santa Ana. In W. L. Leap (Ed.), *Studies in Southwestern Indian English.* San Antonio, Tex.: Trinity University Press, 1977. (a)

———. Sociolinguistic analysis of English diversity among elementary-aged students from Laguna pueblo. Doctoral diss., American University, 1977. (b)

Stout, S. O., & Erting, C. Uninflected BE in Isletan English reconsidered: Implicational scaling and the relationship of Isletan English to other ethnically identifiable varieties of English. In W. L. Leap (Ed.), *Studies in Southwestern Indian English*. San Antonio, Tex.: Trinity University Press, 1977.

Toukomaa, P., & Skutnabb-Kangas, T. *The intensive teaching of the mother tongue to migrant children at pre-school age*. University of Tampere, Department of Sociology and Social Psychology, Research Reports, No. 26. Tampere, Finland: University of Tampere, 1977.

Valdés-Fallis, G. Early day communicative relations of the Mescalero Apache with Spanish speakers, 1540–1846. In B. L. Dubois & B. Hoffer (Eds.), *Southwest areal linguistics then and now*. San Antonio, Tex.: Trinity University Press, 1977.

Wolfram, W., Christian, D., Leap, W. L., & Potter, L. *Variability in the English of two Indian communities and its effect on reading and writing: Final report on NIE grant NIE-G-77-0006*. Arlington, Va.: Center for Applied Linguistics, 1979.

III | Spanish in the Borderlands

OVERVIEW

Much remains to be done in the study of Borderland Spanish. Although the Spanish of the Southwest has received some scholarly attention, there have been few studies investigating the Spanish of northern Mexico. Anecdotal accounts have indicated that this Spanish has much in common with the Spanish of the Southwest. For example, even features that have been labeled as "interference" from English are found in the Spanish of northern Mexico. Further studies in this area are greatly needed.

The pages in this section review previous studies of Southwest Spanish and provide data on particular features of it. Florence Barkin addresses the need for a more comprehensive and focused approach to the study of Spanish dialects in the Borderlands. She urges linguists interested in studying the Spanish of the area to coordinate their efforts to describe these dialects. She also provides researchers and students with a detailed list of phonological features of Southwest Spanish which will enable them to determine its salient features and design future research projects.

Mary Beth Floyd's contribution on syntactic variables also reviews the state of the art. She emphasizes the need for more research in the field of syntax. While it has been pointed out that Southwest Spanish syntax exhibits variability, this variability needs further description and specification. In addition, many areas have not been studied at all. Floyd suggests that further studies be undertaken in order to provide descriptions of what has been called Chicano Spanish and seek explanations of its variability.

June A. Jaramillo and Garland D. Bills contribute a focused study on a single variable, the use of the phoneme /ch/ in Southwest Spanish. They find a tendency for the younger generation to use [ch], rather than [š]. This inter-

esting fact, according to the authors, reflects the educational level and awareness of formal registers on the part of the speaker.

James P. Lantolf also addresses a topic of interest to researchers of Spanish
dialects, that of *para* reduction and its relationship to social factors. He finds
that both sex and age come into play in determining whether *para* will be
reduced to *pa*.

John T. Webb describes the interesting and difficult task of classifying lexical items and writing a dictionary which reflects all of their social and semantic meanings. He is involved in developing a system which documents the various uses of words in the *caló* of the Borderlands.

Guadalupe Valdés, Herman García, and Diamantina Storment discuss sex-
related speech accommodation among Mexican-American bilinguals in Las
Cruces, New Mexico. They determine that there are differences between male
and female bilingual servers in accommodating to the language choice (Spanish or English) of a customer. Their study raises important questions about
language use among males and females and about the nature of bilingualism.

9 | Research in the Phonology and Lexicon of Southwest Spanish

FLORENCE BARKIN
Arizona State University

Southwest Spanish, the Spanish spoken in the Borderlands, has been characterized as a dialect of Spanish in its own right. There are no specific linguistic features which are found only in Southwest Spanish; rather, it combines particular phonological, lexical, and syntactic features of Spanish into a unique whole. The one factor clearly distinguishing the Spanish of the Southwestern United States from that of northern Mexico is Spanish-English bilingualism. Most speakers of Southwest Spanish are bilingual to some degree, yet their speech contains characteristics which are independent of English. While some linguists have used the dialect as a point of departure for discussions of particular evidences of language change, few have attempted a broad-based description. The Teschner, Bills, and Craddock bibliography (1975) provides a valuable source for the study of the Spanish and English of United States Hispanics. However, the student of the Spanish of the Southwest cannot help but be disturbed by the fragmentary, disconnected research presented therein, underscoring the fact that Southwest Spanish has not received adequate attention.

THE STATE OF RESEARCH

Southwest Spanish has always intrigued researchers because of its tenacity of archaisms, as well as constant renovation and change by the surrounding vital English- and Spanish-speaking communities. Nevertheless, the investigator is struck by the lack of systematic research on Borderland Spanish; one finds documentation for an isolated lexical analysis here, a phonological study of the distribution of a particular phoneme there, or an inventory of lexical items found in an isolated rural town. In addition to the lack of systematic investigations in geographical areas, one notes an even greater paucity of method-

This paper is an outgrowth of a paper presented at The Mini-Conference of Border Linguistics held in El Paso in the summer of 1978.

ological approaches. To try to characterize the majority of research projects in Southwest Spanish, I would have to agree with Bills (in his introduction to the bibliography), who claims that the most striking characteristic of the gamut of United States Spanish research is the influence of the Hispanic linguistic tradition and the "relative lack of influence of contemporary scholarship in American and European linguistics." He lists the traits of the Hispanic tradition as follows (p. vi):

> (1) Interest in the accumulation of speech fragments with little concern for linguistic or sociological context; (2) almost exclusive interest in deviations from standard Spanish; (3) historical explanations of deviations in phonological-comparative terms; and (4) a lack of interest in theoretical issues regarding the analysis of language data or the implications of these data for the understanding of language as a human phenomenon.

There is growing evidence that the tide of Southwest Spanish research is changing. Recent conferences and workshops have encouraged an exchange of ideas on both general and specific topics. Particularly noteworthy are conferences that aim at seeking solutions (or at least at discussions which may lead to solutions) for issues of concern, be they practical or theoretical. The Mini-Conference of Border Linguistics held in El Paso in the summer of 1978 utilized such an approach. Scholars with interests in border linguistics spoke on topics of immediate concern to all, emphasizing needs for future research, rather than particular areas of interest or proficiency. This led to a valuable exchange of ideas and the joining of forces to initiate future research projects which cross not only lines of the disciplines but also state and national boundaries, just as linguistic varieties ignore the same artificial criteria in their inception and development. Another evidence for the latest resurgence of communication is SWALLOW (Southwest Areal Language and Linguistic Workshop), whose quality and workshop characteristics are being revitalized. SWALLOW was initiated by Jack Ornstein in 1972 in an attempt to foster communication among scholars of Southwest language and linguistics. In addition, publications are becoming more numerous each day; conferences in the fields of linguistics, psychology, sociology, and education make way for studies of language and bilingualism.

Phonology

While there are lists of phonological variables for New Mexico earlier in the century (Espinosa, 1909, 1930), and for Texas (Post, 1934; Poulter, 1970), and many other areas (Florida, Arizona, California), we have little or no data on which varieties occur where, with whom, or when. In addition, approches to fieldwork and linguistic analyses also vary. We have no knowledge of how language variables are used (if they are used at all) by the various members of Southwest communities. Which features do various social groups have in common with other groups of the same socioeconomic class in Mexico and in other parts of Latin America, as well as with those in the Southwest? As Canfield points out in his introduction to Resnick's *Phonological Variants* (1975, p. ci),

> Attempts to delineate geographical dialect zones on a phonological basis for Spanish America have met with little success. . . . Distinctions in the Spanish of America today . . . are products of many factors; except for vocabulary, these have little to do with zones on the map of America. One thing that is certain is that there is a tenacity of structural features in the Spanish of America.

He goes on to criticize writers who describe one area without knowledge of other parts of Spanish America and with limited perspective, and who assume that what they have described cannot exist in another area 2,000 miles away. With this in mind Resnick has decided to look at all available data on phonological traits of the total area: "Then by using distinctive feature techniques of discrimination, [Resnick] proceeds to break down the entire corpus into binarily specifiable units of information which, by virtue of the presence or absence of a phonological characteristic, make a dialect" (p. xii). Resnick contends that the successful organization and comparison of phonological dialect data does not necessarily require the classification of the dialects into zones. He suggests beginning with the notion of one large corpus—the totality of Latin American Spanish—and establishing a system for dividing this into the greatest number of minimally distinguishable dialect units, each unit ideally corresponding to a meaningful socioeconomic or geographical entity, such as town or city, and within these, a social class. Each such sociogeographical unit identified in this way would contain a unique combination of specified phonological features, a combination which would distinguish it from all other such units (p. 5). Since he is primarily relying on data which have seldom been transcribed and, when they have, often in a system of transcription unknown to the scholar using the literature, we have to rely on the validity of his interpretations. Unfortunately, for this reason the global intent of his approach cannot be distinguished from other more limited studies of phonological variables in Spanish-speaking America.

   In their article on linguistic diversity in southwest Spanish, Bills and Ornstein (1976) emphasize the importance of a good dialect questionnaire. They provide a tentative listing of some phonological, morphological, syntactic, and lexical variables that they believe will exhibit both regional and social variation in Southwest Spanish. Their list of 40 variables includes about 15 which may be considered phonological (or morphophonemic) and about 16 that represent lexical variation. As is the case with all documentations of linguistic variables in Spanish, no one variable is unique to the Spanish of the Southwest. However, it is the sociolinguistic distribution of such variables which distinguishes one dialect of Spanish, or one social class (as reflected by speech), from another. Bills and Ornstein point to the necessity of achieving two general objectives in the analysis stage: "(1) a precise characterization of the number and location of geographical dialects and (2) a generalized picture of the variations in social dialects, the results of which would aid in determining the similarities and differences between social dialect variation and compartmentalized sociological and geographical boundaries" (pp. 13–14).

In her study of variations from standard Spanish in the written and spoken Spanish of 30 Chicano students at the University of Texas at Austin, Sánchez (1972) presents significant data on phonological variables. Although she does not provide sociolinguistic correlations, the extensiveness of her listings proves particularly valuable in and of itself. In the area of consonants, Sánchez also enumerates categories which up until that time had gone undocumented. It is unfortunate that Sánchez does not provide contextual information and interpretations of the data presented. Nevertheless, her seminal article must be read and studied by investigators and educators of Spanish-English Southwestern bilingualism.

Another approach to the study of the phonology of Southwest Spanish is found in Foster's article of 1976. He provides explanations of certain phenomena found in the corpus of data provided by the Cross-cultural Southwest Ethnic Study Center of the University of Texas at El Paso. Foster gleaned his data from tape-recorded interviews with students reading their own compositions or assigned texts. He admits that he made "no attempt . . . to present an overall schematic description of the phonology of this dialect" (p. 17). Of particular interest is his recognition of the importance of considering what have been labeled stylistic varieties—that is, "largo, andante, allegretto, and presto" (1974a, p. 8). In addition, in Foster's study of Southwestern varieties, his comments, in a generative vein, on stress, his explanations of the fronting of /a/ under stress in open syllables (e.g., *casa, mañana*), the dominance of [ɛ] over [e] in a closed syllable, and his discussion of /y/ and /l/ are noteworthy. Foster proves realistic in his disillusionment with scholars' (including his own) inability to sufficiently characterize the "dialect" labeled Mexican-American Spanish or Southwest Spanish, to "isolate it from other dialects or to characterize it in general" (p. 22). Dialect features, he admits,

> do present a thorny problem for phonological characterizations; the degree of the problem, however, depends on the extent to which the features at issue affect the underlying systematic phonemic analysis (as is true for those dialects of English in which *not* and *naught* are homophonous) or merely the rules that produce the systematic phonemic description. (p. 22)

He suspects (and with reason) that the above may be true in the case of Chicano Spanish, and that therefore there is no need to examine systematic phonemics in this dialectal context.

Harris (1974b) approaches two features of New Mexican Spanish from a generative phonological point of view: diphthongization of *e* and *o* and *-nos* for *-mos*, and antepenultimate stress on first-person plural verb forms. He stresses the importance of a morphophonemic approach to language change through the formulation of rules of ongoing linguistic change. His study is an attempt at developing theoretical models for linguistic phenomena while at the same time concerning himself with areal issues. For Harris, Southwest Spanish serves as an appropriate model for developing his theory of morphophonemics.

Phillips, in his dissertation on Los Angeles Spanish (1967), correlates sociological variables such as sex, age, relative use of English and Spanish, and social class with phonetic relativizations of various phonemes. He offers a thorough description of syllabic vowels. For example, he lists the three allophones of the phoneme /i/ which are in complementary distribution: [i] (high-front, nonrounded vowel); [j], a high-fronting on-glide or semiconsonant; and [i̯], which is a high-fronting off-glide or semivowel. He also notes two variant pronunciations of [i]: the slightly raised [i˄] and the slightly lowered [i˅]. The [i] (with its two variants) is the only allophone which may be a syllable nucleus, while the other allophones are used only as margins to syllable nuclei. Not surprisingly, Phillips notes that stressed /i/ produces the [i] allophone with very little variation among informants. However, when unstressed, the /i/ is realized in various ways: [i], [i˅], and [i˄]. He further discusses nasalization (nonphonemic), even when the vowel is not in contact with a nasal consonant: [sĩ] or [ĩ]. However, its occurrence is not predictable, although it is "almost always found any time a vowel is in contact with a nasal consonant, and certainly always if the vowel is between two nasals" (p. 114).

Except for Phillips and for Espinosa (1909, 1930), who elaborate upon the five vowel phonemes in Spanish, other Southwest Spanish researchers do not discuss them nor their allophonic realizations. In addition to his detailed analysis of the vowels in Latin American Spanish, Phillips contributes an elaborate quantitative investigation of /b/, addressing himself to the ever-present need to seek an explanation for linguistic variation in a designated community. In the case of certain phonemes (e.g., /b/), he succeeds in attributing variation to the interaction of several nonlinguistic factors. Phillips also provides a complete inventory of phonemes of Los Angeles Spanish, analyzing them as pronounced by the informants in varying environments. He does not attempt to prove the phonemic status of the various sounds, since he finds nothing to indicate that Latin American Spanish differs in its phonemic structure from other dialects of Spanish in the Western Hemisphere. He does note, however, that a few English sounds are used sporadically. In addition to this study on phonology, Phillips provides some sound spectrograms of recordings. Although there prove to be some problems in sound quality, the spectrograms serve to illustrate certain points visually.

In her study of realizations of three English sounds in Tucson Spanish, Merz (1980) examines labiodental [v] and the bilabials [b] and [β], fricative [š] for affricate [č], and retroflex [r] for alveolar tap [ɹ].

She concludes that [ɹ] is the only one used consistently by all informants. The use of [š] ranges from none to frequent, while [h] use is rare. Merz attributes more frequent use of [v] to English dominance; however, she does note that "these phones have existed in Spanish for many centuries." She claims that while English may not be the origin of these phones, their presence in English "facilitates the reinforcement of any tendencies from within the [Spanish] language" (p. 418).

In their paper on [ch] in Tomé, New Mexico (this volume), Jaramillo and Bills point out that [č] and [š] are about equally prominent in the data collected from their study. They note that there is "only one conditionary factor of importance: /ch/ is always realized as the affricate [ch] following a nasal or lateral consonant (e.g., *en chorros, planchar, el chile, colcha*). In their discussion of contextual factors, their data contradict those of Espinosa (1909) and Bowen (1952), who claim that [š] occurs only in rapid speech. Rather, they find that social characteristics, principally age, education, and formal study of Spanish are factors coming into play in informants' choice of [č]. The direction of change is [š] to [č], and not the reverse. The authors do caution the reader that the interview may have elicited a variety of Spanish appropriate to semiformal contexts, which would call for [č], the standard form.

In a study of /s/ in the Spanish of Arizona, Allen and Chaves (1980) concluded that /s/ aspiration and deletion were more common in men than women. As in the Bills and Jaramillo study of /č/, their investigation also notes that educational level is a key factor in choice of a more "standard" form in this case [s]. They also point out that when deletion does not result in morphological or semantic confusion, it will be more likely to occur.

By far the most complete description of the phonology of any variety of Southwest Spanish is that of Espinosa (1909). It includes all of the above-mentioned characteristics, in addition to others (see appendices, pp. 135–37). The Spanish translation (1930), along with its introduction and elaborate notes by Alonso and Rosenblat, represents a milestone in dialect studies of the Southwest. It documents phonological variants in New Mexico and southern Colorado and notes their occurrence in other areas of the Spanish-speaking world. Espinosa's monumental work provides scholars with data from which to discuss and develop new theoretical models and investigate sociolinguistic correlates. In addition, it can be used as a historical documentation of the Spanish of the area at the turn of the century. Dworkin (1977) suggests various ways in which the specialist in the history of Spanish can best use synchronic descriptions. Researchers can investigate language drift, or "unconscious selection on the part of its speakers of those individual variations that are cumulative in some special direction" (Sapir, 1921, p. 155). Dworkin alerts students of language that "there is no way to predict whether a shift observable in popular speech will eventually constitute part of the *norma culta*," or educated standard (p. 2). Espinosa's study contributes data which could assist linguists to systematically describe the drift of contemporary Spanish.

Lexicon

Much of what I have alluded to in the previous discussion on phonological variables also pertains to lexical variables. Lexical studies have been abundant in the Southwest. However, systematic analyses have been absent. I recommend joining together in order to facilitate the task of uncovering the specific and universal characteristics of Southwest Spanish.

In the realm of the lexicon, most studies have been devoted to the influence of English. What is interference in the speech of one speaker may be the norm in the speech of a certain community. The term interference may imply that the feature has a transitory nature, and thus is a sporadic and somewhat unpredictable occurrence. However, once such features become regularized and predictable, they have become part of the ideolect of the speaker. The same holds true in the speech community. Once the speech of the members of the community is characterized by what some have labeled interference in a consistent and frequent fashion, it represents the norm for that community. Naturally, the situation and its description are not quite so simple. What linguists have labeled interference may never have been interference at all, or may, on the other hand, have originated as interference but subsequently become part of the "code," and the fact that it resembles a particular structure in English is now an interesting fact—but that is all. One characteristic of the Spanish of the Borderlands is the fact that features that seem to be examples of lexical interference among bilinguals on the United States side are part of the dialect of northern Mexico. They are learned as Spanish, not English, terms. This, of course, may be the case on the United States side as well. Craddock has provided a "provisional taxonomy of interference types that can be considered lexical" (1976, p. 46). He follows the general classification introduced by Haugen, although he changes the terminology somewhat, categorizing interference types as: 1) direct insertion of English words; 2) assimilated loanwords; 3) Spanish-English blends; and 4) meaning shifts in Spanish words to fit, in part or wholly, the semantic range of English counterparts (calques, or loan translations, fit here). Haugen's categorization is more complex, dividing lexical items into 1) pure, unassimilated, partially assimilated, and wholly assimilated loanwords; 2) loanblends and loanshifts—homophonous, homologous, and synonymous. His terminology clearly identifies lexical items according to phonological and morphological characteristics. This terminology proves particularly useful when the linguist is faced with the task of sorting out lexical items.

Teschner (1972) follows Haugen's classification in his listing of anglicisms in Spanish. His study offers a valuable resource for lexical items reflecting English influence throughout the Spanish-speaking world. Unfortunately, his comprehensive cataloging does not provide much information about the phonological shape of individual loanwords, since his sources seldom avail themselves of phonetic transcription. In his dissertation, Teschner provides the scholar with two or three separate studies: 1) a cross-referenced guide to the study of anglicisms; 2) an analysis of the influence of English on the Spanish of Chicago Chicanos; 3) an analysis and interpretation of borrowing phenomena. He is to be admired for providing the context for items recorded. Craddock (1977) urges scholars and researchers to report lexical data contextually, since:

> Theoretical revolutions come and go, so that works limited to presenting analytical results from an unpublished corpus are often no better than the theoretical underpinnings that sustain the analysis. If the theory collapses, then the analysis is likely to be useless. On the other hand, carefully presented primary data, besides being a thing of beauty in the eye of the linguistic beholder, lend themselves to any sort of analytical approach. The field worker cannot anticipate all the uses to which his material might be put; let him therefore publish his interviews in extenso and make his tape recordings and notebooks available to fellow scholars. The discipline would be better for it.

Beltramo (1972) uses the criteria provided by Haugen, competently commenting on phonological and morphological aspects of borrowing. His classification and analysis of borrowing include a persuasive and skillful account of lexical interference.

When isolated from sociological, demographic, and stylistic factors, lexical items remain mere description without any immediate application. Haugen's categorization has been used by linguists to clarify the complexity of lexical influence of English on L_2. It has proven useful in the study of gender of loanwords, categorization of code switching according to lexical and sociological characteristics (Barkin, 1981), and syntactic, phonological, and semantic influence under the guise of lexical interference, as with loanshifts (see Barkin, 1979).

Linguists must be leery of how they classify lexical items alone. In criticizing Tzuzaki's use of the category of loanshifts (1970), Craddock cautions the linguist to avoid the "absurdity of mechanically assuming that if a loanword matches the phonological shape of some word found in the dictionary, it therefore constitutes a loanshift" (p. 87). In his critical annotation in the Teschner,

Bills, and Craddock bibliography (1975), he lauds Beltramo's discussion of "loan homonyms" (p. 221):

> Since however, there is no common semantic ground between these words, we do not say that Spanish *carpeta* ("letter file") was either extended in meaning or shifted in context to acquire the meaning "carpet." *Carpeta* is simply a different word, adapted in the same manner as *cuilta* ("quilt"). What must be demonstrated is that the word in question exists in the speaker's dialect and acquires a new meaning through English interference. (p. 122)

Rissel's (1976) "Implications of Differences in the Organization of a Lexical Domain in Spanish and English" sheds new light on how lexico-semantic studies can be utilized to illustrate differences in cognitive styles between mono- and bilinguals. By avoiding the traditional belief in language interference/ integration alluded to in Craddock, Haugen, and others, and choosing to consider the entirety of the speaker's speech capabilities, and their manifestations (i.e., the speaker's performance), linguists can go beyond analysis of specific features of the lexicon and attempt to discover criteria used by people to classify their environment (p. 34). In this way we can examine the interaction of languages, whether they represent one code, two codes, or a multiplicity of codes. The result is a picture of the repertoires and linguistic possibilities available to the speaker.

Responding to the need for further research in English lexicon among the Mexican Americans of Texas and the serious criticism of the "validity and reliability of previous dialect methods in the United States," Villarreal-García (1978, p. 49) investigated the distribution of regional vocabulary in Brownsville, Texas. Unlike investigators who carry out traditional dialect studies, which simply present percentages of the occurrence of each word investigated and maps that display the geographical distribution of groups of words, Villarreal-García uses revised procedures for stimulus presentation, sampling techniques, social classification of informants, and other sociological variables such as location of residence and school, inter–ethnic group contact, and ethnicity. She sets out to answer six basic questions:

1. What are the differences in the use of regional vocabulary by speakers in Brownsville, as a function of ethnicity?
2. Do informants representing different socioeconomic levels differ in their use of regional vocabulary?
3. Does an informant's language background act as a factor in his use of regional vocabulary?
4. Is residence a factor in the use of regional vocabulary?
5. Does inter-ethnic-group contact in the community have any bearing on the distribution of regional vocabulary?
6. Does regional vocabulary differ as a function of topic?

By applying sociolinguistic methodology to dialect geography, Villarreal-García has demonstrated the feasibility of an interdisciplinary approach.

As in the area of phonology, Espinosa aspires to provide a lexicon of New Mexican Spanish. Unfortunately the manuscript has never been published, although a short article reveals his rigorous methodology (Espinosa, 1930).

Bibliographies such as Teschner, Bills, and Craddock's (1975) and classifications of lexical and phonological items such as those of Teschner (1976) and Harris (1974) represent a beginning in the challenging accumulation of linguistic and nonlinguistic data on the Spanish of the Southwest. Nevertheless, the tendency for isolation has not been eliminated.

Sociolinguistics and Dialectology

In his article on sociolinguistics and Hispanic dialectology, Lope Blanch (1976) refutes Rona's claim that dialectology differs from sociolinguistics in that the former concerns itself with regions, while the latter deals with various levels of language in the same region: "Si la dialectología tiene como finalidad general el estudio de hablas, deberá atender tanto a sus variedades regionales como a las sociales, tanto al eje horizontal como al vertical" (p. 71). He adds:

> En consecuencia, la dialectología atenderá a esas dos estructuras sociales a través de sendos métodos idóneos: el socio-dialectal para estudiar las hablas de una sociedad local, vertical, y el geo-dialectal para estudiar las hablas de una sociedad regional, horizonal. No se trata, pues, de dos diferentes ramas de la lingüística, sino solo de dos métodos diversos de la dialectología.

Recognizing the importance of correlating dialect variation with sociolinguistic factors is the first step in designing an appropriate model which illustrates the interaction of horizontal and vertical elements. As Sankoff, in her review of dialectology (1973), points out,

> The past decade has seen a marked growth in the cross fertilization between dialectology and various other traditions in linguistics. Linguists have generally become more interested in problems arising from a perspective which views language as a socially situated vehicle of communication, and have found dialectologists able to contribute insights of importance in this area. (p. 171)

In the same vein, one should emphasize that any system of phonological description must account for sociolinguistic variation in patterns of phonotactic and morphophonemic patterning.

We are at a very critical point in the analysis of linguistic variation: Study of linguistic variables as representative of the linguistic community's verbal repertoire must now supersede specification of isolated linguistic features which may or may not display any stylistic or sociolinguistic regularity. Not only would studies of this nature aid the linguist and teacher of Spanish in the Southwest to appreciate the richness of the Spanish of the region, but they would provide students of language throughout the world with a greater understanding of variability and regularity, in both bilingual and monolingual speech. Such rule-governed stylistically and socially conditioned linguistic behavior can be taught in our foreign-language classrooms, thereby creating more realistic practical language-use situations.

DIRECTIONS FOR FUTURE RESEARCH

Since descriptions of dialects of Southwest Spanish have not been systematic, either in terms of the choice of register under study or even, in many cases, in geographical area, I have chosen to avoid presenting a typology of Southwest Spanish—where a variety is spoken and by whom. I hope that one of the tasks of future research will be a more organized, all-inclusive approach to language description. On this note, I recommend certain very basic tasks be undertaken in order to facilitate this larger goal. While we have important sources of data, they sometimes are inaccessible to people with practical concerns, whether because of their unavailability or their degree of technicality. The appendices to this chapter (pp. 135–37) deal with the phonology of Southwest Spanish and list Southwest Spanish phonemes and their allophonic realizations, and examples of phonemic change. Since in the area of phonology no one dialect feature proves unique in the Spanish-speaking world, it would be of interest to compare this data with documented occurrences of such forms in other areas. Since specification of Southwest Spanish must rely upon documentation of cooccurrence patterns of various phonological phenomena, I encourage studies linking research on individual phonemes, their realizations, and cooccurrence with other phenomena in the same dialect (or register). Such research might serve as a model for future attempts at delineating Southwest Spanish.

In addition to reviewing and restructuring previously documented data, I recommend that linguists concentrate on border linguistics, as well as on the varieties found in northern Mexico. Rather than a strict frontier, I suspect that even though Sonorans, for instance, may not be bilingual, or as bilingual as Texans, New Mexicans or Arizonans, their Spanish still retains much in common with that of the American Borderlands. Let us not commit the error of defining linguistic variation within the confines of political borders. Once we have at our disposal an accessible reference list of phonological features already documented in Southwest Spanish, we can proceed to the next step: a chart demonstrating the interaction of certain sociolinguistic correlates with linguistic data. For instance, does a speaker who aspirates /p/ also aspirate /t/ in certain, or all, environments? Is there any correlation between the aspiration of voiceless stops and the use of /v/? In addition, are there sociolinguistic correlates which prove significant once an individual's ideolect has been determined?

APPLICATION OF RESEARCH

In addition to the previously mentioned scholarly concerns in the study of linguistic variation, we, as investigators, must be aware of the applications of our research. Rather than ignoring possible implications of our findings, we must face up to the fact that we may be in the public limelight. With this in mind, we should attempt to predetermine our goals, both theoretical and practical. Aguirre (1978) notes that "the academic cannot proceed with his research program without the special knowledge of members of the group to be studied and their unique perceptions of the conditions in which they live" (p. 96). He suggests a cooperative approach linking the scholar's intellectual aims to the communities' practical needs, achieved "by involving the users of language in the scholarly process, not only as the objects of research and planning but as participants in those activities that are normally considered to lie within the province of the trained professional" (p. 96).

What we now need is to consolidate our ideas and methodologies so that we may begin to seek out a definitive, structured picture of linguistic variation, its regularity and its diversity, quantitatively identifiable through factors such as social stratification, educational level, sex, age, and other important intra- and extra-linguistic factors. Teachers must be aware of the wide-scale variability of the linguistic features in the Spanish of the Southwest. A thorough knowledge of sociolinguistic theory and its implications proves more useful than the recording of isolated oddities in the speech of Southwest Spanish speakers.

I propose, then, a thorough reexamination of our academic and practical goals and a revamping of our methods and priorities, so that we can begin to relate details about linguistic realities to the concept of the speech community, which is both the object and the participant in our important search for a more complete picture of Spanish and Spanish/English bilingualism in the Southwest. Approaches to research addressing bilingual interference and substandard dialects should be abandoned in order to make way for more complete treatment of the full verbal repertoire of the Southwest Spanish–speaking community.

APPENDIX 1: PHONOLOGY OF SOUTHWEST SPANISH

Phoneme	Allophones	Common Distributions	Examples
/p/	[p]	all positions	*papá, pero*
	[pʰ]	before /i/	*pienso, pior*
/t/	[t]	all positions	*toro, foto, fruta*
	[tʰ]	before /i/	*tiempo*
/k/	[k]	all positions	*vaca, corre, pescado*
	[kʰ]	before /i/	*quien*
/b/	[b]	after juncture and nasal	*vaca, ambos*
	[β]	elsewhere	*recibo, pobre, el vino*
	[v]	free variation, except word interior nasal	all but *hombre, tumba*
/d/	[d]	after juncture and nasal	*doce, anda*
	[ð]	elsewhere	*boda, jugo de naranja*
	[ð]	elsewhere	
	[φ]	esp. past participle	*hablado, gustado*
/g/	[g]	after juncture and nasal	*engañar, un guía*
	[g]	elsewhere	*jugo, me gusta*
	[φ]	before /w/	*agua, saguaro*
/č/	[č]	free variation	*muchacho, pecho, chile*
	[š]	free variation	
/y/	[y]	free variation	
	[j]	free variation	*silla, yerba, llego*
	[φ]	free variation	
/f/	[f]	all positions	*jefe, grifo, foto*
	[h]	before /w/	*fui, fue*
/s/	[s]	before vowel and voiceless consonant	*dice, sol, este*
	[z]	before voiced consonant	*mismo, desde*
	[h]	syllable final and before /r/	
	[ç]	syllable final and before /r/	*los rayos, las raices, esta*
	[φ]	syllable final and before /r/; when context is clear	
/x/	[x]	free variation	*jefe, flojo, proteger*
	[h]	free variation	
/m/	[m]	before vowel and bilabial consonant	*fama, hombre*
/n/	[n]	all positions except below	*vino, pienso*
	[n̪]	before dental consonant	*treinta, mundo*
	[ŋ]	before velar consonant	*naranja, engañar*
/ñ/	[ñ]	intervocalic	*niño, acompañar*
/l/	[l]	all positions	*loco, lento*
	[l]	see example	*sol*
	[ɫ]	syllable final	*talco, vuelta*
/r/	[ɾ]	before vowel	*toro, paro, pobre*
	[r]	all positions (English influence)	
	[r̄]	as infinitive ending	*correr, parar, llegar*
	[r̄]	as infinitive ending	
/rr/	[rr]	before vowel, word initial	*perro, burro, ropa*
	[r̄]	before vowel, word initial	

APPENDIX 2: ATTESTED PHONOLOGICAL PROCESSES

Examples of Metathesis

/u/	ciudad-cuidad
/r/	pobre-probe
/g/	estómago-estógamo
/n/	váyanse-váyasen
/i/	nadie-naide
/m/	hudamera-humadera
/d/	modorro-morrodo

Examples of Epenthesis

gn-n	ignorante-inorante
ni-n	demonio-demono

Consonant Substitution

b-g	bueno-güeno
b-x	boato-juato
b-m	bermejo-mermejo
d-l	datil-latir
f-x	fui-jui
g-b	gorrión-borrión
b-f	calibre-califre
b-p	súbito-súpito
n-d	nomás-domás
n-l	nos-los
n-ñ	nudo-ñudo
k-g	cogote-gogote
x-f	juéz-fuéz
x-g	girafa-guirafa
s-ch	sinsonte-chinchone
cl-cr	Clotilde-Crotilde
m-b	demasana-debasana
k-g	traficar-trafigar
t-d	rete-rede
d-g	ladrar-lagrar
d-b	Federico-Feberico
d-l	admitir-almitir
d-r	Leonidas-Lionires
g-d	migaja-midaja
l-r	alquilar-arquilar
m-n	tengamos-ténganos
r-l	retórico-retólico
r-s	burla-busla

Deletion of Consonants

d	-ado (past participle), puedo-pueo
g	luego-[lwo]
b	no ha vuelto–[noawelto]
k	lector-letor
l	albricias-abricias
n	constante-costante
m	invierno-ivierno
p	adaptar-adatar
r	mira-mia, pero-peo

Deletion of Vowels

a	traer-trer
e	sonreir-sonrir
i	diario-dario
o	ópalo-opal
u	prueba-prebo

Vowel Substitution

Stressed

a	establo-esteble, paraguas-pariague
e	idéntico-intico (also entico)
o	divorcio-divurcio
u	murmullo-mormollo

Unstressed

a-e	citara-citera
a-i	carnaval-carnival
a-u	machacar-machucar
e-a	ermitano-almitano
e-i	vestido-vistido
e-o	elogio-ologio
i-e	visita-vesita
o-a	ocupar-acupar
e-a	Enrique-Anriques
i-a	Ildifonsa -Aldifonsa, Lifonsa
i-e	Cristina-Crestina
o-u	Romulo-Romolo

Vowel Becomes Consonant

u-b	jaula-jabla

Consonant Becomes Vowel		Strengthening	
k-i	accion-aisión, facción-faisión	*Insertion*	
k-u	carácter-caráuter, activo-autivo	g	vea-veiga, crea-creiga
b-u	absoluto-ausoluto	n	mucho-muncho
p-u	adaptar-adautar	y	caer-cayer, deseo-deseyo
p-i	aceptar-aceitar	*Diphthongization*	
		i	tenga-teinga

REFERENCES

Aguirre, A., Jr. Chicano sociolinguistics. *Bilingual Review,* 1978, 5(1/2), 91–99.

Allen, R., & Chaves, M. Estudio de la /s/ final en el español de Arizona. Paper prepared for class in Spanish in the Southwest, Arizona State University, Florence Barkin, professor, 1980.

Barkin, F. Loanshifts: An example of multilevel interference. In A. Lozano (Ed.), *SWALLOW VII.* Boulder: University of Colorado, 1979.

———. The role of loanword assimilation in gender assignment. *Bilingual Review,* 1981,*8,* 1–13.

Beltramo, A. F. Lexical and morphological aspects of linguistic acculturation. Doctoral diss., Stanford University, 1972. Dissertation Abstracts International, 1973, 33, 4379-4380A.

Bills, G., & Ornstein, J. Linguistic diversity in Southwest Spanish. In J. D. Bowen & J. Ornstein (Eds.), *Studies in Southwest Spanish.* Rowley, Mass.: Newbury House, 1976.

Bowen, J. D. The Spanish of San Antonito, New Mexico. Doctoral diss., University of New Mexico, 1952.

Craddock, J. Lexical analysis of Southwest Spanish. In J. D. Bowen & J. Ornstein (Eds.), *Studies in Southwest Spanish.* Rowley, Mass.: Newbury House, 1976.

———. New World Spanish. Unpublished manuscript, 1977.

Dworkin, S. N. Some sound shifts in New World Spanish and the reentry of phonological rules. Paper given at the Symposium on Hispanic and Luso-Brazilian Linguistics, University of Hawaii, July 1977.

Espinosa, A. M. Studies in New Mexican Spanish. Part 1, Phonology. *Bulletin of the University of New Mexico,* 1909, *1* (Second Language Series), 1–161.

———. Estudios sobre el español de Nuevo Méjico. *Biblioteca de dialectología hispanoamericana. Parte 1: Fonética.* Buenos Aires: University of Buenos Aires, 1930.

Foster, D. W. The phonology of Southwest Spanish. In J. D. Bowen & J. Ornstein (Eds.), *Studies in Southwest Spanish.* Rowley, Mass.: Newbury House, 1976.

Harris, J. W. Morphologization of phonological rules: An example from Chicano Spanish. In L. R. J. Cambell, M. G. Goldin, & M. C. ton Wang (Eds.), *Linguistic studies in Romance languages.* Washington, D.C.: Georgetown University Press, 1974. (a)

——. Two morphophonemic innovations in Chicano Spanish. Unpublished paper distributed by Bloomington, Ind., University Linguistics Club, 1974. (b)

Lope Blanch, J. La sociolingüística y la dialectología hispánica. In F. M. Aid, M. C. Resnick, & B. Saciuk (eds.), *Nineteen-seventy-five colloquium on Hispanic linguistics*. Washington, D.C.: Georgetown University Press, 1976.

Merz, G. Realizations of three English sounds in Tucson Spanish. In F. Barkin & E. Brandt (Eds.), *Speaking, singing and teaching: A multidisciplinary approach to language variation. Proceedings of the Eighth Annual Southwest Areal Languages and Linguistics Workshop.* Anthropological Research Papers, No. 20. Tempe, Ariz.: Arizona State University, 1980.

Phillips, R. N., Jr. *Los Angeles Spanish: A descriptive analysis.* Doctoral diss., University of Wisconsin, 1967.

Post, A. C. *Southern Arizona Spanish phonology.* University of Arizona Bulletin, Humanities Bulletin No. 1, Vol. 5, No. 1. Tucson, Ariz.: University of Arizona, 1934.

Poulter, V. L. Comparison of voiceless stops in the English and Spanish of bilingual natives of Fort Worth–Dallas. In G. G. Gilbert (Ed.), *Texas studies in bilingualism.* Berlin: Walter de Gruyter, 1970.

Resnick, M. *Phonological variants and dialect identification in Latin American Spanish.* The Hague: Mouton, 1975.

Rissel, D. A. The implications of differences in the organization of a lexical domain in Spanish and English. *Bilingual Review,* 1976, *3*(1), 29–35.

Sánchez, R. Nuestra circumstancia lingüística. *El Grito: A Journal of Contemporary Mexican-American Thought,* 1972, *6*(1), 45–74.

Sankoff, G. Dialectology. *Annual Review of Anthropology,* 1973, *2*, 165–77.

Sapir, E. *Language* (2nd ed.). New York: Harcourt, Brace & World, 1921.

Teschner, R. V. Anglicisms in Spanish. A cross-referenced guide to previous findings, together with English lexical influence on Chicago Mexican Spanish. Doctoral diss., University of Wisconsin, 1972.

Teschner, R. V., Bills, G. D., & Craddock, J. R. *Spanish and English of United States Hispanos: A critical, annotated, linguistic bibliography.* Arlington, Va.: Center for Applied Linguistics, 1975.

Tzuzaki, S. M. *English influences on Mexican Spanish in Detroit.* The Hague: Mouton, 1970.

Villarreal-García, J. The regional vocabulary of Brownsville, Texas. In H. H. Key, G. G. McCullough, & J. B. Sawyer (Eds.), *Proceedings of the Sixth Southwest Areal Language and Linguistics Workshop.* Long Beach, Calif.: California State University, 1978.

10 | Syntactic Research in Southwest Varieties of Spanish

MARY BETH FLOYD
Northern Illinois University

Of the several varieties of Spanish identified in the United States, it is generally recognized that the "Southwest" or "Chicano" variety has been investigated most thoroughly (Craddock, 1973; Teschner, Bills, & Craddock, 1975). Despite this acknowledgement, however, it must be noted that until 1967 the syntax of the Southwest variety or varieties of Spanish remained a little-considered phenomenon.

During the past quarter of a century, reviewers of the literature have noted the need for syntactic investigations of not only Southwest Spanish but of U.S. Spanish in general (Woodbridge, 1954; Craddock, 1973; Bills, 1975). In the early literature on Southwest varieties of Spanish, references to syntax in general or even observations of specific syntactic phenomena were very sparse. Significant among the earliest descriptive studies were investigations of the Spanish of New Mexico and southern Colorado by Hills (1906/1938) and Espinosa (1914, 1946). Later studies included Bowen's (1952) comprehensive structuralist study of New Mexico Spanish, Ornstein's (1951) article on southern New Mexico Spanish, Barker's (1950) sociological study of Pachuco, the Tucson, Arizona, caló of the 1940s, and Coltharp's (1965) investigation of a similar argot in south El Paso, Texas.

In these early studies of varieties of Spanish in the Southwest, which spanned some 60 years, allusions to syntax characteristically took the form of occasional observations regarding supposed English influence on apparent Spanish calques (e.g., *tener buen tiempo*), comparisons of a generalizing nature between the "structure" or the "syntax" of one apparent dialect and that of another, or occasional observations regarding a particular isolated syntactic phenomenon. Allusions to syntax in general or to specific syntactic phenomena seemed to be founded on limited personal observation or general impression. Even among those studies considered to be serious descriptive efforts (e.g., Hills, 1938) and among those hailed as the most comprehensive of any existing descriptions of U.S. Spanish (Espinosa, 1946; Bowen, 1952), syntactic descriptions were entirely lacking.

139

While descriptive studies of phonological, morphological, and lexical characteristics of Southwest varieties of Spanish had been reported for over half a century, no thorough analysis and description of the syntax of any single Southwest variety of Spanish had been reported in the literature prior to 1967. Phillips' (1967) investigation of Los Angeles Spanish is considered to mark the first significant descriptive study of syntax of a Southwest variety of Spanish. Since then, that is during the last decade or so, syntactic investigations of Spanish in the Southwest have been forthcoming. It is from the studies of these past few years, then, that needs for future syntactic research in Southwest varieties of Spanish may be formulated.

REGIONAL STUDIES

While the Spanish of certain geographic areas of the Southwest has been studied, that of many other regions remains untouched. It has been noted, for example, that before Phillips' study there was a "veritable poverty" of research on the Spanish of California (Bills, 1975, p. xv). Phillips attempted to describe all levels of Los Angeles Spanish, including syntax, based on data deriving from 31 informants selected for their heterogeneity and intended to be representative of the East Los Angeles Spanish-speaking community. Although this major study for Los Angeles exists, major descriptions of syntactic characteristics of Spanish spoken in other areas of California have not been reported in the literature, to my knowledge.

Texas, particularly south Texas, has received attention from several investigators. Lance (1969) and his assistants undertook an exploratory study of the bilingualism of 11 speakers in Bryan, Texas, 9 of whom represented three generations of one family. Marrocco (1972) attempted a description of all grammatical levels of the Spanish of Corpus Christi based on taped material deriving from interviews and group-speaking situations involving several informants, among them 7 members of one family. Sánchez (1972) described characteristics of Texas Spanish based on written compositions, taped interviews, and personal observations of University of Texas–Austin students. In another study, Sánchez (1974) undertook a generative analysis of the grammar of Southwest Spanish, considered to be a popular dialect, and a standard Mexican dialect, deriving both from one underlying system. Solé (1977) analyzed variants in Texas Spanish in data deriving from questionnaires administered to university students.

Although the Spanish of speakers in New Mexico received much attention in the earliest studies, none of these "classic" investigations, as mentioned earlier, involved syntax. In more recent literature there is little evidence of continuing efforts to describe the Spanish of adult New Mexican speakers.

Although in the early literature southern Colorado was treated as an extension of northern New Mexico, studies of the Colorado region per se have only recently been reported. Ross (1975) attempted a description of all levels of the language, including syntax, based on data deriving from 10 informants from San Luis, the "majority" of whom were farmers or ranchers, over 50 years of age, with a fourth-grade education. In my own study (Floyd, 1976) taped interviews with a subsample of 12 university students who met selectional criteria regarding comprehension of Spanish, residence, and limited exposure to classroom Spanish provided spontaneous and structured data for an investigation of verb usage in relation to the expression of tense, mood, and aspect. Certainly grammatical investigation of Spanish in Colorado has only begun.

While morphosyntactic features of the Spanish of Arizona children have been studied (Martínez-Bernal, 1972), syntactic investigations of the Spanish of adult speakers in Arizona have not been reported in the literature to my knowledge.

Certainly, then, the syntax of adult Spanish speakers in many areas of the Southwest remains almost entirely unrepresented in past research. Even in those cases in which a study of a specific area may exist (e.g., Los Angeles), the Spanish of a larger area (e.g., California), cannot be considered to have been described, regardless of how meritorious or comprehensive any single study may be. A multiplicity of investigations is needed if we are to have a reliable perspective of the variety or varieties of Spanish characteristic of adult speakers in such a large geographic area as the Southwest. With the possible exception of south Texas, multiple investigations have not been carried out for any particular region of the Southwest.

It might be noted, too, that while the Spanish of a few of the large urban areas of the Spanish-speaking Southwest has been studied, namely El Paso and Los Angeles, the Spanish of speakers from many other large urban areas of the Hispanic Southwest has received little attention in the linguistic literature. Certainly the concentration of Spanish-speakers in cities such as San Francisco, Albuquerque, Denver, Phoenix, not to mention San Antonio and other areas within Texas, warrants such investigation and offers an exciting prospect for future researchers.

Not only is there a need for syntactic studies of particular geographic areas; needed as well are studies of a comparative type in which syntactic phenomena are investigated across geographic regions. For example, one might compare findings between different areas on the use of the inflected future as opposed to the periphrastic *ir a* construction, or on the maintenance of the aspectual distinction between preterite and imperfective indicative. Such comparisons could profitably be made within specific areas of the Southwest or perhaps between Chicano speakers in the Southwest and Cubans or Puerto Ricans in other areas of the Spanish-speaking United States. Sorely needed as well are studies which investigate language variation in U.S. Spanish in relation to language variation among Mexican and Latin American speakers of Spanish.

The literature on the Spanish of the Southwest includes a growing number of descriptive studies. The need prevails, however, for much more investigation before we can consider that the syntax of Southwest Spanish has been definitively or adequately described. The research of the last decade can provide many ideas for syntactic topics which warrant further descriptive study. It is suggested, however, that the focus of future descriptive studies be narrowed from that of those earlier investigations. Instead of attempting a comprehensive study of the phonology, the morphology, the syntax, and the lexicon of Arizona Spanish, for example, one might limit the investigation to one level. Within the broad area of syntax, one might limit the focus to a specific area of usage— for example, pronominal usage or certain noun-phrase phenomena. Studies in which particular syntactic areas of interest are isolated, allowing a more in-depth investigation of the grammatical phenomenon in question, could contribute significantly toward our knowledge of Southwest varieties of Spanish.

SOCIOENVIRONMENTAL FACTORS

Coexisting with the need for more descriptive studies is the need for investigations which go beyond the purely descriptive and attempt to offer explanations of language behavior. Inquiry into possible relationships between linguistic features or "variables" of Southwest varieties of Spanish and nonlinguistic realities of speakers' lives offers one such promise of explanation.

Jacob Ornstein, reporting on an ongoing research project (Sociolinguistic Studies on Southwest Bilingualism) undertaken at the University of Texas at El Paso in 1968 and 1969, has long encouraged this type of inquiry for the Spanish-speaking Southwest (Ornstein, 1970, 1971a, 1971b, 1972, 1973, 1974a, 1974b, 1975). On the basis of data deriving from students at the University of Texas at El Paso, most of whom were natives of El Paso, Ornstein has suggested linguistic variables, in some cases syntactic, which warrant attention in future sociolinguistic investigations. Hensey (1973, 1974), undertaking analysis of the El Paso data, identified morphosyntactic features considered to be the most common "deviations" from standard Spanish as grammatical "variables" deserving of investigation in future sociolinguistic research. Hensey (1976) later hypothesized that such features were actually sociologically conditioned variables.

One might consider that the notion of geographic area represents an indirect index of socioenvironmental factors which may be more related to language variation than is the general notion of geography alone. For example, degree of Spanish-language maintenance, proximity to the influence of Mexico and

Mexican monolingual speakers, concentration of Spanish-speakers in a particular area, and patterns of out- and in-migration are only some of the many factors which may relate to the Spanish of speakers in the Southwest and may account in some meaningful way for language variation. Systematic and thorough investigations of possible relationships between nonlinguistic factors and syntactic features characteristic of speakers in the Southwest remain rare, if they exist at all in the literature.

A survey of existing studies of Spanish-language maintenance and language loyalty among speakers in the Southwest suggests certain extralinguistic factors which warrant future investigation in relation to language data. Studies of language maintenance in rural and urban south Texas (Skrabanek, 1970), in Austin, Texas (Thompson, 1974), and in urban Los Angeles (López, 1978), for example, have shown a relationship between maintenance of Spanish and the factor of residence in an urban, as opposed to a rural, community. Rarely, however, has this factor or complex of factors been analyzed with specific respect to language structure. Brisk's (1972) observations regarding differences between surface structures in the Spanish of 5 rural children and 2 urban children in New Mexico is an exception. Other factors, such as generation, degree of language use in the home, or language loyalty within the family or community might be expected to bear some relationship to language structure. Investigations of language maintenance and loyalty among speakers in the Southwest have indicated a relationship between maintenance of Spanish and the factor of age (Skrabanek, 1970; Thompson, 1974). The factor of generation has been seen to bear significantly on maintenance of Spanish among speakers in the Southwest. Studies by Thompson for Austin, Texas, by Ortiz (1975) for northern New Mexico, and by López (1978) for Los Angeles have reported differences in language maintenance by generation. Ethnic identity has been suggested as a factor which may relate to differential language maintenance among various groups of Spanish-speakers in the United States (Solé, 1979).

Recently attempts have been made to relate such factors as these to actual Spanish-language proficiency. Hudson-Edwards and Bills (1980) investigated the relationship between self-reported proficiency in Spanish and English among speakers in 55 Chicano households in Martineztown, New Mexico, in relation to informants' ages, composition of household, and generation. In a recent study I explored the relationship between the socioenvironmental factors of age, years of formal study of Spanish, parental use of Spanish in the home, and region of Colorado and young, bilingual, Colorado Spanish-speakers' use of Spanish at home, Spanish listening comprehension, and self-report of Spanish language skills (this volume, "Spanish-Language Maintenance in Colorado"). Although attempts to relate language data from Southwest Spanish to nonlinguistic factors have thus begun, sociolinguistic studies in which actual syntactic data are analyzed vis-à-vis factors such as those mentioned above have not yet appeared in the literature on Southwest Spanish, to my knowledge.

One comment might be made at this point with respect to those data-based investigations of the past 10 years or so which constitute the bulk of the work to date on the syntax of Southwest varieties of Spanish. A significant number of the descriptive studies have resulted from doctoral dissertations by graduate students. The comprehensive and descriptive nature of these studies probably precluded the possibility of investigation of nonlinguistic factors in relation to language data. Nevertheless, the descriptive work which has been undertaken to date provides suggestions regarding linguistic variables which might profitably be investigated for possible relationship to extralinguistic realities. For example, in the area of verb syntax, linguistic variables such as the use of the morphological or inflected future or conditional verb forms or the maintenance of subjunctive could be systematically studied in relationship to nonlinguistic factors such as generation, language use in the home, or degree of formal education in Spanish, to name a few.

If one considers that extralinguistic factors might reasonably bear some relationship to varieties of Southwest Spanish, and hence might suggest explanations of language variation within the area of Southwest Spanish, as well as with respect to U.S. Spanish or even American Spanish, it would seem that the future offers boundless possibilities for such sociolinguistic inquiry.

DEVELOPMENTAL STUDIES

With the exception of university-age speakers of Spanish, often studied, perhaps because of the accessibility of such informants for faculty or graduate students involved in research, the only age group of speakers of Spanish in the Southwest which has received any particular attention in the literature is that of preschool or primary-school–age children. Notable among these are syntactic studies of children's Spanish in Texas (González, 1971), New Mexico (Brisk, 1972), Arizona (Martínez-Bernal, 1972), and California (Merino, 1976). González attempted to establish tentative norms for developmental stages of Spanish grammar among Mexican-American children in his study of 27 Texas children representing various age intervals between 2 and 5. Brisk studied the development of the linguistic performance of 7 New Mexican 5-year-old children, 2 from urban Albuquerque and 5 from a nearby rural area. Martínez-Bernal, analyzing children's percentage of "correct" responses to elicitation items, attempted to measure morphological structures of 26 Mexican-American children in Tucson, Arizona, whose ages ranged from 5 to 8. One developmental study, that by Merino, investigated the acquisition of later-developing syntactic structures among 41 bilingual children, aged 5 to 11, in the San Francisco area. Cohen's (1976) comparative analysis of errors in stories of 45 "bilingually schooled" and 45 "comparison" Mexican-American children also contributes to the literature on children's syntax. While study of the acquisition of Spanish grammar by bilingual children in the Southwest has begun, the number of studies remains limited. The fact that existing studies have been cross-sectional rather than chronological studies and that a relatively small number of children at each age level have provided the data suggests the need for further investigation of the development of Spanish grammar among bilingual children in the Southwest.

So far, primarily children between the ages of 5 and 8—that is, the age at which a child enters school and the early primary-school years—have been studied. However, results of investigations of the development of Spanish grammar among monolingual Spanish-speaking children suggest that later stages of development also need to be investigated. The findings from Kernan and Blount's (1966) study of three groups of children between the ages of 5 and 7, 8 and 10, and 11 and 12, from Jalisco, Mexico, Gili Gaya's (1972) study based on data deriving from Puerto Rican children aged 4 to 7 and others in first and fourth grades, and Echeverría's (1975) syntactic study of the linguistic comprehension of 55 monolingual Chilean children aged 5 to 10 suggest that even for monolingual children in more optimal linguistic circumstances the process of acquisition, and certainly the mastery of syntactic structures, is by no means an accomplished fact even at age 10 or 12. There remains a critical need, then, for studies which investigate later stages of syntactic development of bilingual Spanish-speaking children in the Southwest. The acquisition and development of Spanish grammar among monolingual as well as bilingual children remains a most exciting area of future linguistic investigation.

CONSIDERATIONS OF ENGLISH INFLUENCE

Another area which warrants serious investigation in the future is the question of possible influence of English structure on that of Spanish in a language-contact situation, that is, among bilingual speakers in the Southwest. While assumptions regarding such influence have abounded and continue to prevail, systematic studies of influence have not been reported in the literature until recently. And even now the reported observations are so varied as to preclude any definitive statements on the subject.

Since the early studies of Southwest varieties of Spanish did not examine syntax, it is not surprising that the phenomenon of syntactic influence of English on Spanish drew no particular attention in the early literature. Occasional observations were made regarding "expressions" considered to be direct translations from English (Hills, 1938; Espinosa, 1946; Ornstein, 1951) or regarding the "mixing" of both languages (Trager & Valdez, 1937). With regard to the same dialect area (i.e., New Mexico), observations regarding grammatical influence of English on Spanish varied; such influence was considered by Hills to be very sparse, while Espinosa considered that it was of very great importance and deserving of further study. Assumptions regarding the apparent influence of English on Spanish were made without systematic investigation of such grammatical influence.

Only in the past decade or so has the question of the grammatical influence of English on Spanish been viewed somewhat more critically. Several recent studies concerned with the syntax of Southwest varieties of Spanish have treated the notion of grammatical influence peripherally. To the extent that such observations have been made, however, the results cannot be considered to be conclusive. Investigators of both adult speakers of Spanish (Phillips, 1967; Lance, 1969; Ross, 1975) and children (González, 1970; Brisk, 1972) have reported that they observed very little syntactic influence of English on the syntax of Spanish. Other investigators, however, have reported perceptible effects and various types of grammatical influence of English on Spanish (Ayer, 1971; Marrocco, 1972; Sánchez, 1972; Solé, 1977).

Although the phenomenon of linguistic influence of English on Spanish has been the specific focus of some studies (Coltharp, 1965; Beltramo, 1972) in the past two decades, such studies have not treated syntax. And while studies of English influence on the Spanish of migrants in Florida (Riegelhaupt-Barkin, 1976) and Mexican Americans in Chicago (Teschner, 1972) have treated syntax, their focus was not the Spanish of speakers in the Southwest, even though among their informants were individuals who originated from the Southwest. It appears that no major study of Spanish in the Southwest has had as its primary focus the investigation of syntactic influence of English as a result of language contact and bilingualism. Certainly this area seems to represent one in which long-held assumptions regarding linguistic influence might well be tested for specific areas of syntax for not only particular groups of speakers in the Southwest but for Southwest Spanish in general.

The phenomenon commonly referred to as "code switching" is one area of inquiry relating to syntactic influence of English on Spanish which has received increased attention in the recent literature (Lance, 1969; Gumperz & Hernández-Chávez, 1971a, 1971b; Redlinger, 1976; Reyes 1976). Gingràs's (1974) generative analysis of intrasentential code switching and acceptability judgements regarding such sentences elicited from 38 young native California Mexican Americans offered support for the notion that code switching is rule-governed among Spanish/English bilingual speakers. Maintaining that only nonlinguistic variables can offer an explanation of why bilinguals switch languages, Timm (1975) hypothesized five syntactic constraints which operate in Spanish/English code switching, on the basis of analyses of excerpts of code switching from taped conversations and prose of three young Mexican Americans. Valdés-Fallis (1976) differentiated several types of code-switching patterns on the basis of an analysis of the language of a 24-year-old Chicana in New Mexico observed in conversational interaction with individuals and groups of individuals and considered such patterns in relation to factors such as setting, topic, and speaker roles. Jacobson (1977), in his analysis of intra-sentential code switching based on data collected by university graduate students deriving from 33 Mexican-American informants, defined several psychological and sociological sources of code switching in attempting a theory of the phenomenon. Both the syntactic limits and the social functions of code switching are examined within a theoretical framework in Wentz's (1977) dissertation study of Mexican-American bilingual children. It is clear, then, that present interest in code switching goes beyond the purely linguistic phenomenon: The social functions of code switching as well as its relationship to social factors continue to be studied. This area of inquiry is one which has captured the imagination of many investigators of Southwest varieties of Spanish and seems likely to remain a viable area of investigation in future research.

SUMMARY

The syntactic literature reveals much variability in the Spanish of speakers in the Southwest. Unfortunately the literature does not fully describe the extent of this variability, nor does it show serious efforts to explain the variability which has been described. While syntactic studies have been undertaken for some areas of the Southwest, there remains a great need for future inquiry. Little or no attention has been paid to syntactic study of many regions of the Spanish-speaking Southwest. And for those areas which have received attention, further study is needed to supplement and clarify the existing literature. Syntactic studies of Southwest varieties of Spanish have generally dealt with the Spanish of one particular area. There exists a serious need in future research to interrelate findings from discrete areas within the Spanish-speaking Southwest. Future researchers might also consider comparative investigations of specific syntactic phenomena not only within various areas of the Southwest, but between the Southwest and other areas of the Spanish-speaking United States. Of great interest would be comparisons between the Spanish of speakers in the Southwest and that of Puerto Rican or Cuban bilinguals in other areas of the United States. A review of past and present investigations of the syntax of Puerto Rican and Cuban speakers of U.S. Spanish would contribute greatly toward stimulating such comparative studies.

There is no doubt that the notion of language variation is an important one with respect to investigation of Spanish in the Southwest. I would suggest, however, that we not allow our efforts to determine the differences which prevail between varieties of Spanish in the Southwest to obscure the need to investigate with equal enthusiasm the commonalities which underlie apparent language varieties. If we are to continue to talk about "Southwest Spanish" or "Chicano Spanish" as a linguistic variety defined by certain characteristics distinct from other varieties of U.S. or American Spanish, we must have a clear understanding of the characteristics that are common to speakers of Spanish in the Southwest, in contrast to the features of other varieties of U.S. and American Spanish—if, in fact, such unique characteristics exist.

Beyond these purely descriptive aims, however, we must begin to seek explanation of the variability which is seen between the language of particular areas or groups of Spanish-speakers in the Southwest. One means to that end is the investigation of extralinguistic factors which may bear a systematic relationship to language variability within Southwest varieties of Spanish. Factors such as age, generation, language loyalty, language development, and ethnic identity might be found to be intimately related to syntactic variation in Southwest varieties of Spanish. Such relationships cannot be assumed; they must be studied before any definitive conclusions can be drawn.

Any type of investigation which involves relationships and explanation will undoubtedly require greater rigor and attention to the reliability and validity of research methodologies by which we study language phenomena. The identification of sound methodological approaches to the study of language in general would benefit our inquiry into the syntax of Southwest varieties of Spanish and may even be considered a major area of needed research at this time.

There exists the need not only for continued investigation of early stages of the language-acquisition process but also for investigation of later stages of syntactic development of Spanish grammar among Spanish-speaking children, both monolingual and bilingual.

Still another research priority should be the systematic and thoughtful investigation of the notion of syntactic influence among bilingual speakers in circumstances of language contact in the United States. By investigating specific areas of presumed syntactic influence, we can begin to test assumptions regarding linguistic interference or influence in situations of Spanish/English bilingualism in the United States.

Serious concern with regard to the present state of syntactic research on U.S. varieties of Spanish, voiced recently by Bills (1979), relates to the relative lack of consideration for theoretical issues in the present syntactic literature. The need for investigations which operate from a theoretical framework or base has been recognized. A closer rapprochement between general linguistic inquiry and areal linguistic study of Spanish in the Southwest, in which regional studies would not only draw from the contributions of general linguistic inquiry but would also contribute and relate to the larger field of general linguistics, could have positive consequences both for the study of language in general and for the investigation of regional or areal linguistics as well. As we know, the approach to language study can take many forms, from the purely descriptive to the sociological, with concern for language loyalty, language maintenance, language attitudes, or to the sociolinguistic, seeking to understand relationships between linguistic and nonlinguistic realities. One might see in the American Southwest a microcosm of language-contact situations, a veritable laboratory in which the study of bilingualism, language contact, language variation, and language change can be studied. Those interested in theoretical aspects of language behavior can seek ways in which to test theoretical notions regarding, for example, language acquisition, language variability, language change, and language universals. While the potential for such inquiry has been recognized by some, it has yet to be developed.

Finally, one very important research goal should be the investigation and determination of how both the variable and the invariable—that is, the differences and the commonalities between and among Southwest varieties of Spanish—relate to features of other Spanish varieties in the Americas. That we recognize the need to interrelate our own observations with those of investigations of Mexican, Central, and Latin American Spanish is of primary importance if we are to maintain a larger linguistic perspective than our particular areal concern for the Southwest.

REFERENCES

Ayer, G. W. Language and attitudes of the Spanish-speaking youth of the southwestern United States. In G. E. Perren & J. L. M. Trim (Eds.), *Applications of linguistics.* Cambridge, England: Cambridge University Press, 1971.

Barker, G. C. *Pachuco: An American-Spanish argot and its social function in Tucson, Arizona.* Tucson: University of Arizona Press, 1950.

Beltramo, A. F. Lexical and morphological aspects of linguistic acculturation by Mexican Americans in San Jose, California. Doctoral diss., Stanford University, 1972. *Dissertation Abstracts International,* 1973, *33,* 4379A–4380A. (University Microfilms No. 73-4465)

Bills, G. D. Linguistic research on U.S. Hispanos: State of the art. In R. V. Teschner, G. D. Bills, & J. R. Craddock (Eds.), *Spanish and English of United States Hispanos: A critical, annotated, linguistic bibliography.* Arlington, Va.: Center for Applied Linguistics, 1975.

——. The study of the Spanish language in the United States: The state of the art. Keynote address, Sixth Annual Colloquium on Hispanic Linguistics, Adelphi University, July 1979.

Bowen, J. D. The Spanish of San Antoñito, New Mexico. Doctoral diss., University of New Mexico, 1952.

Brisk, M. E. The Spanish syntax of the pre-school Spanish American: The case of New Mexican five-year-old children. Doctoral diss., University of New Mexico, 1972. *Dissertation Abstracts International,* 1973, *34,* 297A. (University Microfilms No. 73-16,585)

Cohen, A. D. The English and Spanish grammar of Chicano primary school students. In J. D. Bowen & J. Ornstein (Eds.), *Studies in Southwest Spanish*. Rowley, Mass.: Newbury House, 1976.

Coltharp, L. *The tongue of the Tirilones: A linguistic study of a criminal argot*. University, Ala.: University of Alabama Press, 1965.

Craddock, J. R. Spanish in North America. In T. A. Sebeok (Ed.), *Current trends in linguistics* (Vol. 10). The Hague: Mouton, 1973.

Echeverría, M. S. Late stages in the acquisition of Spanish syntax. Doctoral diss., University of Washington, 1975. *Dissertation Abstracts International*, 1976, *37*, 942A. (University Microfilms No. 76-17, 457)

Espinosa, A. M. Studies in New Mexican Spanish. Part 3: The English elements. *Revue de dialectologie romane*, 1914, *6*(3/4), 241–317.

——. Estudios sobre el español de Nuevo Méjico. Parte II: Morfología (A. Rosenblat, trans.). *Biblioteca de dialectología hispanoamericana* (Vol. 2). Buenos Aires: University of Buenos Aires, 1946.

Floyd, M. B. Verb usage and language variation in Colorado Spanish. Doctoral diss., University of Colorado, 1976. *Dissertation Abstracts International*, 1977, *37*, 5092A. (University Microfilms No. 77-3182)

Gili Gaya, S. *Estudios de lenguaje infantil*. Barcelona: Bibliograf, 1972.

Gingràs, R. C. Problems in the description of Spanish-English intrasentential code-switching. In G. D. Bills (Ed.), *Southwest areal linguistics*. San Diego: Institute for Cultural Pluralism, 1974.

González, G. The acquisition of Spanish grammar by native Spanish speakers. Doctoral diss., University of Texas at Austin, 1970. *Dissertation Abstracts International*, 1971, *31*, 6033A. (University Microfilms No. 71-11,540)

Gumperz, J. J., & Hernández-Chávez, E. Bilingualism, bidialectalism, and classroom interaction. In J. J. Gumperz (Ed.), *Language in social groups*. Stanford, Calif.: Stanford University Press, 1971. (a)

——. Cognitive aspects of bilingual communication. In W. H. Whiteley (Ed.), *Language use and social change*. London, England: Oxford University Press, 1971. (b)

Hensey, F. Grammatical variables in southwestern American Spanish. *Linguistics*, 1973, *108*, 5–26.

——. Two current trends in sociolinguistic research. In B. L. Hoffer & J. Ornstein (Eds.), *Sociolinguistics in the Southwest*. San Antonio, Tex.: Trinity University, 1974.

——. Toward a grammatical analysis of Southwest Spanish. In J. D. Bowen & J. Ornstein (Eds.), *Studies in Southwest Spanish*. Rowley, Mass.: Newbury House, 1976.

Hills, E. C. El español de Nuevo Méjico (P. Henríquez-Ureña, trans. and rev.). In P. Henríquez-Ureña (Ed.), *El español en Méjico, los Estados Unidos y la América Central*. Biblioteca de dialectología hispanoamericana (Vol. 4). Buenos Aires: University of Buenos Aires, 1938. (Originally published, 1906)

Hudson-Edwards, A., & Bills, G. D. Intergenerational language shift in an Albuquerque barrio. In E. L. Blansitt, Jr., & R. V. Teschner (Eds.), *A Festschrift for Jacob Ornstein*. Rowley, Mass.: Newbury House, 1980.

Jacobson, R. The social implications of intrasentential code-switching. *New Scholar,* 1977, *6,* 227–56.

Kernan, K. T., & Blount, B. G. The acquisition of Spanish grammar by Mexican children. *Anthropological Linguistics,* 1966, *8*(9), 1–14.

Lance, D. M. *A brief study of Spanish-English bilingualism.* Final Report, Research Project ORR-Liberal Arts 15504. College Station, Tex.: Texas A & M University, 1969.

López, D. E. Chicano language loyalty in an urban setting. *Sociology and Social Research,* 1978, *62,* 267–78.

Marrocco, M. A. The Spanish of Corpus Christi, Texas. Doctoral diss., University of Illinois at Champaign-Urbana, 1972. *Dissertation Abstracts International,* 1973, *34,* 751A–752A. (University Microfilms No. 73-17,312)

Martínez-Bernal, J. A. Children's acquisition of Spanish and English morphological systems and noun phrases. Doctoral diss., Georgetown University, 1972. *Dissertation Abstracts International,* 1973, *33,* 3619A–3620A. (University Microfilms No. 72-34,186)

Merino, B. J. Language acquisition in bilingual children: Aspects of syntactic development in English and Spanish by Chicano children in grades K–4. Doctoral diss., Stanford University, 1976. *Dissertation Abstracts International,* 1977, *37,* 6319A–6320. (University Microfilms No. 77-7132)

Ornstein, J. The archaic and the modern in the Spanish of New Mexico. *Hispania,* 1951, *34,* 137–41.

———. Sociolinguistics and new perspectives in the study of Southwest Spanish. In R. W. Ewton, Jr., & J. Ornstein (Eds.), *Studies in language and linguistics.* El Paso, Tex.: Texas Western Press, 1970.

———. Language varieties along the U.S.–Mexican border. In G. E. Perren & J. L. M. Trim (Eds.), *Applications of linguistics.* Cambridge, England: Cambridge University Press, 1971. (a)

———. Sociolinguistic research on language diversity in the American Southwest and its educational implications. *The Modern Language Journal,* 1971, *55,* 223–29. (b)

———. Toward a classification of Southwest Spanish nonstandard variants. *Linguistics,* 1972, *93,* 70–87.

———. Toward an inventory of interdisciplinary tasks in research on U.S. Southwest bilingualism/biculturalism. In P. R. Turner (Ed.), *Bilingualism in the Southwest.* Tucson: University of Arizona Press, 1973.

———. Mexican-American sociolinguistics: A well-kept scholarly and public secret. In B. L. Hoffer & J. Ornstein (Eds.), *Sociolinguistics in the Southwest.* San Antonio, Tex.: Trinity University, 1974. (a)

———. The sociolinguistic studies on Southwest bilingualism: A status report. In G. D. Bills (Ed.), *Southwest areal linguistics.* San Diego, Calif.: Institute for Cultural Pluralism, 1974. (b)

———. Sociolinguistics and the study of Spanish and English language varieties and their use in the U.S. Southwest. In J. Ornstein (Ed.), *Three essays on linguistic diversity in the Spanish-speaking world.* The Hague: Mouton, 1975.

Ortiz, L. I. A sociolinguistic study of language maintenance in the northern New

Mexico community of Arroyo Seco. Doctoral diss., University of New Mexico, 1975. *Dissertation Abstracts International,* 1976, *37,* 2159A. (University Microfilms No. 76-22,156)

Phillips, R. N., Jr. Los Angeles Spanish: A descriptive analysis. Doctoral diss., University of Wisconsin, 1967. *Dissertation Abstracts International,* 1968, *28,* 2667A. (University Microfilms No. 67-10,644)

Redlinger, W. E. A description of transference and code-switching in Mexican-American English and Spanish. In G. Keller, R. V. Teschner, & S. Viera (Eds.), *Bilingualism in the bicentennial and beyond.* Jamaica, N.Y.: Bilingual Press, 1976.

Reyes, R. Language mixing in Chicano bilingual speech. In J. D. Bowen & J. Ornstein (Eds.), *Studies in Southwest Spanish.* Rowley, Mass.: Newbury House, 1976.

Riegelhaupt-Barkin, F. The influence of English on the Spanish of bilingual Mexican American migrants in Florida. Doctoral diss., University of New York at Buffalo, 1976. *Dissertation Abstracts International,* 1976, *37,* 2834A-2835A. (University Microfilms No. 76-26,502)

Ross, L. R. La lengua castellana en San Luis, Colorado. Doctoral diss., University of Colorado, 1975. *Dissertation Abstracts International,* 1976, *36,* 5264A-5265A. (University Microfilms No. 76-3947)

Sánchez, R. Nuestra circunstancia lingüística. *El Grito,* 1972, *6*(1), 45–74.

———. A generative study of two Spanish dialects. Doctoral diss., University of Texas at Austin, 1974. *Dissertation Abstracts International,* 1974, *35,* 2971A. (University Microfilms No. 74-24,930)

Skrabanek, R. L. Language maintenance among Mexican-Americans. *International Journal of Comparative Sociology,* 1970, *11,* 272–82.

Solé, Y. R. Continuidad/descontinuidad idiomática en el español tejano. *Bilingual Review / La Revista Bilingüe,* 1977, *4,* 189–99.

———. Hispanic organizational interest in language maintenance. *Journal of the Linguistic Association of the Southwest,* 1979, *3,* 90–102.

Teschner, R. V. Anglicisms in Spanish: A cross-referenced guide to previous findings, together with English lexical influence of Chicago Mexican Spanish. Doctoral diss., University of Wisconsin, 1972. *Dissertation Abstracts International,* 1973, *33,* 3625A. (University Microfilms No. 72-23,339)

Teschner, R. V., Bills, G. D., & Craddock, J. R. (Eds.). *Spanish and English of United States Hispanos: A critical, annotated, linguistic bibliography.* Arlington, Va.: Center for Applied Linguistics, 1975.

Thompson, R. M. The 1970 U.S. Census and Mexican American language loyalty: A case study. In G. D. Bills (Ed.), *Southwest areal linguistics.* San Diego: Institute for Cultural Pluralism, 1974.

Timm, L. A. Spanish-English code-switching: El porqué y how-not-to. *Romance Philology,* 1975, *28,* 473–82.

Trager, G. L., & Valdez, G. English loans in Colorado Spanish. *American Speech,* 1937, *12,* 34–44.

Valdés-Fallis, G. Social interaction and code-switching patterns: A case study of Spanish/English alternation. In G. Keller, R. V. Teschner, & S. Viera (Eds.),

Bilingualism in the bicentennial and beyond. Jamaica, N.Y.: Bilingual Press, 1976.

Wentz, J. P. Some considerations in the development of a syntactic description of code-switching. Doctoral diss., University of Illinois at Champaign-Urbana, 1977. *Dissertation Abstracts International,* 1978, *38,* 6104A. (University Microfilms No. 7804192)

Woodbridge, H. C. Spanish in the American South and Southwest: A bibliographical survey for 1940–1953. *Orbis,* 1954, *3*(1), 236–44.

11 | The Phoneme /ch/ in the Spanish of Tomé, New Mexico

JUNE A. JARAMILLO and GARLAND D. BILLS
University of New Mexico

In recent years a sociological and educational awakening has been taking place with regard to the Spanish language spoken in the Southwest region of the United States. Descriptive linguistic research has, quite understandably, failed to provide the basic knowledge required of this more general awareness. The distinctive New Mexican Spanish dialect, spoken by the Hispanic inhabitants of southern Colorado and the northern two-thirds of New Mexico, has been the primary subject of Southwest Spanish linguistic study for over 70 years, beginning with the important early works of Hills (1906) and Espinosa (1909) and continuing through such salient contributions as Rael (1937) and Bowen (1952). Unfortunately, most substantive linguistic studies of New Mexican Spanish have been oriented toward describing a linguistic relic. Few have examined this dialect as a living sociological phenomenon. In an attempt to provide a modest contribution to our knowledge of New Mexican Spanish as a societally complex system of communication constantly in the process of change, this paper explores a single aspect of the phonology of this dialect, the phoneme /ch/, as used in a single community, Tomé, New Mexico.

Tomé is a rural community of approximately 1,500 inhabitants located 26 miles south of Albuquerque in the Rio Abajo (the lower Rio Grande valley of this area). It is a long-established Spanish-speaking community founded in the mid-1660s by one of the earliest groups of Spanish colonists in the region. Tomé has remained a culturally and linguistically homogeneous community for 300 years. Today virtually all of the inhabitants are speakers of Spanish, and a number have no functional command of English. Tomé now appears, however, to be experiencing a period of transition, with today's younger generation exhibiting more and more formal education, greater mobility, and diverse lifestyles.

The data reported here are based on interviews with 36 Spanish-speaking residents of Tomé. All were born and raised in the community or had moved there from another rural area in the vicinity by age 15 to 20. Each subject claimed, to the best of her or his knowledge, to be a descendant of one of the founding families that settled the Rio Abajo. The speakers were specifically selected to provide balanced representation by sex and age: 18 males and 18 females, equally divided among three adult age groups of 12 subjects each. Other relevant information solicited from each speaker included place of birth, changes of residence, occupation, education, and amount of formal instruction in Spanish.

The interviews were of the "free-conversation" type, but the interview situation was sufficiently structured to elicit speech of roughly the same style—generally "semiformal"—from all consultants. The interviews were conducted in the subjects' homes by the principal author, then a 23-year-old nonresident native of Tomé, with the assistance of a 45-year-old woman who was a closer acquaintance of all of the subjects. The conversation was only loosely guided by the interviewers through a range of informal to semiformal topics. Topics of discussion varied from concrete subjects, such as day-to-day living, to topics of intermediate abstraction, such as the comparison of the present to life in the past, and finally to topics of greater abstraction, such as the significance of bilingual education, the use of astronomical principles in sheep-grazing, and the role of religion in one's life. The consultants were told that the purpose of the interviews was to collect information on different cultural manifestations in Tomé. They were not informed that their speech was of primary interest, and no attempt was made to specifically elicit examples of /ch/. All interviews were recorded on a high-quality cassette tape recorder, with recording time ranging from an hour to an hour and a half per interview.

THE PROBLEM

Phonological descriptions of Standard Spanish (e.g., Bull, 1965, p. 60; Navarro Tomás, 1963, pp. 125–127) typically point out that the phoneme /ch/, which occurs only in syllable-initial position except in rare borrowings, is invariantly realized as a voiceless palatal affricate [ch]. It is often noted, however, that a voiceless palatal groove fricative [sh] occurs as an additional allophone of /ch/ in varied regional varieties of Spanish, in Spain (Lapesa, 1959, p. 328) as well as in the New World, particularly in the Caribbean area (Dalbor, 1969, p. 87). This [sh] is also a notable feature of the Spanish of the Southwest. Though not noted in such basic studies as Phillips (1967), Post (1932), and Poulter (1973), its frequent occurrence is widely reported from Texas (e.g., Elías-Olivares, 1976, p. 6) to California (e.g., Lastra de Suárez, 1975, p. 63).

In the Spanish of New Mexico, the fricative allophone [sh] is widely, though not universally, used. Early in this century, Espinosa (1909) noted that the use of [sh] "seems to be limited to the districts south of Albuquerque" (p. 101). A similar statement is provided by Duncan (1956): "El foco de este fenómeno parece estar en la cuenca del Río Grande al sur de Albuquerque, pero se encuentra también en algunos lugares apartados y remotos. En Albuquerque no se da con frecuencia, mientras que en Belén, unas 34 millas al sur, los niños no hablan de otro modo" (p. 228). In the speech of Tomé, just a few miles upriver from Belén, the [sh] allophone of /ch/ occurs frequently, but not in the categorical fashion implied by Duncan. Indeed, the fricative and affricate allophones are about equally prominent in the data collected for our study. Of 3,126 clear instances of /ch/ in the corpus, 1,320 (42.4%) were realized as [sh].

Explanations of the occurrence of the two allophones of /ch/ are diverse and usually vague. Many studies (e.g., Dalbor, 1969, p. 87; González, 1969, p. 4) avoid the issue of explanation in simply making the observation that [ch] and [sh] are in free variation, but others have attempted to relate this variability to conditioning factors, both linguistic and nonlinguistic. Hernández-Chávez and his coauthors (1975, p. xviii), for example, report that [sh] occurs most commonly when /ch/ precedes a front vowel. Espinosa (1909, p. 101) and Bowen (1952, p. 25) both assert that rapid articulation is related to the realization of /ch/ as [sh]. Bowen also notes, however, that in an area of New Mexico not too distant from Tomé, the use of [sh] is primarily characteristic of the speech of the young.

The purpose of this paper is to explore some of the possible explanations for variation in the realization of /ch/. The observations of others indicate that there are three principal factors that might be related to the choice of one allophone or the other: phonological, contextual, and sociological factors. We will consider in order each of these broad areas of explanation.

Phonological Factors

An examination of many aspects of the phonological environment yielded only one conditioning factor of importance: /ch/ is always realized as the affricate [ch] following a nasal or lateral consonant (e.g., *en chorros, planchar, el chile, colcha*). Of the 1,149 instances of /ch/ in this environment, there was not a single [sh] pronunciation. This restriction appears to be a part of the more general rule of Spanish that permits only the stop variant of /d/ after nasals and laterals and of /b/ and /g/ after nasals. It is surprising that this unsurprising manifestation of homorganic assimilation has not, to our knowledge, been previously noted. Cedergren (1973, p. 68) finds that the [ch] variant is more frequent after consonants than after vowels in Panamanian Spanish, but she does not report on the effects of different consonants or consonant classes. In the Tomé data, there is no significant difference in the variability of /ch/ after a vowel (66.4% [sh]) and after a consonant other than a nasal or lateral (68.3% [sh]).

Hernández-Chávez and his coworkers, as noted above, state that a following front vowel favors the fricative variant. A preliminary investigation of the potential influence of adjacent vowels in the Tomé data revealed no significant variation related to the type of vowel either preceding or following /ch/.

In Tomé, a preceding nasal or lateral accounts for some of the allophonic variation of /ch/, but there remains a great amount of variation that apparently cannot be attributed to the influence of the phonological environment. Eliminating the postnasal and postlateral instances of /ch/, we are left with 1,977 cases, of which 1,320 (66.8%) are realized as the fricative variant [sh]. The remainder of this paper will be limited to a consideration of variation in environments other than following a nasal or lateral.

Contextual Factors

A preliminary examination of a portion of the data was carried out to ascertain the importance of two contextual factors, speed of utterance and topic of conversation. Both Espinosa (1909) and Bowen (1952) propose that the realization of /ch/ is related to utterance speed, namely, that [sh] occurs only in rapid speech. In the Tomé corpus, however, rapidity of articulation appears to have no discernible effect on the realization of /ch/.

The formality level of the topic of discussion also is often an important contextual variable. Cedergren (1973), for example, shows its significance with regard to /ch/, though she finds, to our surprise, that the [sh] variant "is seen to increase in those conversational topics that are more formal in context" (p. 70). Nonetheless, the Tomé data reveal no strong correlation between the variant realizations of /ch/ and formality shifts in subject matter (for example, the subject of the preparation of healing herbal teas as opposed to that of the importance of bilingual education).

It must be noted, however, that the format of the interviews was designed to provide as much consistency as possible in the style of language used in order to maximize cross-subject comparability. No attempt was made to promote contextual differences. Therefore, although no important contextual variation of /ch/ with regard to speed and topic was found in the present corpus, more contextually sensitive elicitation could result in variation. Indeed, considering the variability related to the sociological factors discussed in the next section, contextual variability can certainly be expected to exist in Tomé.

Social Factors

In order to examine the relationship between social factors and allophones of /ch/, the consultants were divided into classes along four scales that were considered to be of potential relevance in this community: age, sex, years of education, and years of formal study of Spanish. As previously noted, the 36 consultants were preselected to provide equal representation by sex: 18 males and 18 females, with 6 of each in 3 age groups. These age groups, 12 consultants in each, were set at ages 17 to 30, 31 to 50, and 51 and above; this predetermined grouping, though somewhat arbitrary, was intended to broadly sample the speech of 3 generations of adult speakers. Groupings for education and formal Spanish study were ad hoc and therefore less balanced. For this grouping, speakers were arbitrarily divided into 3 unequal groups according to the highest year completed in the American school system: zero through sixth grade (5 subjects), seventh through twelfth grades (20 subjects), and postsecondary education (11 subjects). They were also classified into 3 groups in accordance with the number of years of Spanish that they had taken during their formal education: none (14 subjects), 1 year (15), and 2 or more years (7).

Table 11.1 presents, for each of the 36 consultants, the use of [sh] as an allophone of /ch/ in all environments except after a nasal or lateral consonant

Table 11.1:   Use of [sh] by Sex and Age

Age		Females				Males	
		[sh] (%)	[sh] :/ch/ (N)			[sh] (%)	[sh] :/ch/ (N)
17–30	YFH1a	95.7	45 : 47	YMH1a		96.7	58 : 60
	YFH1b	100.0	40 : 40	YMH1b		100.0	57 : 57
	YFC1a	1.6	1 : 63	YMC1a		2.4	1 : 42
	YFC1b	13.8	8 : 58	YMC1b		97.3	36 : 37
	YFC2a	21.3	23 : 108	YMC2a		3.0	1 : 33
	YFC2b	15.6	7 : 45	YMC2b		0.0	0 : 46
Average/Total		34.3	124 : 361			55.6	153 : 275
31–50	AFH0a	88.4	38 : 43	AMH0a		96.3	52 : 54
	AFH0b	96.3	26 : 27	AMH0b		78.4	76 : 97
	AFH0c	81.1	77 : 95	AMH1		100.0	13 : 13
	AFH1a	100.0	22 : 22	AMC1		97.3	36 : 37
	AFH1b	100.0	40 : 40	AMC2a		26.5	27 : 102
	AFH1c	78.6	11 : 14	AMC2b		96.1	73 : 76
Average/Total		88.8	214 : 241			73.1	277 : 379
51 +	EFG0a	87.4	104 : 119	EMG0a		98.9	87 : 88
	EFG0b	79.4	54 : 68	EMG0b		80.0	24 : 30
	EFH0a	100.0	45 : 45	EMG0c		4.8	3 : 62
	EFH0b	100.0	47 : 47	EMH0		96.9	62 : 64
	EFH0c	8.3	4 : 48	EMH1		93.6	44 : 47
	EFH1	100.0	19 : 19	EMH2		70.2	59 : 84
Average/Total		78.9	273 : 346			74.4	279 : 375
General Average/ Grand Total		64.5	611 : 948			68.9	709 : 1029

(and except utterance-initially, a position that yielded too few examples to provide reliability in analysis). The consultants are listed in table 11.1 in a mnemonic code of four symbols representing the speakers' characteristics for the four sociological variables. The initial letter signifies age group: *Y* (mnemonically "young") = age 17 to 30, *A* ("adult") = age 31 to 50, and *E* ("elderly") = age 51 and over. The second letter represents sex: *F* = female and *M* = male. The third signals education: *G* = grade school (up to sixth grade), *H* = junior high or high school, and *C* = some college. The fourth symbol, a number (*0, 1,* or *2*), indicates the number of years of formal study of Spanish. A final *a, b,* or *c* is employed simply to distinguish between otherwise identical code identifications.

SEX

The data on the pronunciation of [sh] by sex are included in table 11.1. Males produce 68.9% [sh], females 64.5%. Although the males in the Tomé sample use a slightly higher percentage of [sh], the difference is too small to be of any significance. The pronunciation of /ch/ does not seem to be a variable related to male/female speech differences (if any) in Tomé society. (What effect the use of female interviewers may have had on these results is, of course, unknown.)

However, if we look at usage by sex within the distinct age groups, we do find significant differences. For example, the young males age 17 to 30 use [sh] considerably more frequently than the young females, 55.6% versus 34.3% (quite similar to the overall results for sex reported by Cedergren, 1973, pp. 71–72). We may also note that the 34.3% [sh] in young female speech is only half of the community norm of 67% [sh]. Could this mean that the [ch] variant is developing as a marker of female speech in Tomé? It is difficult to make such an interpretation, for the pattern is reversed in the speech of the older speakers. Thus, in the 31 to 50 age group the females produce 88.8% [sh] and the males just 73.1%, and in the 51+ group there is a minimal difference of 78.9% [sh] for females and 74.4% for males. The differential use of [sh] by males and females, particularly in the youngest age group, cannot be considered of great importance here; the differences may well be a problem of small sample size in the subgroups.

AGE

Turning to the use of [sh] by age groups without regard to sex, however, we encounter an even more striking differentiation, as indicated in table 11.2. These data reveal that the youngest group of consultants (age 17–30) use [sh] 43.6% of the time, and make the standard realization, [ch], more than half of the time (56.4%), twice as often as the two older age groups (less than 24% combined). This age grading in the differential realization of /ch/ does not

Table 11.2:   Use of [sh] by Age
                  Groups

Age	[sh] (%)	[sh] : /ch/ (N)
17–30	43.6	277 : 636
31–50	79.2	491 : 620
51 +	76.6	552 : 721

hold true between the two older groups in table 11.2. Note, however, in table 11.1, that in the elderly group (51 + years of age) there are two highly atypical speakers, EMG0c and EFH0c, who employ [sh] only 4.8% and 8.3% of the time, respectively. This sharp contrast with the general tendency exhibited by their peers could well be due to the fact that both consultants, a husband-wife pair, are highly literate in Spanish, an achievement attained solely through informal instruction and personal dedication. If we eliminate the data for this aberrant couple, a clear age gradation in the use of the [sh] variant emerges: 44% in the youngest group, 79% in the middle group, and 89% in the oldest group.

These findings suggest that age is an exceedingly important social variable to consider in seeking an explanation for the two realizations of /ch/ in Tomé. We may interpret these results to be an indication of an historical sound change in progress: The once almost categorical use of [sh] seems to be giving way through time to the more standard pronunciation [ch]. The sound-change interpretation is not unreasonable. What is unexpected is that the direction of the change is the opposite of what is generally reported. For example, Elías-Olivares (1976) states that in the Spanish-speaking community of Austin, Texas, "a process of change seems to be in progress in which there is a reduction of [ch] to [sh]" (p. 6). This same direction of change is also posited by Cedergren (1973, p. 79), who found a sharp increase in the use of [sh] by the two youngest of her four age groups of Panamanians (pp. 72–75). Even in New Mexico, only findings contrary to ours have been reported. Bowen (1952) found in a community just 50 miles from Tomé that "the use of [sh] seems to be more a characteristic of the younger than of the older speakers" (p. 25). Duncan (1956) believed the use of [sh] to be a sporadic phenomenon "en el habla de personas menores de veinte años," adding that "en general no se halla sino entre los jóvenes. No he oído un solo caso entre la gente de más de cincuenta años de edad" (p. 228). It must be remembered, however, that Espinosa (1909) noted the occurrence of [sh] in this region 70 years ago. Our interpretation of the direction of sound change does not contradict the historical evidence provided by Espinosa.

EDUCATION

Whether or not we accept the plausibility of this historical-change interpretation of the data, we must ask why there is such a clear trend toward greater use of [ch] by the younger speakers. Amount of education can be expected to provide part of the answer. There is a strong tendency in Tomé, as almost universally, for the younger people to have attained more education. The speaker characteristics summarized in table 11.1, for example, reveal that of the 11 persons with education beyond the secondary level, 8 are members of the youngest age group. Furthermore, all 5 of those having no more than an elementary-school education belong to the oldest age group.

Data on the use of [sh] by the three educational-level groups are provided in table 11.3. As might well be expected, those with exposure to postsecondary education show much less use of [sh], only 33%, the smallest percentage that we have yet seen for any group. Moreover, if we discard the data for three atypical speakers of this highest educational group (YMC1b, AMC1, and AMC2b, table 11.1), the incidence of [sh] falls to just 13.7%. Recall, however, that most of the members of the college group are also members of the youngest age group. Discarding the data for these three atypical speakers results in throwing out 2 of the 3 nonyoung members of the college group. Nevertheless, exposure to college is clearly and significantly correlated with diminished use of [sh]. Even though there is a great overlap between the two groups "young" and "college-educated," the college-educated use much less [sh] (33%) than the young (44%). Indeed, examining solely the speech of the young group. the 8 who have had exposure to college use only 17.8% [sh], while the other 4 use 98% [sh].

Turning now to usage by the other two educational groups, it will be noted, perhaps with surprise, that those with 7 to 12 years of schooling produce more [sh] (87%) than the least educated (74%). This difference is largely attributable to the aberrant behavior of the couple previously referred to, EMG0c and EFH0c. Although these two speakers are in separate education groups, EMG0c's impact on the small (5-member) grade-school group is much greater than his wife's impact on the large (20-member) high school group. Conse-

Table 11.3:   Use of [sh] by
Educational Level

	[sh] (%)	[sh] : /ch/ (N)
Grade school	74.1	272 : 367
High school	86.7	835 : 963
College	32.9	213 : 647

quently, if we eliminate the data from this couple, the grade-school group exhibits 88.2% [sh] and the high school group a minimally different 90.8%. It seems clear, then, that with regard to the pronunciation of the phoneme /ch/, the years-of-education variable represents only a 2-degree scale, those who have been to college and those who have not. The former use predominantly [ch], the latter predominantly [sh].

FORMAL SPANISH
Since [ch] is considered the single allophone of /ch/ in Standard Spanish, one would expect that exposure to Standard Spanish could have a negative effect on the fricative [sh] realization, at least in formal and semiformal situations. A quantitative specification of "exposure to Standard Spanish" (like the specification of "socioeconomic class" used in many sociolinguistic studies, e.g., Cedergren, 1973) requires much more precise background data than were gathered for this study. However, one of the principal avenues for gaining familiarity with Standard Spanish in northern New Mexico is the formal study of the Spanish language in school. This is the only measurement of exposure to Standard Spanish that can be explored here.

Variability in the use of [sh] according to the number of years of formal study of Spanish in the schools is illustrated in table 11.4. Predictably, there is a notable increase in [sh] production with greater exposure to classroom Spanish. Once again, a disruptive effect is created by EMG0c and EFH0c, who had extensive informal instruction in Standard Spanish outside of school. If their data are omitted, the no-formal-Spanish group's use of [sh] jumps to a high 89.1%, revealing a still stronger gradation along this scale.

The significance of the formal Spanish variable, however, is somewhat attenuated by the considerable overlap with both the age and education variables. All 12 members of the young age group, for example, had at least 1 year of Spanish, while 9 of the 12 in the oldest age group had never studied Spanish in school. Similarly, with regard to education, none of the 5 members of the grade-school group, but all 11 members of the college group, had studied formal Spanish.

Nevertheless, the data presented in table 11.4 are of great importance in

Table 11.4: Use of [sh] by Formal Study of Spanish

Years of Study	[sh] (%)	[sh] : /ch/ (N)
None	78.8	699 : 887
1 year	72.3	431 : 596
2+ years	38.5	190 : 494

gaining an understanding of the variable realization of /ch/ in Tomé. While 2 or more years of school Spanish correlates with over 70% [ch] use, less than 2 years of such study is reflected in over 70% [sh] use. Interestingly, only 1 year of Spanish in school appears to have minimal effect; the 72% use of [sh] by this group is still above the community norm of 67%.

CONCLUSIONS

In the Tomé speech community, there is considerable variation in the pronunciation of the /ch/ phoneme. This study has demonstrated that this variation is subject to both linguistic and extralinguistic constraints. On the linguistic side, a categorical phonological rule allows only the affricate variant [ch] when preceded by a nasal or lateral consonant. Given the naturalness of this phonetic constraint in Spanish generally, it seems likely that it would exist in other areas where /ch/ is sometimes [sh], but the present study appears to be the first documentation of such a constraint.

In other phonological environments, the phonetic realization of /ch/ is constrained by extralinguistic factors, the social characteristics of the speaker. Persons under the age of 30, those who attended college, and those who have had 2 or more years of formal study of Spanish tend to favor the affricate variant [ch]; others tend to use predominantly the fricative [sh]. The speaker's sex, however, does not seem to be related to the /ch/ variable.

The clear stratification of the /ch/ variants with regard to age seems to signal the existence of a phonetic change in progress in this speech community. Contrary to the findings of other observers of New Mexican Spanish (Bowen, 1952; Duncan, 1956), the [sh] variant is the prevalent, and apparently a long-established, variant in Tomé. Furthermore, the direction of change—[sh] to [ch]—is the reverse of that perceived in other Spanish-speaking regions. In this community, while the two oldest groups of subjects heavily favor [sh], the youngest group exhibits a preference for [ch]. The fact that the membership of this young group overlaps greatly with the college group (73% young) and with the 2-years-of-formal-Spanish group (57% young) provides an indication of the basis for this change. Members of the latter two groups show an even clearer preference for the [ch] variant than the members of the young group. The perceived sound change appears to simply reflect sociological change related to education. Higher education and formal training in Spanish tend to result in a more standardized pronunciation. And it is primarily the young who have received, and are receiving, such education and exposure.

Such interpretations of community performance must, however, be tempered by considerations of individual performance. Although the community norm in environments other than after a nasal or lateral is 67% [sh], a cursory examination of table 11.1 will reveal that each individual in this survey demonstrates a decided preference for one of the phonetic variants and varies from this preference no more than 30% of the time. There are no "fence straddlers" in the 30% to 70% range. Moreover, two-thirds of them show less than 10% variation, and fully one-fourth use a single variant exclusively. Individual behavior is more consistent, shows less variation, than the group behavior considered here. It is also clear from the individual data in table 11.1 that an explanation of the variability solely in terms of the sociological constraints will not predict individual performance. Individual constraints are also needed.

Insights into the constraints on individual performance can be gained by careful probing of contextual factors. But significant variation by context was not found in the corpus for this study. A broader range of data-collection procedures would no doubt have revealed differences in individual competence underlying the documented differences in performance. The central aspect of this competence difference to be tapped is biloquialism (or bidialectalism). Informal observations suggest that the use of the [ch] variant, especially by the young, is reflective of the operative processes of biloquialism. Some younger consultants were intensely careful during the interview sessions. Some tended to perceive the semiformal interview as a test of their speaking abilities. Interestingly, one consultant with a high percentage of standard [ch] produced a few [sh] at points in the conversation where a close rapport was established. Such observations lead us to conclude that in more casual contexts many speakers, and particularly the younger ones, would have produced a higher frequency rate of [sh]. In fact, it seems reasonable to conjecture that the historical change posited above is not a change of competence, but an expansion of competence. Through education and exposure to Standard Spanish, some residents of Tomé may be expanding their command of different varieties of Spanish. It may well be that the present study sampled only (or primarily) that variety of Spanish individually appropriate to semiformal contexts. Additional research with contextually more sensitive elicitation is clearly needed to adequately explore the extent and role of biloquialism in Tomé.

The present study has provided some new information and observations on the Spanish language in the Southwest. In the final analysis, however, the importance and implications of our findings reside in the universal need for a more positive and enlightened outlook on the function of language in human societies. Language, in the process of ever-constant change, is the product of unique linguistic and social evolutionary patterns in any given geographical region.

REFERENCES

Bowen, J. D. The Spanish of San Antoñito, New Mexico. Doctoral diss., University of New Mexico, 1952.

Bull, W. E. *Spanish for teachers: Applied linguistics.* New York: Ronald Press, 1965.

Cedergren, H. The interplay of social and linguistic factors in Panama. Doctoral diss., Cornell University, 1973. *Dissertation Abstracts International,* 1973, *34,* 6614A–6615A. (University Microfilms No. 74-6373)

Dalbor, J. B. *Spanish pronunciation: Theory and practice.* New York: Holt, Rinehart & Winston, 1969.

Duncan, R. M. Algunas observaciones sobre la fonología de la *s* palatal en el español de Nuevo Méjico. *Acta Salmanticensia,* 1956, *10*(2), 223–28.

Elías-Olivares, L. *Language use in a Chicano community: A sociolinguistic approach.* Working Papers in Sociolinguistics, No. 30. Austin: Southwest Educational Development Laboratory, 1976.

Espinosa, A. M. *Studies in New Mexican Spanish. Part 1: Phonology.* Albuquerque: University of New Mexico Press, 1909.

González, G. *The phonology of Corpus Christi Spanish.* Austin: Southwest Educational Development Laboratory, 1969.

Hernández-Chávez, E., Cohen, A. D., & Beltramo, A. F. (Eds.). *El lenguaje de los Chicanos.* Arlington: Center for Applied Linguistics, 1975.

Hills, E. C. New Mexican Spanish. *Journal of the Modern Language Association of America,* 1906, *21,* 706–53.

Lapesa, R. *Historia de la lengua española.* Madrid: Escelicer, 1959.

Lastra de Suárez, Y. El habla y la educación de los niños de origen mexicano en Los Angeles. In E. Hernández-Chávez, A. Cohen, & A. F. Beltramo (Eds.), *El lenguaje de los Chicanos.* Arlington, Va.: Center for Applied Linguistics, 1975.

Navarro Tomás, T. *Manual de pronunciación española.* New York: Hafner, 1963.

Phillips, R. N., Jr. Los Angeles Spanish: A descriptive analysis. Doctoral diss., University of Wisconsin, 1967. *Dissertation Abstracts International,* 1968, *28,* 2667-A.

Post, A. C. Southern Arizona Spanish. Doctoral diss., Stanford University, 1932.

Poulter, V. L. A phonological study of the speech of Mexican-American college students native to Fort Worth–Dallas. Doctoral diss., Louisiana State University, 1973. *Dissertation Abstracts International,* 1974, *35,* 1082-A.

Rael, J. B. A study of the phonology and morphology of New Mexican Spanish based on a collection of 410 folk-tales. Doctoral diss., Stanford University, 1937.

12 | Speaker Sex and *Para* Reduction in Chicano Spanish

JAMES P. LANTOLF
University of Delaware

As is well known, sociolinguistic research has demonstrated that factors beyond the bounds of the linguistic system itself influence the shape and incidence of linguistic forms in actual speech.[1] The work of linguists like Labov and Bernstein, for example, has confirmed that the socioeconomic background of speakers constrains their speech patterns. Linguists have likewise found that extralinguistic variables such as the speaker's age, ethnic group, and geographic origin also govern speech patterns. For some time, linguists have also been aware of sex-related differences in language use.[2] However, the early studies of sex-differentiated speech patterns were primarily based on the so-called exotic languages of Africa, the Pacific, and the Americas. In such languages the differences between male and female speech were easily observed and described, because the languages in question tend to be "sex-exclusive" languages in which one sex uses linguistic forms not used by the other sex (Bodine, 1975, p. 131).[3]

Not until recently have scholars undertaken in-depth empirical research on sex-related linguistic differences in the European languages. The belatedness of interest in investigating this aspect of the European languages is, in all probability, due to the widely held assumption that language in Western society is essentially an androgenous phenomenon (Swacker, 1975, p. 76). Newly uncovered evidence, however, has revealed that while Western languages cannot be classified as sex-exclusive in nature, they at the very least display a strong inclination to be "sex-preferential" languages; both sexes share the same linguistic patterns, but one sex uses certain patterns more extensively than the other sex. Because of the sharing of linguistic patterns by men and women, differences predicated on speaker sex have not been as transparent in the European languages as they have been in the exotic languages. The purpose of the present study is to discuss a case in which speaker sex was indeed found to govern what otherwise appears to be a case of linguistic free-variation in the Spanish of the Chicano community of San Antonio, Texas.

166

DESCRIPTION OF *PARA* REDUCTION

Among the linguistic features which appear in Chicano Spanish is the reduction of the preposition *para* to *pa*, as illustrated in example 1:[4]

1. Me voy para San Antonio → Me voy pa San Antonio

Although the most common environment for the preposition is *pa(ra)* + *ir* + locative, it is also attested when *ir* is replaced by other motion verbs, as in these examples:[5]

2. Nos cambiamos pa Leesville
   Vinieron pa Laredo

As the items given in example 3 illustrate, *para* reduction also operates in matrices containing an element other than a locative in postposition.

3. ... pa acabar (infinitive)
   ... pa quedarme aquí (infinitive)
   ... pa la cena (noun phrase)
   ... pa ese tiempo (temporal adverb)
   ... pa que fuera (adverbial clause)
   ... pa que tenga (adverbial clause)

When *pa(ra)* is followed by the masculine singular definite article *el*, *pa* and *el* emerge to form the contraction *pal*, as in example 4.

4. Ibamos pal town
   Lo tengo pal día que ...

If the locative slot is filled by a noun marked as [+human], the form which appears is *panca*:[6]

5. Iba para la casa de mi tía → Iba panca mi tía
   Se fueron para la casa de la suegra → Se fueron panca la suegra

In cases in which the prepositional object is masculine singular and the definite article is *el*, the contracted form *pancal* appears:

6. Fuimos pancal negrito
   Pa irnos pancal primo

In a series of acceptability studies, García (1977, 1979) presented a set of sentences containing the preposition *pa* to speakers representing several American dialects of Spanish, including Chicano Spanish. She discovered that although the *pa* sentences were rated as acceptable to some extent by many of her informants, the Chicano speakers accepted the sentences with much greater regularity than did the speakers of the other dialects.[7] García's intent, however, was not to determine if any extralinguistic constraints played a role in influencing the shape of the preposition in actual speech. The sole aim of the present study, as stated at the outset, is to report on a specific extralinguistic variable (i.e., speaker sex) which appears to constrain the use of *pa(ra) in natural speech*.

ANALYSIS OF DATA

The data for the present study were obtained from a series of taped interviews with 171 informants conducted from 1972 to 1978.[8] The informants were either natives of the San Antonio area or residents who had been living in the

Table 12.1: Biographical Data

	Number of Informants	Percentage of Informants Using pá
Age		
20	50	29
30	61	36
40	22	13
50	33	19
60	5	3
Sex		
Male	77	45
Female	94	55
Education		
Grade school	31	18
Some high school	19	6
High school graduate	59	35
Some college	38	22
College graduate	8	5
Graduate work	23	14
Occupation		
Student	8	5
Housewife	21	12
Professional	19	11
Blue-collar	37	22
White-collar	84	50

Note: Two respondents did not furnish information on educational background, and two did not furnish information on occupation.

Table 12.2:   Average Frequency of
Para Reduction (Variable = Sex)

Male	Female	Difference
42% (77)	23% (94)	19%

Note: Number in parentheses represents total
number of male or female respondents interviewed.
Percentage = average frequency of *pa* in all
interviews.

region for a minimum of 10 years at the time they were interviewed. During
the interviews, the respondents were free to discuss a wide variety of topics,
including personal histories, jobs, Chicano customs, and so forth. Each respondent provided his or her interviewer with the biographical data summarized in
table 12.1.

In analyzing the data, a clear pattern emerges in which male speakers show
a greater propensity to employ *pa* than do their female counterparts (table
12.2). From table 12.2, it can be seen that there is a 19% difference in the
average frequency of *para* reduction between male and female speakers, with
males favoring the more innovative *pa* and the females preferring the norma-
tive *para*. As will become apparent, however, when speaker age, education, and
occupation are taken into consideration, the difference between the sexes
diminishes at certain points along the variable scale.

Table 12.3 shows the percentages obtained for *para* reduction when speaker
age is taken into account. As table 12.3 illustrates, men at any age level are
more likely to use *pa* than are women. Males at either end of the age spectrum
(i.e., groups 1, 4, and 5) employed *pa* with an average frequency approximat-
ing 50%. Among the female speakers, the highest incidence of *para* reduction
occurred in the youngest age group (30%), but even here there is a difference

Table 12.3:   *Para* Reduction (Variables
= Sex and Age)

Age	Male	Female	Difference
20	50% (19)	30% (31)	20%
30	32% (32)	23% (29)	9%
40	30% (8)	7% (14)	23%
50	53% (13)	16% (20)	37%
60	45% (5)	—	—

Note: Number in parentheses is total number of
male or female respondents interviewed for each age
group. Percentage = average frequency of *pa* for all
interviews in each age group.

of 20% between the sexes in their respective preference for the nonstandard form of the preposition. For males in the middle age groups (groups 2 and 3), the frequency of *pa* diminishes to approximately 31%. In other words, for these respondents the more standard *para* appeared in nearly 70% of the cases. It is not clear, however, why men in their thirties and forties should prefer *pa* to a lesser extent than males at other points along the age gradient. It does not seem that the appearance of *pa(ra)* is merely a function of an age variable in which younger speakers favor the innovative form while the older speakers maintain the standard form of the preposition. The male respondents in groups 4 and 5 were, in fact, closer to their counterparts in group 1 in using *pa* than to the chronologically closer groups 2 and 3. It may well be, as will be discussed below, that education plays a role in determining the form of the preposition, since male speakers identified as members of groups 2 and 3 had generally attained a higher level of education than had the remaining groups.

The graph in figure 12.1 compares male and female informants with respect to *para* reduction using age as a variable factor. The education and occupation variables are interrelated, since an individual's level of education usually has an effect on the occupational category into which that person falls. Table 12.4 shows *para* reduction in relation to both sex and education; table 12.5 shows *para* reduction in relation to sex and occupation. From these tables it can be observed that once again the female informants were less innovative in their use of the preposition at all points on the educational and occupational scales than were the male respondents. The percentages in tables 12.4 and 12.5 indicate that there is an inverse relationship between education and occupation, on the one hand, and the form of the preposition used on the other. As one ascends the educational and occupational scales, the difference in use of *pa(ra)* between the sexes decreases, with both sexes favoring the standard form of the preposition. For example (table 12.4), males with a grade-school education used *pa* 68% of the time, while females falling into the same educational category used *pa* only 29% of the time, a difference of 39%. For those speakers with some college experience, the difference between males and females decreases to 19%. The percentages relating to those respondents holding a college degree may not present a clear picture, since the number of speakers falling into this category is relatively small, especially in the case of females. Although the incidence of *pa* declines by 15% for men between categories 4 and 5, the decline for women between the same two categories is 22% (i.e., 22% in category 4 to 0% in category 5). Since the drop for women is steeper than for men, the result is a net increase of 7% in the difference between the sexes from category 4 to category 5. A more suitable set of figures is obtained if we examine those speakers who have pursued graduate studies. The number of respondents classified into group 6 increases by 14 from the previous category. In this case, the difference between male and female speakers is only 7%. The relationship between education, sex, and *para* reduction is summarized in the graph given in figure 12.2.

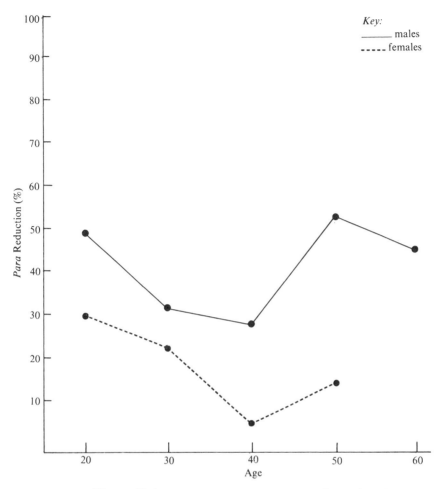

Figure 12.1: *Para* Reduction (Variable = Sex and Age)

Table 12.4: *Para* Reduction (Variables = Sex and Education)

Education	Male	Female	Difference
Grade school	68% (16)	29% (15)	39%
Some high school	65% (6)	39% (4)	26%
High school graduate	43% (18)	25% (41)	18%
Some college	41% (15)	22% (23)	19%
College graduate	26% (5)	0% (3)	26%
Graduate work	7% (15)	0% (8)	7%

Note: Number in parentheses is total number of male or female respondents interviewed for each educational level. Percentage = average frequency of *pa* for all interviews in each category.

Table 12.5:   *Para* Reduction (Variables = Sex and Occupation)

Occupation	Male	Female	Difference
1. Student	18% (5)	10% (3)	8%
2. Housewife		21% (21)	
3. Blue-collar	68% (28)	20% (9)	48%
4. White-collar	41% (30)	21% (54)	20%
5. Professional	8% (13)	3% (6)	5%

Note: Number in parentheses is total number of male or female respondents interviewed for each occupational category. Percentage = average frequency of *pa* for all interviews in each category.

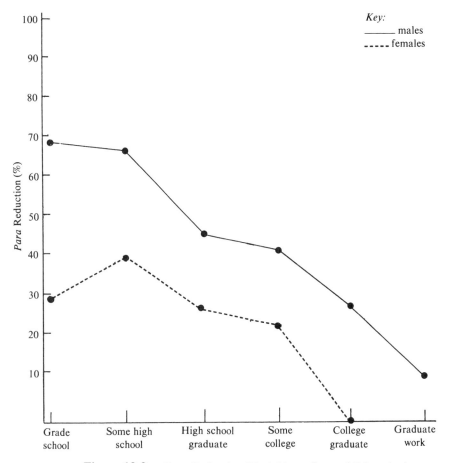

Figure 12.2:   *Para* Reduction (Variable = Sex and Education)

Turning to the occupation variable in more detail (table 12.5), we observe the aforementioned parallels between its effect on *para* reduction and that found for the education variable. Male blue-collar workers utilized *pa* 68% of the time, while females falling into the same occupational category favored *para* reduction in only 20% of the cases, a difference of 48%. At the white-collar and professional end of the scale, however, the difference between the sexes declines substantially, to 20% for white-collar workers and 5% for professionals. Figure 12.3 relates sex and occupation to the frequency of *para* reduction.

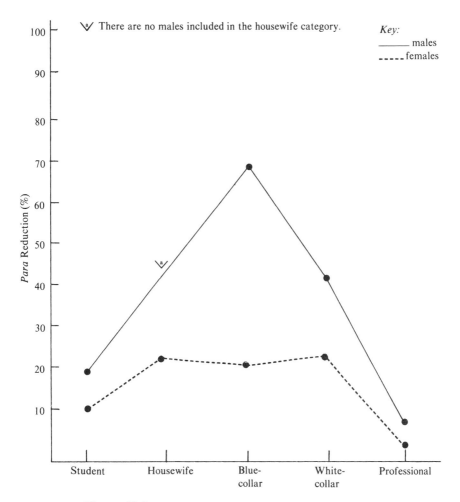

Figure 12.3:   *Para* Reduction (Variable = Sex and Occupation)

It is clear that both education and occupation have more of an effect on males than on females. Females are much more consistent in their preference for the standard form of the preposition than are males. Females with a grade-school education used *pa* 29% of the time (see table 12.4), but those with a college degree or graduate experience did not use *pa* in a single instance. On the other hand, males with a grade-school education utilized *pa* in 68% of the cases, while those males with graduate school experience used the reduced form of the preposition only 7% of the time, a decline of 61%.

Female blue-collar workers chose to use *pa* 20% of the time, but those women with a professional position used the innovative form in only 3% of the cases (table 12.5). For male speakers, however, we again note a much greater discrepancy between the same two occupational categories. That is, male blue-collar workers used *pa* 68% of the time, while professional men employed the same form only 8% of the time, a difference of 60%.

SUMMARY

Although San Antonio is often cited as this country's tenth largest city, its Hispanic community has generally maintained a more provincial and tradi- tional set of social norms than perhaps one would anticipate in a modern urban center with a population approaching one million.[9] In a comparative study of the Chicano communities of San Antonio and Los Angeles, Grebler, Moore, & Guzmán (1973) found that the San Antonio community consistently favored a more conservative position than did its Los Angeles sister community with respect to such current issues as divorce, birth control, male and female social roles, and the like. The most noteworthy conclusion of the study, as far as it relates to the present discussion, is that while a tendency toward sexual egalitarianism has begun to emerge in San Antonio, the community by and large continues to foster the notion of a male-dominated social framework. The presence of a marked distinction between male and female social roles goes a long way toward explaining the differences between male and female patterns of *pa(ra)* usage.

According to Trudgill (1974) and Thorne and Henley (1975), the fact that women's speech habits are frequently more standard than those of men is a reflection of a social division between the sexes. Women undertake to compen- sate for their subordinate social position by signaling status through linguistic means. Men, on the other hand, employ less standard speech forms as an index of masculinity and male exclusivity or solidarity.

Nowhere in the present study is the notion of male solidarity and exclusivity reflected more graphically than it is among those respondents who identified themselves as members of the working class (see table 12.5). The reason for such divergent male/female speech patterns among blue-collar workers is, according to studies reported on by Thorne and Henley, the heightened importance placed on sex-role distinctions and male dominance within the working class. To be sure, variations in prepositional usage also appeared between men and women holding white-collar and professional positions. Linguistic differences between the sexes at this end of the occupational scale may well arise from the extension of male working-class speech habits as stereotypical indices of masculinity or *machismo* (Thorne and Henley, p. 18). It will be recalled, however, that the differences between the sexes with regard to *pa(ra)* usage were not as pronounced among non–working-class speakers as they were in the case of blue-collar workers (see table 12.5). The explanation for this may be traceable to the effect of education (see table 12.4), which often insulates white-collar workers and professionals from working-class norms and ideals.

NOTES

1. I would like to thank Maryellen García for her insightful comments on and criticisms of an earlier version of this paper. The author accepts full responsibility for any shortcomings of the present version.

2. In a well-known case cited in numerous writings on the relationship between language and speaker sex, European settlers reported the discovery of a tribe inhabiting the Lesser Antilles which appeared to have separate languages for men and women. In later investigations of the supposed languages, it was found that the differences between the men's speech and that of the women were superficial, and what seemed to be two different languages turned out to be two varieties of the same language, with each sex using distinct lexical items.

3. The fact that one sex is assigned exclusive use of certain linguistic forms in a given society does not mean that the other sex has only a tacit knowledge of the patterns belonging to the other sex. Bodine (p. 146) discusses Haas's findings that among Koasati speakers, an adult of either sex can correct the sex-inappropriate speech of a child of either sex by using the linguistic forms befitting the child's sex.

4. The reduction of *para* to *pa* is by no means limited to Chicano Spanish. It has been attested in a number of Spanish dialects throughout Latin America (see Alonso, 1938).

5. García (1979) found that use of the verb *andar* with *para* may be ungrammatical when the context is ambiguous with regard to physical motion. Thus, *¿andaba pa Seguin?* may be ungrammatical, since it need not entail direction toward a specific point but movement within a location, as in the sentence *andaban en Seguin.* When it is clear that direction is involved, however, *para* can be preceded by *andar,* as in *vamos a andar pa casa.*

6. According to Galván and Teschner (1977), *panca* represents a contraction of *para + la casa de.* Maryellen García (personal communication) contends that the form derives from *para en casa de.* Garciá believes that prior to the generalization of *para* as a prelocative preposition, the phrase *en casa de* evolved to become *enca,* with the meaning of 'over at X's house', as in *¿Onde está? Está enca me tía;* 'Where is she?'

'She's over at my aunt's house'. Later, when *para* could be used to introduce a locative phrase, the two forms *para* + *enca* combined to yield *panca.*

7.   In her 1979 study, García found that sentences containing *pa* were rated as acceptable by an average of 78% of her Chicano respondents and by 19% of her Mexican informants. In her 1977 article, she reports that an average of 43% of the Chicanos studied accepted sentences with *pa,* while 28% of the Mexican and 6% of the other Spanish-American respondents who participated in her study accepted sentences with the reduced form of the preposition.

8.   The data for this study are taken in large part from the San Antonio Data File established by Prof. R. Joe Campbell and his students.

9.   A major factor contributing to the relative conservatism of San Antonio's Chicano community may well be the city's proximity to the agricultural regions of the Rio Grande Valley. Many families continue to nurture close kinship bonds with relatives living in the conservative rural areas of southern Texas and northern Mexico (see Madsen, 1973).

REFERENCES

Alonso, A. Introduction. In P. Henriquez-Ureña (Ed.), *El español en Méjico, los Estados Unidos, y la América Central.* Biblioteca de dialectología hispanoamericana (Vol. 4). Buenos Aires: University of Buenos Aires, 1938.

Bodine, A. Sex differentiation in language. In B. Thorne & N. Henley (Eds.), *Language and sex: Difference and dominance.* Rowley, Mass.: Newbury House, 1975.

Galván, R. A., & Teschner, R. V. *El diccionario del español chicano.* Silver Springs, Md.: Institute of Modern Languages, 1977.

García, M. Chicano Spanish/Latin American Spanish: Some differences in linguistic norms. *Bilingual Review,* 1977, *4,* 200–209.

——. *Pa(ra)* usage in United States Spanish. *Hispania,* 1979, *62,* 106–14.

Grebler, L., Moore, J. W., & Guzmán, R. C. The family: Variations in time and space. In L. I. Duran & H. R. Bernard (Eds.), *Introduction to Chicano studies: A reader.* New York: Macmillan, 1973.

Madsen, W. *The Mexican-Americans of south Texas.* New York: Holt, Rinehart & Winston, 1973.

Swacker, M. The sex of the speaker as a sociolinguistic variable. In B. Thorne & N. Henley (Eds.), *Language and sex: Difference and dominance.* Rowley, Mass.: Newbury House, 1975.

Thorne, B., & Henley, N. (Eds.). *Language and sex: Difference and dominance.* Rowley, Mass.: Newbury House, 1975.

Trudgill, P. *Sociolinguistics: An introduction.* Middlesex, England: Penguin, 1974.

13 | Lexicology and Border Spanish (or *Caló*)

JOHN T. WEBB
University of Illinois at Chicago

Samuel Johnson, in his dictionary of the English language, defined *network* as follows: "Any thing reticulated or decussated, at equal distances, with interstices between the intersections" (1755). Bergen Evans, in turn, commented: "Of all Johnson's definitions, this excited most ridicule. But the obvious is not easy to define; of necessity, the simplest must be defined in terms less simple. This remains one of the best definitions of *network* we have" (1968, p. 483). Now, I say that if the obvious is difficult to deal with, we need to empathize with both the lay person and with the professional. *Reticulated* ('divided into a network of small squares of intersecting lines') and *decussated* ('arranged, forming with crossing [right-angle] lines, like an *X*') are common terms to some people; for others, they might come from Mars. *Chévere* is everyday Spanish for many speakers—completely unknown to others. The teaching of terms, standard or nonstandard, to the uninitiated sometimes takes more than "just" knowledge or "just" skill. In England, foreign learners of English might consult a dictionary for the term *network* and find: "complex system of lines that cross ... connected system"; here they would get elucidation, without reticulation or decussation—but is it sufficient?

Border Spanish is best known by its *users* for what it is and what it isn't, yet, their school teachers may not only impose labels on its usages, but may also be the persons most likely to want a reference book of it. The lexicographer, then, has the double task of making accurate interpretation of language that often is not written, and of putting that language into writing which means something to those who already "know" such speech, as well as to those who want to know about such usage.

No matter how fluent he is in Spanish, the speaker raised in the United States and educated only in English may never have heard *quiubo* or *quiúbole* outside the ghetto, and thus normally spells it *q-vo*. In alphabetized listing, should the lexicographer responsibly record it under the Spanish-orthography informal pronunciation, under the Anglicized so-called spelling, under *qué* (knowing that it comes from *¿qué hubo?*), or under *haber*? Perhaps it should

177

be in all these places. Then, what about *quiúvanas*? It is my contention that the expression should be alphabetized in all the forms the dictionary-user may reasonably be expected to look for (if it occurs in written form). One central variation should be chosen by the lexicographer (according to criteria provided to the reader) as the locus for all necessary explanatory data, and all other variations should, in turn, be referred to the main one. Unless there are good reasons for a different choice (and they should be explained to the reader), the central variation should be that one most likely to be found in print, preferably in standard-language orthography. The central variation should be referenced to a form in Spanish or some other standard language, so that the reader may find further background information, if necessary. We must let the reader know what is being done. We need also to know for ourselves just what we are trying to do. How can we put a fence around our material? What is our enclosed corpus?

"Slang" is a kind of language easily recognized by speakers of United States English, and the term has been applied to many kinds of Spanish. But, just as the native-English–speaking person has great difficulty defining the limits of slang, so the Spanish-speaker often has to work out any agreement with *conciudadanos* on what to include, and what not to include, in Argentina's *lunfardo,* Venezuela's *calé,* Peru's *replana,* or Aztlán's *caló.* Manuel Alvar, when he translated Iordan's introduction to Romance linguistics, felt obligated to add a special note to the discussion of jargons and argots: "In Spanish the following distinctions tend to be made: *germanía* 'old *jergal* speech' and *jerga* or *argot* 'modern *jergal* speech', while *caló* is the 'language of the Gypsies', only quite late has *caló* come to be used from time to time as '*jerga* of malefactors'" (Iordan, 1967, p. 636, n. 18). Despite his and others' legitimate concern with clarifying exactly what they are talking about, serious students of language may maintain that *germanía* is a label that may be applied to a type of language used in Puerto Rico, and that *lunfardo* is no longer alive and well in Argentina. Neither the American speaker of English nor the knowledgeable linguist studying categories of usage can afford to be smug; only very recently has there been a major attempt to define, with any precision, American slang (Dumas & Lighter, 1978). Only recently have lexicographers and their critics faced the inadequacy of labeling in American dictionaries (Creswell, 1975 [1978]).

I here briefly review, with a nuts-and-bolts approach, my experience with making a dictionary of a specific type of nonstandard Spanish, *caló,* and hope that a few developments, when placed in context, can profitably be used by other students, in any language system. In an appendix to this chapter (p. 181), I present the introductory material to my dictionary of *caló* to serve as reference.

In the process of reaching toward meaningful recording and definition of

Mexican and Chicano *caló* with the help of live speakers, and by comparing and contrasting oral and printed opinions of other students, as well as looking at types of French *argot,* Italian *gergo,* and Portugese *calão* and *gíria,* I have evolved the definition of *caló* shown in section 1 of the appendix (p. 181).

In attempting to find out how the users might limit their own language, I proceeded to test specific form and content, again from both spoken and written sources, against criteria that obviously might not fully satisfy anyone. Little by little, over a number of years, preponderance began to tell. Guesswork became "harder" data, confirmed by opinion, by trial and error, and by confirmation in testing against my own records and examinations of others. With some assurance, then, selection of informants, judging of their reliability, and corroboration of their data became increasingly sure, describable, and organizable. The next stage involved evaluating and interpreting the data in a way that could be understandable to an optimum number of people and in a way that would reach those who could use the information. One obvious dichotomy is preparation of materials for the requirements of an academic press as opposed to the needs of a popular press. For example, a popular publisher would not normally want to be concerned with page after page of citations; an academic publisher of a recent Chicano dictionary would not accept the manuscript that contained palpably offensive material, even knowing that the language reflected is everyday usage, responsibly collected with enviable scholarship. Further, as the reader will see in section 2.1 of the appendix (p. 182), informants often do not see a direct correlation between spoken and written forms, which suggests prejudice from both literacy and nonliteracy. This is not to quibble over whether or not a letter *u* should or should not have two dots on top, but, more important, to ponder such situations as whether *de una vez,* pronounced rapidly and with change of stress to become *diunávez* (*diunaves*), really "means" something different (or is peculiar to given people or situations). An additional consideration, unfortunately quite important, involves the amount of paper and ink at stake. Can the lexicographer responsibly combine forms and contents in a way that saves space yet also makes the material comprehensible and available to the intended audience? Can the conscientious lexicographer "correct" for what seem to be misunderstandings or mistakes in pronunciation, spelling, typography, or apparently meaningless conventions? Does *furriz* exist as a variant of *furris*? Is *foete* hypercorrection for *fuete*? Just how far does "completeness" lead the student in recording all possible variations on a theme? For example, should /xájna/ as a pronunciation be cross-referenced to spelling *h-y-n-a,* with full knowledge that English-language schooling may be "at fault"? Or, another example, should we be concerned with probable interference of rapid pronunciation, and possible interference of informal education, when *abajo de ala* and *abajo de hola* (*a-l-a* and *h-o-l-a*) are confirmed as variants of each other? Where do we stop?

Section 2.2 of the appendix (p. 183), brings us to the question of "too little" or "too much" information. Most important, if we truly want to provide what most users may expect, is the definition, the gloss. If *j-o-t-o* is defined as 'urning, physical homosexual', the reader may not have another dictionary that defines *urning,* and may accuse the lexicographer of being overly pedantic; yet, the term normally implies 'sensually perceptible', and a person who presents no physical evidence of "other" sexual orientation could not, in most circumstances, be considered *joto.* For such reasons, I have found it necessary to state standards, as in note 5, p. 185, which may not satisfy all possible users, but which do, at least, provide points of departure.

Abbreviated grammatical information must be clear and consistent. I suggest, for instance, that *adj.* indicates adjectives, and also adjectival constructions that have potential for use as substantives or adverbs and that follow normal written and spoken conventions of Spanish adjectives; that *mf.* should indicate 'taking either the masculine or feminine form (if such falls within normal expectations), according to the sex of the living referent'; and that *m +* *f.* should refer to an 'invariable form taking either gender'.

In providing usage data indicating how broadly or narrowly an expression ordinarily is or has been used, we are, of course, treading on thin ice. Time, place, persons involved, all can affect how an expression may carry a message. Speakers and interlocutors interpret in a particular environment, and we are all aware that speech is often taken (or given) in or out of context. Only in those cases, therefore, where some frequency takes form or content out of their usual settings, can we legitimately indicate that *nel* [normally 'no'] may "mean" 'yes', or that *chingón* may have positive rather than negative connotations. Consider, similarly, how we might accurately encode American English usage of *bad* to mean 'good' (how? where? when? why? by whom? with what frequency?).

When we provide information on definition and usage, a sentence frame from living language must *exemplify* the explanatory information. This means, for instance, that a verb marked transitive must show transitivity in the example, and particularly so if the form of the verb does not follow standard-language conventions. If an overtly "reflexive" verb, such as *agujerarse,* 'to "needle" oneself', can be used transitively, we should make every effort to find a valid frame, such as *agujératemelo* ("needle" it to me), even if we have to strain ourselves (or our informants' patience) in such exemplification.

In the matter of citations (sec. 2.3, p. 183), a major consideration is the accessibility to the reader of at least one dependable written source, if that is possible. For example, one source cited by Galván and Teschner (1977) is a mimeographed report by Keever, Vasquez, and Padilla (1945), which is probably available from the Library of Congress; the paper possibly can only be "found" for members of Congress, and even then it is accompanied by the notation "Do Not Duplicate"; such a source should not be the only one cited.

For a sample entry, I have chosen a family of words that, for most readers, probably has strong emotional and political overtones. Since informants will confirm different glosses for different times and places, we should separate the glosses (my preference would be chronologically) if they should be separate, divide them by semicolons when they are separate but equal, or divide them by commas when they may blend together.

A dictionary serves to get a certain body of information, made accessible in a certain order, to a certain population. Lexicographers must find what to do and what not to do, and be consistent in approach. The better we can ascertain the likes and dislikes of the intended audience, the more reasonably we can structure a dictionary's material to make it meaningfully accessible; this includes knowing what to put in and what to leave out. As a famous king once said: "Begin at the beginning, . . . and go on till you come to the end: then stop" (Carroll, 1963, p. 158).

APPENDIX: FRONT MATTER FOR A DICTIONARY OF *CALÓ*

Introduction

1.1   Definition.   The present dictionary of *caló,* a special type of Spanish, is an expansion of my dissertation (Webb, 1976); it is also the result of many years of interesting, often pleasurable experience with language. Caló, similar to, but not identical with "slang" as defined for United States English (Dumas & Lighter, 1978), is used especially in the setting of urban poverty, with relative homogeneity in Mexico and in the United States, and with greater fluency by people with a mastery of informal Mexican Spanish.

1.2   Criteria.   After lengthy examination of the literature and extensive conversation with consultants and informants (often the same person), the following usage criteria were established. *Two* or more of them must be in effect for an expression to be considered *caló* by its speakers.

1. Deflation of dignity: The uttering of such an expression will markedly deflate, at least temporarily, the assumed dignity of the wider community's formal speech. The positing of such dignity may be made either by the speaker or by the community, or by both.

2. Nonconventionality: The expression implies a strikingly humorous or nonconventional view of reality. The more evident such an implication is, the more lively is the potential for lowering the dignity of formal speech.

3. Group intimacy: The expression signals the speaker's special intimacy with a type of language which he views as *caló,* or with a group of people who normally use such terms. To be sure, the concept of *caló* is an elusive one; expressions at one time considered *caló* may eventually, through excessive use, become normal in popular Spanish or even in English, and thus cease to serve for in-group identification.

4. Status recognition: Terms taboo in ordinary discourse with persons believed by the speaker to be of higher social status may continue to be thought *caló* despite great popularity. Preeminent in this category is the family of words headed by *chingar;* they

retain the flavor of strong taboo, are used by the bulk of Spanish-speakers only in situations calling for emphasis of ghetto cultural values, and are normally associated in the wider community with persons choosing, or restricted to, poverty and delinquency.[1]

1.3   Selection.   A given expression, nevertheless, is not recorded here unless confirmed as *caló* by:

   1. *Two* or more informants deemed sufficiently conversant in this type of language; such informants were identified as such only if they could recognize and at least generally define ("gloss") a given set of expressions (adequately understood and fluently used, under "normal" conditions, only by monolingual Spanish-speakers in an urban-poverty setting); or by,

   2. *One* or more informants who corroborated data of apparently reliable first-hand investigators, such as Amor, Islas, or Wagner; or by,

   3. *Three* or more informants, despite other standard-language use. Whenever possible, an effort was made to verify that sources were independent of each other (preferably not known to each other), and to find independent corroboration of use (at least 10 years each) in Mexico and in the United States. Further, and as circumstances allowed, an attempt was made to determine at what level of popularity an expression would normally be used in a Spanish-language context.

Guidelines for Use of the Dictionary

2.1   Arrangement.   The principal part of this dictionary, arranged in the form of an index, is a master list of lexically relevant morphemes and words which follows both the Spanish and English alphabets (some forms, therefore, for the reader's convenience, may appear twice).[2] Further, the index may ignore word boundaries when there has been any question as to how many words form a given expression (thus *larache* [or *la rache*?] 'night'/'noche' before *laredo* 'side'/'lado'), and therefore involves occasional "repetition." Forms bearing diacritical marks immediately follow those without them: Thus *arrañarse* comes after *arranarse,* and, similarly, *nor, ñor, nora, ñora, . . . tirili, tírili.*

   Detailed information is normally provided and studied only once, in the form of entries (articles that may include definitions, derivations, pronunciations, examples of usage, etc.). All relevant morphemes and words are cross-referenced to an entry-article, which is headed by the most "original" or most important form (word) of all those studied in the particular group. Each entry begins with that *caló* form (or a Spanish form, if recognized by informants as directly related), for which I adopt either the conventional orthography of standard Spanish or the most common form from published sources, or, failing that, my estimate of how literate users would expect to find it in print;[3] thus, *alfiler* heads an entry which includes the blending of *filo* into such a form as *afilorear,* the included forms also appearing at the appropriate alphabetized places elsewhere in the dictionary, and cross-referenced back to *alfiler.*

   In this way, the enlarged entries form groups or families of words containing the same root morpheme, according to my own or my informants' best judgment. Family membership determines the order of descriptive presentation of the lexical items collected, and in most cases their position suffices to explain their provenance; therefore strictly etymological considerations are introduced only apropos of the most important word, while separate analyses of other individual members of the family are carried out only when special problems arise. Thus, the entry for *ahora* contains discussion of monodiphthongization or loss of the initial syllable(s), while subentries *órale* (with variant *hórale*) and *oranas* have cross-referenced studies of affixation and affectivity.

Subentries, indented, are generally ordered from simple to increasingly complex use of the root morpheme. Those of similar complexity are alphabetized by the next most important (that is, most common) word. Thus, under *agua* (with variant *aguas*) are listed *agua bendita, agua de calcetín, como agua, como agua para chocolate, dar (su) agua (a)* [and *dar (su) agüita (a)*], *de agua, debajo del agua, echar agua (a), en el agua, hacer agua la canoa a, mover el agua (a), tirar el agua (a),* and so forth.

2.2   Detailed Entries.   The entry form (with variants) is followed by syntactic and other grammatical information (phonological specifications only as needed); such information indicates conformity with rules and conventions of literary or colloquial Spanish, unless otherwise indicated.[4] Next I have placed English and Spanish glosses ("definitions"),[5] enclosed in single quotation marks (' ') and separated by a slanted stroke (/).

The body of the entry may contain the following categories: 1) secondary meanings of the form or phrases containing the main word being defined; 2) syntactic usages differing from the principal one; 3) formulas or idiomatic phrases (with glosses) containing the form in question; and 4) attestations ("sentence frames") from informants or from relevant literature, enclosed in double quotations marks (" ").[6]

Usage data have been encoded immediately before the attestations. "I" designates forms provided by informants, but not found in published sources; within these two categories I make the following subdivisions: "1": form considered by informants as part of popular, informal Spanish of Mexico or the Southwest; "2": form considered by informants as part of the Spanish that reflects urban poverty; "3": form considered by informants as limited to delinquent cant. In addition, "PC" points out those forms from published sources confirmed by informants; while "PR" designates published-source forms recognized by at least two informants as *caló,* but for which they failed to provide sentence frames.

2.3   Citations.   Citations of published material are given in chronological order of the earliest reference to each author, the intent being to demonstrate the diachronic trajectory of each term. Where I refer to an author for more than one source, all citations immediately follow the date of his earliest publication. Of the authors cited in the bibliography, some survey material from larger areas (e.g., Latin America) but only incidentally record data from Mexico or from Aztlán (here, Spanish-language areas of Mexican cultural heritage in the United States); I have cited them exclusively when inadequate confirmation is furnished by sources that concentrate on Mexican-Chicano material. In the case of authors with more than one "last name," I cite only the first of these (e.g., Blanco = Blanco S., Fernández = Fernández de Lizardi, García = García Icazbalceta, Galván = [Roberto] Galván and [Richard] Teschner), the indicated year providing sufficient clarification.

In all cases I respect the orthography of published sources (with due consideration of misunderstanding and possible typographical errors), which, I feel, normally represents all relevant phonological detail.[7]

2.4 Sample Entry.

chicano   adj. 'Mexican, of Mexican ancestry or heritage, militantly proud of ties with Mexican culture'/'mexicano, de ascendencia o herencia mexicanas, de orgullo militante por sus lazos con la cultura mexicana.'

            PC1 "Me siento muy chicano" Quirós 1928:346; Kercheville 1934:19; Keever 1945:10; Storz 1945:26; Barker 1950:19, 41; Ornstein 1951:139; Trejo 1951:19; Madsen 1964:11; Coltharp 1965:148; Baker 1966:52; Phillips 1967:66; Fody 1968:xvi, xviii–xix, Jan. 1970:44, 86, 185–186; Sharp 1970:218; Blanco 1971:558; León 1971:6; Rosales 1973:1.181–82, 2.227; Reyes 1974:1; Galván 1975:25, 1977:35.

            -Sp. *mexicano* 'Mexican'; cf. pop. Sp. *méchica/mésica(n)* 'Mexican' (Espinosa 1913:279; 283, n. 2; 316, n. 7). While there is no reason to discount the English influence posited by Espinosa, the internal Spanish $/x/ \sim /č/$ (cf. *jocoqui chocoque, empujar empuchar,* in Bowen 1952:165, 178) can adequately account for the sound change. Additionally, Mex. *chicana* 'trick, artifice, stratagem' (Fr. *chicane;* Inclán 1865:1.130; Ramos 1895:163; García 1899:147; Santamaría 1959:373; Rosales 1973:1.181) is an influence.

chicanada   f. 1. 'all (United States) *chicanos* '/' todo *chicano* (estado-unidense).'

            PC1 "Ahora escucha al gringo cuando habla la chicanada" Prieto 1971:58–59.

            2. (var. *chicaneada, chicaniada*) '(wily) *chicano* custom'/ '(mañosa) costumbre *chicana.*'

            PC2 "Aviéntale una chicanada" Rosales 1973:1.181; Galván 1975:25, 1977:34–35.

            Cf. Mex. *chicana* 'bad or shameless action' (Chabat 1956:38; Usandizaga 1972:19).

chicanero   adj. 'normally using *chicanas* or *chicanadas*'/ 'que acostumbra hacer *chicanas* o *chicanadas.*'

            PC2 "Son unos *batos* chicaneros" García 1899:147; Santamaría 1959:373; Fuentes 1962:120.

            Cf. Mex. *chicantana* 'rabble, riffraff' (Ramos 1895:164; Santamaría 1959:373).

NOTES

1. These criteria permit a rough identification of *caló* material. The outsider may classify much of this language as unsavory or taboo. For the *caló*-speaker, however,

the purpose in using *caló* is manifold: An expression may be substituted for a well-known conventional equivalent in order to: 1) protect the *speaker* from the discomfort caused by the conventional word or words, 2) protect the *speaker* from self-disclosure, or 3) create discomfort for the *listener*. The expression may invite the sympathy of ghetto-dwellers who also wish to avoid the intervention of the outsider or to inhibit his ease of action. The outsider is often unable to decipher the nuances of *caló,* whose interpretation requires a certain amount of inventiveness. For many users, more relevant than a creative tongue is a creative ear; the listener's interpretation reaches beyond the perception of thoughts and feelings consciously transmitted by the speaker.

Euphemism as a psychological interdiction also plays a part in *caló,* and must be differentiated, by its relation to the unconscious, from purposeful deformation and enciphering in the strictly technical language of delinquents and professional criminals. Furthermore, chance phonological, morphological, and semantic similarities can lead to the formation of new expressions, amply demonstrated in the lexicon.

2. "Word" is defined by informants as to boundaries; in cases of doubt, all elicited boundaries are shown, following the guidelines of Chao (1968, pp. 136–93). Native speakers will appreciate the difficulty, at times of separating *sino* from *si no.* Menéndez Pidal (1953, p. xiii) suggests that the Spanish Academy return to its original alphabetic norm, "international uniformity" (thus avoiding the difficulties of the *"abecechario"* of standard Spanish).

3. "Spelling" with, and alphabetization of, phonological symbols is difficult at best (see Wolf, 1960); I provide supplementary phonological specification if needed. In every instance, by reproducing the orthography of published sources, I enable the reader to locate cited material. Cf. Espinosa (1913, p. 251): "The inconsistencies of modern orthography clothe the written language with a Latin garb which seems to separate it widely from the popular pronunciation, but this is frequently not the case, the dialectologist having in many cases only to transcribe faithfully the words in question, using the traditional alphabet."

4. I have indicated, for instance, that verbs in *-ear/-iar* nearly always diphthongize syllables where the second of two vowels is stressed (thus: *jurneo,* but *jurniamos, jurniemos, jurnié,* etc.). In the case of *jurnear,* however, my informants confirm "regular" and "irregular" conjugations (e.g., *jurneo* and *jurnio*); I have, therefore, separate entries for *jurnear* and *jurniar.*

5. In the interests of precision and of intelligibility, "exact" synonymy is sought, but, where too abstruse, subdefinitions may be offered. The division, for English, is based on the *Oxford Advanced Learner's Dictionary* . . . (Hornby, 1975); for Spanish, the *Diccionario ideológico* . . . (Casares, 1966). Sometimes I will make fine practical distinctions, necessary for the reader and not always obvious to the native speaker; the reader's understanding, in such cases, takes precedence over "scientific" semantics.

6. Meanings, usages, and formulas are presented in their probable order of development (for a situation where that may be questioned, see *alfiler*). Of orally elicited sentence frames, the one providing optimum clarification of the gloss is given; only by coincidence would it duplicate one drawn from relevant literature. When the sentence frames, as well as lexical entries, contain *caló* terms other than the one at issue, these are marked by *underlining.* The reader may then consult the appropriate entry for any supplementary information.

7. Allophonic variants (e.g., *güey* for *buey*) are ignored in sentence frames, as

they would in no example here analyzed improve understanding of the *caló* lexicon (see also n. 3, above). For Romanés, which lacks an orthographic tradition, I use a modified International Phonetic Association system of transcription.

REFERENCES

Blanco S., A. *La lengua española en la historia de California*. Madrid: Cultura Hispánica, 1971.
Carroll, L. [Charles L. Dodgson]. *The annotated Alice* . . . (M. Gardner, Ed.) Cleveland: World, 1963.
Casares [y Sánchez], J. *Diccionario ideológico de la lengua española* (2nd ed.). Barcelona: Gili, 1966.
Chao, Y. R. *A grammar of spoken Chinese*. Berkeley: University of California Press, 1968.
Creswell, T. J. *Usage in dictionaries and dictionaries of usage*. Publication of the American Dialect Society, Nos. 63–64. University, Ala.: University of Alabama Press, 1975 [1978].
Dumas, B. K., & Lighter, J. Is slang a word for linguists? *American Speech, 1978, 53*(1), 5–17.
Espinosa, A. Studies in New Mexican Spanish: morphology. *Revue de dialectologie romane, 1913, 4*, 251–86.
Evans, B. (Ed.). *Dictionary of quotations*. New York: Delacorte, 1968.
Fernández de Lizardi, J. J. *El periquillo sarniento*. México, D. F.:Edinal, 1961. (Originally published, 1815–16).
Galván, R. A., & Teschner, R. V. *El diccionario del español chicano*. . . . Silver Spring, Md.: Institute of Modern Languages, 1977.
García Icazbalceta, J. *Vocabulario de mexicanismos*. México, D.F.: La Europea, 1899.
Hornby, A. S. *Oxford advanced learner's dictionary of current English* (3rd ed.). London: Oxford University Press, 1975.
Iordan, I. *Lingüística románica*. (M. Alvar, Ed. and trans.). Madrid: Alcalá, 1967.
Johnson, S. *Dictionary of the English language*. London: Strahan, 1755.
Keever, M., Vasquez, A., & Padilla, A. F. Glossary of words and expressions, irregular in form or meaning, encountered in the examination of Spanish mail on the Mexican border. Mimeographed. El Paso, Tex.: U.S. Office of Censorship, 1945.
Menéndez Pidal, R. El diccionario que deseamos. In S. Gili y Gayá (Ed.), *Diccionario general*. Madrid: VOX, 1953.
Webb, J. T. *A lexical study of caló and non-standard Spanish in the Southwest*. Ann Arbor, Mich.: University Microfilms International, 1976.
Wolf, S. *Grosses Wörterbuch der Zigeunersprache*. Mannheim, Germany: Bibliographisches Institut, 1960.

14 | Sex-related Speech Accommodation Among Mexican-American Bilinguals: A Pilot Study of Language Choice in Customer-Server Interactions

GUADALUPE VALDÉS, HERMAN GARCÍA, and
DIAMANTINA STORMENT
New Mexico State University

RESEARCH IN THE AREA OF WOMEN'S USE OF LANGUAGE

Within the last decade, increasing attention has been given to the study of women's use of language. Essentially, this research has presented two conflicting views: (1) that women do indeed habitually use speech patterns which are unique to them and which mirror their insecurities in general, and (2) that women's use of language patterns varies according to the situation, context, and interlocutors involved.

The first position views women as intrinsically (or by long conditioning) more sensitive (Argyle, Salter, Nicholson, Williams, and Burgess, 1970; Rosenthal, Archer, DiMatteo, Koivumaki, and Rogers, 1974), more aware of nuances in a variety of areas, and in general more likely to respond to both verbal and nonverbal cues in communicative exchanges.

The second position, on the other hand, has maintained that if and when there are differences in language use which suggest greater insecurity, efforts at politeness, and so forth, in women as opposed to men, these differences are related to the perceived social status, rank, and role of a specific woman vis-à-vis a specific man or to the social context which requires a particular style from female participants. Such speech differences, this view holds, are found among

Research for this project was supported by a Postdoctoral Fellowship for Guadalupe Valdés sponsored by the National Institute of Education–New Mexico State University Project on Minorities and Women.

all persons who interact and whose role relationships, perceived or actual status, and so forth, make wise use of a conscious or unconsciously differential speech style from one of the members of the interactive dyad. Thus, rather than peculiar to female speech, patterns which suggest insecurity, obsequiousness, and the like are also typical of men as they interact with other men or women who are perceived to be more "powerful."

MEXICAN-AMERICAN WOMEN'S USE OF LANGUAGE

In the study of the use of language by bilingual Mexican-American women, one specific feature, speech accommodation, has been focused on as a type of behavior which might again mirror an inherent desire to please found in all females, or which might simply be typical of all individuals who find themselves interacting with an interlocutor whose approval they desire to court.

Speech accommodation can be defined as the attempt by a member of an interactive dyad to adopt or reject the speech patterns of the person to whom he or she is speaking. Speech accommodation (convergent behavior) as it has been studied by Giles, Taylor, and Bourhis (1973) is essentially a subtle, generally unconscious process which has little to do with the social norms surrounding the speech exchange and a great deal to do with the speaker's desire to win the approval of an interlocutor. Among bilingual speakers, positive speech accommodation may involve relative blend and frequency of switches into the other language or the very choice of base language for carrying out the interaction. In two recent studies of the speech of Mexican-American bilinguals (Valdés-Fallis, 1978a, 1978b) a speaker is said to have *accommodated* to the language choice of an interlocutor if, having initially selected a language, he or she honors the other speaker's choice entirely or interjects utterances in this language which show an awareness of the other's preferred code.

QUESTIONS RAISED BY THE STUDY OF SPEECH ACCOMMODATION AMONG MEXICAN-AMERICAN BILINGUALS

The results of two studies (Valdés-Fallis, 1978a, 1978b) which have focused on speech accommodation by Mexican-American women have been as inconclusive as those which have examined the speech of monolingual American women. The first study examined the speech behavior of each of 4 women as they were engaged in interaction with 6 different persons of both sexes. Attention was given to the phenomenon known as code switching, and the number and frequency of switches for all 4 speakers were counted. It was determined that, when speaking with males, Mexican-American women tended to follow a language switch initiated by a male and also tended to imitate the relative frequency of language switching, as well as the kinds of switching patterns, selected by a male speaker throughout a conversation. Such accommodation was notably more limited, or nonexistent, in the speech exchanges involving any 2 female speakers.

The second study sought to explore speech accommodation in code-switching styles by Mexican-American men and women in response to the speech of three male speakers. The study was conducted in an experimental setting, and speakers were asked to respond to the taped speech of 3 male individuals whose style of switching had been carefully controlled. It was conjectured that in such an artificial setting, where no relationship existed between the taped speakers and the respondents, no difference would be found in the speech accommodation of men and women. The study did indeed conclude that speech accommodation occurs in both men and women if speakers perceive that there are potential rewards available to them in the form of approval from the other speaker or, in this case, from the experimenter. In an artificial setting, there seemed to be no difference in this feature between men and women.

A number of questions were raised by these studies. In the first case, the range of relationships which resulted in women's wishing to court male approval could not be determined. At the same time, a parallel set of tapes for male speakers was not available, a fact which made comparison impossible. In the second study, there was some uncertainty concerning the use of stimulus tapes. Again, it could not be determined how individuals responding to these tapes perceived their own role and status with regard to that of the taped speakers. The basic question of whether speech accommodation in bilinguals occurs predominantly among women because of inherent or conditioned attitudes or whether it occurs because of the power relationship as it is perceived between any two individuals was not answered.

THE PRESENT PILOT STUDY

The purpose of this pilot study was to investigate further the relationship between speech accommodation and sex among Mexican-American bilinguals. The study sought to examine this connection in naturalistic interaction in a context in which the power relationship between individuals might be kept constant. It was conjectured that in service encounters, that is, in interactions between clerks and customers in business establishments, the relationship between individuals would be stable, similar, and due primarily to the fact of the business exchange. Essentially, it was also conjectured that of the two individuals involved in such interaction, the server, especially if he were following the general maxim that the customer is always right, might be expected to view power as residing primarily in the customer. The study was intended to examine the difficulties to be encountered in determining

1. Whether male and female servers accommodate equally or unequally to the language choice of a male, as opposed to a female, customer
2. Whether different responses are related to age differences among servers
3. Whether bilingual servers of different ages or different sexes seek to determine the language strengths of a customer before selecting a base language
4. Whether final language choice is made by the server because of the perceived language preference of the customer or because of personal strengths, preferences, or limitations of the server

This pilot study primarily sought to identify how effective the manipulation of a standard communicative event might be in shedding light on a real-life problem. The study was designed, as will be explained below, in such manner as to require that two decoy customers (a man and a woman) select a specific language of exchange in order that the instances of accommodation or lack of it might be examined. It was conjectured that by using such manipulation, in a setting which otherwise kept constant the relationship between speakers, one might more directly determine the connection between sex and speech accommodation.

Design

The study was carried out in Las Cruces, New Mexico. A previous study of the same community (Valdés-Fallis, 1974) had established the fact that bilingual service personnel in the shopping centers of the community expected to be addressed in English. However, it was established also that Spanish was heard as frequently as English among shoppers and store personnel and that the use of either English, Spanish, or both seemed appropriate to all individuals surveyed.

For this pilot study, two Mexican-American bilinguals, 1 man and 1 woman of approximately the same age, general personality characteristics, and skin color, visited a number of business establishments located in the largest shopping center in the community. At 1-week intervals, the two individuals played the role of customers and interacted with servers in order to determine whether these individuals would or would not accommodate to their use of Spanish as a base language. During the first week, the female bilingual interacted with 10 servers who were obviously Mexican American and who could, given the general characteristics of the community, be assumed to be bilingual. A week later, the male bilingual retraced the previous week's route and interacted with as many of the same servers as were available. Of the 10 servers, 7 were available.

All interactions between decoy customers and servers were recorded. The customers wore small wireless FM transmitters which were capable of transmitting interaction occurring within a 5-foot radius. An FM receiver and cassette recorder were used at some distance from the decoy customers to record the speech exchange. Permission was obtained from all business establishments to record on the premises. The exact nature of the study was not disclosed.

Server Selection and Speech Manipulation: Details

Servers were selected jointly by the 3 authors of this study, who were, in fact, the 2 decoy customers and the individuals responsible for recording all interactions. Servers were selected arbitrarily within establishments which had given the investigators permission to record. The key factors in such selections were: (1) the physical characteristics of the individual; that is, he or she was required to be identifiably Mexican-American in appearance, and (2) the accessibility of the individual, that is, he or she must be in a position where response to customer questions was expected. Attention was given to the selection of an equal number of men and women.

Having selected the servers, the decoy customer approached the individual and spoke in Spanish in order to initiate the communicative exchange. Each customer was free to begin such interaction as he or she saw fit. It was only required that the customer retain Spanish as his or her base language.

ANALYSIS

The quality of the tapes obtained by means of the process described above varied. Interference from other sources resulted in heavy static, surrounding noise was loud, and the individual responsible for recording found herself in somewhat awkward positions at times in order to keep within the transmission range of the concealed microphone. However, in spite of background noise and static, enough of all the interactions was recorded clearly so that transcriptions of all tapes could be made. For each interaction, the first 8 turns of speaking were transcribed, using as a basis the system developed by Sacks, Schegloff, and Jefferson (1974).

The samples available included 10 interactions between the female researcher and the servers and 7 interactions between the male researcher and 7 of the *same* servers approached by the female researcher. Each transcribed sample was studied, and the server's use of language choices was determined for each of the first 5 turns of speaking. Samples 1 and 2 below will illustrate the process of analysis and comparison. The appendix (p. 196) contains additional samples.

1. TG&Y Store.   Saturday, 27 October 1979. Server: female, 22–25.
                                 Customer: female.

Turn 1   C: Señori : : ta—¿no venden tights para niños?
               S: ¿Qu'és eso?

Turn 2   C: tights
               S: O : : tights—no, uh uh.

Turn 3   C: No venden.
               S: No vendemos nada.

Turn 4   C: No venden leotards.
               S: Uh uh.

Turn 5   C: ¿Tampoco?
               S: We sure don't—un un—no—we sure don't.

Turn 6   C: Mu : chas gra : cias.
                   (Exchange ends.)

2. TG&Y Store.   Saturday, 3 November 1979. Server: female 22–25.
                                   Customer: male.

Turn 1   C: ¿Qué tal?
               S: Fine.

Turn 2   C: ¿Cómo stás?
                S: Bien, gracias.

Turn 3   C: Ando buscando material para cubrir los asientos de mi carro—
                   ¿ tienen—material?
               S: U : : m

Turn 4   C: ¿Para cubrir los asientos del carro?
               S: Se me'hace que sí (*pause*) allí onde estáquel material—junto del
                   (*inaudible*)

Turn 5   C: Sí.
               S: Más para ya—delante de allá—está una mesa y allí tienen dob-
                   lado—de no sé si es el clase que busca usté—pero.

Turn 6   C: Bue :no—déjeme ir a buscar allá a ver que
               S: OK:ay.

Turn 7   C: Bue :no gra :cias.
               S: A : : ja : : .
                   (Exchange ends.)

RESULTS

A comparison of the speech accommodation of the same 7 servers to the language choice of the male and female customers is summarized in table 14.1

Table 14.1: Accommodation by Servers to Language Choice of Customers

No.	Server Sex	Approx. Age	Store Name	Sex of Customer	Turn 1	Turn 2	Turn 3	Turn 4	Turn 5	Turn Where Accommodation Occurred
2	M	18–21	Safeway	Female	Engl.	Engl.	Engl./Span.	Ambig.	Engl.	3
				Male	Ambig.	Engl.	Engl.	Engl.	Span./Engl.	5
3	M	30–40	Skaggs	Female	Engl.	Engl.	Engl.	Engl.	Engl.	8
				Male	Span.	Span.	No resp.	Span.	Span.	1
5	F	18–21	Anthony's	Female	Span.	Span.	Span.	Span.	Span.	1
				Male	Span.	Span.	Span.	Span.	Span.	1
6	M	22–25	Anthony's	Female	Inaud.	Span.	Span.	Span.	Span.	2
				Male	Span.	Span.	Span.	Span.	Span.	1
7	F	50–60	Singer	Female	Span.	Span.	Span.	Span.	Span.	1
				Male	Span.	Span.	Span.	Span.	Span.	1
8	M	18–21	Kinney's	Female	Engl.	Engl.	Engl.	Engl.	Engl.	a
				Male	Engl.	Span.	Span.	Span.	Span.	2
9	F	22–25	TG & Y	Female	Span.	Ambig.	Span.	Ambig.	Engl.	1
				Male	Engl.	Span.	Ambig.	Span.	Span.	2

a. Did not occur.

193

below. For each turn of speaking, only responses by servers which could be identified clearly as English or Spanish or a combination of both were labeled. Responses such as "um : : : :" or "a : : : :" were classified as ambiguous.

Only 2 of the 7 servers for which a comparison was possible accommodated at the same turn of speaking with both the male and the female customer. These individuals were server 5 and server 7. All other servers accommodated to the language chosen by each of the customers at a different turn. One server (no. 8) did not accommodate at all to the choice of the female customer.

A comparison of the occurrence or nonoccurrence of speech accommodation for interaction with males and with females is contained in table 14.2. A binary system was used for this comparison, so that positive accommodation was given a rating of 1 and failure to accommodate was given a rating of 0. It will be noted that accommodation occurred with males 100% of the time, as opposed to 85% of the time with females.

Table 14.3 contains a less meaningful comparison, given the number of individuals involved, but one which might indicate a trend to be studied further. In this table, the turns at which accommodation occurred in speaking to both the male and the female customer are summarized, and the mean turn at which accommodation occurred for the male and the female customer is shown. It will again be noted that accommodation to the preferred choice of the female customer seems to have occurred at a later turn overall.

Table 14.4 focuses on male and female servers separately, giving the incidence of accommodation and the mean turn of accomodation in interaction with the male, as opposed to the female, customer. While again, one cannot be certain of the significance of these findings, given the small number of respondents, it does appear that male servers accommodated 100% of the time with the male customer and only 75% of the time with the female customer.

Table 14.2: Incidence of Occurrence of Accommodation

Server	With Male Customer	With Female Customer
2	1	1
3	1	1
5	1	1
6	1	1
7	1	1
8	1	0
9	1	1
Average	100%	85%

Table 14.3: Mean Turn at Which Accommodation Occurred

Server	With Male Customer	With Female Customer
2	5	3
3	1	8
5	1	1
6	1	2
7	1	1
8	1	Did not occur
9	2	1
Mean	1.85	2.67

Note: Accommodation occurred = 1. No accommodation accurred = 0.

Table 14.4: Accommodation by Male and Female Servers

	With Male		With Female	
Female Server	Incidence	Mean Turn	Incidence	Mean Turn
5 (F/18–21)	1	1	1	1
7 (F/50–60)	1	1	1	1
9 (F/22–25)	1	2	1	1
	100%	1.33	100%	1.00

	With Male		With Female	
Male Server	Incidence	Mean Turn	Incidence	Mean Turn
2 (M/18–21)	1	5	1	3
3 (M/30–40)	1	1	1	8
6 (M/22–25)	1	1	1	2
8 (M/18–21)	1	2	0	[a]
	100%	2.25	75%	4.33

a. Did not occur.

DISCUSSION

It was determined that the manipulation of a standard communicative event in the terms attempted in this study could indeed shed light on a real-life problem. All servers involved in the recorded interactions showed no particular reaction to the choice of Spanish by the decoy customers nor to the retention of this language for the extent of the interaction. All responded as they might to any one of a series of similar interactions.

While the natural limitations of this pilot study do not permit wide generalizations about the speech behavior of Mexican-American bilinguals, certain trends were revealed which made further study promising. It does appear, for example, that both male and female servers accommodate somewhat differently to the language choice of male and female customers. Accommodation seems to occur later in interaction with female customers and cannot always be expected to occur. On the other hand, accommodation always occurred in the interaction with the male customer. Additionally, these preliminary findings suggest that there is some difference between male and female servers in accommodating to the language choice of a customer. Female servers always accommodate to the language choice of the customer, regardless of sex, while male servers accommodate 100% of the time to the choice of the male customer, but not to that of the female customer.

It is clear, also, that the techniques employed in this study will elicit information concerning the relationship between age and response of individuals. In this very small sample, differences between same-age males were evident.

The techniques employed in this study will also provide information about the other questions raised. They can reveal much, for example, concerning the strategies employed by different individuals in determining language strengths of other interlocutors. While the tapes were not examined from that perspective, such examination is possible.

In essence, this pilot study has provided some initial evidence that both males and females do accommodate to the choice of a more "powerful" interlocutor. However, it has also pointed to the fact that personality differences, as well as language limitations, may be factors. In order to answer the broad question posed at the beginning of this study, it will become increasingly important to determine what factors take precedence for bilingual speakers. It will be necessary to establish, for example, how limited the skills of a speaker must be before he or she refuses to interact in his or her weak language, how individuals consider the merits of accommodating as opposed to that of preserving their own comfort, and finally, how sex, age, status, and the like weigh in this decision-making process.

Clearly, additional work needs to be done. It will be difficult to isolate factors, but continued attention to the questions raised here is exciting in what it can reveal, not only about differences in the use of language by men and women, but, more important, about bilingualism itself.

APPENDIX: SAMPLE TRANSCRIPTIONS OF CUSTOMER-SERVER INTERACTIONS

A.   Server no. 3 and another employee [E].   Location: Skaggs.   Sex: male.   Age: 30–40.

---

1. *Interaction with female customer*

    Turn 1   C: ¿Tienes el perfume "Jungle Gardenia"?
              S: I might *(inaudible)* one. *(Walks to another part of store and addresses another employee. Customer follows.)* Janet—have you seen "Jungle Gardenia"—in the perFUMES?
              E: Jungle of the *(inaudible)* Gardenia—you want jungle? Who makes it? Do you know?

    Turn 2   S: *(Addressing customer)* Do you know who
              C: No.
              (Pause. Employee continues looking. Customer addresses server.)

Turn 3   C: ¿Usteś el majoydomo?

           S: No—I resigned de de warehouse manager—I was the warehouse manager, then I resigned in January to go back to school; I said

Turn 4   C: Yahora qué está haciendo?

           S: AH : : I'm

Turn 5   E: I'm sorry ... *(Second server interrupts to speak to customer.)*

           C: Thank you.

           S: I came back full time y antonces en en January I'm going to cut out again; I'm just gonna work Saturdays and Sundays.

Turn 6   C: Y : : : : : :Y : : : : : que stá haciendo en la escuela.

           S: Management—I'm getting my degree in management.

Turn 7   C: ¿Ya mero termina?

           S: O : : : in : : by May *(inaudible)*.

Turn 8   C: ¿Y lo qué va' cer?

           S: Ah : : *(inaudible)* me me voya quedar con la compañía—porque pagan muy bien.

              (Exchange continues. Spanish use predominates.)

2. *Interaction with male customer*

Turn 1   C: No tiene shampú de *(inaudible)*.

           S: Nnnn : : no sé *(pause. Speaks to another customer.)* Hi—how are you? How's everything going? Pues ay quemándome *(laughter. Speaks to another employee)* Do you have any *(inaudible)* shampoo?

              (Pause. Server chats and laughs with same employee he addressed while she looks.)

Turn 2   C: Y tambień necesito un un shampú para ninõs—¿tiene?—pero que sea muy débil—que no sea fuerte.

           S: A : :para ninõs ¿si?

Turn 3   C: Sí.

           S: *(Speaks to same employee again.)* You don't have any? *(Continues talking with same person.)*

Turn 4   C: ¿Sabe cómo se usa éste? ¿Me puede decir cómo se usa?

           S: Ah : :*(Pause. Looks at container and reads instructions.)*

Turn 5   C: Porque dice shampú especial.

           S: Okay—se lo pone la primer vez—eh—entonces se lava el cabello tallándose el caspa y todo bien—y antonces se da su enjuague yantonces se guelve a dar otra-tallada con más shampú y entonces se lo deja por un poquito tiempo.

Turn 6   C: Aja : : : okey.
             S: Y : : yentonces—unos tres—cuatro minutos—me entiende—y
                  entonces se lo.

Turn 7   C: Me lo enjuago
             S: Se lo enjuaga completamente—okay?

Turn 8   C: Bue : no de regre : so lo levanto—Aquí va'star¿verdá?
                  (Exchange continues in Spanish.)

B.   Server no. 2.   Location: Safeway.   Sex: male.   Age: 18–21.

---

1.   *Interaction with female customer*

Turn 1   C: Oiga—¿no sabe dónde está el stroganoff?
             S: What's that?

Turn 2   C: D'esos que nomas se le—se le añide—tú sabes—ah ah carne
                  molida.
             S: Ah huh *(inaudible)*. I know where it is—but I can't—hold on—
                  let me check. *(Pause: Walks away. Addresses other employee.
                  Customer follows.)* Do you know where the stroganoff is? *(Hears
                  answer.)*—yeah—*(Leads customer to right aisle.)* I don't know
                  what it looks like.

Turn 3   C: Es una caja y dice—ah—stroganoff—y—es como hamburger
                  helper pero no—
             S: ˘   Oh.

Turn 4   C: ¿Tú nun : :ca's comido—stroganoff?
             S: I just know—¿qué quieres?—I don't know what it is.

Turn 5   C: No lu'has comido nunca.
             S: No.

Turn 6   C: U : :pos—si la—si la hallamos t'enseño lo que parece *(pause)*.
                  Mira—se parece a esto—Ves : :
             S: Oh yeah—like noodles.

Turn 7   C: Si nomás que tiene carne y—lo—tiene como—hongas—
                  (Pause) sabes lo que son hon : :gas *(laughter)*.
             S: No.

Turn 8   C: Mushrooms.
             S: Oh! mushrooms—it sounds good!

Turn 9   C: Ah huh.
             S: Oh good—okay—I've never tried it.

Turn 10   C: No? *(Both individuals search shelves.)*
             S: No.

Turn 11   C: Pues parece que no tienes por eso no lu'has comido. No la ve : :o.
           S: No : : nomás e:se.

Turn 12   C: ¿Es todo verdad? Mira aQUÍ—pero no es—otra ves estamos
               con noo : : :dles—mira—pero no—mira lo que tienes
               aqui': :pero no SON.
           S: Oh—that's—yeah—

Turn 13   C: ¿Deso sí has comido?
           S: Si hamburger pero no desa clase nomaś está. I never try it. I
               don't like to try things. I don't eat.

Turn 14   C: Pero si nunca lo—apruebas como vas a saber si está bueno o no
               (pause) yo creo que no tienes.
           S: No.

Turn 15   C: Ándale pues . . . mu : : chas GRAcias.
               (Exchange ends.)

2. *Interaction with male customer.* Customer talks to two employees: older male 55
    to 60 and young male 18 to 21. They are identified below as OS (older server)
    and YS (younger server). YS is server no. 2.

Turn 1   C: Si—no no—digo—voy—estoy planeando un—uh—viaje para
                ir a cazar venados y nicisito comida que no se me haga fea.
           OS: Ah no.
           YS: No.

Turn 2   C: ¿No sabe en dońde pudiera consequir?
           OS: No sé oiga.
           YS: Maybe Furr's.

Turn 3   C: ¿Dónde?
           YS: Back in—Furr's or Albertson's.
           OS: Pueda qu'ellos—

Turn 4   C: ¿Dónde queda eso? ¿puede darme direcciones?
           YS: Ah—si—Albertson's—Albertson's *(pause)* nomaś—you go
                through the lights right here—straight down El Paseo—next
                light *(inaudible)* make a turn.

Turn 5   C: D'esta luz que queda aquí—
                                                     ¿queda una luz aquí?
           S: Aquí mero queda una luzes y—after you turn you go straight
                down esta to the next light.

Turn 6   C: Y—ah—lo me voy derecho.
           S: Ah—right.

Turn 7   C: Volteo a la derecha digo.
            YS: Sí.

Turn 8   C: Cuando llegue a la luz.
            YS: Sí sí.

Turn 9   C: ¿Aquea?
            YS: Yeah—mira. *(Leads customer to part of store where intersection outside can be seen.)*

Turn 10   YS: Te vas por ésa—a tu left—nomás que das derecho.
            C: Sí.

Turn 11   YS: En the next light ay stá.
            C: Sí—gracias.
                  (*Exchange ends.*)

REFERENCES

Argyle, M., Salter, V., Nicholson, H., Williams, M., & Burgess, P. The communication of inferior and superior attitudes by verbal and nonverbal signals. *British Journal of Social and Clinical Psychology,* 1970, *9,* 222–31.

Giles, H., Taylor, O. M., & Bourhis, R. Y. Towards a theory of interpersonal accommodation through language: Some Canadian data. *Language in Society,* 1973, *15,* 87–105.

Rosenthal, R., Archer, D., DiMatteo, R., Koivumaki, J. H., & Rogers, P. L. Body talk and tone of voice: The language without words. *Psychology Today,* 1974, *8,* 64–68.

Sacks, H., Schegloff, E. A., & Jefferson, G. A simplest systematics for the organization of turn-taking for conversation. *Language,* 1974, *50,* 696–735.

Valdés-Fallis, G. Language choice in the Las Cruces area. Report to the Research Center, College of Arts and Sciences, New Mexico State University, 1974.

——. Code-switching among bilingual Mexican-American women: Towards an understanding of sex-related language alternation. *International Journal of the Sociology of Language,* 1978, *17,* 65–72. (a)

——. Speech accommodation in the language of Mexican-American bilinguals: Are women really more sensitive? Paper presented at the annual meeting of the Modern Language Association, New York, 1978. (b)

IV | Teaching and Learning

OVERVIEW

Researchers have pointed out that there may be great differences between what is taught and what is learned. This section focuses on the educational implications of bilingualism and language contact. As Kroskrity has demonstrated, the outcomes of language contact and bilingualism are always social. Educational programs focus on product and outcome sometimes to the exclusion of process.

Carole Edelsky and Sarah Hudelson show that this was clearly the case in one elementary-school bilingual program whose aim was to help all of the children to become bilingual in English and Spanish. The outcome was that while the Spanish-speakers acquired English, the English-speakers acquired very little, if any, Spanish. The authors attribute this to the children's awareness of the linguistic reality of the larger society, where English is the standard language and the language of prestige, and also to the teaching methods employed and the "political" atmosphere in the schools.

In a similar vein, Richard Teschner points out that even in a city as bilingual as El Paso, Texas, students whose native language is English but who have been exposed to Spanish throughout their elementary-school education are unable, if not unwilling, to use Spanish in more than a minimal way. He attributes this to a number of factors, especially to the students' frustration at being unable to speak Spanish after having studied it so long. Teschner suggests that some of the findings of Rosario Gingràs and his fellow authors (Gingràs, Ed., *Second-language Acquisition and Foreign Language Teaching,* 1978) might be used to develop new teaching methods to help these students.

The learning and teaching of Native American languages has often been a frustrating experience for those involved. J. Anne Montgomery attributes this to the clash between the syntactic structure of the majority of these languages and language-teaching methods derived from Indo-European languages, which have a very different syntactic structure. She criticizes the audio-lingual, cognitive approach and reports on an indigenous method developed by Native American speakers that incorporates attitudes toward teaching and learning that are accepted in many Native American cultures. This method uses natural texts and discourages early solo performance. The speech behaviors and learning strategies she reports for the Chippewa have been reported for many southwestern Native American speakers (see Kroskrity, this volume), and thus it is particularly appropriate to include this paper. In addition, the discovery of a method that appears to work is clearly important.

Marla Scafe and Gretta Kontas discuss the classroom implications of the differences between white and Native American rhetorical patterns described by Cooley and Lujan (this volume). Scafe and Kontas suggest that greater awareness of differing expectations for speech organization, on the part of speech teachers, could lead to a more flexible approach to the evaluation of speeches and to a more satisfying classroom experience for both teachers and Native American students.

15 | The Acquisition (?) of Spanish as a Second Language

CAROLE EDELSKY and SARAH HUDELSON
Arizona State University

BACKGROUND TO THE PRESENT STUDY

For some time, we have been concerned that most studies of second-language acquisition ignored the political nature of the second-language learning situation. Since researchers almost always investigate the acquisition of a target language which dominates the native language of the learner in the situation in which the learning is supposed to occur, we wondered if different second-language–learning strategies would be displayed if we looked at a situation wherein the usual relationship between the dominant target language and the less powerful native language was reversed. In the fall of 1977, then, we began a school-year–long study of three Anglo first graders supposedly acquiring Spanish as a second language in a bilingual classroom near Phoenix, Arizona (Edelsky & Hudelson, 1979). Although the goals of that school district did not include explicit attention to mutual second-language learning on the part of both Anglos and Chicanos, the teacher in our target classroom expressed that desire and made plans for it to occur. We did limited observations in that classroom in order to find out who was addressing Spanish to our subjects, for what purposes, and under what conditions. Every 2 weeks, with Sarah Hudelson (SH) posing as a monolingual Spanish-speaker, we audiotaped our subjects, each paired with a bilingual peer, in language-testing and play sessions. We left the room for about 20 minutes during those half-hour sessions, leaving the tape recorder on, in order to have samples of uninterrupted interaction, between the children.

Our findings were: 1) that no Spanish was addressed individually to these children by anyone except us during our biweekly sessions (i.e., that the Span-

An earlier version of this paper was prepared for the Southwest Areal Language and Linguistics Workshop of 1979 and was published as "Acquiring Spanish as a second language in a bilingual classroom," in Florence Barkin and Elizabeth Brandt (Eds.), *Speaking, singing and teaching: A multidisciplinary approach to language variation,* Anthropological Research Papers, No. 20 (Tempe: Arizona State University, 1980), pp. 33–41.

203

ish-speakers did not take the language-teacher role); 2) that during classroom activities conducted in Spanish, when they were part of a large group, and in our taping sessions, our English-speaking subjects "tuned Spanish out" in a variety of ways (i.e., they did not take the language-learner role); and 3) that, with the exception of a few color and number words, no Spanish was acquired (Edelsky & Hudelson, 1978). We felt that, unfortunately, our original hypothesis that the political relationship of target and native language might have some influence on strategies for second-language acquisition was verified in the extreme. The "influence" appeared to be that if a speaker of the school's usual, taken-for-granted, conducting-of-business language (an *un*marked language) (Fishman, 1976) was expected to learn a language on whose behalf special efforts had to be made so that it could appear as a school language (a marked language), little or no second-language acquisition would occur. A considerable influence! Additionally, it appeared that the unmarked/marked language distinction was responsible not only for differences in ultimate acquisition, but also for differences in conditions for acquisition. These conditions included a double standard in societal expectations for second-language acquisition and for playing out the role of learner and teacher, differential code-choice norms, and assymetrical reactions to both the "quantity" and authenticity of what was acquired (Edelsky & Hudelson, 1978).[1]

Despite what seemed to us to be a very clear set of findings, we hoped that we were wrong, that genuine, mutual second-language learning could occur if the conditions were optimal. We realized that in the 1977–78 study, acquisition of Spanish as a second language was not the goal of all the educational personnel and that Spanish was not used as the vehicle of instruction for anywhere near half the instructional time. Therefore, in 1978–79, we continued our search for strategies in the acquisition of a marked language as a second language in what we thought would be a more effective setting for second-language acquisition.

RESEARCH QUESTION

Our research question was altered to include two parts: 1) What is the context for acquisition of the marked language (What classroom interactions occur in what language, for what functions)? and 2) What strategies are used by learners in order to interact in, make sense of, and hopefully acquire a marked language?

SETTING

This time, we chose a classroom in a district near Phoenix in which one of the explicit goals of the bilingual program was to produce bilinguals among both

Spanish- and English-speaking children. Not only was this the rhetoric, but the district had instituted systematic second-language instruction in each language, and it assessed second-language proficiency in each language with a test (the Primary Acquisition of Language Test [PAL], a test devised for use in the El Paso Title VII Bilingual Project). Moreover, almost all of those involved in the bilingual program (principals, teachers, aides, children, parents of the English-speakers) were aware that both groups of children were supposed to be learning a second language.

The language schedule in this first-grade classroom was also different from that in 1977–78. The teacher studied in 1978–79 elected to use an Alternate Days model, continuing the delivery of content, rather than translating it; one day was English Day, the next was Spanish Day. We assumed that this would result in a greater quantity of Spanish being spoken in the classroom than resulted from the subject-matter scheduling model that we studied in 1977–78, when a smaller overall number of whole class events were conducted in Spanish than in English and when the Spanish activities suffered from much switching into English.[2]

There were 22 children in the class: 10 were bilinguals or monolingual Spanish-speakers who were bussed in from a *barrio*. Twelve lived in the neighborhood and were English monolinguals or English-dominant children with some limited ability to produce Spanish. Of the 12 neighborhood children, 5 were Anglos; 7 were Chicanos.

As in our first study, SH posed as a monolingual Spanish-speaker. Her almost weekly presence in the classroom for observation and participation was another deliberate effort on our part to maximize the possibilities for acquisition of Spanish. With "la Señora Spanish" (as one bilingual called her) there, the English-speakers would not only be assured of getting some Spanish directed to them occasionally on a one-to-one basis, but, if they wished to interact with her, they would have to attempt to understand her and to accommodate to her monolinguality.

METHOD AND SUBJECTS

Rather than gathering most of our data from special sessions with pairs of children, this year we also participated and observed in the classroom for one-half to a full school day at least 3 times each month, from October through early April. There were three observers: the two authors and a graduate student.[3] In deference to the teacher's wishes, often only one observer was present on a given day. All observers paid special attention to code choice, functions of language, and examples of sense-making, participation, or withdrawal by Anglophiles in relation to Spanish interactions.

In the classroom, we interacted with all of the children, helped them with their work, had casual conversations with them, played with them, helped the teacher at her request—in other words, acted as both adult volunteers and as observers. We carried notebooks with us and took notes even during our participating time. Whenever possible, we tried to record verbatim exchanges.

We selected 3 of the Anglo children—Kathy, Katie, and Nathan—and two Chicanos—Vince and Anita—for close observation (though other children were also studied). According to testing, our observations, and the teacher's, Vince and Anita were very close to being monolingual in English. Their personal histories indicated, however, that Spanish was used around them at home occasionally, or at family events. We reasoned that, given a second-language–learning environment where the target language is marked, perhaps some familiarity with the "tune" of the language, possible prior understanding of some social routines, and associations of the language with intimate family events would provide the extra push that would result in major progress for these two children in the ability to produce that language for real communicative purposes. Therefore a gross comparison of the 3 Anglos and the 2 Chicanos was planned. One *un*-planned-for difference between the 1977–78 and 1978–79 investigations was that the children studied in the current investigation appeared to be of higher socioeconomic class status.

In addition to observing the children in the classroom, as in the previous study, we took each of these 5 subjects, with a Spanish-speaking peer, to a separate room where we gave them a comprehension and repetition task. They were asked—in Spanish, of course—to show SH the picture of the big boy, little boy, and so forth, and to repeat sentences such as *es un muchacho grande (this is a big boy)*. After SH tested them, she played with them, using Play-dough, puppets, magic slates, and other toys. Again, during the playtime, we left the children alone for several minutes. The sessions were conducted entirely in Spanish and were audio-tape-recorded with a Pioneer KD-11 cassette recorder. One child wore the Realistic Condenser microphone. The other researcher, Carole Edelsky (CE), sat in the background and whispered observations of the context into a second tape recorder. In the current study, we held only 3 of these testing sessions, since, on the basis of our previous findings, we no longer expected that the grammar acquired would be changing so rapidly that frequent documentation would be necessary.

FINDINGS

The Second-Language–Learning Context

The features that seemed noteworthy about the context in which the acquisition of Spanish was supposed to occur were: the functions for which Spanish was used; the circumstances under which Spanish and English each crept into the other language's "day"; the children's perception of the nature of the systematic second-language (SL) instruction; and the effect of the presence of the "monolingual" Spanish-speaking adult in the classroom.

Our observations show that "Public Spanish" from a child (the use of Spanish to several people or to one person in front of an audience) was used only by those children who were bussed from the *barrio,* and then only if both the addressee and all members of the audience were bilingual. Public Spanish from children was used for a wide range of cognitive and social functions—directing, predicting, informing, teasing, threatening, explaining, consoling. Public Spanish from the teacher and two aides (interactions involving SH will be discussed separately from those of the other adults in the classroom) was restricted functionally by the teacher role that the adults were playing. Exchanges where the function was directing, reprimanding, explaining, entertaining (storytelling), keeping order, providing transitions between activities, establishing social contact, and conducting classroom routines (taking attendance, collecting lunch money) were noted.

Spanish that was directed individually to our subjects (not in a public setting) or to other English-dominant children was much more rare than Public Spanish, and much more limited in function. It was predominantly used for social routines such as greetings *(buenos días)*, for reprimands, and for directions when the activity could also be signalled nonverbally. It was not used by adults for explaining, joking, warning, or "making conversation" during any momentary stepping out of the teacher role. With almost no exceptions, it was not used at all by children. The exceptions were all produced by two Mexican immigrants (Eréndida and Lily) who were monolingual in Spanish in August. Once, Eréndida gave Anita a short direction in Spanish which she followed without pause with an English paraphrase. During a test session, Lily and Kathy provided the only evidence of any overt negotiations by children over code choice.

(1) Kathy: What's she doing?
    Lily: Dice tú—(She says you—)
    K: Don't say in Spanish. English.
    L: Que, te digo español. (That, I tell you Spanish.)
    K: English!
    L: Nope.
    K: Say it in English!
    L: No. *(The argument was ended by our resumption of the testing.)*

In an Alternate Days bilingual program, the "rule" is one language per day. Nevertheless, loudspeaker announcements are made daily in English, Spanish-speakers talk to each other in Spanish every day—in other words, no day is "language pure." However, the frequency and extent of the other language's intrusion was not symmetrical in this classroom. Spanish was used very infrequently on English days. Outside of Spanish reading time for Spanish-speakers, adults used no Public Spanish on English Day. What they did use was one-to-one Spanish, directed only to Spanish-dominant children, either as a reprimand or in response to an initiation in Spanish by a child. Spanish used between children on English Day seemed slightly but not obviously diminished.

The picture for the intrusion of English into Spanish Day was vastly different, not only in comparison with the use of Spanish in English Day, but also in comparison with the use of Spanish during Spanish Day. English was used publicly to all, not merely to English-dominant children, on Spanish Day. It was used for the same functions as was Public Spanish on Spanish Day, but additionally it was used for ensuring the understanding of the Anglophiles, with the teacher asking, "Do you understand?" and providing an explanation in English if necessary. There was no comparable checking on English Day, with ¿entienden? along with a Spanish explanation for the Spanish-dominant children. On Spanish Day, whenever adults referred to a meaning that could not be pointed to, acted out, or predicted, they switched to English *(Now when you get finished, wait for someone to come around and help you; There's going to be a surprise tomorrow)*. Sometimes, English was used to "frame" or announce a verbal activity *(I'll explain this first in English and then Spanish)*. Like Spanish, it was sometimes used for transitions and to announce routines *(O.K., English reading group now)*, and for some directions and checking of plans between the teacher and an aide. It was always used to conduct activities in other rooms in the school and in the presence of nonbilingual outsiders who might come in to make announcements. It was even used by Spanish-dominant children to the "monolingual" researcher. Whereas Public Spanish on Spanish Day was limited in function, English on Spanish Day was not. While Spanish on English Day occurred only in relation to the language competence of the addressee, English on Spanish Day appeared for more varied reasons.

Another aspect of the second-language–learning context was the provision of second-language instruction by the audio-lingual method, for both English and Spanish, and a "booster" program for development of the weaker language in bilinguals. ("Special English" was provided for children who scored badly on the English version of the PAL test. Some Spanish-surnamed children, who appeared to us to be native English speakers, went to Special English. There were no comparable "Special Spanish" classes.) The children were aware of the divisions in the language teaching program and in the class generally. They referred to "the kids who come on the bus"; they would name which children went to Spanish as a Second Language (SSL), to ESL, and to Special English; they sometimes commented on which children were potential after-school playmates (for logistical reasons, at least, it was not those who left on a bus); they knew which children could be used as translators.

Their perception of the special second-language lessons also became part of the context. To them, the lessons and the routines learned were to be used as games or performances one could dredge up to entertain or impress another. Kathy occasionally approached SH with cards showing fruits, articles of clothing, and so forth, pointed to the cards and to the adult, said *'spañol,* and tried to elicit card-naming in Spanish as a game. Nathan once said that though he could not speak Spanish, he could say *es un abrelata* [sic], *(it's a can opener).* That the phrase *es un (it's a)* was perceived as a frame in a game or routine, rather than as a productive way to express a labeling or referential function, is shown by its total absence at any time when our subjects were intending to label. This perception was foregrounded for us by a comment made by Kathy. In one taping session, SH was asking Kathy about what the children did in the SSL class.

(2) SH: ¿De qué platican? (What do you talk about?)
     K: *(Laughs)* What?
     Lily: Que ¿qué platican? Sorda! (She says what do you talk about, you deaf thing!) They say what you, what you talk in Ms. V.'s class en español.
     SH: ¿De qué platican? (What do you talk about?)
     K: Es un. (It's a), *(spoken with terminal intonation contour.)*

Perceptions of the artificiality or communicative uselessness of the SSL activities were similar for ESL activities. When Lily, Kathy's taping-session partner, told SH that in ESL they talked and played the "radio" (probably a record player), SH asked what the "radio" was for.

(3) Lily: Inglés, para que aprendamos inglés. Dicen "I'm a fireman." Dicen así. (English, in order to learn English. They say "I'm a fireman." They talk like that.)

The usual intent of second-language instruction is to highlight "patterns" (syntactic constructions, phoneme boundaries, etc.) within a language and speed up their acquisition. However, all that this Spanish-as-a-second-language instruction seemed to be facilitating was the learning of a few lexical items from various categories (body parts, articles of clothing, kitchen items, occupations) for use in answering questions and for adding a routine to the children's playing-school games.

The occasional presence of a "monolingual" Spanish-speaker (SH) in the classroom was a factor we had deliberately placed in the context in order to provide an objective need for children to accommodate to the demands of an interlocutor who did not understand them, whether or not they perceived this need. However, we did not anticipate that her presence would also influence the functions of language to which they were exposed in Spanish. Since SH was not responsible for directing activities or maintaining order in the classroom, she could engage children in casual conversation, something the teacher and aides never did, owing to their roles in that setting. While "shooting the breeze," then, SH (but no other adult) used Spanish both publicly and individually, in order to get information, to make social contact and open a conversation, to get translations, to joke, to compliment. Though the "monolinguality" imposed a pressure to maintain a pretense, it relieved a pressure to avoid violating a code-choice norm. In other words, because speaking in Spanish "couldn't be helped," it was easier for SH to avoid switching to English when the topic could not be pointed to or when the addressee displayed a lack of comprehension. Once every other week, then, our subjects received persistent, situated Spanish input carrying a range of intentions.

Language Acquisition (?) in This Context

Findings on our subjects' responses to the second-language–learning context can be grouped into four categories: 1) display of metalinguistic awareness; 2) taking the learner role in comprehending; 3) not taking the learner role; and 4) producing Spanish.

METALINGUISTIC AWARENESS

Our subjects appeared to have developed a striking awareness of language as an entity, of the existence of multiple languages, of a relationship between language, ethnicity, and geography, and of second-language learning as something which occurs in relation to need. Sometimes, this awareness was stated neutrally; sometimes it was accompanied by positive or negative statements (the opposing affects often expressed by the same child). In class, Kathy and Katie were engaged in a bit of competition.

    (4)   Kathy: I can speak three languages—English, and Spanish, and Indian.
           Katie: Well I can speak four—English, and Spanish, and Scotland, and Jewish.
           Kathy: So! I'm gonna learn Flagstaff.

Anita let SH know that since the same idea can be expressed differently in different languages, synonyms with certain phonological characteristics (such as *pony* and *horse,* where pony sounds faintly Spanish) might actually be translations.

    (5)   Anita: *Pony* in English is *horse.*

We heard many comments like the following:

(6) *(After we had left the room during a taping session:)*
Nathan: Finally, we can speak English. I hate Spanish.

(7) Andrés *(Nathan's peer partner):* You know how to talk Spanish.
N: Nope, only in English.
A: But you're trying, you're trying.
N: Yup, cause I *want* to talk in Spanish.

(8)   I don't talk Spanish. I just know the colors.

(9)   Do you speak English? Then why don't you speak it?

(10) *(Responding to an encouraging remark from her peer partner about learning Spanish:)*
Yeah, I'm learning because I *got* to learn. Every day I go home my dad teaches me how to talk Spanish 'cause we're going to Mexico to meet my dad's cousins, my mom's cousin.

TAKING THE LEARNER ROLE

In order to acquire a second language, to use the language input to construct one's own hypotheses about underlying rules, one must do at least two things: make sense out of nonsense—bring meaning *to* sounds, since, by definition, one is unable to get meaning *from* them (Macnamara, 1973); and be a participant in interactions, presenting oneself as a legitimate receiver of input (Wong-Fillmore, 1976). Primary aspects of the learner role, then, are to use clues to guess at meanings and to stay in an interaction by taking one's conversational turn.

In both classroom and taping sessions, our subjects often took this role. They would watch faces intently, matching facial expressions with the speaker, with a split-second delay. They took their turns using head nods, shrugs of shoulders, giggles, and requests for clarification. More interesting was their verbal turn-taking, which often included uncanny guesses at the speaker's meaning. These guesses seemed to be based on various combinations of verbal and visual clues, along with clues from their "real-world knowledge" (which might mean knowing that there is a great likelihood that an adult in an interview setting is asking a child a question, that some questions are more likely than others in relation to given topics, that topics tend to be maintained across several turns, that certain behaviors are expected in school or testing settings, etc.).

Our subjects used at least 8 of these combinations of clues. Many of their efforts masqueraded as comprehension of Spanish. Others showed the masquerade up for what it was, sophisticated sense-making, even if it was wrong. In the examples which follow, we will present exchanges which make it look as though the subject is comprehending the language. Our inferences concerning

the children's presumptions about the likely questions they are being asked in
certain contexts is in brackets.

1. Gesture + likely question
    (11)   SH: *(Points at "Grease" written on Nathan's T-shirt.)* ¿Qué
                 dice aquí? (What does this say?)
           N: [If an adult in school is pointing at print, she is probably
                 asking me to read it] Grease.
    (12)   *(During play part of the taping session; they are working with
           playdough:)*
           SH: ¿Qué vas a hacer ahora, Katie? (What are you going to
                 make now, Katie?)
           K: [If an adult is looking at something I'm doing as part of
                 an adult-initiated activity, the question is probably
                 about what I am making.] A pillow.

2. Names + likely question (we are assuming that children's first names
    and adults' titles + last names are often comprehended, salient items
    in a string of strange speech sounds.)
    (13)   *(During play session:)*
           SH: Anita. ¿estudias español con Ms. V.? *(the SSL teacher.)*
                 (Anita, do you study Spanish with Ms. V.?)
           A: [The topic concerns Ms. V. . . .] *(No response.)*
           SH: ¿Qué hacen? ¿Platican? (What do you do? Talk?)
           A: *(Nods head.)* Yes.
           SH: Sí. ¿Qué dicen? ¿De qué platican? (Yes, What do you
                 say? What do you chat about?)
           A: *(No response.)*
           CE: ¿Quienes más van contigo al cuarto de Ms. V.? Kathy?
                 ¿Quien más? (Who else goes with you to Ms. V.'s room?
                 Kathy? Who else?)
           A: [The topic concerns a category including Kathy and Ms.
                 V. The likely question is Who else is in that category?]
                 Rolando. *(Anita is right.)*
    (14)   *(During play session:)*
           Andrés *(to SH):* Él *(Nathan)* tiene hermanos. (He has
                 siblings.)
           SH: ¿Cómo se llaman? (What are their names?)
           A: Ronnie . . .
           SH: Nathan, ¿quién es Ronnie? (Nathan, who is Ronnie?)
           N: [The topic concerns Ronnie. A likely question is Who is
                 Ronnie?] My brother. *(Goes back to writing on the
                 Magic Slate.)*

3. Language clue (other than names) + gesture + likely question or expectation
    (15) *(At the moment when the test task changed from 'point to the picture' to 'repeat the phrase':)*

    SH: Ahora, las muchachas están corriendo. (Now the girls are running.)

    K: *(Points to correct card.)*

    SH: Esta vez, vas a decir lo que digo yo, eh, Katie? Di, es un muchacho chiquito. (This time, you're going to say what I say, O.K., Katie? Say "es un muchacho chiquito.")

    K: [SH has slowed the speed of one phrase. Her chin is jutting out, and her head tilt remains constant, as though her utterance is incomplete. One section of sounds is familiar from SSL—"es un." The likely request is, as in SSL, for me to repeat the "es un" phrase.] Es un muchacha (sic) chiquito.

    (16) *(Katie is drawing a picture of a man and a woman:)*

    SH: ¿Es tu mamá? Cómo es el pelo de tu mamá, Katie? (It's your mom? What's her hair like?)

    K: [The topic concerns my mom.] *(No response.)*

    SH: (Points to own hair.) Tiene mucho pelo, mucho cabello? (Does she have a lot of hair?)

    K: *(No response.)*

    SH: Katie, ¿de qué color es el pelo de tu mamá? (Katie, what color is your mom's hair?)

    K: [The topics have to do with mama and hair. One string of sounds is familiar and signals an understandable question—"de qué color." The question probably refers to the topics mama and hair.] Rojo. *(Katie is right.)*

4. Language clue + likely question
    (17) *(Writing on Magic Slates:)*

    Eréndida: Yo sé escribir mi nombre en letra corrida. (I know how to write my name in cursive.)

    SH: ¿Quien te enseñó? (Who taught you?)

    E: Mi Mamá. (My mom.)

    SH: Y tú Anita, ¿Quién te enseñó a escribir así? (And you, Anita, who taught you to write like that?)

    A: [The topic includes Mamá. Adults in school often ask a question with many right answers and then expect children to take turns giving answers to the same question. A likely question is What else goes with mamá?] Papá.

5. Another child's actions + likely question or direction
   (18) *(At end of comprehension/repetition task:)*
      SH: Es todo. Ahora, ¿con qué quieres jugar? ¿Plastilina? Títeres? (That's all. Now what do you want to play with? Playdough? Puppets?)
      Nathan: *(No response.)*
      SH: ¿Qué quieres tú, Andrés? (What do you want, Andrés?)
      Andrés: Plastilina. (Playdough.) *(Points at can.)*
      SH: *(Gives can of Playdough to Andrés.)* ¿Y qué quieres tú? (And what do you want?), *(to Nathan.)*
      N: [Adults in school often expect the same behavior from each child in turn. Andrés chose materials. It is now my turn. The likely expectation is for me to make a choice.] *(Points to Playdough.)*
   (19) *(During comprehension/repetition task:)*
      SH: Nathan, di "es un muchacho chiquito." (Nathan, say "es un muchacho chiquito.")
      N: [The direction has been to point to one of the cards, up until now. The likely direction is to continue the pattern.] *(Points to card of little girl.)*
      SH: Esa es una muchacha chiquita. Di la frase tú. "Es un muchacho chiquito." (That's a little girl. *You* say the phrase "es un muchacho chiquito.")
      N: [Absence of the formula "muy bien" means I didn't choose right. The likely direction is to try again.] *(Points to card of little boy).*
      SH: *(To Andrés)* Tú di la frase primero y luego Nathan. (You say the phrase first, and then Nathan.) "Es un muchacho chiquito."
      A: Es un muchacho chiquito.
      SH: Ahora tú, Nathan, "Es un muchacho chiquito." (Now you, Nathan. "Es un muchacho chiquito.")
      N: [Adults in school often expect the same behavior from each child in turn. Andrés repeated a phrase. It is now my turn. The likely direction is to repeat the phrase.] Es un /nut ate kidit o/.

6. Another child's actions + language clue + likely question
   (20) Hector *(Vince's peer partner, to SH):* ¿Puedo ir al excusado? (Can I go to the bathroom?)
      SH: O.K.
      H: *(Leaves room.)*

SH: ¿No tienes que ir, Vince, al baño? (You don't have to go, Vince, to the bathroom?)

V: ["Excusado," in combination with Hector's leaving, means he went to the bathroom. Adults in school often expect the same behavior from all children. The likely question is do I want to go also.] Na unh, I don't have to.

7. Knowing the topic from having initiated it + continuing one's own topic (based on the interactional knowledge that topics often continue over several turns)

   (21) *(Vince has brought up the topic of being in the taping room before, since it had been his room in kindergarten.)*

   SH: ¿Qué es "kindergarten"? (What's "kindergarten"?)

   V: *(No response.)*

   SH: ¿Quién era la maestra? (Who was the teacher?)

   Hector: Mrs. L.

   V: (My topic is my kindergarten experience. Mrs. L. is a name I recognize, but she doesn't fit my topic.) That wasn't our teacher. We had another one.

   Hector: Mrs. L.

   V: [My topic is my kindergarten experience. Mrs. L. is a name I recognize, but she doesn't fit my topic.] That wasn't our teacher. We had another one.

   CE: ¿Cómo se llama? (What's her name?)

   V: [My topic is my kindergarten teacher. A likely question is, What's her name?] Mrs. M.

   CE: Ms. M. ¿Está en esta escuela todavía? Sí? ¿no? (Is Ms. M. still in this school? Yes? No?)

   V: [My topic is Ms. M. I will tell more about Ms. M.] She moved to another work. She's working—she gives people food. She serves people.

8. Knowledge of likely demands made by someone acting out the teacher or interviewer role

   (22) SH: *(Puts two picture cards out in front of Nathan at our first testing session.)* ¿Ves los dibujos, Nathan? Quiero que me enseñes el muchacho grande. (Do you see the pictures, Nathan? I want you to show me the big boy.)

   N: [Teachers and interviewers often test children with pictures. During these tests, children have to choose one of the pictures by circling, underlining, or pointing.] *(Points to picture of the little girl.)*

Most of the preceding examples make it seem that our subjects had already acquired enough Spanish to understand the language, not merely the context. Our contention, however, is that they were simply doing what is necessary in order to *begin* to acquire a second language; namely, participate, guess the general gist of an extended exchange, and guess the specific communicative demand of a particular turn. Evidence for that position comes from the children's failure to respond correctly when SH deliberately withheld gestures; from the great number of times when at first they responded with shrugs, and then responded appropriately to the same questions when translated by one of the bilingual children; from their failure to respond at all to any "there/then" topic which could not be tipped off by a person's name (with the exception of one answer from Vince); and, most important, from the times when they took a guess, but their guess missed the mark. The fact that these outright errors in comprehension can be accounted for through inferring what topic or question the subjects thought they were answering is the basis for the claim that a guessing strategy, based primarily on nonlanguage clues, was at work in other responses also. Examples of these missed-the-mark responses, along with the clue combinations which we believe were being used (identified by the numbers used in the previous listing) are:

1. Gesture + likely question
   (23) SH: *(Leans forward and looks at Anita's cursive writing of her name.)* ¿Quién te enseñó a escribir así? (Who taught you to write like that?)
         A: [The topic being posturally identified is my writing. The likely question in relation to written symbols is, What does it say?] Anita.

4. Language clue + likely question
   (24) *(Preceding references have been to Katie's picture of her mother and father and her sister, Carrie.)*
         SH: ¿Cuántos años tiene? (How old is she?)
         K: [I recognize *cuántos* as meaning 'how many'. The general topic has concerned members of my family. The likely question is How many children are there?] *(Holds up two fingers. Carrie is actually 9 years old.)*
         SH: Dos. Tiene dos años, dos años. (Two. She's 2 years old, 2 years.)
         K: [I understand "dos." The adult is reiterating my elicited answer that there are 2 children in my family. I will further elaborate that response.] Me and Carrie.
   (25) SH: ¿Tienes hermanos, Anita? (Do you have siblings, Anita?)

A: *(No response.)*
Eréndida: Trae una hermana. (She has a sister.)
SH: ¿Es más chica o más grande? (Is she younger or older?)
A: *(Shrugs shoulders.)*
E: Grande. (Bigger.)
SH: Ah, ¿cuántos años tienes, Anita? ¿Seis años?
A: [I'll answer yes in response to a word I recognize, like "seis."] *(Nods yes.)*
SH: Sí. ¿Y tu hermana? ¿Ocho años? (Yes. And your sister? Eight years old?)
A: [I like to answer yes when I recognize a word like *ocho*.] *(Nods head yes.)*
SH: Sí. ¿Cómo se llama? (Yes. What's her name?)
A: [I recognize the *como se llama* string as having to do with names. The likely question is What's your name?] Anita.
SH: Tú te llamas Anita. Pero tu hermana. ¿Cómo se llama ella? (*Your* name is Anita. But what's your sister's name?)
A: [A repeated question about a name probably refers to who else is present.] Eréndida. *(not true)*
(26) SH: Y Katie, ¿cómo esta tu papá? (And Katie, how is your father?) *(She had told us the month before that he had hurt his back.)*
K: *(No response.)*
SH: ¿Mejor? ¿Se siente mejor? (Better? He feels better?)
K: [I recognize "papá," which must be the next topic. A likely question concerning my father is, What does he do for a living?] Makin' insurance.

5. Another child's actions + likely question or direction
(27) *(During the first comprehension/repetition task session:)*
SH: Enséñame el muchacho grande. ¿Cuál es el muchacho grande? (Show me the big boy. Which is the big boy?)
Kathy: *(Shrugs her shoulders.)*
Lily: No sabe cuál es. (She doesn't know which one it is.)
SH: ¿No sabe? (She doesn't know?)
L *(To K):*   A boy big.
K: [Lily has just said a phrase backwards about one of the cards. Adults in school often expect similar behavior from each child in turn. I will try a backward phrase about another card.] Girl big.

L: A boy.
K: [The pattern must not be backwardness. I will try rep-
      etition.] A boy.
SH: Enséñame. (Show me.)
L: Touch it. Put, put your fingers.
K: *(Points at correct picture.)*

7. Knowing the topic from having initiated it + continuing one's own
    topic
    (28)   Katie *(Playing with Playdough):*   You know what I'm gonna
            get for my birthday September 10? *(Conversation con-
            tinues about her anticipation of receiving a waterbed.)*
            SH: ¿Quién te la va a dar? (Who's going to give it to you?)
            K: *(Shrugs shoulders.)*
            SH: ¿Tienes un novio, Katie? *(New topic.)* (Do you have a
                  boyfriend?)
            K: Mmmmmm.
            SH: ¿Quién es tu novio? (Who's your boyfriend?)
            K: [My topic is the waterbed. That is also what I'm making
                  out of Playdough. I'll repeat when I'm going to get this.]
                  My birthday.

8. Knowledge of likely demands made by someone acting out the teacher
    or interviewer role
    (29)   *(Katie is making a model of the waterbed she expects to receive.
            There are other toys available to go along with the Playdough;
            cookie cutters, small dolls, etc. SH does not gesture toward
            these objects.)*
            SH: ¿Quieres otra cosa, Katie? ¿Quieres más? (Do you want
                  something else, Katie? Do you want more?)
            K: [Adults in school often ask children to name what they
                  are making.] /Maͥ ya/ cama. (My bed.)

On a few occasions, we are quite certain that for Vince, the meaning-hypoth-
esizing about an entire exchange was less dependent on the strategy of assessing the nonverbal context. For example, after his class had moved to a new
room SH asked him which room he liked better, the old or the new one (a
there/then topic difficult to indicate by gesture). After he nodded his head in
response to *el nuevo (the new one),* he was asked why. He answered *más grande
(bigger),* which was also one of his two multiword utterances in Spanish in 7
months. In the classroom, SH once asked him what he *had* to do next *(¿Qué
tienes que hacer ahora?).* He responded in English with "I *have* to do this." Of
course, these instances were balanced by the times when he totally failed to
respond and by his inappropriate responses. Still we would speculate that
Vince's responses may have been based on a combination of "true" language

comprehension and context-guessing, while those of the others were based almost entirely on their use of non-Spanish clues.

NOT TAKING THE LEARNER ROLE

There were many times when the subjects either simply failed to take their turn and try to guess at the meaning of talk or when they refused outright to take part or comprehend. Absence of turn-taking or guessing occurred when the Spanish-speaker

1) used certain WH (where, what, who, how, why, when) questions,

> (30) SH: ¿Cuándo te platican en español? (When do they talk to you in Spanish?)
> V: *(No response; looks at wall.)*

2) asked about there/then topics (coupled with a WH question),

> (31) SH: ¿Cómo se siente tu papá? (How does your father feel?)
> K: *(No response.)*

3) initiated new topics which were not accompanied by gestures or supporting context,

> (32) CE: ¿Sabes el cuento do los tres osos? (Do you know the story of the Three Bears?)
> K: *(No response.)*

or 4) barraged the child with language:

> (33) SH: ¿Tienes hermanos, Katie? ¿Y hermanas? Tienes una mamá y un papá. Y hermanos y hermanas no tienes? ¿Quién está en tú familia? ¿Tú y quién más? (Do you have brothers, Katie? And sisters? You have a mom and a dad. And you don't have brothers and sisters? Who is in your family? You and who else?)
> K: *(No response.)*

The children sometimes even failed to follow the lead of the other child and respond in a similar fashion after we had set up the Spanish-speaking child as a model. At other times, their guessing appeared to break down badly, despite the provision of good clues.

> (34) *(Nathan has just written his whole name:)*
> SH: *(Looks at writing, then points at Nathan.)* Ah, tú te llamas Nathan Hughes. (Ah, your name is Nathan Hughes.)
> N: No. My sister's.

In class, when an unfamiliar story was read in Spanish without a preceding synopsis of the plot in English, the English-dominant children (including our subjects) would quickly escape through misbehavior or physical withdrawal.

There were other instances of non–turn-taking and supposed nonsense-making which were more emotionally loaded than were the above examples. In these cases, our subjects played on their monolinguality in order to defy an adult or to express their frustration. For example, Nathan had misbehaved and was being physically shepherded by one of the aides to another seat, accompanied by her repetition of *siéntate acá (sit here)*. Glowering, he said, "I don't even know what you mean!" Another day, the class was playing Hokey Pokey in Spanish for the first time, but using the same melody, same sequence of body parts being "put in and out and shaken all about." Nathan wailed, "*I don't understand this.*" During our test sessions, Kathy refused to repeat a phrase even after she knew what she was being asked to do.

> (35) SH: Y ahora "es un muchacho chiquito." (Now "es un muchacho chiquito.")
>   K: I said it. I said it with myself, like this *(moves her lips, goldfish style)*.
>   SH: Es un muchacho chiquito.
>   Lily: Say, Kathy.
>   K: I did. Really *(laughs)*.

PRODUCING SPANISH

In class, except for interactions with SH, the only Spanish produced by these 5 children was color words, number words, *adiós,* and song lyrics. SH's language "handicap," however, along with her availability for casual talk and child-initiated, non-instructional game-playing elicited additional Spanish (mostly, a broader lexicon) from all of the English-dominant children, including those Chicanos from the neighborhood who were designated as "limited" bilinguals and who did not use Spanish with any other school adult.[4] Even to SH, though, the Spanish production of our targeted children was mostly single words. There were a few exceptions. Once, Kathy constructed a whole sentence, either in order to give SH information or to open a conversation *(esa clase we learn spañol,* pointing to the SSL room). This example is unique both for its length and its informing or social/interactional function. The other children used Spanish only when they were responding to a question or topic initiation by SH.

In the taped sessions, though more Spanish was produced, it was hardly a frequent occurrence, and there, too, it usually consisted of single words. At least once, each child answered an either/or question by producing one of the choices presented in Spanish. They correctly used several color or number words, sometimes when not responding to a question. On those few occasions, they were addressing their peers. *(I'm not negro; I'm blanco/I want dos yellow/ Lemme have the rojo.)* There were expressions of some SSL-originated words *(bed, face, jacket)* from Katie, and the use of *mamá* and *papá* instead of *mommy* or *daddy.* After SH showed lack of comprehension, Anita once converted "this is a *hot dog*" to the single word *taco.* A few times, the single lexical item that a subject produced was inserted into a phrase. Early in the year, for example, Kathy and Katie each used the beginnings of a "mixed code" that combined the two languages or that Hispanicized English words (Engspan?). For example: *ma'ya/ cama (my bed); dos people (two people); boy in cama (boy in bed); me strelita (my star).* Usually, however, their limited production was delivered in one-word utterances, not merely single Spanish words in a longer phrase.

When we left the children alone with the tape recorder on, they produced less Spanish than when we were present. Neither Kathy nor Katie produced even one Spanish word in this situation. Nathan used a number and a color word in January. Vince said *tortilla, masa,* and *bruja* once each, and had one exchange with Hector involving taboo words.

(36) V: I know what's *poop* in Spanish.
      H: What?
      V: It starts with a *p.*
      H: Let's see—
      V: *P-e-pedo.*
      H: No. *Pedo* is fart, and *poop* is *cagada.*
      V: You know you're not supposed to say those bad words in school. They'll send you to Mr. B.

In our absence, Anita gave us our only example of Spanish nonsense syllables. (These initiated the utterance in example 10).

(37) A: /ke ka la a na mo do/
      Eréndida: Huh?
      A: /a ma na ka kos lo ro/
      E: You just talk a little bit of Spanish, huh?
      A: Yeah, a little bit. Not very much.
      E: 'Cause you're learning, huh?
      A: Yeah, I'm learning, 'cause I got to learn.

The 5 children, then, used language about language quite frequently. They acted out at least parts of the second-language learner role in relation to receiving Spanish, though not consistently. And they produced some Spanish when responding to particular people who addressed it to them. Did these efforts result in major gains in Spanish acquisition between October and April?

Changes in Spanish Performance

When we first met these children, they already knew some color and number words, a song about the date on the calendar, the names of some letters, and two social routines *(adiós; buenos días)*. Although we are certain that the Anglos were monolingual in August, it is possible that the Chicanos could understand certain utterances in Spanish before entering first grade. After only 6 weeks of school, though, the children could produce what we have reported and, through using different combinations of clues, some of the time they could respond appropriately to spoken Spanish.

Six months later, the two Chicano children showed a rarely occurring understanding of there/then topics and knowledge of a few more lexical items. Each also used a two- or three-word Spanish formulaic phrase once or twice. (Possibly, they knew the few additional words and the formulae in October and simply had not revealed this earlier.) Their performance on the comprehension/repetition tasks did not change in the 6 months. We can hardly say, then, that being in this bilingual classroom resulted in any significant acquisition of Spanish syntax, morphology, or even lexicon for these 2 children. More important, if this more narrowly conceived linguistic acquisition is dependent on acquisition of certain discourse strategies (Hatch, 1978), neither Vince nor Anita demonstrated any increased inclination to initiate or sustain interactions with Spanish-speakers, using Spanish. Being Chicano, and having a headstart through prior exposure and some already established abilities in Spanish, did not result in the great leap forward that we had hoped these children would take.

Of the three Anglos, Nathan showed only one change—he learned (and used it to show off) an SSL routine, *es un abrelata* [sic] *(It's a can opener)*. Though Kathy's performance on the comprehension/repetition talk did not improve, and she did not produce any "SSL words," she was the only one of the 5 who ever used Spanish to convey her own meaning and intentions over more than one turn in an interaction (always with SH) on more than one occasion. A few times, she attempted to get SH to play an SSL card-naming game by saying her own name in Spanish, pointing to the cards, and repeating "'spañol, 'spañol." Once, she tried to get SH to cross her name off a list.

    (38)   K: *(Pointing to self)*, Katerina.

            SH: Ah, tú te llamas Katerina en español. (Ah, your name is Katerina in Spanish.)

            K: *(Takes SH by the hand and takes her to a list of names on the board, alternately pointing to herself, SH, and the list.)* Spañol.

            SH: Sí, veo "Kathy" en la lista. (Yes, I see "Kathy" on the list.)

> K: Katerina *(points to name on list, runs SH's finger*
> *through name, points at SH)*. Katerina. 'Spañol. Take it
> off.

Katie appeared to "stay with" Public Spanish longer than the others. Once, when trying to follow a public exchange between the teacher and some other children, she selected herself as next turn-taker, and made a clarification request using Spanish *(¿dos people?)*. Katie was the only child whose comprehension task-performance improved. In fact, by March, she was always correct in her choices, though under less constrained conditions (during class or during the playing part of the taped session), when the input was less predictable, her comprehension seemed no better as the months passed. We changed the order of the items and repeated many in order to rule out some memorization of a sequence. She never failed. Perhaps, with the major comprehension problem of task and topic determination eliminated by her familiarity with the card-choosing part of our routine, she could display the hypotheses she had correctly constructed concerning masculine/feminine and singular/plural endings. On the other hand, she might have been constructing hypotheses about some other aspect of the test statements, as some nonreading 3-year-olds do in relation to a total context of print, color, smudge marks, and other identifying features, in order to pick records or books out of a pile—a feat that makes it appear that they are reading print alone. Katie also made the greatest gains in production of SSL lexical items (4 items). Essentially, however, the three Anglos made no greater or lesser improvement than the Chicanos did.

It is important to note that while these 5 children were making minimal, if any, progress in Spanish, the Spanish-speakers were taking giant steps in English. They produced long English strings, used English to convey their own meanings (as opposed to merely responding to others' questions), and attempted to follow extended exchanges and stories which were not augmented by Spanish translations. English was their increasing choice for use with other Spanish-speakers, both adults and children (once, we heard Andrés and Hector discussing in English the Spanish reading group's worksheet, which was written in Spanish), as it was for their labeling of school-taught concepts (rectangle, circle, etc.), despite presentation of these concepts in both languages, and for their use of social routines with "monolingual" SH. This was a repeat of what we saw the previous year, when the Mexican immigrants' learning of the second language extended even to Anglicizing their own names.

COMPARISON OF FINDINGS: 1977–78, 1978–79

Did our attempts to find a setting which differed from that in the 1977–78 setting result in different findings? The question actually has three parts: 1)

Did this setting produce a different second-language learning context? 2) Did the subjects behave differently as potential second-language learners? and 3) Was there any difference in what was acquired? At this point, we must distinguish between second-language acquisition, the induction of the deep, underlying structure of a language, and second-language learning, the conscious awareness of pedagogical rules and close-to-the-surface items (Krashen, 1976).

The setting under discussion did indeed provide a different second-language–learning context—that is, if the marked/unmarked language relationship is exempted from a discussion of context. There was a greater use of Public Spanish in the second class studied, and it was used for a wider range of functions. The amount of Spanish directed individually to non-Spanish-speakers increased from none to some. Though we had not predicted it, SH's presence supplied some interaction in less schoolish speech events (chitchat, playing make-believe games, etc.). While she was present on an average of only 2 school days per month, this provided, again, an increase from none (in the 1977–78 study) to some (in the 1978–79 study) in the number of times children were exposed to a real demand for the use of Spanish.

There were also great differences between the subjects in the two studies in relation to their willingness to take on a second-language–learning role, or at least to use strategies that are deemed necessary to that role. Though neither group was consistent (the 1977–78 subjects occasionally took their turns in interactions and guessed at meaning; the 1978–79 subjects sometimes did not), the current 5 used these strategies far more frequently and used a greater variety of clues for their guesses. Akin to the preceding year, within the present group of children, individual differences contributed to a greater or lesser use of these strategies. Katie, for example, did the best school work and was a pattern-deriver *par excellence*. (The teacher and aides reported that she would perceive a school scheduling or behavior routine after only one run-through and would then verbalize that, often to the annoyance of the adults) And it was Katie who used the greatest variety of clues for guessing at meanings. Vince, on the other hand, seemed to approach schoolwork hesitantly, wanting reassurance that he was right before he would commit anything to paper. Despite his ability to occasionally understand new topics which could not be predicted on the basis of context clues alone, he often opted out of taking his turn.

We would like to be able to say that the differences in the two settings (sharedness of program goals among parents and school-district personnel, Alternate Days model, persistence of the teacher, etc.) which produced differences in the second-language–learning context were also the antecedents of the differences among the two groups of subjects taking the second-language–learner role. The children in the two studies, however, were also different in socioeconomic status. Perhaps the 5 middle-class children from the 1978–79 study took the second-language–learner role more readily and more adeptly because they came to school more primed to play all aspects of the school game. Perhaps it was a combination of middle-class priming, along with a setting maximized for second-language–learning of a marked language, which was the primary causative factor in the differential use of learning strategies.

Despite the differences in context and second-language–learning behaviors of the subjects, there were almost no "bottom line" differences in acquisition of Spanish. When we first met the children, it appeared that these 5 understood and produced more Spanish (even if it was merely number words and a few songs) than the 3 from the previous study did after a comparable length of time in the bilingual first-grade class; that is, they had *learned* more surface routines. When we look at their *acquisition* from October through March, however, there was essentially no difference between the two groups in relation to the gains they made. From our first meeting with them to our last, both groups appeared relatively unchanged.

CONCLUSION

If children were exposed to a second language both in a naturalistic setting and through direct instruction; if others used that second language with them in one-to-one interactions; if the children themselves took interactional turns and tried to derive the meaning of second-language utterances—why didn't they make more gains in second-language acquisition? We could answer with an appeal to quantity (there wasn't enough one-to-one interaction in the second language, there weren't enough functions for which the second language was used) or to time (6 months was not long enough—though it was long enough for the Spanish-speakers to make great strides in English). We believe, however, that the political position of the second language in the institution where learning is to take place is a more useful explanatory factor. Evidently, individualized input from teachers and the use of second-language–learning strategies by children, though necessary, was not sufficient in any sense. The marked language was used less in the classroom. There were no pressures, no authentic reasons, to use the marked language outside the classroom, let alone outside the school. There were no expectations that the marked language would be used by unmarked language speakers to initiate topics or for sustained interaction.

From our experiences in two different bilingual first grades over a 2-year period, we must conclude that even under highly favorable conditions, acquiring a marked language as a second language is going to be problematic. What is more likely is that children will *learn* lexical items and rote routines. (By October of each year, the subjects had attained most of this repertoire.) In order to learn how to communicate one's own intentions through a second language—that is, to acquire that language—even "favorable conditions" appear to be insufficient.

Markedness is a dimension that has its source outside the school. That dimension could be upset in a limited way through the establishment of an immersion program. Short of an immersion program, however, it seems that for mutual, rather than one-way language learning, bilingual programs must be accompanied by truly heroic efforts. What the nature of "heroic efforts" would be—how to turn ordinary school people into heroes or heroines—we have no answers to those questions here. What we have in relation to research on second-language acquisition is a new question; not *how,* but *whether* genuine second-language acquisition of a marked language can occur at all among children.

NOTES

1. Of course, child speakers of English do attain near-native proficiency in Spanish in naturalistic settings—when the child moves to a Spanish-speaking speech community. Spanish has then become an unmarked language. Another setting for successful acquisition of Spanish by English-speakers is immersion programs. What is unique about immersion programs, however, is that they reverse the markedness distinction, making the marked language into an unmarked one within the confines of that program. In other words, markedness cannot be determined by comparing one language to another in terms of its general power in the world at large. A language is unmarked or marked in relation to particular domains or institutions in particular speech communities. It is possible that a politically weak language of low prestige in one community is the unmarked language in a school somewhere else. We would expect the learning of that language as a second language to proceed in very different ways in those two communities.

2. It may appear throughout that we are being either covertly or overtly critical of the bilingual adults, especially the teachers, who were involved in these two studies. On the contrary—we are not surprised by their code switching and ensuing lack of awareness of which language they were using within a given topic in the school domain (Kjolseth, 1977, reports on Fishman's findings of high validity for self-report and, therefore, self-awareness, of language choice across domains, but low validity within domains). Moreover, we praise them for their motives and their efforts to make bilingual education a two-way street. Especially noteworthy is the extraordinary amount of energy the teacher in the 1978–79 study must have expended in order to persist in violating code-choice norms against using a marked language to monolingual speakers of an unmarked language, to persist in doing what was often followed by signs of incomprehension by her students (just the opposite of what a teacher hopes for) in the name of a larger principle, to provide the amount of Spanish that she did when all around her the push was toward greater use of English, and to maintain her Spanish-maintenance desires in the face of absence of support for that goal from many non-bilingual program personnel. It is hard to imagine that anyone could have provided

more interaction with the marked language without changing the entire politicolinguistic context and making the marked language into an unmarked one (i.e., by setting up an immersion program).

3. We are greatly indebted to Gary Moorman for the classroom observations he made with us, for his perceptions, and for his suggestions during our data analysis.

4. The "limited" bilingual children signalled their understanding of many of SH's questions and comments about topics dealing with other times and places, abstractions, and some jokes by responding appropriately in English. Their Spanish production, though of phrase length, was telegraphic in character (uninflected, missing articles, etc.).

REFERENCES

Edelsky, C., & Hudelson, S. Acquiring a second language when you're not the underdog. Paper presented at Los Angeles Second Language Acquisition Research Forum, University of Southern California, Oct. 1978.

———.Resistance to the acquisition of Spanish in a bilingual setting. *Journal of the Linguistic Association of the Southwest,* 1979, *3*(2), 1102–11.

Fishman, J. *Bilingual education: An international sociological perspective.* Rowley, Mass.: Newbury House, 1976.

Hatch, E. Discourse analysis and second language acquisition. In E. Hatch (Ed.), *Second language acquisition.* Rowley, Mass.: Newbury House, 1978.

Kjolseth, R. Bilingual education: For what and for whom? *Language in Society,* 1977, *6*(2), 247–62.

Krashen, S. Formal and informal linguistic environments in language learning and language acquisition. *TESOL Quarterly,* 1976, *10*, 157–68.

Macnamara, J. The cognitive strategies of language learning. In J. Oller & J. Richards (Eds.), *Focus on the learner: Pragmatic perspectives for the language teacher.* Rowley, Mass.: Newbury House, 1973.

Wong-Fillmore, L. The second time around: Cognitive and social strategies in second language acquisition. Doctoral diss., Stanford University, 1976. *Dissertation Abstracts International,* 1976, 37, 6443A. (University Microfilms 77-7085)

16 | Second-Language Acquisition and Foreign Language Teaching: Spanish Language Programs at a University on the U.S.-Mexican Border

RICHARD V. TESCHNER
University of Texas at El Paso

FINDINGS OF THE GINGRÀS VOLUME

At issue is which process—*learning* or *acquisition* (as these terms have been used since the early work of Jean Piaget)—does a better job in the facilitation of what I will henceforth call *language getting* (the need for a neutral term is now obvious, since *learning* and *acquisition* take on particular and separate definitions in the present context). The issue is one which is dealt with convincingly and at length in the collection of papers by Stephen Krashen, Kari Sajavaara, and others, edited by Rosario Gingràs and entitled *Second-Language Acquisition and Foreign Language Teaching* (1978).[1]

It is the goal of the present paper to discuss the Gingràs volume in terms of its applicability to the University of Texas at El Paso's (UTEP's) language-getting programs in Spanish intended for English monolinguals (as contrasted with its language-expanding/language-refining programs in Spanish aimed at Spanish-English bilinguals typically fluent in Spanish but lacking advanced or "school" lexicon and more at ease in writing English than Spanish).

As Krashen puts it, a major goal of his own research and that of the scholars he cites is

> to determine the true contribution of conscious learning. . . . Whatever the quantity of its contribution to adult second-language performance, the Monitor Model predicts that it is in one domain only, as a conscious Monitor. Conscious learning does not initiate utterances or produce fluency. It also does not contribute directly to acquisition. (p. 23; hereafter all page references are to Gingràs, Ed., 1978, unless otherwise indicated)

228

Sajavaara seconds this, refining the role which acquisition plays in bringing the language-getter up to an acceptable state of fluency:

> Acquisition and learning seem to be different in that acquisition leads to skills which are automated for the most part. After acquisition the programs and plans which are necessary for the execution of tasks require a minimum of attention. Learning mainly provides for storage of separate items and ingredients of sub-tasks whose retrieval from long-term memory requires highly complicated and capacity-consuming processes; the number of readily available plans is small. . . . What is decisive here is that unless the plans and programs necessary for the execution of a task are "acquired," the planning device will have to resort to learned items, which requires more processing and consumes more capacity. (pp. 58–59)

Crucial to our understanding of the programmatic implications of Krashen and his coauthors' thinking are the increasingly well-known terms *affective filter, input, intake,* and *explicit* as opposed to *implicit* language getting. *Affective filter* refers to attitude, conscious and unconscious. *Input* consists of all target-language materials directed at or heard by the language-getter, while *intake* is what the language-getter actually "takes in," that is, submits to meaningful processing and comprehends. The *explicit* versus *implicit* distinction parallels the one between learning and acquisition.

A prime goal of language teaching must be to mitigate the influence of the affective filter, which operates both to obviate the integrative motivation (to the extent that integrative motivation is necessary for language-getting) and to enhance those feelings of self-consciousness which, following the onset of adolescence, contravene the willingness to experiment in an area as central to the core of human personality as language. Thus Krashen notes that "the 'right' attitudinal factors, the presence of an integrative motivation and an optimal amount of self-confidence, produce two effects: They encourage intake, or useful input, and they allow the acquirer to utilize this intake for acquisition" (p.9). His comments regarding adolescent self-consciousness complement the above:

> Around age 12, according to Inhelder and Piaget (1958), the child grows significantly in his ability to think abstractly; for the first time, he is able to relate abstract constructs to other abstractions. . . . This newly-entered into "Formal Operations" stage may indirectly contribute to the typical adult's inability to acquire a second language perfectly, since it may be at least partially responsible for psychological changes that cause an increase in the affective filter. (p. 14)

Concern about the affective filter is evident throughout the Gingràs volume and is emphasized by the editor himself in his introduction (p. ix): "In particular, research is needed on how teachers can 'lower the affective filter' so that L_2 acquirers are more open to the language they hear and understand." Further comments on affective filtering will appear below, especially in relation to its effect on non–native English-speaking students at UTEP.

Observers of child language development note that children acquiring second languages generally go through (as Krashen puts it) a " 'silent period' during which they may be building up acquired competence via active listening. Their output during this period consists, for the most part, of prefabricated rather than creative language. . . . This stage may correspond to the adult use of the first language as a 'filter' " (p. 13). Krashen also notes that interference, or first-language influence, "is most prevalent in acquisition-poor environments, such as foreign-language situations. It is rare in normal ('playground') child second-language acquisition. . . . Too early production before sufficient acquisition is built up results in the use of the surface structure of the first language" (p. 13). This is a phenomenon which all language teachers constantly experience—plenteous "anglicisms" in Spanish or "hispanisms" in English persist well into the advanced levels of language instruction among students subjected to the sort of classwork that demands manipulation of structures immediately upon their presentation.

In view of the importance Krashen attaches to acquisition-rich instructional environments ("It is my view that one of our main responsibilities—if not our most important one—is to provide the adult acquirer with intake, either inside the classroom or outside" [p. 18]), a fuller explanation of what he means by "intake" will be helpful. For Krashen, "intake" is language that is understood by the acquirer; language that is at or slightly in advance of the acquirer's current stage of grammatical competence; language that is sequenced, and which gets progressively more complex; and, last, language that constitutes, or at least approximates, natural communication.

If intake is what does most to facilitate acquisition, then language-class activities must be analyzed in terms of whether they promote intake or not. This Krashen does at length (see pp. 18–19). He discusses, in turn, free conversation, mechanical exercises, manipulation drills, and other techniques. One drawback of free conversation is that it "is often not understood, may or may not be at the acquirer's level or just beyond it and is practically never progressive" (p. 18). Manipulation or mechanical exercises are uses of language in isolation which "may be understood for their propositional content, but soon lose this effect. Paulston (1972) warns that overuse of this drill type produces tedium, and Lee, McCune and Patton's study (1970) of the rapid decline of orienting response to mechanical drill confirms this as well. [The requirement for] natural communication is not met at all" (p. 18). This, incidentally, is a point which Savajaara, Gingràs, Valdman, and the other contributors make haste to echo; the consensus is that the *sole* virtue of mechanical exercises is to drill pronunciation and to provide the least secure students with the illusion of language production. As for drills, Krashen and the others favor only what he terms "meaningful and communicative drills, activities in which students can tell the truth or role play [since such drills] have the potential for satisfying all the characteristics listed: They are designed to be understood, may be put at any level, may be progressive, and may involve real communication or something close to it. These types should be the most effective for acquisition" (p. 19). They are, however, as Krashen warns, "the most difficult to construct."

If the conclusions reached so far appear to have tied our hands, the knot is cut by realizing that what we should be after is not intake for the sake of immediate feedback as speech production, but intake *for its own immediate sake*—intake that is to be stored as eventual material for output. As Krashen points out, "There is little doubt that speaking is very useful for acquisition, but its main function is that it allows conversation which *encourages intake*" (p. 20, emphasis in the original). Such reasoning is fully consonant with several recent studies which show that delaying speech in second-language acquisition, when active listening is strongly emphasized, causes no delay in attaining proficiency (ultimate oral, as well as aural, proficiency), and may even be of greater benefit; among the citable studies are Gary (1975) (for child acquisition) and (for adults) three pieces by Asher (1965, 1966, 1969), and the definitive work of the late Valerian Postovsky (1974, 1977), which demonstrated that students of Russian *not* availed of a direct opportunity to perform orally actually *exceeded* an oral-involved control group in all four basic language skills, *including* oral production.

If by delaying oral production (both free and audio-lingual or patterned), the primary emphasis is to be put on aural comprehension, then how does one facilitate it? In part by explicitly teaching certain of its components. What Gingràs has in mind is the explicit presentation of both vocabulary and sound system, two sine qua nons of aural comprehension. He says:

> Understanding can be aided by the early internalizing of vocabulary as well as by direct guidance to the surface phonetic system of the L_2. Research suggests that the early learning of *vocabulary* is of great importance since such ... appears to facilitate the comprehension of listening activities.... Pronunciation instruction is probably best limited to explicit instruction that allows the students to recognize and produce recognizable instances of the vocabulary items they will be learning. (pp. 90–91)

With vocabulary taught and pronunciation drills utilized for recognition purposes, "active listening" can then be given the emphasis it deserves. Gingràs has some specific suggestions as to how to promote active listening: "The vocabulary items should be known by the students (as a result of previous presentation) and the context of the conversation should provide enough hints so that students understand what the conversation is about" (p. 95). Earlier he had insisted that since the focus should be on comprehension, topics that students are unfamiliar with should be avoided; specific unfamiliar topics to be avoided involve foreign cultural patterns and artifacts, presentation of which should be made in English. What makes this type of listening any more active than, say, the reading of short passages, followed by "questions," that instructors perform in class regularly? Except for the central role assigned the activity, and the intensity with which it is carried out, only the type of desired response distinguishes this from present practices; as Gingràs notes, "Students should give some evidence they understand the conversation presented by way of short answers in the L_2, or even by allowing responses in the native language if students feel very uncomfortable producing utterances in the L_2" (p. 95).

Sajavaara expands on these themes by stressing the need to develop listening skills, no matter which method of instruction is employed. Language teaching, he says, has traditionally emphasized "the production of acceptable chains of utterances. Communication, however, involves constant switching over of the converse roles of the speaker and the hearer. In many cases, communication fails, not because the speaker-hearer is unable to produce signals that can be interpreted in the right way, but because he is unable to adjust to the signals which he is receiving." (pp. 53–54). In this regard, he insists that language-getters be exposed to "real" speech at normal or near-normal rates from the very beginning, and that if the rate of speech needs slowing down, this should be done by lengthening pauses or, if mechanical reproduction is involved, by means of speech-expanded devices. Savajaara also emphasizes (as does Saville-Troike) that those using active-listening exercises should do everything possible to focus on message, not structure for its own sake. The main task of the teacher, then,

> is to bring in communicatively meaningful materials. This is the area where most language teaching methodologies have failed, not primarily because they were wrong as methods, but because teachers have seen themselves mainly as teachers of *language*—language meaning the grammar and vocabulary of the language concerned. From very early on, it is the natural tendency of a human being to focus on message, [whereas] academic language teaching . . . has emphasized form. (p. 67)

So to sum up: The consensus from the Gingràs volume is that successful language instruction involves deemphasizing the Monitor (though Krashen cautions that "for the optimal Monitor users, the application of conscious rules to one's output *can* result in a real increase in accuracy" [p. 25]); lowering in adolescents and adults the restrictive workings of the affective filter; providing judicious input; and, above all, transforming input into maximal intake, so as to speed the all-important process of acquisition.

However, as Muriel Saville-Troike reminds us, "The success of particular methods, teachers, texts and even goals of instruction and models for curricular organization is likely to prove relative to particular social and cultural settings and socio-cultural and psychological characteristics of students" (p. 70). With this in mind, and since the purpose of the present paper is to discuss the Gin-gràs volume in terms of both how and why it is applicable to language teaching on the U.S.-Mexican border, let us now focus on local conditions.

APPLICATION OF THE FINDINGS AT UTEP

Both the applicability of these methods and the necessity for considering them derive from the following two considerations: the presence, within the El Paso/Ciudad Juárez "internationalplex" (to borrow the media term), of a full bilingual continuum covering all possible points; and, chiefly among the English-monolingual products of El Paso's public school systems, the suspected presence of a stronger-than-healthy affective filter vis-à-vis Spanish. It is the genesis and the effects of the filter that I will now discuss.

One of the major causes of the negative affectivity that Spanish still produces locally in the El Paso/Ciudad Juárez area and, of course, throughout the Southwest and beyond is highly salient and easy to recognize. I refer here to interethnic tension, even in a city such as El Paso, with its comparatively high degree of social integration between the Hispanic majority (ca. two-thirds of the population) and the Anglo minority. Less self-evident, though, is how affective factors deriving strictly from ethnic circumstances would affect performance by anglomonomatriphones (monolingual speakers of English as a mother tongue) in a Spanish course at the university level. I submit that the effect would be negligible. On the one hand, we know from the work of Teitelbaum, Edwards, and Hudson (1975) that among Anglo students of Spanish at the University of New Mexico, no relationship could be discerned between positive attitude toward the local Hispanic community and performance in Spanish in the classroom. On the other hand, it is logical to assume that anglo-monomatriphones bearing specific ill will towards Hispanics and, by extension, the Spanish language would probably elect French, German, Russian, or some other language, not Spanish. Ethnic factors thus can be largely ruled out as constituting the core of the negative affectivity I perceive to exist among many of our non-native-speaker students. What I do judge a prime cause is one that can be laid directly at the doorstep of the mandatory (from early elementary grades onward) Spanish programs of the FLES (Foreign Language in the Elementary School) sort that have been operant since the 1950s in all public schools in El Paso.

We all know this type of program: thirty minutes of language a certain number of times per week (seldom daily), utilization of a strictly cognitive codal methodology—in short, exactly the sort of system against which the English-Canadian parents of St. Lambert rebelled in the mid-1960s, and which gave way to what was (for the North American continent at least) a genuine innovation: the immersion program, or "home-school language switch," which, as is widely known, succeeded precisely where FLES had failed. FLES, however, is alive and sick in El Paso, Texas, and continues to produce students such as those I encounter semester after semester signing up for (or, worse, being placed into) *first*-semester Spanish at the university level—students who despite 30 minutes per day times however many hundreds of days are unable to recognize (let alone produce) more than one verb tense, if that; cannot handle object pronoun constructions; cannot count beyond 100; and on and on. One hardly needs to ask why their filters are "affected": It is because the chief lesson they have learned is that they are unable to communicate in the language they have studied. From this it follows that since these students succeed in reaching young adulthood without either having mastered the city's second language or having seen a need to do so, they come to view Spanish as a language they have successfully done without and can therefore avoid learning ever, at no cost to their lives or their careers. I should add that with certain exceptions, our twin city Ciudad Juárez offers up exactly the same situation vis à vis English; in Juárez, English is a required subject in all state-sponsored elementary schools, is taught deductively, is confined to short semidaily periods, and is mastered by no one save those youngsters whose livelihoods force them into frequent contact with monolingual English-speakers.

Perhaps some of these students exposed in vain to Spanish are enrolling in our university-level courses in hopes that somehow at this level the communicative miracle can take place (but compare the results of an impromptu survey presented below). No miracle can occur, however, unless the negative affectivity justifiably born of a linguopedagogically wasted childhood of frustration and nonacquisition can be overcome by a method one of whose chief virtues is that it does not expect the language-getter to produce language until the ability to comprehend language is highly developed. Other ramifications of a comprehension-centered system are likewise obvious: The frustrated, long-time nonacquirer is especially insecure about the sounds he or she produces in Spanish; thus any emphasis on oral production, until such time as the student is aware of having made actual progress with the language, may actually be counterproductive, reinforcing negative affectivity.

If the typical sections of courses described in our catalogue as "Spanish One/Two/Three/Four for Non-Native Speakers" were effectively limited to students whose sole home-acquired language has been English, then the effects of the particular negative affectivity which derives from "fear of speaking" among those who know that their Spanish phonology is far from native would at least be attenuated. However, these effects are actually exacerbated, thanks to that second local fact of sociolinguistic life mentioned earlier—the presence here of a complete bilingual continuum. That is to say, the absence of anything resembling a clear-cut division between "natives" (native Spanish-speakers) and "nonnatives" (nonnative Spanish-speakers) makes a mockery of our department's attempts to apportion off students into just these two tracks. Individual location at a point on the continuum is the product of a seemingly interminable list of factors—social, economic, generational, residential, and personal—the recounting of which is easily the subject of a monograph. For present purposes, however, it suffices to say that despite our department's mandatory Spanish placement system, it will never be possible for us to achieve nonnative sections that are totally free of persons who have experienced childhood acquisition of Spanish on the home front.

Before placement became mandatory, the typical nonnative class was roughly 33% native or seminative. The placement examination now delivers up nonnative classes about 15% of whose students possess some native-speaker background. This is a reduction of more than half from previous totals, but it still leaves a perceptible native component in the nonnative track. My experience in El Paso has shown how very attuned our locals are (and local students comprise 89% of our undergraduates) to who is what, socially and linguistically. Where physical appearance fails to reveal linguistic background (this is especially true of the products of interethnic marriages, of which there are many), and where ways of speaking English likewise fail to do so, ways of speaking Spanish will almost always reveal a history of home acquisition as opposed to school nonlearning.[2] Anglomonomatriphones "know," then, how many of "us" and how many of "them" there are in a given Spanish class within minutes of the first oral drill. This constitutes yet one more argument favoring an instructional methodology which delays or at least deemphasizes oral production.

A third argument favoring adoption of speech-production-delayed programs in our nonnative track likewise derives from the facts of life on the local continuum. Briefly put, some form of self-pacing, and therefore individualized, instruction ought to be instituted, given the wide diversity of backgrounds of students. The ideal would be a large number of self-paced topic-specific "units" or "packets" loosely supervised by a combination of professors, teaching assistants, and language-laboratory workers. The reality is that in a department (typical of so many) with few teaching assistants and many tenured faculty, nearly all of the lower-division classes are taught entirely by the latter, and the single-teacher, teacher-centered, same-group-of-students format is vocally preferred by the majority of faculty members. Emphasizing aural comprehension would serve as a compromise, since prerecorded aural comprehension exercises are individualizable but yet readily retain the teacher as the focus of attention, since instructors must be on hand (as Gingràs insists) to teach and drill the vocabulary and the sound system.

These pedagogical recommendations are also entirely consonant with my perception of the sort of language behavior that is expected by the internationalplex's rules of speaking. As is well known, El Paso/Ciudad Juárez is the world's largest bilingual international twin city, and also the U.S.-Mexican border's busiest crossing point. Of the two political units, Juárez is easily the larger (ca. 700, 000 people to El Paso's ca. 425,000). There is at least as much south-to-north traffic in search of goods and services as there is north-to-south. Various degrees of bilingualism can be said to exist among Juárez residents (for details see Ornstein, Valdés-Fallis, and Dubois, 1971; also Valdés, this volume), but my general impression is that most *juarenses* are proficient in English only to the extent that they have undergone extensive schooling in El Paso. As a consequence (and also because Spanish monolingualism is by no means limited to Juárez), the immediate area is home to considerably more Spanish than English monolingualism. Thus Spanish is a de facto requirement for many private and public service positions. And while in general, north-of-the-border Hispanics lacking English or weak in it appear willing to tolerate an English-medium exchange or wait for bilinguals to attend them, my impression is that this is much less the case among Juárez residents, especially wealthier ones, who are quick to assert their wish for service in Spanish (as, of course, has long been the custom with respect to English among most Anglos visiting Juárez). The implications of this for persons lacking Spanish are obvious.

Spanish-getting, then, is to be taken seriously. This is especially true in places like El Paso where Spanish increasingly must be learned for commerce, but it is becoming true elsewhere as well; and in any event, to offer, in classes purporting to teach language, anything less than actual steps toward genuine acquisition is to mislead the student. That is what informs my partial disagreement with one of the Gingràs volume's contributors, Professor Albert Valdman, who admits to a "distinctly pessimistic view" about what can be achieved in language classes for adolescents and adults. Basing his conclusion on the work of Krashen and the other authors in the volume, he asserts that

> the current emphasis on communicative competence appears incompatible with basic language instruction. ... The level of communicative ability attainable under ordinary classroom circumstances is relatively low, and emphasis on that objective requires special instructional features such as small groups of students, the simulation of natural conditions of language use, etc. (p. 81)

In consequence, communicative ability is beyond reach, so foreign language (FL) teaching "should retain its traditional stress on language learning and on analytic skills" (p. 81). Valdman thus prescribes what he terms a "little language course," defined as a

> basic FL course that stresses realizable goals—language learning and the teaching of language concepts—while providing for some degree of language acquisition. But in that instructional scheme, language acquisition would serve an

exemplary function only; there is no illusion about the learner's acquiring proficiency sufficient to use the FL for instrumental purposes. (p. 81)

That Valdman's minimalist solution is not unduly pessimistic can be corroborated in part by an impromptu survey I recently administered to all 53 students present on the third day of the semester in my two sections of first-semester nonnative Spanish.

The survey requested respondents to "put a checkmark alongside the *one* statement that best describes *why* you are taking Spanish 4101, and *what* you expect to get out of the [four-semester] sequence." Complete anonymity was demanded so as to obviate responses of the ingratiating sort; to that end, the questionnaires were collected by a student, who was instructed to shuffle the papers before turning them over to me. The choices, together with the number and percentage of the total responding to each statement, were:

1. I strongly want to learn Spanish; I expect to be able to speak it fairly well by the end of Spanish Four. *2 (= 3.77%)*
2. I strongly want to learn Spanish; I expect I will need further coursework beyond Spanish Four in order to speak it fairly well. *7 (= 13.21%)*
3. I have a moderate, average interest in learning Spanish; I expect to be able to speak it fairly well by the end of Spanish Four. *2 (= 3.77%)*
4. I have a moderate, average interest in learning Spanish; I expect I will need further coursework beyond Spanish Four in order to speak it fairly well. *0 (= 0.00%)*
5. I have little or no interest in learning Spanish; I expect to be able to speak it fairly well by the end of Spanish Four. *3 (= 5.66%)*
6. I have little or no interest in learning Spanish; I expect I will need further coursework beyond Spanish Four in order to speak it fairly well. *39 (= 73.58%)*

Respondents were also asked to indicate "true" or "false" for the following: "If my degree plan did not require a language, I would not be taking this class." Responding "true" were 42 persons (= 79.25%); 11 (= 20.75%) responded "false."

It is highly significant (and also rather disturbing) that nearly 8 out of every 10 students were enrolled solely because a language was required of them as a result of having chosen a certain major field. Unsurprising, then, is the absolute correlation between involuntary enrollment (42 persons) and the attitudes of little or no interest in learning Spanish (responses nos. 5 and 6—the very same 42 respondents).

Of the remaining approximately 20%, the clear majority (9 students) indicated a "strong" desire to learn Spanish; only 2 specified "moderate, average" interest. The majority of the strongly desirous are also strongly realistic (response no. 2); they are aware that 4 semesters of 3 hours per week × 15 weeks = 45 hours × 4 semesters = 180 class hours is hardly sufficient time in which to master a language so as to speak it "fairly well." They may also intuit that a class in which 80% of the students are not interested in the subject matter is no ideal setting for rapid progress.

On the basis of both the survey and my 11 years in the classroom, I would be forced to agree with Valdman that within the constraints imposed by the inadequate amount of class time presently available, a "little" language course must always remain an option. Nonetheless, and for all the reasons earlier adduced, a yet-to-be-designed acquisition-centered program must also remain an option (an ideal?) until proven unworkable. To my knowledge, no published longitudinal study has empirically compared full-scale cognitive-code, deductive programs with acquisition-centered inductive programs in a normal American university setting subjected to the well-known twin constraints of classroom time and student attitude. It should be recalled that Postovsky's (1974) study was performed at the Defense Language Institute, whose students are self-selected, and which reserves the right to weed out poor performers.

Until such an empirical study is undertaken, various alternatives for improving morale and enhancing language getting will surely include the usual intensive programs, fast tracks, and summer institutes. It is likely, though, that these would mainly appeal to that "strongly desirous" 20%, who, siphoned off into separate programs, would leave behind students in the regular classes as depressed as ever, or perhaps more so. Nor is there any guarantee that all the 20-percenters would remain strongly motivated throughout their special program.

The chief disadvantage to teaching a "second" language in an area where it is in daily public use by a significant number of readily encountered persons is that since one is immediately able to put the class-learned material to use outside the classroom, one is easily frustrated by the inevitable disparity between the limited amount that can be mastered in a classroom—even the best of classrooms—and the total command of the language shown by its native speakers. Perhaps this fact makes postchildhood second-language teaching intrinsically more difficult in a stable bilingual area such as ours. More difficult, but not for any of that less urgent.

NOTES

1. All quotations in this chapter from this work are used by permission of the Center for Applied Linguistics. For the six papers in the volume by Gingràs, Krashen,

Sajavaara, Saville-Troike, Schumann, and Valdman, see the bibliography to this chapter.

2. I have no statistics on this, but I would estimate that among UTEP undergraduates who are fully Hispanic ethnically, about half can and regularly do produce an English that is entirely devoid of "Chicano English" features, or nearly so.

REFERENCES

Asher, J. The strategy of the total physical response: An application to learning Russian. *International Review of Applied Linguistics,* 1965, *3*, 291–300.

——. The learning strategy of the total physical response: A review. *Modern Language Journal,* 1966, *50*, 79–84.

——. The total physical response approach to second language learning. *Modern Language Journal,* 1969, *53*, 3–17.

Gary, J. S. Delayed oral practice in initial stages of second language learning. In M. Burt & H. Dulay (Eds.), *On TESOL '75.* Washington, D.C.: TESOL, 1975.

Gingràs, R. C. Second-language acquisition and foreign language teaching. In R. C. Gingràs (Ed.). *Second-language acquisition and foreign language teaching.* Arlington, Va.: Center for Applied Linguistics, 1978.

Gingràs, R. C. (Ed.). *Second language acquisition and foreign language teaching.* Arlington, Va.: Center for Applied Linguistics, 1978.

Inhelder, B., & Piaget, J. *The growth of logical thinking from childhood to adolescence.* New York: Basic Books, 1958.

Krashen, S. The Monitor Model for second-language acquisition. In R. C. Gingràs (Ed.), *Second-language acquisition and foreign language teaching.* Arlington, Va.: Center for Applied Linguistics, 1978.

Lee, R., McCune, L., & Patton, L. Psychological responses to different modes of feedback in pronunciation testing. *TESOL Quarterly,* 1970, *4*, 117–22.

Ornstein, J., Valdés-Fallis, G., & Dubois, B. L. Bilingual child-language acquisition along the United States–Mexican border: The El Paso–Ciudad Juárez–Las Cruces triangle. *Word,* 1971, *1–3*, 386–404. (special issue, *Child Language—1975,* edited by W. von Raffler-Engel.)

Paulston, C. B. Structural pattern drills: A classification. *Foreign Language Journal,* 1972, *4*, 187–93.

Postovsky, V. Delay in oral practice in second language learning. *Modern Language Journal,* 1974, *58*, 229–39.

——. Why not start speaking later? In M. Burt, H. Dulay, & M. Finocchiaro (Eds.), *Viewpoints on English as a second language.* New York: Regents, 1977.

Sajavaara, K. The Monitor Model and monitoring in foreign language speech communication. In R. C. Gingràs (Ed.), *Second-language acquisition and foreign language teaching.* Arlington, Va.: Center for Applied Linguistics, 1978.

Saville-Troike, M. Implications of research on adult second-language acquisition for teaching foreign languages to children. In R. C. Gingràs (Ed.), *Second-language acquisition and foreign language teaching.* Arlington, Va.: Center for Applied Linguistics, 1978.

Schumann, J. G. The Acculturation Model for second-language acquisition. In R. C. Gingràs (Ed.), *Second-language acquisition and foreign language teaching.* Arlington, Va.: Center for Applied Linguistics, 1978.

Teitelbaum, H., Edwards, A., & Hudson, A. Ethnic attitudes and the acquisition of Spanish as a second language. *Language Learning,* 1975, *25,* 255–66.

Valdman, A. Implications of current research on second-language acquisition for the teaching of foreign languages in the United States. In R. C. Gingràs (Ed.), *Second-language acquisition and foreign language teaching.* Arlington, Va.: Center for Applied Linguistics, 1978.

17 | Natural Texts and Delayed Oral Production: An Indigenous Method for the Teaching of American Indian Languages

J. ANNE MONTGOMERY
University of Notre Dame

> In polysynthetic languages a large number of distinct ideas are amalgamated by grammatical processes and form a single word, without any morphological distinction between the formal elements in the sentence and the contents of the sentence. (Boas, 1966)

It is often the mystic attraction and possibly the formidable complexity of the sentence-length word which catches the attention of English-speaking students of an American Indian language and forces upon them the realization that they are dealing with a syntactic structure very different from any of the other Indo-European languages with which they may have become familiar. It is likely, however, that the language teaching methodology which presents the Indian language to students is one which has been developed within the context of the Indo-European inflecting language, under the assumption that what works for Spanish will serve as well for Chippewa. This has presented such a problem for English-speaking students that the introductory texts for Indian languages frequently acknowledge the "difficulty" of learning the Indian language and advise students to persevere and persist in their efforts to master what the author recognizes to be inherently difficult.[1] This is something rarely done for other contemporary languages, certainly not for those which are commonly taught. The potential for making American Indian language study an option for American students (of Indian or non-Indian ethnic origin) has never

---

An earlier version of this paper was prepared for the Southwest Areal Language and Linguistics Workshop of 1979 and was published as "An 'indigenous' method for the teaching of Native American languages," in Florence Barkin and Elizabeth Brandt (Eds.), *Speaking, singing and teaching: A multidisciplinary approach to language variation,* Anthropological Research Papers, No. 20 (Tempe: Arizona State University, 1980), pp. 235–38. Used by permission.

been realized in American educational systems. An occasional Indian-language course is offered in a college located near an Indian community, while elsewhere only the students of linguistics or anthropology are likely to become acquainted with an Indian language.

In the face of the imminent disappearance of their remaining ancestral languages, many American Indian communities have turned to the academic linguists who have already worked on these languages to prepare teaching materials for them. Based in part on observations of native speakers of American Indian languages who were engaged in the teaching of their own languages to monolingual, English-speaking Indian children, the following discussion questions the applicability of the audio-lingual/cognitive approach to the teaching of many polysynthetic Indian languages, and further suggests that teaching by means of natural texts is, in many instances, a preferable method.

The American Indian languages have greatly interested language scholars since the time when they were discovered by Western European linguists some 300 years ago. A strong Americanist tradition is now built upon twentieth-century exploitation of the language laboratory provided by the relative isolation and fecund diversity of the American Indian population's native languages.[2] The academic community whose discipline has been founded on these languages has rather generously responded to the requests from American Indians to share the resulting scholarship with the Indian peoples, that is, to make it accessible to the Indian community, specifically to teachers and students as they pursue enterprises such as language maintenance, language retrieval, and native-language literacy. This response of the academic community has largely taken two forms: a call for training native speakers as linguists and a call for the preparation of materials intended for use in language teaching situations. Neither enterprise has been particularly successful in any significant proportion to the great number of requests for them which have been heard at academic conferences and read in professional publications over the last 15 years. There are very few Indian-language courses which propose to teach North American Indian languages, fewer still with a record of success and signs of continuing viability, and only a handful of academically trained Native American linguists. The general public is still required to study linguistics and anthropology in order to have access to the academic laboratories where, in some cases, the only evidence of a people's ancestral culture lies buried as ethnolinguistic data.

THE STANDARD PEDAGOGICAL METHOD: ASPECTS OF CULTURE AND SYNTAX

The phenomenal lack of noticeable results in the teaching of Indian languages calls into question the assumption that the methods based on, and used for, the teaching of Indo-European languages will serve for the American Indian languages. The standard pedagogical approach for the teaching of second languages in the United States is often referred to as the cognitive or audio-lingual approach. While it does tolerate an occasional eclectic element, this is fundamentally a package consisting of the beginner's text (story or dialogue) in the target language, syntactic models and paradigms, example utterances, and an associated drill structure which includes audio-lingual exercises. The text which the student first meets is an artificial one composed by the linguist, that is, the designer of the teaching materials. It is a passage artificially constructed so as to present minimally complex grammatical elements in a serial order which will progress slowly toward a maximum of morphosyntactic complexity. The lexical items, selected for their phonological and morphological simplicity and their presumed interest to a particular age group, dictate the subject matter of the text. The student is frequently made to begin oral language production immediately by participating upon demand in imitation and substitution drills. The assignment of written work in the target language is generally a function of grade level and its actual classroom use varies greatly among instructors.

At the Wisconsin Native American Languages Project (WNALP, 1973–75)[3] elementary teaching materials were developed for Chippewa, Menominee, Oneida, Potawatomi, and Winnebago, using elements of the standard method sketched above. Native speakers were trained extensively in using the teaching materials, and they conducted field trials of the materials in several Wisconsin public schools. Many of the suggestions put forth below are based on observations of these teachers in the classroom and on subsequent discussions with them and the WNALP staff.[4]

Morphosyntactic Considerations

Lesson-designers who prepare teaching materials for polysynthetic languages following the traditional models for Indo-European languages are immediately aware of unique morphosyntactic problems. For one, the words and concepts typically included in the primary lexicon are not only lengthy, but phonologically and morphologically complex—the names of classroom objects and simple commands, for example. The Menominee word for pencil is *asāqcekamāhtek*. To possess the pencil in the first person becomes *netawaqcekanahtekom* (Miner, Ed., 1975). Thus the six-syllable word stem undergoes a fairly complicated alternation in vowel quality, as do a great number of Menominee words (but not all of them, nor are the words which do so predictable), and, furthermore, it acquires a prefix and a suffix in the possessive morpheme. The intricate build-up drills designed to introduce these words slowly, syllable by syllable, were consumed very quickly by primary-grade–level students of Menominee. The students, in fact, very quickly progressed to the point where dwelling on such drills gave undue emphasis to meaningless syllables and threatened to actually hinder acquisition of the word, rather than enhance it. The adult students, on the contrary, became dependent upon such introductions to polysyllabic words and were interested in dwelling on the derivations of the constructions. In addition, the older students required a significantly modified explanation of the change in vowel length. Kenneth Miner solves this problem by introducing a set of learner's diacritics which are used to signal changes in vowel length. Presumably these are to be discarded after the student learns the forms by memory or manages to learn the phonological rule which describes the environment of such sound changes (Miner, 1975).

Returning for a moment to the older student's pursuit of derivations, the lesson-designer must adopt a theoretical position as to the extent of the transparency of word derivations in a polysynthetic language and how to best handle the problem for students (Kroeber, 1911; Sapir, 1911). Inflections for person and number, possession, tense, and so forth, are familiar to the student, or, if they are not, can easily be demonstrated in English. With the exception, however, of the obvious compound words and a few recurring prefixes of Latin origin, the English lexicon's derivations are largely opaque. The sentence-length words of the polysynthetic language force recognition of noun incorporation processes on the student's attention, and soon meaningful roots begin to appear everywhere. The point here is—where does one stop (or start) in analyzing a word to help the student learn it? One would not want to overlook the obvious mnemonic usefulness of recognizing derivations in order to acquire vocabulary. Compare the Menominee *asaq-,* 'to write'; *maeqtek,* 'piece of wood'; *awāqcekamāhtek,* 'pencil'. A balance must be struck between providing students with useful clues and overloading them with too much information at once.

The choice of citation forms is also a pedagogical problem when constructing syntactic rules for these languages. The citation form of a morpheme for purposes of entering it into a vocabulary list or dictionary may be an abstract representation which must undergo significant changes when it is combined with other morphemes to form actual utterances. Consider this situation in Cree (Wolfart & Carroll, n.d.). The citation form for the 'familiar animal', either a dog or a horse, is given as *atim.* The incorporation form is -*astimw-.* The citation form for 'to lose an animate possession' is *wanih-. Wanih-,* when inflected for third person and singular number and combined with -*astimw-* becomes *wanishastimwēw,* 'he loses his dog/horse'. The cognitive rules which will enable the student to account for this construction are infinitely more complex than they would be for equivalent sentences in the commonly taught Indo-European languages. But mere complexity is no argument for abandoning a necessary and useful explanatory concept: The rule can always be presented in parts and in stages suitable for the student's comprehension. Consider, however, that the other person- and number-inflection morphemes will occasion still other phonological changes, and so will the animate/inanimate distinction, and so forth. These also are not insurmountable complexities, but they greatly reduce the productivity of substitution drills. Slots cannot simply be filled in these sentences without considerable morphophonemic readjustments. Students furthermore cannot be encouraged to produce novel sentences by analogy until they have mastered a great deal of material. The teacher must hold students' interest and motivate them for a considerably longer period while they learn the basic morphophonemic processes. Their contact with real language is deferred for so long that many a student will give up the effort.

Sociocultural Aspects

The social and cultural aspects of using the traditional audio-lingual methodology for teaching polysynthetic languages are as significant as the morphophonemic problems, if not more so. The imitation drills, the slot-filler drills, and the combinatory exercises all require that students attempt to produce language forms upon demand, usually solo, and in front of their peers. Willing students must suspend their sense of personal language intimacy and risk producing almost certain error in public. Differences among students as to the rate and ease of acquisition are quickly apparent to all. Some students find this process not only uncomfortable, but should they stoically participate in good faith, they ultimately find their efforts to have been unproductive. They often do not feel that they have acquired skills proportionate to their work; the proficiency they have acquired is often found to be short-lived.

While this is acknowledged to be the case for a number of students among the population as a whole, it may be even more of a problem for Indian students who are monolingual speakers of English and who are seeking to study their own ancestral languages. Indian "styles" of learning which differ considerably from those of the Anglo-American tradition have been observed. Among these are the reluctance to compete in class against friends, reluctance to perform solo in front of the group, and particular uses of silence (Cazden & John, 1971; Dumond, 1972; John, 1972; Phillips, 1972). What these studies clearly demonstrate is that the student's own traditional style of learning is very important in the formal educational setting. Standards for language behavior in public do vary among cultures, as among individuals. Some codes of behavior call for speaking out quickly and clearly, without hesitation, even if one is uncertain about his response. Others require careful reflection before speaking, perhaps even silence until certain about one's performance. When students are required by their teacher to break a code of language behavior, the task of learning is obviously made more complicated.

When a conservative elder Indian finds himself teaching a disappearing language, problems arise which are unique to his situation. When the language of a culture is the sacred language and there is no secular dialect, when the natural native texts involve material upon which the culture itself sets restrictions,[5] then neither the distillation of the syntax into rules nor a noisy, error-ridden drill performance is appropriate. It was a case such as this which prompted a WNALP Menominee language teacher, Wallace Pyawasit, to suggest that linguists designing language materials observe the native tradition of teaching Indian children to perform ceremonial drumming. The student spends hours sitting behind performers as they drum, perhaps for several months. The student is finally invited to join the circle of drummers and to keep up with the songs by tapping lightly with small straight sticks on the edge of the drum, again for an unspecified period of time. Eventually the student will be provided with real drumming sticks and allowed to participate in the performance. Never was the drumming process analyzed into component structures and presented to students, nor were they made to perform elementary, preliminary songs. Never were students forced to perform before they were ready, nor did the occasion arise to criticize them for their efforts, however constructive that might have been.

As language teachers, Wallace Pyawasit and his colleagues modified the audio-lingual language lessons they had been given in such a way as to suggest a parallel with the traditional style for the teaching of music. This emergent methodology discourages early solo performance of the language by the student. The language materials which the student meets from the first are real language—that is, a spontaneous, natural text produced by a native speaker on a topic, or a legend, or a history. The students' motivation is derived largely from the powers of the text which is recited for them or read aloud to them. In actual practice, students of various ages and of all levels of competence were grouped together in an informal manner in the classroom. Older students were occasionally asked to recite words or phrases. The youngest students sometimes wandered in and out during a class, although all in attendance were expected to pay respectful attention to the speaker. Similar textual material was presented in successive classes. The texts were translated by the teacher, and commentaries, which were sometimes anecdotal, were offered on them. Students who wanted to spoke along with the speaker when they recognized words and phrases. Faulty performance was discouraged without any explanation of the nature of the student's error. Students of various ages voluntarily and regularly attended these classes, and the classes appeared to be successful.

In summary, the standard and traditional methods for second-language teaching are problematic for both the producer of the teaching materials and the student. With the traditional teaching methods, one of the most *promising* features of the language, its polysynthetic nature, is considered as a barrier, which will delay the student's access to the language, rather than as an attraction, which may draw the learner's interest. If this text is to be retrieved and exploited, a new methodological approach is called for.

NATURAL TEXTS AND DELAYED ORAL PRODUCTION

The best argument for the use of a natural text, that is, language produced by a native speaker, with or without mediation by a linguist, lies in its inherent capacity to motivate students, to fix their attention, and to maintain their interest. When a text is artificially assembled so as to employ all and only the syntactic constructions which have been previously taught and is dependent upon a similarly controlled lexicon, no real language experience can result. The context of the artificial text must, in fact, be rejected by the student. With a natural text, however, the content of the text can be safely retained as cultural information. Not only are language forms presented, but the sociolinguistic context for the use of that language is accessible to the student. As an example, consider what is frequently an early lesson in the elementary language curriculum: words and phrases for greeting persons and initiating conversations. A dialogue is generally constructed to present this material. The speakers are identified by common names, something like Peter and Mary. These names are only markers for sex, because Peter and Mary are not known persons with social, economic, cultural, and intimate rank. Their greeting interaction is only a stiff model of a greeting paradigm. When, in a natural text, speakers are observed engaging in an act of greeting, much of the sociolinguistic information necessary for the choosing of the appropriate behavior under similar circumstances is present. The student can keep this information for future reference.

Another argument for the use of natural text grows out of language-maintenance and language-retrieval projects, cases where the last speakers of a language are the elderly and other persons who are uncomfortable with, or hostile to, the cognitive/audio-lingual approaches to language teaching. They are already competent in natural language discourse and can present it much more easily than they can be trained as linguists or taught to use these teaching methods under protest. A very important consideration here is that linguists who are preparing the texts, whether transcribing or adapting them, act as mediators or assistants in the process of the transmission of language, not as creators of artificial texts in a language of which they may very well have only a limited knowledge (see Reibel, 1969).

The question remains as to what to do with a natural text and a class of students, especially if early language production is to be avoided. A distinction should be made between asking students to produce faulty renditions of language out of context in front of their peers and the alternative types of oral language production. First, however, the use and abuse of oral language drills should be considered. There is considerable evidence that imitation, repetition, and rehearsal do not contribute so significantly to the acquisition of a second language that they should be crucial to lesson design (see Ervin-Tripp, 1970; Postovsky, 1970; Craik & Watkins, 1973). In fact, the classroom observer will often find that language drills serve more as a disciplinary framework in the classroom of the overtaxed teacher than as a teaching device. Having 20 people caught up in the repetition of sentences and obliged to listen closely for key words so as to produce the required response does have the appearance of a language-learning activity. It provides feedback for the teacher, as Ervin-Tripp has suggested, and solo performance supposedly provides a chance for diagnosis and measurement in the learning process. What is ultimately measured, of course, is not so much the amount of language acquired as the ability to perform exercises on demand, two different phenomena.

Oral production, in the sense of choral repetition after a model, that is, repeating discourse after the native speaker or reading aloud from a text, allows students to become familiar with the phonetic system of the new language on their own terms and without public exposure of their progress. The memorizing of established texts (natural texts of cultural significance) is, contrary to popular expectations, generally welcomed by the contemporary student. If students have memorized a fair amount of text, they have access to a great deal of paradigmatic information and know these language forms in a natural discourse context as well. Dictation is also a productive technique, and one which the untrained or relatively novice teacher can perform with relative ease. Translations are, of course, primarily from the target language into English, with translations into the target language and novel production of it reserved for intermediate and advanced states of acquisition.

LINGUISTS AND THE PREPARATION OF NATURAL TEXTS

The preparation of the natural text in a language for which there are no native writers (as opposed to native speakers) is left to the linguists, and in many cases this is the role for which they are best suited. The derivation of this text by linguists is a very serious problem. One aspect of this problem is the rendering of a phonemic inventory and the establishing of an orthographic system which the Indian communities can accept. Speakers of the languages can then, in theory, transcribe texts from traditional materials, as well as produce new ones of their own. It is the case where linguists will bear the primary responsibility for deriving texts for a language not their own which is the most sensitive. In the course of doing so, they must choose one of a number of dialects, thus giving that dialect permanent status above its competitors. Consequently, there are social and political implications in their actions. The use of archival language materials for language learning is an issue which deserves careful consideration of such points as the accuracy of the texts, the circumstances of their collection, and the cultural restrictions on religious or otherwise restricted materials. In cases where there are few speakers or only speakers with incomplete knowledge of the language, when linguists must draw on archival resources to supplement their contemporary material, they are in fact not only designing materials, but giving shape to the future of the language itself.

The use of natural texts appears to be a promising approach, not only for the teaching of American Indian languages but for others as well. It is a clear alternative for the teaching of students whose major interest is in acquiring access to cultural history through the language, rather than obtaining oral fluency. When combined with techniques of delayed oral production, it also promises to serve the student who is uncomfortable with the traditional methods which demand early oral production. This method allows the natural attraction of an unknown language to motivate the students and leaves the teacher as master of the language—not master of the student.

NOTES

1. For three very different approaches to the problem of advising students on the difficulties presented by Indian languages, see Goosen, 1967; Andrews, 1969; and Wolfart & Carroll, n.d.

2. See Haugen, 1976; Hymes, 1976; and Voegelin & Voegelin, 1976, for discussions of the use of American Indian languages as a laboratory and the linguists' resulting sense of responsibility toward the Indian people.

3. A Title IV, Department of Health, Education, and Welfare language project of the Great Lakes Inter-Tribal Indian Council and the University of Wisconsin at Milwaukee.

4. While the assistance and inspiration of the WNALP staff and the language teachers are gratefully acknowledged, they are not responsible for any errors in this interpretation of Indian language pedagogy.

5. One example of such a restriction concerns the use of religious texts as teaching materials. While the Lord's Prayer is commonly taught as a text to students of Old English, to hear a sacred song analyzed for its syntax may well disturb and offend the Indian community.

REFERENCES

Andrews, J. R. *An introduction to classical Nahuatl.* Austin: University of Texas Press, 1969.

Boas, F. Introduction. In P. Holder (Ed.), *Handbook of American Indian languages.* Lincoln: University of Nebraska Press, 1966.

Cazden, C. B. & John, V. P. Learning in American Indian children. In M. Wax, S. Diamond, & F. O. Gearing (Eds.) *Anthropological perspectives on education.* New York: Basic Books, 1971.

Craik, F. I. M., & Watkins, M. J. The role of rehearsal in short-term memory. *Journal of Verbal Learning and Verbal Behavior,* 1973, *12,* 599–607.

Dumond, R. Learning English and how to be silent: Studies in Sioux and Cherokee classrooms. In C. B. Cazden, V. P. John, & D. Hymes (Eds.), *Functions of language in the classroom.* New York: Teachers College Press, 1972.

Ervin-Tripp, S. Structure and process in language acquisition. In J. E. Alatis (Ed.), *Bilingualism and language contact.* Washington, D.C.: Georgetown University Press, 1970.

Goosen, I. W. *Navajo made easier.* Flagstaff, Ariz.: Northland Press, 1967.

Haugen, E. Introductory remarks. In W. L. Chafe (Ed.), *American Indian languages and American linguistics. Papers of the Second Golden Anniversary Symposium of the Linguistic Society of America, Berkeley, 1974.* Lisse, Belgium: Peter de Ridder Press, 1976.

Hymes, D. The Americanist tradition. In W. L. Chafe (Ed.), *American Indian languages and American linguistics. Papers of the Second Golden Anniversary Symposium of the Linguistic Society of America, Berkeley, 1974.* Lisse, Belgium: Peter de Ridder Press, 1976.

John, V. P. Styles of learning—styles of teaching: Reflections on the education of Navajo children. In C. B. Cazden & D. Hymes (Eds.), *Functions of language in the classroom.* New York: Teachers College Press, 1972.

Kroeber, A. Incorporation as a linguistic process. *American Anthropologist,* 1911, *13,* 577–84.

Miner, K. *A Menominee reference grammar.* Milwaukee, Wis.: Great Lakes Inter-Tribal Council and the University of Wisconsin-Milwaukee, 1975.

Miner, K. (Ed.). *Omaeqnomemew-Kiketwanan.* Milwaukee, Wis.: Great Lakes Inter-Tribal Council and the University of Wisconsin-Milwaukee, 1975.

Phillips, S. W. Participant structures and communicative competence: Warm Springs children in community and classroom. In C. B. Cazden, V. P. John, & D. Hymes (Eds.), *Functions of language in the classroom.* New York: Teachers College Press, 1972.

Postovsky, V. Effects of delay in oral practice at the beginning of second language learning. Doctoral diss., University of California, Berkeley, 1970.

Reibel, D. Language learning analysis. *International Review of Applied Linguistics,* 1969, *8,* 283–94.

Sapir, E. The problem of noun incorporation in American Indian languages. *American Anthropologist,* 1911, *13,* 250–82.

Voegelin, C. F., & Voegelin, F. M. Some recent (and not so recent) attempts to interpret semantics of native languages in North America. In W. L. Chafe (Ed.), *American Indian languages and American linguistics.* Lisse, Belgium: Peter de Ridder Press, 1976.

Wolfart, H. C., & Carroll, J. F. *Meet Cree.* Edmonton: University of Alberta Press, n.d.

18 | Classroom Implications of Culturally Defined Organizational Patterns in Speeches by Native Americans

MARLA SCAFE
Central State University

GRETTA KONTAS
University of Oklahoma

In their chapter in this volume entitled "A Structural Analysis of Speeches by Native American Students," Cooley and Lujan (pp. 80–92) examine a series of speeches given by Native Americans. Their analysis centers on the question of organizational structure and the white tendency to respond to Native American speeches as rambling or disorganized. Investigations of audiotaped speeches presented by Kiowa, Creek, and Cherokee tribal elders and 8 Native American college students indicated that it is not a lack of organization which confuses the white listener; rather it is a lack of awareness of an unfamiliar structural foundation.

This perspective suggests that some of the negative classroom experiences for Native American and other minority students might be rooted in differing sets of communication patterns and interactional norms (Lujan and Dobkins, 1978). The authors note that any of the conclusions or recommendations made in their analysis are based on data gathered from Kiowa, Creek, and Cherokee

This paper originally appeared in an earlier version as "Classroom implications for awareness of evaluations of culturally defined differences in Native American speeches," in Florence Barkin & Elizabeth A. Brandt (Eds.), *Speaking, singing, and teaching*, Anthropological Research Paper no. 20 (Tempe: Arizona State University, 1980), and is used by permission. A later, expanded version of this paper, by M. Scafe, G. Kontas, and R. Cooley, "The impact of teacher evaluations on Native American persuasive speech presentations," appeared in the *Indiana Speech Journal, 16,* 1981, 1–6. The speech data from which we base our conclusions in this chapter were collected by Ralph Cooley and Philip Lujan and are used here with their permission. These data are discussed in their chapter in this volume.

tribal elders and a small group of Native American college students and that any attempts to generalize to other, or all, Native Americans or other minority groups should be avoided by the reader, as they have been avoided by the authors.

Siler and Labadie-Wondergem in their chapter in this volume entitled "Cultural Factors in the Organization of Speeches by Native Americans" (pp. 93–100) posit cultural reasons for Native American speech structure. They operate from the premise that communication behaviors which are valued in the Native American culture are different from those which are valued in white culture. They discuss white expectations of linear progression from one topic to the next which often result in confusion for the white listener, because the Native American organizational pattern is analogous to the spokes of a wheel. "The speaker proceeds through the speech, moving along the rim to offer the audience a series of different perspectives on the subject" (p. 98). Siler and Labadie-Wondergem discuss the respect that is accorded any tribal elder who is selected to give a ceremonial speech. Their analysis of the same data base of speeches examined by Cooley and Lujan indicates that the tribal elders' speech behaviors were models for the college students.

TEACHER AWARENESS OF EXPECTATIONS AS CULTURALLY BASED

This discussion is concerned with the teacher, his or her expectations, and the subsequent effect of these expectations on written and oral evaluations of Native American speakers. In a bicultural or multicultural class, effective instruction and constructive feedback is dependent upon 1) the teacher's awareness of his or her own expectations as being culturally based and 2) the expansion of these expectations to adapt to students from differing cultures, with the explicit affirmation that several alternative ways of speaking are valid, depending on the situation.

Teachers need to increase their awareness of their cultural expectations. About 15 years ago, Lynn Osborn (1967) correlated survey data received from mailings to 241 bicultural public high schools in 17 states. The survey asked what problems teachers encountered while teaching in a bicultural classroom. The replies of these bicultural classroom teachers were then placed into categories of "problems." Among the writing problems identified were 1) comparatively inadequate training and background of the Indian pupil in necessary research techniques; 2) difficulties with idea development; and 3) lack of organizational skills (p. 188). But are these phenomena really "problems," or are they simply an artifact of student performances being evaluated by a white cultural standard? The teacher influenced by white educational standards may see deficiencies in Native American communication behavior because she or he is not aware of the criteria according to which the Native American speaker has modeled his performance.

WHITE CULTURAL EXPECTATIONS

As Cooley and Lujan explain, the dominant white culture prescribes that informative and persuasive speeches be 1) an interpretation of the available data, which relates to the problem noted by Osborn of the need for research techniques; 2) compact units of thought, which relates to Osborn's problem of the need for idea development; and 3) linear in topic progression, which relates to Osborn's problem of the need for organizational skills.

These cultural prescriptions are exemplified in textbooks. We conducted a survey of 14 recently published basic public speaking and introductory speech communication textbooks and compiled guidelines of white expectations for public speaking. The survey revealed the belief that public speeches should be organized on two levels: macrostructure and microstructure.

Macrostructure

The macrostructure of a public speech refers to the introduction, body, and the conclusion. The texts suggest ways of introducing a speech. Some prescribed introductory devices are: personal reference, narrative, reference to the audience, reference to the occasion, anecdotes, startling statements, apt quotations, and citation of statistics. The student speaker is encouraged to present himself as competent and confident from the beginning of his presentation. He is warned about the negative effects of disclaimers on his credibility. "He [the speaker] need make no apologies for his ideas or his desire to share those ideas" (Connolly, 1974, p. 70). In fact, the speaker is urged to remind the audience of any special qualifications which he has that might enable him to speak on the topic.

The data suggest that while Native American elders, on the one hand, use references to the audience and the occasion, Native American students, on the other hand, tend to persuade by not referring to themselves as experts, but as humble offerers of an opinion. One of the Indian students shows traces of this way of speaking by indicating his relationship to the topic (see "Example 1," ll. 9–10, p. 83 of this volume): "I was supposed to talk over brainwashing techniques that the cults used." This concept of disclaiming is more overtly exemplified in one of the elder's speeches (see "Example 5," ll. 5–9, p. 88 of this volume): "I have been asked to speak, and yet my words fall short. I may not measure up to what you already know, and I may not even add to what you already know. But because this time has been allotted me, I'm going to try to fulfill the wishes of the people here."

The structure of the body of the speech can take many forms. The organizational structures most often taught in classrooms by white teachers include: temporal or time-order sequence, spatial or geographical sequence, topical classification order, order of increasing difficulty, cause and effect, ascending and descending order, problem and solution order, comparison and contrast, structure and function relationship, and a sequence determined by man's anticipated order of reasoning. When students are evaluated on the organization of their public speeches, they are graded largely on whether or not the organizational pattern of the content is clearly discernible to the teacher.

The conclusion of the speech typically takes the form of a summary of the main points, a recapitulation or restatement of the main ideas. The student may find an apt quotation, illustration, or anecdote which succinctly ties the ideas together. Often the student is also encouraged to provide an added inducement, a personal challenge, or a statement of personal intention to enhance a persuasive appeal.

These three elements, the introduction, body (with the content arranged in a recognized organizational pattern), and the conclusion, comprise the typical macrostructure of the white public speech. Any deviation from this format is evaluated negatively by the white teacher.

Microstructure

This format continues to be a problem in the microstructure of the speech. The microstructure of a white public speech includes supporting subpoints under major topic headings, amplification of major points, and style—the manner of moving through the speech. An outline of the macrostructure depicts the microstructure filling in the gaps of the definitely linear progression. Linear progression is not embraced by the Native American culture; instead, as we have mentioned, the organizational structure of the speeches in this data base appears to take the form of spokes of a wheel. The organization is more of an implicit collage of related topics than a very explicit listing of one major premise and three to five subordinate premises, such as are found in the microstructure of white public speeches. For instance, one student's speech on suicide among Indian students was a discussion of three distinct topics: reservations, urban areas, and the problems associated with boarding schools.

Teachers also need to be aware that verbal topic-change devices are not used in the same way by Native Americans and whites in public speeches. Topic-change devices are the portions of speeches and papers that connect one topic with another. They serve a transitional purpose, making a smooth switch from one idea or thought to another. Examples of typical verbal topic-change devices taught by white public-speech teachers are phrases such as "not only," "but also," "in the first place," "the second point is," "in addition to," "notice that," "more important than all of these is," "in contrast to," "similar to this is," "this last point raises a question," "keeping these three things in mind," and so forth. Most white teachers regard public speeches that lack topic-change devices as choppy. The analysis of the Native American students' speeches indicated, for the most part, that these speeches lacked verbal topic-change devices. The Native American elders' speeches included some implicit topic-change devices. Future videotape analysis may show that the Native American public speeches include nonverbal topic-change devices. Nonverbal topic-change devices could very likely be culturally favored over the more explicit verbal transitions which whites employ.

Another difference between the expectations of the white culture and what actually occurred in these Native American presentations involves reported speech. Because the white culture is highly conscious of time and has a "scientific" bent, expectations are that speech students should provide proof for their statements. Presenting proof is the "process of using evidence to secure belief in an idea or statement" (Bettinghaus, 1972, p. 15). The material which provides the proof is referred to as evidence.

The ways of presenting evidence that the white culture and these Native American speeches appear to share are: 1) comparisons and contrasts, which may include figurative and literal analogies; 2) descriptions; and 3) restatement. Areas of white expectations which were not found in the Native American speeches are: 1) definitions, to make the meaning of a word clear; 2) statistics or numerical data; and 3) quotations using other people's words to clarify or verify ideas. White teachers expect that the student will not only give the cited person's name and note his credentials as they relate to the topic, but will also state when and where the cited source made the statement. The white teacher also expects that the student will indicate the source of his evidence. The speaker is required to indicate to his audience the relevance and significance of the supporting ideas that he advances. "Relevance suggests that the idea or reason pertains to the general proposition; significance suggests that the reason is an important one" (Allen & McKerrow, 1977, p. 152). Native American elders, on the other hand, appear to present the material and let the audience decide the relevance and importance for themselves.

EXPANSION OF EXPECTATIONS

In analyzing the classroom situation—especially the role of the teacher whose expectations lead to written and oral evaluations of speakers—the authors have already noted that effective instruction is dependent upon the teacher's awareness of his or her own expectations as being culturally based. An additional prerequisite for meaningful instruction in the bicultural or multicultural classroom is the expansion of these expectations into a recognition that differing cultural values are viable. The expansion of expectations should, in turn, create interest in establishing alternative sets of criteria for student evaluation. It is vital that the teacher explicitly affirm that, depending on the situation, one of several alternatives are appropriate. "What must happen is an increase of cultural sensitivity on the part of the individual instructor. In dealing with minority students, the instructor must be aware of his own assumptions about classroom performance and be ready to interpret the behavior of the student on a much broader range of possibility" (Lujan and Dobkins, 1978).

It appears that in the presentations which were analyzed, Native American students model a speaking performance that is not linear in progression. The elders find it more acceptable to their audience when the oral presentation begins with a disclaimer. Because of their stature, tribal elders may not be required or expected to explicitly verify their material or sources of proof. Credence is not determined by citing written proof because for generations transmission of the Indian culture was maintained through the spoken word.

Expansion of teacher expectations may necessitate exposure to a variety of bicultural or multicultural experiences. But exposure is not a sufficient condition for effective instruction. Pedagogical training is also necessary. This training might enable teachers to prepare instructional materials which would more accurately evaluate culturally diverse public-speaking styles. When the teacher acknowledges that an organizational structure other than linearity is appropriate for some situations, he or she could heighten the awareness of all class members. The awareness could range in scope from adopting an attitude of tolerance for different ways of speaking to pride in an increased repertoire of public-speaking skills.

Without awareness of his or her own expectations and the evaluative criteria derived from them as being culturally based and without expansion of these criteria to adapt to students from differing cultures, how well can teachers meet the needs of Native American and other minority students? Teachers gain insight from exposure to different speaking styles. This insight can then be given direction through training programs. Further research in the development of these training programs would seem to be a fruitful area of research to pursue at this time.

REFERENCES

Allen, R. R., & McKerrow, R. E. *The pragmatics of public communication.* Columbus, Ohio: Charles E. Merrill, 1977.
Bettinghaus, E. P. *The nature of proof* (2nd ed.). New York: Bobbs Merrill, 1972.
Connolly, J. E. *Public speaking as communication.* Minneapolis, Minn.: Burgess, 1974.

Cooley, R. Language attitudes and policies in the United States: Their impact on Native American culture. Paper presented at the Fifth Annual Convention of the Society of Intercultural Education, Training, and Research (SIETAR), Mexico City, Mar. 1979.

Lujan, P. & Dobkins, D. Communicative reticence: The Native American in the college classroom. Paper presented at the meeting of the Speech Communication Association, Minneapolis, Nov. 1978.

Osborn, L. The Indian pupil in the high school speech class. *Speech Teacher*, 1967, *16*, 187–89.

V | Language Maintenance, Language Shift, and Language Use

OVERVIEW

Because of the uniqueness of the Borderlands as a multilingual, multiethnic, and multinational geographical area, the maintenance of individual languages there becomes an important social, cultural, and, sometimes, a political issue.

Jon Amastae's and Adalberto Aguirre's contributions deal with the maintenance of Spanish in locations that are close to the political border between the United States and Mexico. Studying the Rio Grande Valley in Texas, Amastae notes that even though Spanish-American speakers shift from Spanish to English in domains outside the home, a shift associated with upward mobility, there is a complementary shift from English to Spanish once high economic and social status are attained. He documents a stable balance of both languages in this area of Texas, where neither prevails. Aguirre's findings for Spanish-American students in a California border town support those of Amastae. He reports extensive use of both languages for various social events, and a marked balance between the use of English and Spanish together in many social interactions.

Contrary to the findings in the two previous studies, Mary Beth Floyd's investigation points to a Spanish-language loss among Spanish-American university students from Colorado. While fearful that the process of language loss in this situation may be irreversible, she recommends intervention by educators and others influential in language maintenance to promote the revival and maintenance of Spanish in Colorado. As might be expected, it appears from these studies that proximity to the border is a major factor in Spanish-language maintenance.

19 | Language Shift and Maintenance in the Lower Rio Grande Valley of Southern Texas

JON AMASTAE
The University of Texas at El Paso

Almost all non–English-speaking immigrants to the United States have failed to maintain their native language longer than a generation or two. So have many nonimmigrant groups who have come into contact with English through conquest, though such groups have often maintained their language for longer periods of time. I consider here, in terms of language maintenance and language shift, the situation with respect to Spanish in the Lower Rio Grande Valley of southern Texas, which is an area of language contact by virtue of conquest, immigration, and proximity to Mexico. The area was conquered and annexed by the United States at a time when the inhabitants were Spanish speaking, and more Spanish-speakers have immigrated since. English has been the official language, though efforts with bilingual education pay at least lip service to the legitimacy of Spanish. Specifically, then, this investigation is an inquiry into the socioeconomic, educational, attitudinal, sexual, and other correlates of maintaining or losing Spanish in this setting, where maintenance and loss are defined in terms of patterns of first language learned, language use, language attitudes, and language skill.

The activity which is the subject of this report was supported in whole or in part by the U.S. Office of Education, Department of Health, Education, and Welfare. However, the opinions expressed herein do not necessarily reflect the position or policy of the U.S. Office of Education, and no official endorsement by the U.S. Office of Education should be inferred. The research reported here has been supported by an Advanced Institutional Development Grant (OEG-0-74-2511) to Pan American University; this support is gratefully acknowledged. I thank Nick Sobin, Dan Alvírez, Bob Wrinkle, and Judy McQuade for helpful comments and discussion. I also thank David Glaser for assistance in the computer analysis of the data. Any shortcomings of this work are strictly my own. A preliminary version of this paper was presented at the World Congress of Sociology, Uppsala, Sweden, Aug. 1978.

PROCEDURE

The data for this investigation have come from a 133-item Sociolinguistic Background Questionnaire administered during fall term, 1976 to a stratified systematic sample ($n = 679$) comprising 7.6% of students attending Pan American University, in Edinburg, Texas. The questionnaire is modeled in some respects after one used at the University of Texas at El Paso (Brooks, Goodman & Ornstein, 1972), and covers several areas, including general background (family structure, socioeconomic status, and history), academic background and aspirations, patterns of language use, language fluency rating scales, and linguistic attitudes.

The sample population was chosen at the beginning of fall semester 1976 by selecting classes out of the fall class schedule. We calculated how many subjects would be necessary to achieve a sufficient sample size, calculated an average class size for the entire university, figured out how many classes we would need to include to be sure of reaching the requisite number, then chose every 40th class in the schedule. In this manner we randomly selected a sample population representative of all divisions of the university and all social class levels. Instructors were contacted to arrange for a class time for the administration of the questionnaire, and the questionnaire data were punched directly into cards and analyzed with the Statistical Package for the Social Sciences on the DEC-10 computer at the Pan American University Computer Center.

We expected that, given the selection process used, we would encounter some students more than once. In reality there was very little duplication, since of 701 questionnaires given out, only 22 students were encountered twice. This indicates the efficacy of our random selection procedure. When the questionnaire was administered, students were informed of the general nature of the investigation and were told that their participation was entirely voluntary and that all information collected would be held in strictest confidence. All cooperated cheerfully, though some chose not to answer, or could not answer, all questions. For this reason, there may be slight variations in the totals of various breakdowns.

All of our statistical tests are crosstabulations giving a probability figure arrived at by means of the Chi-square test. Though this test is not the most powerful statistical test available, it was chosen because of the overwhelming amount of nominal and ordinal data elicited by the questionnaire. We decided, therefore, to use the method of analysis most suited to both types of data, the Chi-square test. In the interest of presenting the data most clearly, tables in this paper are summaries showing percentages of respondents in each group. The appendix to this chapter (pp. 274–75) gives the confidence level for each tabulation. Readers who desire the Chi-square figure and the number of degrees of freedom may contact the author. Gamma is not reported, in contrast to some recent usage, since its validity now appears to be questionable (cf.

Berry, Jacobsen, & Martin, 1976). Also, since the creation of too many cells is a problem in crosstabulations, categories have been conflated where necessary. Correlations with large numbers of cells in the crosstabulation are reported as significant only where a second or third test with related categories conflated also shows significant correlation.

BACKGROUND OF THE SAMPLE

The sample has the following general characteristics. Of the 679 students surveyed, 76.7% had Spanish surnames. Surname is a substantially accurate, but not perfect, indicator of actual language background, since 2.1% of those with Spanish surnames claimed to speak no Spanish, and 9.1% of those with non-Spanish surnames claimed to speak Spanish (3.8% of those with non-Spanish surnames claimed to have either learned Spanish first or to have learned both languages simultaneously). These figures show that Pan American University is a highly bilingual community, and compare with approximately 30% Spanish-surnamed students reported at the University of Texas at El Paso.

Of the sample, 47.4% were freshmen, 19.0% sophomores, 16.5% juniors, 15.6% seniors, which accords closely with the general university breakdown, though there is perhaps a greater proportion of freshmen in our sample than in the general university population. Of the sample, 48.9% are male, 51.1% female. Among the respondents 75.3% were in the primary university age bracket, 18 to 23. Single students (75.6%) outnumbered married ones (20.7%). Those who had graduated from high school in the Lower Rio Grande Valley constitute 81.2% of the sample. In terms of majors, 24.3% are in education, 22.4% in social sciences, 14.7% in business, 13.4% in nursing or other health-related professions, 11.6% in science and mathematics, 8.7% in humanities, and 5% in other, special programs. These are approximately the proportions that the registrar gives for the total university for that term, though they are a bit low for education and business and high for nursing. Of those surveyed, 66% said they intended to attend graduate or professional school after earning a baccalaureate degree.

Though a vast majority of all Pan American University students come from the immediate area, significantly more non-Spanish-speaking (NSS) than Spanish-speaking (SS) students "come from" (either were born or attended school) out of the immediate area. There are few differences in the occupational goals of the NSS and SS students, though slightly more NSS stated a major or occupational goal in a traditionally professional area such as law, medicine, or engineering, while slightly more SS have chosen education or civil service. There are no differences between the two major groups in terms of their expectations of attending graduate or professional school, although NSS expect to earn more.

Of all the PAU students in this sample, 48% work, 7% earning as little as $1.50 per hour, 65% earning $2.10 to $2.50 per hour, and 12.3% earning $3.60 per hour. There are no differences between ethnic groups in terms of amount of earnings. However, NSS tend to work more hours per week. Only 30% of Pan American University students are not paying some of the costs of their education themselves (there are slightly more NSS in this bracket). Veterans constitute 14.4%, and 12% are receiving GI benefits of some form. Those receiving some sort of financial assistance through the university make up 76.4%, which indicates that the primary group served by the university is of lower to lower-middle socioeconomic status. Indeed the 1970 Census shows that the immediate area is among the poorest in the nation, having a median income of $3,994 for SS familites, as opposed to $8,490 for Texas as a whole and $9,590 for the entire nation.

This portrait of the socioeconomic background of students is corroborated by the data for other items, such as education of parents and parents' earnings, though important ethnic-group differences emerge here. Of the sample, 55.4% have fathers who completed less than 8 years of school (68.4% of the SS as opposed to 16.7% of the NSS), and the fathers of the SS are more likely to hold jobs in skilled or nonskilled labor, while more NSS are likely to hold professional jobs. Salaries vary accordingly, with 63.9% of the SS fathers having incomes of less than $8,000 a year, as opposed to 23.9% for the NSS. Similar patterns hold for mothers, with SS showing less schooling, lower occupational status, and lower income levels. Finally, the SS students come from significantly larger families.

The data also reveal certain trends of emigration. The fathers of 36.3% of the SS students were born in Mexico, and so were 34.9% of their mothers. In terms of schooling, some 26.7% of their fathers attended school in Mexico, as did 29.2% of their mothers. Despite this evidence of recent emigration, many students (79%) visit Mexico only once a month or less, and 60% visit there twice a year or less. Slightly more than half, 53.4%, reported that they only go to the border towns, and that they never travel to areas in Mexico beyond the border. There appear to be no significant differences between ethnic groups in frequency of travel to Mexico.

EVIDENCE FOR LANGUAGE SHIFT

Given the nature of this sample of Pan American University students outlined above, it is clear that the University acts as a means to social mobility. The question now is, what does this social mobility imply for the two languages involved?

It is undeniable that there is some evidence that the population under study is failing to maintain Spanish. Indeed, much of this population acknowledges the concern, since 53.2% of the Spanish-speaking respondents think that the younger generation is moving away from the use of Spanish. Other evidence can be gleaned from examination of language attitudes, language use, and language skill ratings.

Table 19.1 shows the terms selected from the questionnaire by all subjects to describe the local varieties of both Spanish and English. Clearly the local variety of English is regarded by all subjects (responses by the NSS group are given for comparisons) as superior to the local variety of Spanish. The proportions of each group selecting the terms *formal, educated style, informal, educated style, Southwest dialect,* and *border slang* reflect much common lore which categorizes the local Spanish as inferior to Spanish found, for example, in Mexico or other Spanish-speaking environments.[1] Commonly heard terms for the local variety are *Spanglish, Tex-Mex, Pocho,* or *Mocho.*

This somewhat prejudicial attitude toward the local variety of Spanish carried over to Spanish-accented English. A majority of both ethnic groups thought that a Spanish accent in English hinders social success (53.5% SS, 63.6% NSS) and that a Spanish accent also impedes finding a job (60% SS, 63.3% NSS).

Obviously, given the disparity in prestige shown by the two languages, and the negative view of traces of Spanish in a speaker's English, it would be likely for the low-prestige language to begin losing ground in terms of the loyalty of its speakers.

The SS respondents were also asked to rate their own ability to speak, understand, read, and write both languages on a 6-point scale of ability: none, slight, elementary, intermediate, advanced, and educated native. The results are given in table 19.2.

These SS respondents clearly view their ability in Spanish as being less than

Table 19.1:   SS and NSS Students' Evaluations of Local Spanish and English Varieties

Terms Used to Describe Local Variety	Local Spanish		Local English	
	SS	NSS	SS	NSS
Formal, educated style	1.4%	0.7%	7.7%	2.1%
Informal, educated style	44.8	22.7	66.0	61.5
Southwest dialect	20.2	16.3	18.1	22.6
Border slang	33.6	60.3	7.3	9.8

Source: Parts of tables 19.1, 19.2, 19.4, and 19.9 are taken from Jon Amastae, "Sociolinguistic background of Pan American University students," in *Bilingual and biliterate perspectives,* ed. by Anthony Lozano (Boulder, Colo.: University of Colorado, 1978), pp. 234–136

Note: Figures represent percentages of sample population (SS and NSS) choosing each term.

Table 19.2:   Language-Ability Self-ratings by SS Respondents

Language Ability	None	Slight	Elementary	Intermed.	Adv.	Educated Native
Speak English		0.8%	3.2%	38.6%	36.9%	20.0%
Understand English		0.8	2.3	31.8	41.6	23.1
Read English		1.5	1.9	30.9	41.3	24.2
Write English		1.5	5.7	40.0	32.2	20.1
Speak Spanish	0.9%	6.6	14.3	46.2	21.1	11.1
Understand Spanish	0.6	4.3	9.8	41.5	29.5	14.3
Read Spanish	3.2	12.0	17.6	35.8	20.8	10.7
Write Spanish	4.3	17.2	16.3	37.1	16.1	9.0

Note: Figures represent percentages of Spanish-surnamed respondents choosing each rating.

their ability in English.[2] The lower rating in the Spanish literacy skills is very likely highly accurate, since Spanish-speaking students have, for the most part, received their education in English. Other studies (e.g., Fishman, Cooper, Ma et al., 1971) have shown that this sort of self-report of linguistic skills is generally accurate. This section was also designed to elicit attitudes about English and Spanish. Whatever these respondents' linguistic skills actually are, they plainly feel a difference in the level of all linguistic skills for the two languages.[3]

This inequality in all skill levels for the two languages, taken together with the prestige levels, might be considered an indication that the bilingual situation under consideration is not a stable one, but a transitional one in which much of the bilingual population is moving away from Spanish toward English.

A third questionnaire section dealt with patterns of language use among the bilingual respondents. Previous investigations have relied heavily on the concept of domain. In Fishman, Cooper, Ma et al. (1971), for example, it was found that use of one language or the other varied systematically according to which of 5 domains, or contexts of usage, conversation occurred in: home, neighborhood, school, work, or religion. Thus a speaker might use mostly Spanish in one domain, English in another. We used these 5 domains, and added 2 others. Since Pan American University is near the border, we surmised that it might also be important to investigate language use in Mexico, and to investigate what we called media use—the amount of each language respondents used in nonschool reading, writing, and television watching or radio listening. The results of this section are summarized in table 19.3.

In these data, several trends are evident. One is an obvious separation of the home domain from the others. The home domain is clearly that in which Spanish is the dominant language. In addition, there appears to be a generational differentiation, since Spanish is used more with grandparents than with parents, and relatively little with siblings. Similarly the neighborhood domain seems to show a shift from the greater use of Spanish with friends to a lesser amount in neighborhood shopping, and a lesser amount yet in shopping out of the neighborhood. In the school domain appears a comparable shift from greater use of Spanish in elementary school to lesser use of it at the university.

Table 19.3:   Language Use by Domains for SS Respondents

Domains	Only Spanish	Mostly Spanish	½ Spanish and ½ English	Mostly English	Only English
Home					
Home, to parents	31.2%	22.2%	27.2%	14.4%	4.4%
Home, from parents	43.7	23.7	22.2	8.0	2.8
Home, to grandparents	75.3	14.8	6.4	1.8	1.8
Home, from grandparents	80.5	13.1	3.3	1.5	1.5
Home, to siblings	7.8	7.8	40.6	31.6	12.2
Neighborhood and downtown					
Neighborhood, to friends	10.4	15.2	40.9	25.0	8.6
Shopping in neighborhood	5.0	7.4	36.1	33.5	18.0
Shopping downtown	3.0	3.6	35.1	37.1	21.1
School					
Elementary school, outside class	8.4	14.4	33.7	24.8	18.6
High school, outside class	5.2	7.5	40.1	32.7	14.5
University, to friends	2.2	9.5	41.5	32.7	14.1
University, to acquaintances	0.6	3.8	30.3	46.6	18.7
University, to bilingual professors	2.7	6.7	30.5	35.8	24.3
Work					
Work, to fellow employees	2.6	9.0	36.9	37.1	14.4
Religion					
Church	8.5	15.8	29.1	29.6	17.1
Confession	8.5	4.6	8.8	27.8	50.3
Language religious leader uses	16.2	14.2	28.8	18.1	23.5
Praying	7.6	6.5	18.9	26.9	40.0
In Mexico					
Visiting border town in Mexico	41.1	35.2	19.7	2.8	1.3
Visiting interior of Mexico	56.2	30.1	9.8	2.8	1.0

Table 19.3   *(continued)*

Domains	*Only Spanish*	*Mostly Spanish*	*½ Spanish and ½ English*	*Mostly English*	*Only English*
Media use					
Watching TV	3.6%	4.6%	29.0%	32.6%	30.2%
Listening to radio	2.8	3.8	20.3	32.9	33.3
Movies	2.0	3.6	23.0	34.9	36.5
Reading newspapers	2.2	1.0	10.8	33.3	52.8
Reading books	1.4	0.4	10.6	36.1	51.6
Reading magazines	1.6	0.4	11.0	35.0	52.0
Writing to friends	4.0	2.2	5.2	30.6	57.9

Source: Florence Barkin and Elizabeth Brandt (Eds.) *Speaking, singing and teaching: A multidisciplinary approach to language variation,* Anthropological Research Papers, No. 20 (Tempe: Arizona State University, 1980), p. 27.
Note: Figures represent percentages of respondents choosing each category.

In no domain other than home can Spanish be said to be the dominant language, judging from these data. All other domains show a preponderance of use of "1/2 Spanish, 1/2 English," "Mostly English," or "Only English." In this, these data seem to support the interpretation often advanced that Spanish is being replaced by English in the bilingual community in the Southwest.[4] This is to say that Southwest bilingualism seems not to be stable bilingualism, but transitional bilingualism, since the apparently complementary distribution of the two languages forms a pattern in which Spanish is associated with the home and English is associated with the "outside" domains of school, work, and the media. Or, to put it slightly differently, English could be said to be primarily associated with social and economic mobility. From these data, then, it seems that Spanish is not being maintained in the bilingual community in the area.[5] However, I will present another view of the data in table 19.3 in the section that follows.

EVIDENCE FOR LANGUAGE MAINTENANCE

This conclusion cannot be seized simply, however, since there is other evidence to consider. Some of this evidence involves other aspects of the data discussed so far, while other evidence involves a consideration of the effect of socioeconomic status on various aspects of linguistic behavior.

While it may be the case that SS respondents do not have a particularly high opinion of much local Spanish, deprecate their own ability in many Spanish skills, and tend to use more Spanish at home than in any other domain, they are still keenly interested in acquiring more skill with the language. Of the total sample, 86% studied Spanish in high school (including 80% of the NSS respondents), and 47% took more than 1 year. This interest continues into the university, where 87% of the SS respondents have studied Spanish. In addition, they report a sharp and balanced aesthetic appreciation. Of the SS respondents, 48% felt that Spanish is the more beautiful language, and 45% reported that English is the more beautiful language. While these figures do not show the respondents to be totally oriented toward Spanish, they do not show an overwhelming orientation toward English. What they do reveal is an appreciation of both languages.

In addition to aesthetic appreciation, the SS respondents show a strong practical appreciation of both languages, as table 19.4 illustrates.

Nor does language use by domain clearly show a shift from Spanish to English. Our questionnaire was limited in its ability to deal with all the determinants of domain. Domain may be determined by the physical setting of the conversation, such as home, school, or other environment. It may also be determined by the topic of conversation or by the type of interlocutors—friends, workmates, colleagues, parents, teachers. Our questionnaire included location and type of interlocutors, but did not include topic, because of length considerations. It is the lack of reference to topic which makes the category "1/2 English, 1/2 Spanish" in table 19.3 difficult to interpret. The respondent's answer may mean that the choice of language depends on the topic, or that regardless of topic both languages are used. The "1/2 English—1/2 Spanish" category may also indicate various combinations of the two languages, ranging from the use of a word or two from one language in an utterance of the other language to rapid and consistent code switching.[6]

There is, however, what seems to me to be a more important factor effecting language maintenance. Recall that one argument for language shift involves social mobility. That is, upward movement in socioeconomic status in the United States correlates with more use of English and less Spanish. Let us, then, examine just this: the correlation in our data of socioeconomic status with other factors such as attitudes, capability ratings, pattern of language use, and first language (see the appendix for probability levels).

Socioeconomic status can be defined in several ways. I take it here to be a

Table 19.4: Practical Benefits of Each Language as Assessed by SS Respondents

Language Chosen	Most Advantageous to Know	Most Advantageous to Know in SW	Most Advantageous to Know Outside SW	Most Useful for Getting a Job
Spanish	11.5%	24.5%	2.2%	1.6%
Both	60.2	66.8	31.8	52.3
English	28.2	8.7	65.8	46.1

Note: Figures represent percentages of SS respondents choosing each description.

generalized construct including income and education, without any attempts to devise a scale for melding both into one index, since the original data show that income and education are not necessarily functional equivalents.

There are no correlations between the income of the SS respondents' fathers and language attitudes. But there is a correlation between fathers' education and the respondents' language attitudes, in that those whose fathers have more education are more likely to assert the necessity of both languages in acquiring a job.

While a majority of SS respondents report learning Spanish (74%) or both languages first (14%), there are some significant relationships between socio-economic status and first language. Those respondents whose parents are of higher socioeconomic status are generally more likely to have used English first and less likely to have used Spanish first, even if the parents were educated in Mexico. However, there are interesting and important differences in types of skills, the determinants of socioeconomic status (income versus education, particularly), and influence of fathers and mothers.

Table 19.5 shows Spanish as first language spoken by U.S.-born SS respondents as a correlate of parents' income. Clearly, increasing income as measured by fathers' income correlates with decreasing likelihood of Spanish as first language. However, in considering the association of mothers' income, we see that the trend reverses itself at the higher income level. Mothers, therefore, appear to influence children slightly more toward Spanish than fathers do, which is seen also in the fact that somewhat more of the respondents whose mothers were born in Mexico report learning Spanish first (90.3%) than respondents whose fathers were born in Mexico (86%). Income level of parents appears to have no association with reading or writing first in Spanish, since for all income levels (for both parents) the proportion claiming Spanish first is between 7% and 11%.

Education as a component of socioeconomic status is also associated with first language, though in this case with reading and writing. Here, there is little difference in the influence of fathers or mothers on the respondents having read or written Spanish first: For both SS and NSS students, respondents whose

Table 19.5:   U.S.-born SS Respondents Claiming Spanish
as First Language Spoken

Father's Income	%	Mother's Income	%
$ 4,000–6,000	87.0	$ 4,000–6,000	75.4
6,001–8,000	78.2	6,001–8,000	66.0
8,001–12,000	73.3	8,001–12,000	50.0
12,001 +	40.4	12,001 +	75.0

parents had more education in Mexico are much more likely to have read and written first in Spanish, as shown in table 19.6.

These sorts of patterns do not show up for respondents with U.S.-educated parents, who, presumably because of lack of education in Spanish, would lack the Spanish literacy skills to pass on to their children. Evidently then, considering also the fact that there is a clear difference in the behavior of those who have at least 12 years of education, a certain threshold of skill is necessary for integenerational transmission outside of school. The important thing, however, is that such transmission does occur.

Socioeconomic status also interacts significantly with language-ability ratings, in ways similar to its interactions with first-language patterns. Again, there are differences between the effects of fathers and mothers on respondents' ability estimates.

There are no significant relationships between fathers' income or education and the respondents' ability ratings. But there are some important relationships between mothers' income and education and language-ability ratings. SS respondents who have mothers with more education tend to rate their ability to speak and read English more highly, as shown in table 19.7.

There is also a relationship between mothers' income and advanced skill in speaking Spanish, although the relationship is a bit more complicated than that for English, as shown in table 19.8. Those whose mother's earnings are in the two lowest of four income categories tend to rate their ability to speak Spanish higher than those whose mothers are in the next-to-highest income bracket. Those with mothers in the highest income bracket then tend to rate their Spanish-speaking ability at a higher level than any of the others.

A similar pattern appears when we examine the relationship between socio-

Table 19.6: U.S.-born SS Respondents Claiming Reading and Writing First in Spanish

Years of Father's Education (in Mexico)	Reading	Writing
1–8	25.0%	21.7%
9–12	34.8	30.9
12+	88.9	88.9
Years of Mother's Education (in Mexico)	Reading	Writing
1–8	19.8%	20.7%
9–12	36.8	36.8
12+	87.5	87.5

Source: Parts of tables 19.6, 19.7, and 19.8 are taken from Jon Amastae, "Family background and bilingualism," *Journal of the Linguistic Association of the Southwest,* 1980, *3*(4), 145, 148.

Table 19.7: U.S.-born SS Respondents Claiming Advanced Ability in English

| Years of Mother's Education | Advanced Ability | |
	Speaking English	Reading English
1–8	52.7%	57.4%
9–12	71.1	81.3
12+	85.2	85.2

Table 19.8: U.S.-born Respondents Claiming Advanced Ability in Speaking Spanish

Mother's Income	Advanced Ability
$ 0–6,000	33.1%
6,001–8,000	28.9
8,001–12,000	9.1
12,000+	37.5

economic status and language use. Respondents with fathers who are more highly educated, who have higher-status occupations, and who earn more report greater use of English in the home domain, but there are no differences in language use between groups with different socioeconomic status in other domains. (Recall that the entire SS sample shows the greatest use of Spanish in the home domain.) The trend of mothers' influence is similar, except that respondents with mothers who are more educated and who earn more also report greater use of Spanish in reading.

I leave for those more trained in the area the fascinating question of the differential influence of fathers and mothers on aspects of children's behavior, since this is inextricably bound up with sociocultural patterns of child-rearing and other aspects of family organization. However, I will remark here that other studies (e.g., Labov, 1966) have shown females to be more concerned than men with the standard dialect of a language. We are not seeing this dynamic here, but we may be seeing one in which there is a clear separation of the effect of sex on linguistic behavior. As fathers' socioeconomic status rises, so does greater orientation to English, though educational level, it is important to note, does not follow this trend. For mothers, the trend is only partial, and, more important, at the highest level of income reverses itself. It thus seems that while economic and educational "advancement" requires greater use of English, it ultimately also involves greater use of Spanish, and that mothers may be the primary means for this second shift to occur.

It might be thought that this trend is basically attitudinal, rather than substantive. It could be that SS, who have lost Spanish as a function of switching to English for socioeconomic reasons, upon reaching a desired socioeconomic status, realize what they have lost and are immediately regretful.[7] There is, however, good evidence that the trend is not only attitudinal, but substantive. The relationship of the higher socioeconomic status and linguistic behavior does not extend only into attitudes and preferences, but into actual background and behavior: Spanish as the first language, reading first in Spanish, and higher levels of ability in Spanish.

There are several explanations for this sociolinguistic trend. First, language is obviously part of ethnic and cultural identity. That, of course, has not been enough to prevent other ethnic groups from assimilating linguistically into the English-speaking society, but the situation on the border is somewhat different. Spanish-speakers in this situation are still in contact with an entire Spanish-speaking country. This contact not only includes models in the most general sense, but also access to television, radio, and printed matter. Many Spanish-speakers have relatives in Mexico whom they see more or less frequently. Secondly, the area is self-renewing with respect to Spanish. There is a constant influx of immigrants who speak no English, but who, of course, must communicate with those already here. Finally, and perhaps most important, considering the trend of socioeconomic status and other factors in linguistic behavior, the area's economy is rather closely linked to Mexico. Jack McNally of the McAllen (Texas) Chamber of Commerce estimates, from research done after the 1976 peso devaluation, that 18% to 23% of retail trade in the McAllen area is the direct result of trade with Mexico. The figure would be somewhat lower for Harlingen (8%–19%), which is somewhat removed from the border, and higher for Brownsville (25%–30%), which is right on the border. Of those who work, 50% of the students noted that they use Spanish "frequently" or "usually" at work. Thus Spanish is very necessary for many aspects of international trade and economic activity, as well as governmental contact.

Given these aspects of the area, it is not too surprising that it is not only low socioeconomic status that involves greater emphasis on Spanish, but also the upper socioeconomic status.

An additional reason that the language-contact situation in the Lower Rio Grande Valley of Texas may be more stable than it would appear at first glance has to do with the attitudes and behavior of the NSS respondents in the sample. Many of these respondents have a well-developed appreciation of both the asethetic and practical aspects of Spanish, in particular, and bilingualism in general. While 47% of the NSS thought English to be the more beautiful language, 33% thought the two languages to be equally beautiful, and 26% thought Spanish to be more beautiful. Of the NSS, 23% would like their children to be bilingual, and 30% do not approve of Mexican Americans who discourage their children from speaking Spanish. In terms of practical benefits, the NSS respondents find Spanish or both languages useful in the ways shown in table 19.9 (cf. table 19.4 for comparison with SS respondents).

It is, of course, not a majority of the NSS respondents which has a positive aesthetic image of Spanish or bilingualism, and it is only a slight majority which avows the practical benefits, but the proportions are larger than I had

Table 19.9:   Practical Advantages of Each Language as Assessed
by NSS Respondents

Language Chosen	Most Advantageous to Know	Most Advantageous to Know in SW	Most Advantageous to Know Outside SW	Most Useful for Getting a Job
Spanish	7.7%	16.3%	0.0%	9.7%
Both	33.1	53.7	14.3	52.8
English	59.2	29.9	85.7	37.5

Note: Figures represent percentages of NSS respondents choosing each description.

anticipated, judging from some local stereotypes. That these proportions of NSS respondents with positive attitudes toward Spanish and bilingualism are as large as they are is very likely an indication that the bilingual situation will change very little.

CONCLUSION

We have seen that there is evidence both for and against language shift, both for and against language maintenance in the Rio Grande Valley of southern Texas. Though the evidence is mixed, the key to interpreting it may lie in not assuming an either/or model. While speakers show a shift away from total use of Spanish, they do not show a shift toward total use of English, but towards a more stable balance of both languages. If they do shift more towards English as a function of upward mobility, they then apparently correct this swing with one back toward Spanish, as a function of having passed through a transitional stage in both socioeconomic status and language patterns.[8]

APPENDIX

Confidence Levels for Tabulations

Socioeconomic Factors	Linguistic Behavior	p
Years father attended school	First language understood	0.0000
	First language spoken	.0000
Father's present occupation	First language understood	.0000
	First language spoken	.0000
Father's annual income	First language understood	.0000
	First language spoken	.0000

Confidence Levels for Tabulations

Socioeconomic Factors	Linguistic Behavior	p
Mother's place of birth	First language understood	.0000
	First language spoken	.0000
	First language read	.0000
	First language written	.0000
Location of mother's schooling	First language understood	.0000
	First language spoken	.0000
	First language read	.0000
	First language written	.0000
Years mother attended school	First language understood	.0000
	First language spoken	.0000
	First language read	.0036
	First language written	.0025
Mother's present occupation	First language understood	.0000
	First language spoken	.0000
Mother's yearly income	First language understood	.0126
	First language spoken	.0178
Amount of mother's schooling	Speak English	.0113
	Read English	.0059
Mother's present occupation	Speak English	.0005
	Read English	.0133
	Write English	.0131
Mother's annual income	Speak English	.0001
	Speak Spanish	.0026
Amount of father's education	Mean home use	.0000
Father's occupation	Mean home use	.0000
Father's annual income	Mean home use	.0050
Amount of mother's education	Mean home use	.0000
	Mean reading use	.0047
Mother's present occupation	Mean home use	.0000
Mother's annual income	Mean reading	.0011

NOTES

1. See Amastae and Elías-Olivares (1978) for more on the attitudes of Mexican speakers toward much Mexican-American Spanish.

2. SS respondents also rate their ability in English lower than NSS do, and rate their ability in Spanish lower than NSS rate theirs in English. See Amastae (1978) for more comparisons between the two ethnic groups.

3. One of the long-range aims of this research project is to attempt to correlate self-reports with actual linguistic behavior. Future reports will describe this aspect of the research.

4. See Solé (1975), Thompson (1973), Grebler, Moore, and Guzman (1970). Ornstein and Goodman (1979) found no such pattern.

5. I am aware that Fishman (1972) has said that it is overlapping function that leads to loss and complementary function that leads to maintenance—precisely the opposite of what I have just said. Given the great imbalance in the use of English and Spanish, however, I don't see that such a slight diglossia as displayed here can be interpreted as a criterion for maintenance. In addition, there is the effect of the border, discussed below.

6. Cf. Elías-Olivares (1977) for more discussion of these sorts of difficulties in interpreting sociolinguistic questionnaire data, and Elías-Olivares (1976) for more extensive discussion of code switching as constituting not just a mixture of language, but an actual linguistic variety.

7. Fishman, Cooper, Ma, et al. (1971) note that among Puerto Ricans in New York "intellectuals, writers, and artists" are much more likely than "ordinary Puerto Ricans" to assert that it is necessary to know Spanish to be Puerto Rican. I do not know that the dynamics for New York Puerto Ricans are exactly similar to those in the Rio Grande Valley, but it is at least noteworthy that parts of what we are seeing here have parallels elsewhere.

8. One limitation of this study is the time lag. Since the respondents were in the primary university age group, ages 18 to 23, many of the trends discussed actually concern the preceding generation. We have no guarantee that these trends will continue with these subjects. However, the societal trends noted have changed little. Additionally, in the last 10 to 12 years, there has been a great deal of discussion of the social, cultural, and educational reasons for bilingual education and bilingualism. Obviously there is a need for a study which will examine the present generation for these trends.

REFERENCES

Amastae, J. Sociolinguistic background of Pan American University students. In A. Lozano (Ed.), *Bilingual and biliterate perspectives.* Proceedings of the Seventh Annual Southwest Areal Languages and Linguistics Workshop. Boulder, Colo.: University of Colorado, 1978.

Amastae, J., & Elías-Olivares, L. Attitudes toward varieties of Spanish. In M. Paradis (Ed.), *Proceedings of the Fourth LACUS Forum.* Columbia, S.C.: Hornbeam Press, 1978.

Berry, L., Jacobsen, R., & Martin, T. Clarifying the use of Chi-square: Testing the significance of Kruskal's gamma. *Social Science Quarterly,* 1976, *57*(3), 687–90.

Brooks, B., Brooks, P., Goodman, P., & Ornstein, J. Sociolinguistic background questionnaire. Unpublished instrument. El Paso: University of Texas at El Paso Press, 1972.

Elías-Olivares, L. Ways of speaking in a Chicano community: A sociolinguistic approach. Doctoral diss., University of Texas, 1976. *Dissertation Abstracts International,* 1976, *37,* 2329A. (University Microfilms No. 76-26, 624)

————. Un cuestionario sociolinguístico: Problemas en la interpretación de datos. In B. Hoffer & B. L. Dubois (Eds.), *Southwest areal linguistics then and now.* San Antonio, Tex.: Trinity University Press, 1977.

Fishman, J. *The sociology of language.* Rowley, Mass.: Newbury House, 1972.

Fishman, J., Cooper, R. L., Ma, R., et al. *Bilingualism in the barrio.* Bloomington: Indiana University Press, 1971.

Grebler, L., Moore, J., & Guzman, R. *The Mexican-American people: The nation's second largest minority.* New York: Free Press, 1970.

Labov, W. *The social stratification of English in New York City.* Washington, D.C.: Center for Applied Linguistics, 1966.

Ornstein, J., & Goodman, P. Bilingualism viewed in the light of socio-educational correlates. In W. Mackey & J. Ornstein (Eds.), *Sociolinguistic studies in language contact: Methods and cases.* The Hague: Mouton, 1979.

Solé, Y. Language maintenance and language shift among Mexican-American college students. *The Journal of the Linguistic Association of the Southwest,* 1975, *1*(1), 22–48.

Thompson, R. Social correlates of regional pronunciation in Mexican-English. Paper presented at the Summer Meeting of the Linguistic Society of America, Ann Arbor, Mich., 1973.

20 | Language Use Patterns
of Adolescent Chicanos
in a California Border Town

ADALBERTO AGUIRRE, Jr.
University of California at Riverside

It is estimated that there are currently at least 14 million Spanish-speakers in the Chicano speech community. Despite the fact that they are clearly the largest linguistic minority in North America, it has only been recently that they have attracted sociolinguistic attention. As a consequence, very little is known about the varieties of language used by Chicanos, patterns of language use, attitudes toward particular language varieties, extent of language loyalty or maintenance of Spanish and English, or for that matter, any other aspect of language within the group. This is true even though their principal language is Spanish, which, in other areas, has had a long history of scholarly interest (Aguirre, 1977b).

The relatively few studies that have been carried out, though useful enough, are largely descriptions of local dialects which base their analyses on deviations from standard, written Spanish. The vast majority have been done by white researchers, many of whom have the barest knowledge of the communities in which they work, and even less of an interest in contributing to their betterment. An indication of the state of affairs in Chicano linguistics is that by far the most comprehensive and accurate work in this area was accomplished nearly 60 years ago by Aurelio Espinosa in his studies of New Mexican Spanish (1917, 1946).

It is usually assumed that most Chicanos are bilingual, approaching native-speaker ability in English only seldom, and using a variety of Mexican Spanish as the language of the home. The persistence of the Spanish language within the Chicano speech community is usually said to reflect the degree of social

This paper is a revised version of a paper presented at the Midwest Sociological Society Annual Meeting in Minneapolis in April 1978. The research was made possible through small research grants from the Educational Testing Service and from the Chicano Fellows Program at Stanford University. The author gratefully acknowledges the assistance and support of Eduardo Hernandez-Chavez on this project.

278

isolation of the group from interaction with the larger society, the close proximity of Mexico and the close relations with relatives in Mexico that many
Chicanos maintain, a continuous arrival of newcomers from Mexico to this
country, and family pressure to retain the "old" ways of Mexico. In brief, the
sociolinguistic situation of the Chicano speech community, as discussed in the
literature, may be summarized as follows (Grebler, Moore & Guzman, 1970;
Skrabanek, 1970, Patella & Kuvlesky, 1973; Dunn, 1975; Lopez, 1976, 1978):

1. Urban Chicano households tend to use less Spanish than rural Chi-
    cano households.
2. There is a tendency for Chicanos living in predominantly Chicano
    neighborhoods to speak inadequate English, while Chicanos living in
    mixed neighborhoods exhibit less of a language handicap in English.
3. Spanish-language radio is more popular than Spanish-language tele-
    vision, and Spanish-language media, in general, are most popular
    among the poor, women, and old people.
4. An inverse relationship between the socioeconomic status of the fam-
    ily and use of Spanish is usually postulated.

There are cogent and powerful reasons to encourage sociolinguistic study of
the Chicano speech community. Seen purely from an academic perspective,
sociolinguistic investigation into the Chicano speech community makes excellent sense. This community is a large group that resides in all areas of the
country, the basic varieties of language use are easily accessible to researchers,
it shares many social characteristics with other groups, and little has been done
(Aguirre, 1977c). In most cases, where attention has been paid to the sociolinguistic situation of the Chicano speech community, it has been sporadic and
nonintegrative with other work. Because of the lack of commitment of the
researchers and community in these studies to one another and the missing
integrative framework, little serious sociolinguistic research on the Chicano
speech community has been produced.

Our purpose in this essay is to present some results that illustrate the range
and type of language use and its functions, for bilingual Chicano adolescents.
This report is part of a larger study focusing on the choice of language for
interpersonal interaction, and on bilingual speakers' ability to separate grammatical from ungrammatical language alternation sentences (Aguirre, 1978).
This is the first stage in a multistage research program for discovering the
social dimensions of language use within the Chicano speech community, and
the first phase of a cumulative research strategy in Chicano sociolinguistics.

SOME PRELIMINARIES

A *bilingual person* may be described in general terms as either a member of
two distinct speech communities or as a member of a stable bilingual com-

munity. In either case, bilingual speakers are characterized by the alternation of languages in accordance with their appropriateness to social situations, or by the alternation of languages within the same utterance. One can also think of a bilingual person, following Weinreich's (1953) suggestion, as an individual who makes regular use of two languages. Similarly, Haugen (1956) views bilinguals as individuals with the ability to produce complete and meaningful utterances in two languages, while Bloomfield (1933) describes the bilingual person as someone with nativelike control of two languages. For our purposes, we employ the popular notion that individuals with a similar proficiency in two languages can be characterized as bilingual.

Secondly, in 1959, Charles Ferguson introduced the term *diglossia* to refer to situations in which either two varieties of the same language or two different languages are used coextensively in a society. It was later extended by Joshua Fishman (1965) to include the use of different languages for specific social functions. For example, Fishman (1966) suggests that for a stable bilingual group, one speech variety is often associated with status, high culture, and ration for upward social mobility (High Language), while the second speech variety corresponds to solidarity, comradeship, and intimacy (Low Language). Regarding bilingual Chicanos, Spanish may be seen as valuable in certain roles and situations and English as valuable in others (Rubel, 1968). Barker (1947) observed in an early study of bilingual Chicanos that Spanish is often identified as the language of intimacy and familial relations and English as the language of formality and social mobility.

Comparatively speaking then, bilingualism refers to the linguistic characteristics of individuals within a speech community, and diglossia refers to the recognition and acceptance of different forms of speech within a speech community (Peñalosa, 1980). We make the distinction because our central purpose in this essay is to examine the association between reported language use and linguistic dominance. By examining the relative degree of diglossia for a small group of bilingual Chicanos, we will be able to describe the range and extent of bilingualism within the group.

PARTICIPANTS AND LOCATION

A total of 75 students, 33 males and 42 females, in the ninth, tenth, and eleventh grades participated in the study. The students are all residents of a California town that borders a rather large metropolitan Mexican city. The population of the Mexican city is estimated by local people to be in excess of 10 times the population of the American border town. The proximity and size of the Mexican city are such that it is not uncommon for residents to suggest that the California border town is actually a surburb of the much larger Mexican city. An indirect observation supporting this is the rather large flow of commercial traffic and labor into the Mexican city from the American border town.

The demographic data gathered indicates that the informants come from predominantly working-class homes, with the parents employed as either laborers, service workers, or farm equipment operators. The educational level of the father, to the extent that the informants were able to furnish information, seems to hover about the sixth-grade, and for the mother it seems to fall between the sixth- and seventh-grade. The majority of the informants reported annual family income as less than $5,000.

The decision to limit this study to a sample of bilingual Chicano adolescents reflects the fact that the bilingualism of this group has seldom been studied. Most of the research on the Chicano adolescent has been limited to an analysis of their psychological adjustment to a dual marginal role (Peak, 1958, Derbyshire, 1968). The duality of cultures, however, is what makes a focus on language behavior intriguing. The social situation of the bilingual Chicano adolescent, in which limited means of attaining socially prescribed goals are presented, too often results in a confusion of identity that forces the adolescent to give up the use of Spanish. In addition, because adolescents tend to be more responsive to peer-group influence than adults, they are also in a state where they are ready to identify with either American or Mexican sociocultural values, rather than both, and consequently, with the use of either English or Spanish.

DATA-COLLECTION INSTRUMENTS

To investigate the relationship between linguistic proficiency and language use, informants were administered the Bilingual Syntax Measure II (BSM II). The BSM II is designed to measure the grammatical proficiency of junior high school to adult bilingual speakers in either or both English and Spanish by using natural speech as a basis for making judgments. The instrument is specifically designed to provide information on linguistic dominance and structural proficiency in English or Spanish.

A questionnaire, patterned after some of the suggestions outlined by Reyburn (1975), was prepared to examine the language use of our informants 1) in the familial context, 2) for given social situations, and 3) for frequency of use of Spanish-language mass media. The questions concerning language choice for various social situations can allow, in aggregate form, for the development of a social language-use matrix for each informant. First, the instrument was field-tested with a group of Chicano junior and senior high school students attending the Barrio Summer School Program sponsored by the Chicano Fellows Program at Stanford Univeristy. Then it was administered to our group of 75 subjects in the California border town.

Table 20.1: Reported Language Use in Different Social Situations by Type of Speaker

Language Pattern	With Friends in School Hallway			On Neighborhood Sidewalk			In Neighborhood Supermarket		
	ED	B	SD	ED	B	SD	ED	B	SD
Mostly English	78%	13%	3%	74%	4%	0	78%	4%	0
Same amount of both	14	65	33	18	61	3%	18	61	7%
Mostly Spanish	8	22	64	8	35	97	4	35	93

$X^2 = 196^*, d.f. = 4$ $X^2 = 289^*, d.f. = 4$ $X^2 = 292^*, d.f. = 4$

Key:
ED = English-Dominant (N = 22)
B = Balanced (N = 23)
SD = Spanish-Dominant (N = 30)

Note:* = significant at 0.05 level

RESULTS

Linguistic dominance and reported language use in given social situations among these students are shown in table 20.1 to be closely associated. As expected, a high percentage of English-dominant speakers report using "mostly English"; a high percentage of "balanced" speakers, those in whom neither English nor Spanish is dominant, report using the "same amount of both"; and a high percentage of Spanish-dominant speakers report using "most Spanish" in all three situations. Results in table 20.2 and table 20.3 also show a close association between linguistic dominance and the language reported as being used most often in the neighborhood and at home.

These results are important because they provide us with some interesting information regarding what an individual can do (i.e., linguistic dominance) and what an individual actually does (i.e., reported language use). On the basis of these results, we can make the observation that the close association between

Table 20.2: Language Spoken Most Often in Neighborhood by Type of Bilingual Speaker

Language Pattern	Type of Speaker		
	English-Dominant (N = 22)	Balanced (N = 23)	Spanish-Dominant (N = 30)
Mostly English	24%	8%	7%
Same amount of both	36	31	20
Mostly Spanish	40	61	73

Table 20.3:   Language Spoken Most Often in Home by Type of
Bilingual Speaker

	Type of Speaker		
Language Use	English-Dominant (N = 22)	Balanced (N = 23)	Spanish-Dominant (N = 30)
Mostly English	41%	0	0
Same amount of both	27	13%	7%
Mostly Spanish	32	87	93

linguistic dominance and language use may serve as support for the method-ological use of self-reports in language study.

The close association between linguistic dominance and reported use of lan-guage agrees with previous research in several respects. On the one hand, it supports the sociolinguistic proposition that language proficiency and language use are positively related (Cooper & Greenfield, 1969; Edelman, 1969), while on the other it suggests that knowledge of the bilingual speaker's grammatical control for each of the languages may be used to predict language choice (Aguirre, 1978).

As would be expected of the English-dominant adolescents, the majority (about 75%) reported speaking English most of the time (see table 20.1). Inter-estingly, the balanced speakers, although most chose Spanish or equal amounts of both languages, reported using English with friends in the school hallways 13% of the time. This compares with only 4% in the verbal encounters on neighborhood sidewalks or supermarkets. Even the Spanish-dominant subjects spoke their greatest percentage of English in the school hallways, albeit only 3% but compared with none in the other two social situations. Figure 20.1 sum-marizes our informants' use of language for three social situations.

An analysis of the statistical association for each social situation by reported language use indicates that a closer association occurs for the two neighbor-hood situations than for the school interaction. (See table 20.4.) These results strongly support the assertion that language choice by bilingual speakers is determined by the nature of the interactional situation and the notion that social situations are associated with certain language behaviors by bilingual people (Fishman, 1965, 1966).

Given these results, we may speculate, as Patella & Kuvlesky (1973) have done, that use of Spanish decreases as distance from home increases. It has not been researched, however, whether the decreased use is a result of a personal desire to assimilate into the larger society. From a social-psychological point of view, use of English in the United States may increase in proportion to dis-tance from one's home because its use may reduce the chances that the person's

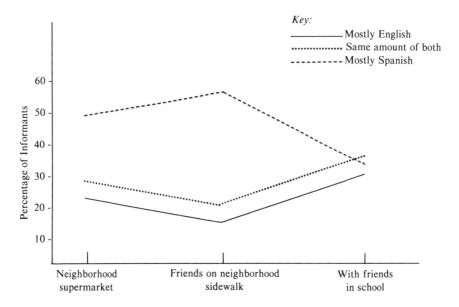

Figure 20.1:   Informants' Reported Use of Language for Three Social Situations

behavior will be perceived as incongruent with the larger social world. For the bilingual Chicano, the shift from the use of Spanish to the use of English may be fruitfully considered not only in terms of generational and chronological changes in language use, but also in terms of a community milieu which may inhibit or enhance the use of Spanish or English. As Lieberson (1970) has

Table 20.4:   Statistical Association Among Social Situations in the Questionnaire

Situation		Situation S_2			Gamma Value	Situation S_3			Gamma Value
		ME	SA	MS		ME	SA	MS	
S_1	ME	90%	16%	8%	0.80351	89%	15%	7%	0.84676
	SA	10%	74%	37%		11%	80%	28%	
	MS	0	10%	55%		0	5%	65%	
S_2	ME	—	—	—		78%	15%	0	0.89542
	SA	—	—	—		16%	70%	7%	
	MS	—	—	—		6%	15%	93%	

Key:
S_1 = School Hallway   ME = Mostly English
S_2 = Neighborhood Sidewalk   SA = Same Amount of Both
S_3 = Neighborhood Supermarket   MS = Mostly Spanish

demonstrated, there is good reason to expect language use to be influenced by the residential pattern of bilinguals.

Informants were also asked to list the members of their immediate household by age, sex, and relationship and to state the language used most often with each person for conversation in the home. Figure 20.2 summarizes our informants' use of language for the familial context and shows the order of decreasing frequency.

Approximately 80% of the informants speak mostly Spanish with their immediate family—mother, father, older brother, older sister, younger brother, younger sister. Although the difference is only 10%, the mother received the highest reported Spanish-language interaction. The lowest number of informants reported Spanish interaction with their older brother, but this was no more than 5% less than for other siblings.

The father and younger sister received the highest number of reports that informants speak the same amount of both English and Spanish (30%). Nearly equal (15%) numbers of the informants speak the same amounts of both, or mostly English, with the mothers. Between 20% and 30% of the informants speak mostly English with their older sister and older and younger brothers.

Two interesting observations can be made from the results in figure 20.2. First of all, it is clear that Spanish is the language most often used for conversation with immediate household members, and that regardless of age, Spanish

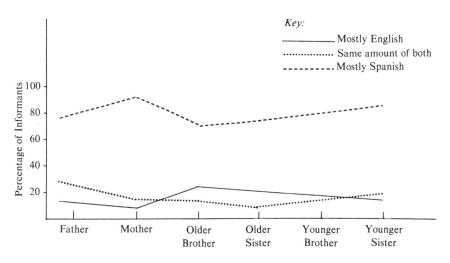

Figure 20.2:   Informants' Reported Use of Language with Other Household Members

Table 20.5: Respondents Reporting Use of Spanish Language Mass Media Sources

Frequency of Use	Radio Programs	Television Programs	Newspapers or Magazines	Books	Movies
Once a week or more	69%	65%	64%	45%	41%
Once or twice a month	7	8	12	16	13
Once every 3 or 4 months	3	11	7	11	12
Once a year	0	4	17	7	7
Not at all	21	12	16	21	27

is the language most often used by siblings amoung themselves (for a contrast see Timm, 1975). Secondly, it appears that regardless of age, brothers are most often spoken to in English, while younger sisters are most often spoken to in Spanish.

Given the rather limited scope of this study, future work would do well to compare the language use of each family member by age and sex. In this manner, cross-sex and cross-age comparisons may enable researchers to evaluate language choice further by topic of conversation, or by social occasion within the familial context. Given this, we may be able to get closer toward analyzing why different family members make different choices between two languages.

Finally, table 20.5 summarizes informants' reported use of Spanish-language mass media. In order of decreasing use, we can see that the following percentages of informants reported that they use the various types of media once a week or more: radio programs (69%); television programs (65%), newspapers or magazines (64%), books (45%), and movies (41%).

Our informants are thus frequent users of Spanish-language mass media. The proximity of Mexico might be a factor accounting for this result. However, regardless of whether this is the case, we can speculate that use of Spanish-language mass media is helping to maintain the use of Spanish within the Chicano speech community and among our bilingual informants. The issue becomes problematic, though, if we begin to consider whether the use of Spanish-language mass media is a good indicator either of the maintenance of the Spanish language or of loyalty toward the Spanish language. The former concern would imply that Spanish was usually spoken by Chicanos, whereas the latter would imply that Spanish is simply the preferred medium of communication, regardless of whether it is used or not (Aguirre & Gutierrez, 1978).

SUMMARY AND DIRECTIONS FOR FUTURE RESEARCH

Given the rather limited scope of this study, we may conclude that the maintenance of, and loyalty to, the Spanish language is present in our sample of

bilingual Chicano adolescents. The close association between linguistic dominance and language use that we found may serve as a sociolinguistic variable
for the contextualization of events or persons by these bilingual speakers. For
example, regarding their linguistic behavior, they are doing that which they
are most likely to know something about.

In all three social situations, there is a reported use of both languages. There
is not a partialing out effect for language use as affected by the social situations. Therefore, there is not a clear diglossic element in the sociolinguistic
behavior of our informants, but, rather, an extensive use of both languages for
various social events or persons.

However, we should not discount the fact that a close statistical association
was present for two of the three social situations. Whether this can be used as
evidence for the presence of diglossia is something that warrants greater attention. In particular, it would be interesting to begin studying the effects of social
situation upon language use, in order to understand when general social forces,
as opposed to specific sociostructural demands, affect language choice (Hill,
1978, see Koenig, 1980). Intervening influences directly related to the size and
proximity of the much larger Mexican city may affect the range and extent of
bilingualism for our informants. Some of these influences are most certainly
going to be produced by the presence of large numbers of Spanish-speakers
there, and the investment in corporate and human capital.

Work which seeks to examine the sociolinguistic situation of the bilingual
Chicano adolescent must be cautious in employing measures of linguistic dominance as indicators of social assimilation, and, consequently, of *language loss*
(e.g., loss of the ability to speak one's mother tongue). For while linguistic
dominance and language use may be closely associated, as our results show,
dominance alone does not serve to define its relationship to language loss, but
may simply serve to identify it. If Fishman's (1966) suggestion that with the
acquisition and development of a second language a person often adopts some
of the values associated with that language is plausible, then we must be able
to identify the relationship of these values to the speaker's development of a
social commitment to the second language. In this manner, we may be in a
better position to examine the various social processes involved in language
loss. For instance, is language loss the result of adopting the values of a second
language and identifying with them? Or, is language loss a necessary condition
for the adoption of values belonging to a second language?

An interesting direction to take in the examination of language use by bilingual Chicano adolescents would be to examine the effects of urban as opposed
to rural residence on language choice. One observation that could be tested is
whether urban bilingual Chicanos have greater flexibility in their social and
functional uses for languages than their rural counterparts (Vigil, 1979). Perhaps the incorporation of retrospective questions into an interview or survey
instrument would allow researchers to observe what life- and world-experiences

are central in the bilingual adolescent's life for the maintenance of bilingualism.

In summary, in order for the relationship between linguistic dominance and language use to be part of an explanatory framework for the association between language loss and social assimilation, future research must consider, in detail, the context of bilingualism, including the effects of 1) residential patterns and location, 2) degree of bilingualism in the neighborhood, 3) general attitudes toward bilingualism, and 4) language use in general upon the bilingual Chicano adolescent's use and choice of language. All of these effects must be outlined in order to observe how such a speaker is socialized to develop a social commitment for one language but not another. For it is among Chicano adolescents that we are going to find a polarization into at least two types of speakers: Those who adopt and follow the dominant elements of middle-class American culture, and those who rebel linguistically and socially (cf. Lance, 1969). For comparative purposes, more research is needed to determine to what extent this is a general tendency among Chicanos and in other populations where bilingualism is a predominant behavioral pattern. These are all researchable issues that must be addressed before we can begin to assert generally valid conclusions regarding the sociolinguistic situation of the bilingual Chicano adolescent.

REFERENCES

Aguirre, A., Jr. Acceptability judgements of grammatical and ungrammatical forms of intrasentential code alternation. Doctoral diss., Stanford University, 1977(a).

———. Language in the Chicano speech community: A sociolinguistic consideration. Paper read at the Annual Meeting of the American Sociological Association, Chicago, November, 1977(b).

———. El lenguaje de los Chicanos: The review as social commentary. *Language in Society,* 1977(c), *6.*

———. *An experimental sociolinguistic investigation of Chicano bilingualism.* San Francisco: R & E Research Associates, 1978.

Aguirre, A., Jr., & Gutierrez, F. The effects of Spanish language media on bilingualism in the Chicano speech community. Paper read at the Twelfth International Congress of World Sociology, Uppsala, Sweden, 1978.

Barker, G. C. Social functions of language in a Mexican American community. *Acta Americana,* 1947, *5,* 182–202.

Bloomfield, L. *Language.* New York: Holt, Rinehart & Winston, 1933.

Cooper, R. L., & Greenfield, L. Language use in a bilingual community. *Modern Language Journal,* 1969, *53,* 179–83.

Derbyshire, R. L. Adolescent identity crisis in urban Mexican Americans in East Los Angeles. In E. E. Brody (Ed.), *Minority group adolescents in the United States.* Baltimore, Md.: Williams & Wilkins, 1968.

Dunn, E. W. Mexican American media behavior: A factor analysis. *Journal of Broadcasting,* 1975, *19,* 3–10.

Edelman, M. The contextualization of school children's bilingualism. *Modern Language Journal,* 1969, *53,* 166–72.

Espinosa, A. M. Speech mixture in New Mexico: The influence of the English language on New Mexican Spanish. In H. M. Stephens & H. E. Bolton (Eds.), *The Pacific ocean in history.* New York: Macmillan, 1917.

——. *Estudios sobre el español de Nuevo Méjico.* Buenos Aires: University of Buenos Aires, 1946.

Ferguson, C. Diglossia. *Word,* 1959, *15,* 325–40.

Fishman, J. Who speaks what language to whom and when? *Linguistique,* 1965, *2,* 67–88.

——. *Language loyalty in the United States.* The Hague: Mouton, 1966.

Grebler, L., Moore, J., & Guzman, R. *The Mexican American people.* New York: Free Press, 1970.

Haugen, E. *Bilingualism in the Americas: A bibliography and research guide.* Publication of the American Dialect Society, No. 26. University: University of Alabama, 1956.

Hill, J. H. Language contact systems and human adaptations. *Journal of Anthropological Research,* 1978, *34,* 1–26.

Koenig, E. L. Ethnicity: The key variable in a case study of language maintenance and language shift. *Ethnicity,* 1980, *7,* 1–14.

Lance, D. M. *A brief study of Spanish-English bilingualism.* College Station, Tex.: Texas A & M University, 1969.

Lieberson, S. *Language and ethnic relations in Canada.* New York: Wiley, 1970.

Lopez, D. E. The social consequences of Chicano home/school bilingualism. *Social Problems,* 1976, *24,* 234–46.

——. Chicano language loyalty in an urban setting. *Sociology and Social Research,* 1978, *62,* 267–78.

Patella, V., & Kuvlesky, W. P. Situational variation in language patterns of Mexican American boys and girls. *Social Science Quarterly,* 1973, *53,* 855–64.

Peak, H. M. Search for identity by a young Mexican American. In G. Seward (Ed.), *Clinical studies in culture conflict.* New York: Ronald Press, 1958.

Peñalosa, F. *Chicano sociolinguistics: A brief introduction.* Rowley, Mass.: Newbury House, 1980.

Reyburn, W. D. Assessing multilingualism. In S. Ohannessian, C. A. Ferguson, & E. C. Polomé (Eds.) *Language surveys in developing nations.* Arlington, Va.: Center for Applied Linguistics, 1975.

Rubel, A. Some cultural aspects of learning English in Mexican American communities. In P. Kazamias & E. Epstein (Eds.), *Schools in transition: Essays in comparative education.* Boston: Allyn & Bacon, 1968.

Skrabanek, R. L. Language maintenance among Mexican Americans. *International Journal of Comparative Sociology,* 1970, *11,* 272–82.

Timm, L. A. The bilingual family. *Studies in Linguistics,* 1975, *25,* 21–33.

Vigil, D. Adaptation strategies and cultural life styles of Mexican American adolescents. *Hispanic Journal of Behavioral Sciences,* 1979, *1,* 375–92.

Weinreich, U. *Languages in contact.* The Hague: Mouton, 1953.

21 | Spanish-Language Maintenance in Colorado

MARY BETH FLOYD
Northern Illinois University

RESEARCH TO DATE

Maintenance of Spanish in the southwestern United States has been of interest to areal linguistic investigators for many years; nevertheless, there has been limited systematic study of the phenomenon or of factors which may relate to the maintenance or loss of the Spanish language in this broad geographic region. Existing research on Spanish-language maintenance in the Southwest is not extensive and pertains largely to the areas of southern Texas (Skrabanek, 1970; Thompson, 1974), New Mexico (Ortiz, 1975; Hudson-Edwards & Bills, 1980), and southern California (Lopez, 1978); less is known about Spanish-language maintenance in other areas of the Southwest. While the patterns of language use described in the existing research have for the most part seemed complementary, general conclusions regarding language maintenance reached by the authors have at times been divergent. The formulation of definitive conclusions regarding maintenance of Spanish in the Southwest on the basis of research done to date might be premature, but consideration of these findings in relation to certain factors that affect language maintenance merits attention in the present study.

Generational differences in the use of Spanish have been noted in previous studies of Spanish-language maintenance in the Southwest. Lance (1969, 1970), in a preliminary study of one family in southern Texas, observed that Spanish was not being maintained by successive generations of Spanish-speakers who are members of a cultural minority in an English-dominant society. Language-maintenance studies by Thompson (1974) for Austin, Texas, by

The author most gratefully acknowledges the assistance of Dr. Sarah S. Fuller in conducting and interpreting the statistical analyses of data presented in this report. This study is dedicated in loving memory to her, a dear friend and an excellent colleague, whose enthusiasm for research inspired this investigation and saw it to fruition. A preliminary and abbreviated report of this study was presented at the Third Symposium on Spanish and Portuguese Bilingualism, University of Massachusetts, Amherst, 17 Nov. 1979.

Lopez (1978) for Los Angeles, California, by Ortiz (1975) for the northern New Mexican community of Arroyo Seco, and by Hudson-Edwards and Bills (1980) for Albuquerque, have reported generational differences in the use of Spanish.

Thompson (1974), in his study of 136 male heads of households in Austin, Texas, examined generational differences in language use in relation to the childhood residence—rural or urban—of the adult informants. The patterns of use revealed that first-generation speakers—that is, those who had had a rural childhood residence—used only Spanish with children in the home. Second-generation fathers, divided between rural and urban childhood residences, were divided as well in their use of Spanish with children in the home: Some reported use of half Spanish or no Spanish, others reported use of all Spanish. Third-generation heads of households, speakers largely of urban childhood residence, tended to report use of half Spanish or less with children in the home (pp. 73–74). In a separate survey, Thompson found that 60% of the children of second-generation families were reported by their parents to use only English in the home and to respond in English even when their parents addressed them in Spanish (p. 75). Thompson concluded that English was becoming the language of the home even in this predominantly Mexican-American area of Austin.

Lopez (1978) reported similar findings in data deriving from a survey of Los Angeles Chicano couples. Examining the current language use in the home of 890 Chicano married women, Lopez found a striking reversal of language between those informants who were first-generation speakers (those born and raised in Mexico) and those who were third generation. He noted: "84% of those born and raised in Mexico ('first generation') continue to speak mostly Spanish at home. . . . In the third generation . . . 84% use mostly English, with most of the rest using both languages" (1978, p. 271). Noting that intergenerational shift from Spanish to English was progressing at a "high rate" and nearly as rapidly among second-generation Chicanos in Los Angeles as it was among the third generation, Lopez concluded that while the loss of Spanish among Chicanos in the future is not inevitable, "in the absence of countervailing institutions it is exceedingly likely" (p. 276).

Ortiz (1975) examined patterns of language use among 48 children and their parents in the rather isolated northern New Mexico community of Arroyo Seco. Ortiz (p. 129) found that while parents and children tended to use predominantly Spanish with each other in the home, children used approximately as much English as they did Spanish in their interactions at home with siblings. It was just this interaction between siblings which Ortiz observed as the vehicle by which English had been introduced into the family setting. Of the 48 children, 36 were judged as able to function well both in English and in Spanish in this traditionally Spanish-speaking community. Indications of intergenerational language change turning an essentially monolingual Spanish community in 1940 into a bilingual community by 1975 included an increase in the number of people in the community claiming both Spanish and English as mother tongue, as well as those claiming equal proficiency in both languages.

Hudson-Edwards and Bills (1980), in their survey of 55 Chicano households in Martineztown, a barrio of Albuquerque, considered mother tongue claimed, self-reported language proficiency, and language use in relation to generational data. Among heads of households (second-generation), 87% claimed Spanish as their mother tongue; among the third generation, 44% claimed Spanish. The authors found the greatest Spanish proficiency reported by informants who were members of single-generation households; next were informants of multiple-generation homes without minor children; members of multiple-generation homes with younger children reported the lowest frequency of Spanish fluency. With respect to the actual generation of the informant, all of the parents of heads of households reported fluent Spanish, 85% of the heads of households did so, and only 33% of the "junior" generation reported fluency in Spanish. The use of Spanish in the home was seen to be greatly influenced by the presence or absence of minor children: The greatest use of Spanish at home was reported by those living in homes without young children. Less than a third of those living with children reported greater use of Spanish at home than English.

The factor of age has also been considered in relation to Spanish maintenance by Chicanos in the Southwest. Skrabanek (1970) noted a "direct relationship" between age and use of Spanish among heads of households in his study of southern Texas, in that those speakers "55 . . . and older made the most use of Spanish, while those between . . . 35 and 54 used Spanish less frequently and those under 35 . . . used it the least" (p. 277). Skrabanek reported similarly that "the younger children . . . tend to use Spanish less than their older brothers and sisters and the older children, in turn, less than the parents" (p. 276). It must be noted, however, that Skrabanek's overall conclusion was that Spanish was being maintained to a high degree among the Texas speakers. It might also be noted that Skrabanek's data predate 1966, deriving from a larger study which was published in that year.

Thompson, in his Austin study, also considered age, and found that the use of "all Spanish" with children in the home predominated among the oldest heads of households—that is, those 60 years of age and older; the youngest, ages 18 to 29, reported use of half Spanish or less, and informants in the middle age groups reported varying degrees of use of Spanish between these two extremes (p. 74).

The greatest single factor fostering the maintenance of Spanish in Arroyo Seco, Ortiz noted emphatically, was its use in the home and family. Yet Ortiz, in considering age, found that older parents of northern New Mexico children reported significantly greater use of Spanish than younger parents in all domains, particularly that of the family (pp. 146–47). An increase in the use of English within the home between siblings was attributed to the greater use, and hence modeling, of English among younger parents and the influence of older siblings who had learned English at school (p. 161). In comparing across age groups, Ortiz found that those who reportedly favored Spanish as the language they spoke "most comfortably" were the oldest adults and the youngest children (p. 153). The overall pattern, Ortiz observed, was one of Spanish monolingualism among the two age extremes—that is, the preschool children and the adults over 60; school-aged children and younger adults who had attended school were characterized by a high degree of bilingualism (p. 154). Although Ortiz observed "considerable evidence of a diglossic relationship between Spanish and English," Spanish being the intragroup language and English the one used for intercultural communication, the diglossic relationship, nevertheless, was a "relatively tenuous" one (p. 198). With respect to the future of Spanish in Arroyo Seco, Ortiz concluded that whether or not the language situation will stabilize further with the passage of time remains to be seen.

With regard to the factor of age, Hudson-Edwards and Bills found a strong positive correlation between increasing age and the claiming of Spanish as the mother tongue. While 90% of the informants over 25 claimed Spanish as their mother tongue, only 38% of those under 25 did so. The authors found age to be highly correlated, as well, with self-reported proficiency in Spanish. While 87% of those 26 and over reported relatively high ability in Spanish, those under age 25 reported a wider range of abilities. Conversely, 86% of the younger members claimed fluency in English, as compared with only 44% of those over 25. The authors conclude in their tables 1, 4, and 5 that intergenerational language shift is very much in evidence in Martineztown.

As already suggested, studies of language maintenance have showed differences in language use related to urban or rural background of the speakers involved. Skrabanek's data (p. 276) reflect a pattern of relatively greater maintenance of Spanish among adults and their children from rural Atascosa county households than among speakers from the contiguous urban area of San Antonio. Thompson's findings with regard to urban, as opposed to rural, childhood residence of the informants have been reported above. It might be noted that it was Thompson's analysis of precisely this variable in relation to other data that revealed that language shift was in progress in Austin. Lopez (p. 273) indicated that although the effect of rural origin was not as great as that of generation, his findings did give "limited support" to the idea of greater maintenance of Spanish in rural areas than in the urban Los Angeles area.

These observations regarding Spanish-language maintenance in southern Texas, New Mexico, and southern California may have implications for other areas of the Southwest as well. It has been noted that the concentration of

Spanish-speakers in the Southwest is highest in those areas nearest the Mexican border and diminishes as distance from the border increases (Christian & Christian, 1966). If a language shift from Spanish to English is in process in southern Texas and southern California, areas near the border, one would anticipate similar observations for an area like Colorado, a state observed to have the lowest percentage of Spanish-speakers in the five states of the Spanish-speaking Southwest (Christian & Christian) and one farther removed from the border. While there have been occasional observations over the years regarding the maintenance of Spanish in Colorado (Graham, 1962; Ross, 1975), apparently no previous research has dealt specifically with the maintenance of the Spanish language in this area.

In comments on the maintenance of Spanish in northern Colorado, Graham (1962) noted that the location and autonomy of the Spanish-speaking people in the area were unfavorable to the maintenance of the language. He further stated, however, that the presence of Spanish radio, television, and movie houses in the area "would seem to indicate a strong language loyalty as well as the presence of a numerically important minority in northern Colorado" (p. 207). On the other hand, Graham concluded (nearly 20 years ago) that in this northern region of Colorado, Spanish was losing ground with each generation and that children "with Spanish names and Spanish-speaking parents tend to speak English among themselves and to take it into the home" (p. 210).

The area of Colorado traditionally considered to be Spanish-speaking is the southern part of the state, particularly that bordering New Mexico. Nevertheless, language maintenance in this region of Colorado has not been given explicit consideration. However, in a recent descriptive study of Spanish in San Luis, Colorado, Ross (1975) made the following observation regarding a marked decrease in the use of Spanish by young people in the area: "A la hora de conversar, son pocos los que lo puedan hacer con facilidad en español. En la casa lo más usual es que sus padres les hablen en castellano y ellos respondan en inglés" (when it's time to talk, there are very few who can do it with ease in Spanish. At home, it's most common for their parents to speak to them in Spanish and for them to answer in English) (p. 12).

These previous observations suggest that the Spanish language is not being maintained among the younger population of the native Spanish-speaking people in this southwestern state. To my knowledge, however, there has been no systematic study of the degree to which the use of Spanish is shifting to English in Colorado, nor have there been efforts to evaluate those factors which may contribute to the maintenance of Spanish or, conversely, to its loss. The purpose of the present investigation is to explore the degree of Spanish maintenance in a sample of Mexican-American university students from Colorado, and further to explore the relationship of parental Spanish-language use, region of Colorado (northern or southern) of childhood residence, age, and years of formal

Spanish study to the informants' maintenance of Spanish as indicated by self-reported use of Spanish in family interactions, scores on a standardized Spanish-language comprehension test, and self-reported Spanish-language skills.

METHOD

Informants

As part of a larger study reported previously (Floyd, 1976), students who had been assumed to be native Spanish-speakers and who were consequently enrolled in a first-semester Spanish course designed for Mexican-American students at the University of Colorado at Boulder completed a Spanish comprehension test, as well as a general questionnaire concerning use of the Spanish language and demographic characteristics. Of the initial group of 67 students, 61 were found to have lived in Colorado for more than 10 years, a criterion considered to indicate those students who were established members of the traditionally Spanish-speaking community of Colorado. Data to be reported herein derived from these 61 Mexican-American university students.

Measures and Procedure

SPANISH-LANGUAGE COMPREHENSION

A modified version of the Modern Language Association (MLA) Cooperative Foreign Language Listening Test for Spanish (Educational Testing Service, 1965) was administered orally during the first week of class to the lecture section of a first-semester Spanish course for bilingual or native speakers of Spanish attending the university. This test for first- and second-semester college groups consists of a tape recording of oral utterances, conversations, and short passages, as well as questions which are asked of the listener. Students were instructed to choose the correct answer to each question, as indicated on test booklets provided. This test and procedure had previously been modified for administration to incoming students of Spanish-speaking backgrounds at the University of Colorado at Boulder.[1] Since the students were not assumed to read Spanish, the printed responses in the booklets were supplemented with an oral presentation of the same. This oral presentation was effected by playback of a previously recorded tape, the voice being that of a Spanish-speaking native of Mexico. Thus, the student was not required to read Spanish responses from the booklet, but could indicate his response by choosing 1 of 4 oral-response alternatives. The original MLA test had also been shortened, and this modified version of the test included only the first 38 items of the original test.

After the administration of the comprehension test, students were asked to complete a one-page questionnaire which included measures of language use, language skills, and background information on age, sex, formal study of Spanish, and geographic location of elementary and secondary schools attended.

SPANISH-LANGUAGE USE

Five of the questionnaire items were designed to elicit information pertinent to the informant's use of Spanish with parents and siblings, and parents' language use with each other and with their children. Possible responses to each question—*no Spanish* or *all English, both Spanish and English,* or *all Spanish,* were scored from 0 to 2 respectively, the score indicating the degree of Spanish use (0 = no Spanish (or all English), 1 = both Spanish and English, 2 = all Spanish). Responses to each question were examined separately; in addition, scores for the two items reflecting the informant's use of Spanish with parents and with brothers and sisters were summed to provide a single index of the informant's use of Spanish. The possible range for this index was 0 to 4. Similarly, scores for the two items concerning parents' use of Spanish with children in the family were summed to form a single index of parents' language use with children. This index also had a potential score of 0 to 4.[2]

SPANISH-LANGUAGE SKILLS

Informants were asked to report their ability to use Spanish by indicating whether or not they could understand, speak, read, and write. Responses to these four questions were examined separately and in combination by summing the number of reported skills. The summated score for language skills, thus, could range from 0 to 4.

REGION OF COLORADO

The earlier study from which the data used in the present report are derived (Floyd, 1976) was designed primarily as a descriptive linguistic investigation and did not purport to be a sociological study of Spanish-language maintenance in Colorado. Nevertheless, frequent references in the early dialect literature to "southern Colorado," that area contiguous to the high Spanish-language maintenance area of northern New Mexico, suggested that informants who had grown up in southern Colorado be distinguished from other informants. For purposes of the present investigation, southern Colorado was considered to be the area including and south of the Arkansas River basin; considered to be northern Colorado was the area north of the Arkansas River basin, including the western slope of the Rocky Mountains. So that childhood residence could be determined, informants were asked to indicate where they had attended elementary, junior, and senior high school. For purposes of subsequent data analyses, the northern region was scored as 0 and the southern region as 1.

OTHER MEASURES

The questionnaire also elicited information pertaining to the informant's sex and age. Two additional questions yielded information on the number of years of formal study of the Spanish language and the number of resident years in Colorado. The latter measure served only to identify those informants who could be considered long-standing residents of Colorado.

RESULTS

Characteristics of Informants

The ages of the 61 informants ranged from 17 to 36 years, with a mean age of 21.30 (SD = 4.38). Of these informants, 56 had been residents of Colorado for more than 15 years and the other 5 had lived in Colorado more than 10 years. The group included 30 men and 31 women. Southern Colorado was considered to be the home of 26 informants, while 34 were found to be from northern Colorado; in one case the information relevant to region of Colorado was not provided. Overall, the informants reported little formal study of Spanish; the mean years of Spanish education was 0.77 (SD = 0.97).

Maintenance of Spanish

An examination of informants' scores on the Spanish listening comprehension test revealed a range of 5 to 34 correct responses out of a total of 38. The mean number of responses showing comprehension of Spanish was 16.46 (SD = 7.92).

Descriptive information pertinent to use of the Spanish language by informants and their parents within family interactions is summarized in table 21.1.

Table 21.1: Use of Spanish by Informants and Parents

| | Language Use of Informant | | | | Language Use of Parents | | | | | |
| | Informant with Parents | | Informant with Siblings | | Parents with Each Other | | Father with Children | | Mother with Children | |
Use of Spanish	(f)	(%)	(f)	(%)	(f)	(%)	(f)	(%)	(f)	(%)
No Spanish	45	74	52	85	23	38	46	75	45	74
Some Spanish	12	20	9	15	21	34	12	20	11	18
All Spanish	4	7	0	0	17	28	3	5	5	8

Note: Percentages do not always total 100 because of rounding error. N = 61.

As is apparent from the table, few of the informants reported active use of Spanish with other members of their families. Of the informants, 45 (or 74%) reported using no Spanish with parents; 52 informants (or 85%) reported using no Spanish with siblings. Although 4 informants (7%) reported using all Spanish in communication with their parents, even these individuals reportedly interacted with their brothers and sisters in both English and Spanish. While 62% of the informants' parents apparently continue to use some or all Spanish with one another, it is evident from table 21.1 that few of these parents are using Spanish in communication with their children. Indeed, 74% of the informants indicated that their mothers used only English with them. Similarly, 75% of the informants reported that their fathers used no Spanish in talking with children in the family.

The self-report of language skills—understanding, speaking, reading, and writing—in Spanish showed that 19 informants, or 31%, possessed no skills in Spanish; 40, or 66%, could understand Spanish; 26, or 43%, indicated an ability to speak the language; 15, or 25%, reported a reading ability; only 10 informants, or 16%, indicated that they could write in Spanish. Of the 42 informants reporting some skill, 13 reported only 1, 16 indicated 2 skills, 6 reported 3 skills; only 7 informants reported abilities in all 4 language skills. The average number of skills reported was 1.49 ($SD = 1.34$).

Variance in Language Maintenance

While the presentation of descriptive data clearly shows the existence of variability in the maintenance of Spanish among these Mexican-American university students, it does not allow elucidation of factors which may account for or contribute to the range of variability observed. In an effort to further understand the data, additional analyses were carried out using a hierarchical model of multiple regression/correlation analysis (Cohen & Cohen, 1975). No assumptions are necessary for the computation of simple correlation and regression coefficients or their interpretation when they are used to describe data available from a given sample; further, it has been demonstrated that the usual significance tests (t and F tests) are robust with respect to failure in meeting distribution assumptions (Cohen & Cohen, pp. 48–49). Thus, it is possible to use inferential statistical techniques even when variables are not normally distributed in the sample data, as was the case in this study.

As a preliminary check on the reliability of the self-report measures of language maintenance, Pearson correlation coefficients were computed between the objective measure of comprehension (modified MLA test) and the self-report measures of informants' Spanish use and Spanish-language skills. Self-reported use of Spanish was found to be correlated significantly with the informants' Spanish comprehension scores ($r = 0.54$, $p < 0.01$) and with reported language skills ($r = 0.47$, $p < 0.01$); comprehension scores were related significantly to reported language skills ($r = 0.63$, $p < 0.01$). These significant interrelationships suggest that the self-report measures were reliable indices of language maintenance.

For purposes of the hierarchical multiple-regression analyses, parents' use of Spanish with children, parents' use of Spanish with each other, region of Colorado, years of formal Spanish study, and age of informant were considered as independent variables and ordered in the sequence stated. The hierarchical order was determined by consideration of the probable influence, from greatest to least, which these factors might have on the informants' maintenance of the Spanish language. Informants' report of their own active use of Spanish in family interaction, informants' scores on the Spanish listening comprehension test, and the number of Spanish language skills reported by the informants were considered as dependent variables. The three hierarchical multiple-regression analyses for these indices of Spanish language maintenance are summarized in table 21.2.

Table 21.2:   Summary of Hierarchical Multiple-Regression Analyses of Indices of Spanish-Language Maintenance

Independent Variables	Informants' Use of Spanish		Informants' Spanish Comprehension		Informants' Reported Spanish-Language Skills	
	Unique Variance (%)	F (1, 54)	Unique Variance (%)	F (1, 54)	Unique Variance (%)	F (1, 54)
Parents' use of Spanish with children	0.1824	21.33†	0.2125	22.16†	0.2455	24.40†
Parents' use of Spanish with each other	.1223	14.30†	.0209	2.18	.0587	5.84*
Region of Colorado	.0004	0.05	.0529	5.52†	.0136	1.35
Years of formal Spanish study	.0306	3.58	.0106	1.11	.0629	6.25*
Age of informant	.2026	23.70†	.1855	19.35†	.0761	7.57†
R^2	0.5383		0.4824		0.4568	

Note: Since data on region were not provided by 1 informant, these analyses are based on an N of 60.
*$p < 0.05$
†$p < 0.01$

As seen in columns 1 and 2 of table 21.2, nearly 54% of the variance in informants' use of Spanish was explained by the 5 independent variables; $F(5, 54) = 12.59$, $p < 0.01$, with the largest proportion explained by 3 variables only. While parents' use of Spanish with children and parents' use of Spanish with each other accounted for significant proportions of the explained variance, it is interesting that age of informants alone explained about 20% of the variance, even after other sources of influence had been partialed. Older informants reported using more Spanish than younger ones. Not surprisingly, greater use of Spanish by parents, both with their children and with each other, was associated with greater use of Spanish by informants. There was no evidence, however, that informants from southern Colorado used any more Spanish than those from the northern region of the state or that formal study of Spanish was associated with greater use of Spanish. It should be recalled, however, that the degree of formal Spanish study in this sample was reported to be quite minimal.

A significant 48% of the variance in Spanish comprehension scores (columns 3 and 4) was also explained by the independent variables; $F(5, 54) = 10.07$, $p < 0.01$. Parents' use of Spanish with children, age of informant, and region accounted for significant proportions of the variance in comprehension. Parents' use of Spanish with each other, however, was not associated with greater language maintenance as indexed by this comprehension measure. Regarding region, informants from southern Colorado showed greater comprehension of Spanish than did those from northern Colorado.

Results of the analysis of reported language skills (columns 5 and 6) are similar to those for the other indices of Spanish maintenance. Nearly 46% of the variance in reported skills was explained by the independent variables; $F(5, 54) = 8.45$, $p < 0.01$. Once again parents' use of Spanish with children and with each other explained significant proportions of the variance in informants' reported language skills, as did informants' age. More skills were associated with greater parental use of the language, and older informants reported more skills than did younger ones. Contrary to the previous analyses, years of formal Spanish study was related significantly to reported language skills and explained a significant proportion of the variance in this index of language maintenance. More detailed examination of these data indicated that informants who had studied Spanish formally were more likely to report being able to read ($r = 0.33$, $p < 0.01$) and write ($r = 0.33$, $p < 0.01$) the language than those who had not, but study of Spanish was not related significantly to reported skill in understanding ($r = 0.05$, n.s) or speaking the language ($r = 0.15$, n.s.). These data suggest that although the aural-oral skills of listening comprehension and speaking may be acquired independently of exposure to formal study of the language, the literate skills of reading and writing are more likely to be acquired through the intervention of formalized study of Spanish.

DISCUSSION

Results of this investigation show that when informants' maintenance of Spanish is measured in terms of active use of the language, listening comprehension, and self-reported language skills, maintenance of the Spanish language among these Mexican-American university students is very minimal. English is the dominant language for the great majority of these informants. All three measures of informants' language maintenance were seen to be significantly related to the use of Spanish at home by parents with children. Yet we have seen that while those parents who reportedly used either all or some Spanish with each other constituted a majority, only a small percentage of those parents used either all or some Spanish with their children. These findings contradict certain assumptions that prevail regarding the use of Spanish in the home environment among Colorado's traditionally Spanish-speaking population. The Colorado data support the notion (Lopez, 1978) that a measure of language use in the home which reflects that used between parents and children is a good indicator of what language is being passed on from generation to generation and in this way a good predictor of future language behavior of the younger generation involved.

The finding that age of informant was positively related to all indices of language maintenance is similar to those findings reported for Texas by Skrabanek (1970) and Thompson (1974), for New Mexico by Hudson-Edwards and Bills (1980), and by Ortiz (1975), and passing observations regarding Spanish maintenance among young people in Colorado by Graham (1962) and Ross (1975). These data would seem to indicate that the Spanish language is being lost, rather than maintained, among members of the younger population of the traditionally Spanish-speaking people of Colorado. These findings for the Colorado informants lend support to the conclusion of some investigators that an intergenerational language shift from Spanish to English is occurring among Chicanos in the Southwest (Hudson-Edwards & Bills; Lopez; Thompson). Further, this shift from Spanish to English seems to be relatively independent of geographic regions within Colorado. Although informants from southern Colorado were found to have greater oral comprehension of Spanish than those from northern Colorado, the statistically significant differences do not seem to represent a major practical influence of region. The minimal, although significant, influence of region in explaining the observed variability in Spanish maintenance suggests that the shift from Spanish to English is as pervasive in southern Colorado as it had previously been thought to be in northern Colorado by Graham.

It is possible, of course, that these Mexican-American university students are not representative of all Mexican-American young adults in Colorado. For example, their admission to the university would suggest a degree of assimilation to the dominant culture that may not be matched by their generational counterparts who do not seek admission to institutions of higher education. At the same time, there is little reason to think that these students would not be representative of other young Chicanos in Colorado who are college-bound. It is also possible that while this group of students may represent those young people who would enroll in an elementary-level university course in Spanish, it did not represent a larger totality which might be expected to include some students whose previous study of Spanish in elementary, junior, or senior high school and whose greater maintenance of the Spanish language at home might have caused them to opt for a more demanding, intermediate-level course. While it is not known what percentage of incoming university students might have opted for intermediate- or advanced-level courses in Spanish, my previous experience as a teaching assistant and associate in Spanish at the University of Colorado at Boulder suggests that the overwhelming majority of incoming Chicano students enroll in beginning-level university Spanish courses.

In referring to these particular university-age students it is more appropriate for us to speak in terms of language loss than of language maintenance. If Spanish is to be revived and sustained among younger speakers of Hispanic background in Colorado, especially among successive generations of speakers, some external intervention would seem to be called for. If recognition and appreciation of the value of maintaining the active use of Spanish in the home could be fostered, doing so might well have a significant and beneficial effect on the abilities of the young to use their "first" language, as well as to pass it on to future generations. An increased understanding on the part of school teachers and administrators of the problems of bilingualism, language contact, language acquisition, and language maintenance might be expected to have a positive effect on retarding, or perhaps even reversing, what some see as an inevitable process of language shift in which Spanish will be forced out, over time, by the language of the dominant society—in this case, English. Whether the chapter on the history of the Spanish language in the late twentieth century in Colorado will be written in terms of the inevitable death of the Spanish language, or, conversely, in terms of the maintenance and continued vitality of the Spanish language in the face of seemingly insurmountable opposing forces has yet to be determined.

NOTES

1. Modifications in the MLA listening comprehension test were made by Prof. Charles Stansfield of the Department of Spanish and Portuguese, University of Colorado at Boulder.

2. In four cases where the informant derived from a single-parent home, a score of 0 was assigned for the Spanish-language use of the missing parent. The same scor-

ing procedure was used in the corresponding circumstances where informants did not give a response to the item relating to parents' use of language with each other. This scoring procedure was deemed appropriate because the absence of a potentially Spanish-speaking parent might indirectly diminish the degree of Spanish-language use in family interactions.

REFERENCES

Christian, J. M., & Christian, C. C. Spanish language and culture in the Southwest. In J. A. Fishman (Ed.), *Language loyalty in the United States.* The Hague: Mouton, 1966.

Cohen, J., & Cohen, P. *Applied multiple regression/correlation analysis for the behavioral sciences.* Hillsdale, N.J.: Erlbaum, 1975.

Educational Testing Service. Modern Language Association Cooperative Foreign Language Tests: Spanish Listening Test. Princeton, N.J.: Educational Testing Service, 1965.

Floyd, M. B. Verb usage and language variation in Colorado Spanish. Doctoral diss., University of Colorado at Boulder, 1976. *Dissertation Abstracts International,* 1977, *37,* 5092A. (University Microfilms No. 77-3182)

Graham, R. S. Spanish-language radio in northern Colorado. *American Speech,* 1962, *37,* 207–11.

Hudson-Edwards, A., & Bills, G. D. Intergenerational language shift in an Albuquerque barrio. In E. L. Blansitt, Jr., & R. V. Teschner (Eds.), *A Festschrift for Jacob Ornstein.* Rowley, Mass.: Newbury House, 1980.

Lance, D. M. *A brief study of Spanish-English bilingualism.* (Final Report, Research Project ORR-Liberal Arts 15504). College Station, Tex.: Texas A & M University, 1969.

———. The codes of the Spanish-English bilingual. *TESOL Quarterly,* 1970, *4,* 343–51.

Lopez, D. E. Chicano language loyalty in an urban setting. *Sociology and Social Research,* 1978, *62,* 267–78.

Ortiz, L. I. A sociolinguistic study of language maintenance in the northern New Mexico community of Arroyo Seco. Doctoral diss., University of New Mexico, 1975. *Dissertation Abstracts International,* 1976, *37,* 2159A. (University Microfilms No. 76-22, 156)

Ross, L. R. La lengua castellana en San Luis, Colorado. Doctoral diss., University of Colorado at Boulder, 1975. *Dissertation Abstracts International,* 1976, *36,* 5264A-5265A. (University Microfilms No. 76-3947)

Skrabanek, R. L. Language maintenance among Mexican-Americans. *International Journal of Comparative Sociology,* 1970, *11,* 272–82.

Thompson, R. M. The 1970 U.S. Census and Mexican American language loyalty: A case study. In G. D. Bills (Ed.), *Southwest areal linguistics.* San Diego, Calif.: Institute for Cultural Pluralism, 1974.

About the Contributors

ADALBERTO AGUIRRE, Jr., assistant professor of sociology at the University of California at Riverside, completed his doctoral work in sociolinguistics at Stanford University in 1977. Dr. Aguirre is author of *An Experimental Sociolinguistic Investigation of Chicano Bilingualism* (1978), *Intelligence Testing, Education, and Chicanos* (1980), and editor of *Essays in Chicano Sociolinguistics* (forthcoming). His articles on sociolinguistics and bilingual education have appeared in *Language in Society, AZTLAN, NABE Journal,* and other journals.

JON AMASTAE, assistant professor of linguistics at the University of Texas at El Paso, was the director of the Language and Linguistics Research Center at Pan American University. He has done linguistic investigation of the creole languages of Dominica, W.I., and San Andrés Isla (Colombia), as well as on language contact in the United States. He has also written on phonological theory, creole languages, and sociolinguistics. He received his Ph.D in 1975 from the University of Oregon.

FLORENCE BARKIN, associate professor of Spanish at Arizona State University, received her Ph.D. from the State University of New York at Buffalo. Her research interests include second-language acquisition, sociolinguistics and applied linguistics, and the social, psychological, and pedagogical implications of bilingualism. Her current research investigates bilingual speech with special reference to language variation in the nuclear family, code switching, gender assignment, and influence of English on Spanish. In a practical vein, she has directed the development and administration of a new Spanish bilingual proficiency examination required of all teachers applying for Arizona State Bilingual Endorsement.

GARLAND D. BILLS, associate professor of linguistics and of modern and classical languages, and holder of the chair of linguistics at the University of New Mexico, received his Ph.D. in linguistics from the University of Texas at Austin in 1969. He is coauthor of the textbook *An Introduction to Spoken Bolivian Quechua* (1969) and of the bibliography *Spanish and English of United States Hispanos* (1975), and editor of *Southwest Areal Linguistics* (1974). His interests include indigenous languages and bilingualism.

ELIZABETH A. BRANDT, associate professor of anthropology at Arizona State University and former anthropology research coordinator for a large, interdisciplinary project in literacy sponsored by the National Institute of Education, received her Ph.D. in linguistics and anthropology from Southern Methodist University in 1970. She is coeditor of *Speaking, Singing and Teaching: A Multidisciplinary Approach to Language Variation* (1980). She has worked with Tanoan languages in New Mexico and with Apache in Arizona. Her research interests are in bilingualism, literacy, cerebral lateralization for speech processing, and the relations between language and culture.

305

RALPH COOLEY, faculty member in the Department of Communications at the University of Oklahoma, received his Ph.D. in linguistics from the University of Michigan in 1974. He is currently engaged in linguistic research in the Delaware language. His interests are in communicative competence in children, especially in multilingual and multidialectal settings, and also in conversational analysis and cross-cultural communication.

CAROLE EDELSKY, associate professor of elementary education at Arizona State University, received her Ph.D. in curriculum and instruction in 1974 from the University of New Mexico. Her dissertation, concerning the acquisition of language and gender stereotypes, won the Popejoy Dissertation Award for 1974–77. Her articles on first-language acquisition, second-language acquisition, and language and gender have appeared in the *Journal of Child Language,* the *Journal of the Linguistic Association of the Southwest,* and *Language in Society.*

MARY BETH FLOYD, assistant professor of Spanish at Northern Illinois University, received her Ph.D. in Hispanic linguistics from the University of Colorado at Boulder in 1976. Her current research interests include syntax, particularly verb usage, U.S. varieties of Spanish, Spanish-English bilingualism, and language acquisition, maintenance, variation, and change with particular respect to Spanish in the Southwest. Related articles have appeared in *The Bilingual Review, Journal of the Linguistic Association of the Southwest,* and *Teaching Spanish to the Hispanic Bilingual,* edited by Guadalupe Valdés-Fallis, Anthony Lozano and Rodolfo Garcia-Moya.

HERMAN S. GARCÍA, recipient of a doctoral fellowship in bilingual education at New Mexico State University, completed a Master of Arts degree in foreign languages and literatures (Spanish) at Washington State University and a Bachelor of Arts in Spanish and social studies at New Mexico Highlands University. His research interests include bilingualism and sociolinguistics.

SARAH HUDELSON, associate professor of elementary education at Arizona State University, completed her doctoral work in reading at the University of Texas at Austin in 1975. She has been involved in pre- and in-service teacher education for bilingual education programs and has published in the areas of Spanish reading, language development, and second-language acquisition. A volume she edited, *Learning to Read in Different Languages,* is being published by the Center for Applied Linguistics.

PATRICIA D. IRVINE is a doctoral candidate in the field of educational foundations at the University of New Mexico. Her major interest is literacy, in theoretical as well as practical perspective. She has conducted ethnographic research on the functions of writing on the Navajo reservation. Currently she is teaching reading and writing at the Technical-Vocational Institute, Albuquerque, New Mexico.

JUNE A. JARAMILLO is a doctoral candidate in Spanish linguistics and Spanish Peninsular literature in the Department of Modern and Classical Languages at the University of New Mexico. Her principal interests are Hispanic descriptive linguistics and sociolinguistics, and Golden Age and contemporary peninsular literature.

GRETTA KONTAS, a doctoral candidate at the University of Oklahoma, is a graduate teaching assistant in the Department of Communication. She has been awarded the

Outstanding Graduate Teacher award and is currently assistant coordinator of approximately thirty sections of the basic speech course. She has written articles concerning Native American "ways of speaking" in both public speaking and small group situations.

PAUL V. KROSKRITY, assistant professor of anthropology at the University of California at Los Angeles, completed his doctoral work in anthropology at Indiana University in 1977. The title of his dissertation was "Aspects of Arizona Tewa Language Structure and Language Use." For the past 8 years, Dr. Kroskrity has conducted ethnographic, ethnohistorical, linguistic, sociolinguistic, lexicographic, and folkloristic research in the Arizona Tewa speech community and in the pueblo Southwest in general. His articles have appeared in the *International Journal of American Linguistics* and in *Anthropological Linguistics.*

DIANE LABADIE-WONDERGEM, marketing analyst for the University of California, Irvine Extension, completed her masters degree in communications at the University of Oklahoma. She has done significant work for the Osage Indian tribe in preserving their oral Indian traditions by recording myths and ceremonies. She is currently studying bilingual education and acculturation of non-American elementary children in U.S. schools.

JAMES P. LANTOLF, assistant professor of languages and literature at the University of Delaware, has done research on the Spanish of the Southwest. Some of his work has focused on the Spanish of San Antonio, Texas. His research interests include a sociolinguistic investigation of *tú, usted,* and *para* reduction in Southwest Spanish, and male/female differences in speech.

WILLIAM L. LEAP, associate professor of anthropology at the American University, Washington, D.C., is also currently the Education Director for the National Congress of American Indians, Washington, D.C. He served as director of Indian Education programs at the Center for Applied Linguistics from 1974 to 1979, and has worked with over 70 tribes and Indian organizations in language-maintenance and -renewal efforts. He also coordinated the publication of the first book of studies about American Indian English in the Southwest, an area which continues to be of great interest to him.

JUAN M. LOPE BLANCH, professor of languages and linguistics at the Universidad Nacional Autónoma de México, and the Programa Interamericana de Lingüística y Enseñanza de Idiomas. As coordinator of the "Proyecto de estudio coordinado de la norma lingüística culta de las principales ciudades de Iberoamérica y de la Península Ibérica," he succeeded in investigating the *norma culta* of Spanish in the principal cities of Latin America.

PHILIP LUJAN, assistant professor in the Department of Communication and director of the Native American Studies Program at the University of Oklahoma, received a law degree from the University of New Mexico. His major interest is in using intercultural communication as an academic vehicle for Native American research that confronts contemporary conflicts between Indian and Anglo cultures.

J. ANNE MONTGOMERY worked from 1974 to 1975 as an education specialist for Indian languages on the Wisconsin Native American Languages Project. After completing her doctoral work in applied linguistics at the University of Texas at Austin, she spent 4 years teaching and conducting research in language acquisition in New Mexico. She is currently teaching at the University of Notre Dame, where her interests include the design of pedagogical grammars and issues in the acquisition of literacy.

MARLA G. SCAFE, assistant professor in the School of Business at Central State University in Oklahoma, received her doctoral degree in communication at the University of Oklahoma. She has been awarded the Outstanding Graduate Teacher award and is conducting dissertation research on teacher effectiveness and communicator style mapping. She has written articles on Native American public speaking styles and on a communicative-competency approach to the teaching of oral English skills to international students.

INA C. SILER, assistant professor of communication studies at Northern Illinois University, completed her doctoral work in the Department of Communication at the University of Oklahoma in 1980. She has served on the faculty at Howard University, Bowie State College, and the University of the District of Columbia. She is the coauthor of *Verbal Language* (1980) and of an article on Native American speaking which appeared in the SWALLOW VIII proceedings (1970).

BERNARD SPOLSKY received his M.A. from the University of New Zealand and his Ph.D. from the Université de Montréal. After 12 years at the University of New Mexico, where he was professor of linguistics, elementary education, and anthropology, as well as dean of graduate studies, he took up a position in 1980 as professor in the Department of English at Bal Ilan University, Israel. He has written or edited eight books and many articles on educational linguistics, language testing, and bilingual education. He is the editor of the journal *Applied Linguistics*. His current research interests are in multilingualism and literacy.

DIAMANTINA PRADO DE STORMENT, a doctoral candidate in curriculum and instruction with emphasis in bilingual education at New Mexico State University, has helped to train teachers in methods of teaching English as a Second Language and methods of teaching bilingual social studies in the state of New Mexico. Her research experience is primarily in bilingualism and language contact in the Borderlands.

RICHARD V. TESCHNER received his Ph.D. from the University of Wisconsin at Madison in 1972. Since 1976 he has been an assistant professor of Spanish at the University of Texas at El Paso. He is the author or coauthor of several publications on a variety of U.S. Spanish topics, including *Spanish and English of United States Hispanos: A Critical, Annotated, Linguistic Bibliography* (1976); *El diccionario del español chicano* (1977); and *Español escrito: Curso para hispanohablantes bilingües* (1978). In 1977–78 he directed the National Endowment for the Humanities–sponsored "Survey of Research Tool Needs in the Hispanic Languages and Literatures" (SRTNHiLL). He is an associate editor of *Hispania* and the book-review editor of *The Bilingual Review/La revista bilingue*.

GUADALUPE VALDÉS, associate professor of Spanish at New Mexico State University, completed her doctoral work in 1972 at Florida State University. Her research focuses on the study of bilingualism, and her publications in this area include studies on Spanish-English code switching. She has also worked extensively in the area of teaching Spanish to students who are bilingual in Spanish and English. She is the author of two textbooks directed at the Hispanic bilingual, and of numerous articles on various aspects of ethnic-language-teaching methodology. Currently she is involved in research on reading under a grant from the National Institute of Education, analyzing Spanish-language texts used in bilingual education programs, and bilingual children's comprehension of them.

JOHN T. WEBB, assistant professor of Spanish-Italian-Portuguese at the University of Illinois, Chicago, finished his doctoral work in romance philology at the University of California, Berkeley, in 1975. His research has focused on the Spanish of the Southwest, and he has done extensive work on professional and "nonstandard" speech. He is currently compiling a diachronic-synchronic dictionary of Mexican-Chicano *caló*.

Index

Abrahams, R., 94
Acoma, NM, 52–53
Affective filter, 229–230, 234
Age-based variation in language, 52–54,
   56–58, 67, 69, 128, 148, 156–164, 166,
   169–171, 190, 195–196, 278–289, 292–
   294
Aguirre, Adalberto, Jr., 134, 259, 305
Alaska, 32, 102–103
Alaska Native Languages Center, 32
Alford, D. K., 105
Allen, R., 128
Allen, R. R., 255
Allières, Jacques, 22
Allophones, 127, 133, 135, 155–158, 185–186
Alonso, A., 128, 175
Alternate Days for languages in school, 205,
   207–208, 224
Alvar, Manuel, 178
Alvarez, Albert, 31, 35
Alvírez, Dan, 261
Amastae, Jon, 259, 305
American Anthropological Association, 29
American Ethnological Association, 29
American Indian pidgin English (AIPE),
   28–29, 36–37, 107
American Institutes for Research, 109
Andersen, N. A., 33–34
Andrews, J. R., 249
Anglo, 93, 203, 205–206, 222–223, 233, 236
Apache, xv, 28, 30–36, 38–39, 49, 52, 55,
   64–67, 69; Chiricahua, 66
Archer, D., 187
Areal studies, 1, 28, 37, 39, 41, 125,
   141–143, 147–148, 261–303
Argentina: status of the Spanish language in,
   21
Argyle, M., 187
Arizona, xv, 28, 33–35, 39, 49, 51–72, 128,
   133, 139, 141–142, 144, 203–227
Arizona State University, 31, 51–72, 73
Arnold, C. C., 97
Artículos gancho, 8
Asher, J., 231

Athabascan, 28, 30, 32, 35, 65, 105
Attestations (sentence frames), 180, 183, 185
Ayer, G. W., 146
Aztec loanwords, 27–28

Babich, R., 81
Bahr, D. M., 35, 39
Barber, C. G., 108
Barker, G. C., 139, 280
Barkin, Florence, 30, 73, 93, 121, 203, 241,
   251, 305
Barth, F., 60–61
Basso, K., 33–34, 39
Bauman, R., 28, 37, 70, 80, 95
Becker, A. L., 81
Beltramo, A. F., 130–131, 146
Berlin, B., 35
Bernstein, 166
Berry, L., 263
Best, E., 75
Bettinghaus, E. P., 255
Bickerton, D., 105
Bilingual Education Act, 73, 103, 109
Bilingualism, passim: definition of, 279–280;
   English/Native American, 28–29, 33,
   101–119; English/Spanish or Spanish/
   English, 3, 8–16, 123–138, 201, 203–227,
   228, 259–303; Mexican/American,
   187–200, 259–289, 291, 295
Bilingual Syntax Measure II (BSM II), 281
Bills, Garland D., 30, 121, 123–126, 128,
   131–132, 139–140, 143, 148, 290–293,
   301, 305
Biloquialism, 164
BIP (Border Industrialization Program), 8
Bittle, W. E., 29
Blacks, 36–37, 41, 94, 102
Bloomfield, L., 280
Blount, B. G., 145
Boas, F., 241
Bock, K. N., 4
Bodine, J. J., 106–107, 166, 175
Bolds, J., 5
Bolinger, D., 58

311

Venezuela: status of the Spanish language in, 21
Vernacular, 73–79
Vigil, D., 287
Villarreal-García, J., 131–132
Vocabulary, 107, 231–232, 235
Voegelin, Charles F., 29, 51, 77, 249
Voegelin, F. M., 29, 51, 249

Walapai, 28
Walker, W., 74
Watkins, Laurel, 32
Watkins, M. J., 248
Webb, John T., 122, 309
Weed, W., 38
Weinreich, Uriel, xv, 52–53, 280
Wentz, J. P., 147
White, J., 74
Whorf, B. L., 27
Williams, M., 187
Williams, Marcellus, 98
Wilson, J., 97
Wilson, R., 51, 53, 57, 67–69, 104

Winnebago, 243
Wisconsin Native American Languages Project (WNALP), 243, 246, 249
Witherspoon, G., 31, 39
WNALP, 243, 246, 249
Wolf, S., 185
Wolfart, H. C., 244, 249
Wolfram, Walt, 101–102, 106, 112
Wong-Fillmore, L., 211
Woodbridge, H. C., 139
Wrinkle, Bob, 261
Writing, 33–34, 40, 75–76, 78, 95, 102, 106, 112–113, 213, 216, 219, 228, 243, 252, 265–266, 268, 270, 296, 298, 300

Yaqui, xv, 30, 33–35, 39, 67, 69
Yavapai, 28, 30, 34
Young, R. E., 81
Young, R. W., 30–31, 33, 74, 76
Yuman, 28, 30, 36

Zaharlick, Amy M., 30–32, 101
Zuni, 28